Gradient Profile Ambergate Station – Bugsworth Station (Renamed Buxworth on 4th June 1930.)

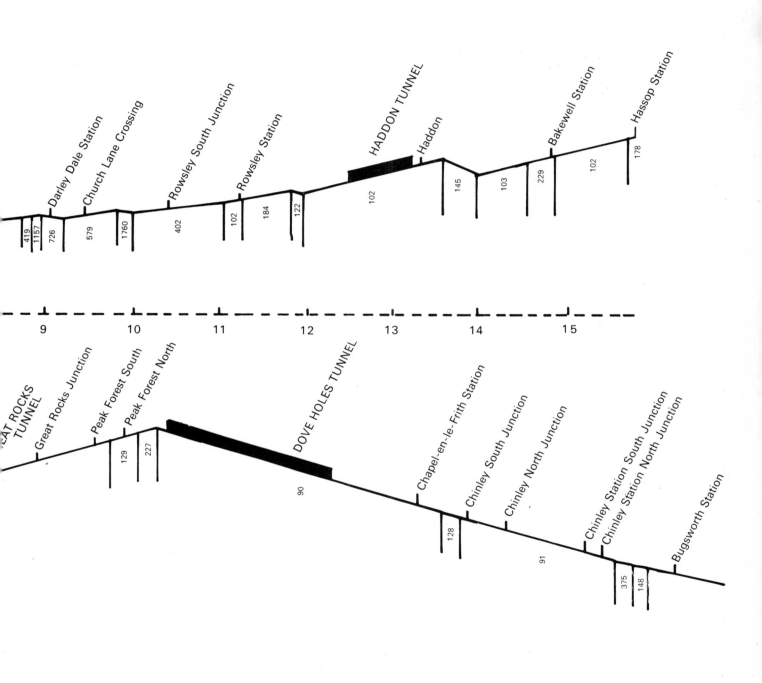

The Peak Line –
Ambergate to Chinley

Frontispiece: Limestone and steam, essential memories of the Midland main line through the Peak. In this view an 8F banker nears the summit behind a Tunstead-Northwich hopper train in March 1966.
(L.A. Nixon)

Through Limestone Hills

The Peak Line – Ambergate to Chinley

Bill Hudson

THE ST PANCRAS–MANCHESTER EXPRESS.

Haynes

Oxford Publishing Co.

LOCATION PLAN
Scale ¹/₄″ to one mile

A FOULIS-OPC Railway Book

© 1989 W. Hudson & Haynes Publishing Group

British Library Cataloguing in Publication Data
Hudson, Bill
  Through limestone hills
  1. Derbyshire. Railway services, British Rail:
London Midland Region. Ambergate-Chinley line, history
I. Title
385'.09425'1
ISBN 0-86093-217-6

Library of Congress catalog card number
89-84304

Published by:
Haynes Publishing Group
Sparkford, Near Yeovil, Somerset. BA22 7JJ

Haynes Publications Inc.
861 Lawrence Drive, Newbury Park, California 91320, USA.

Printed by J.H. Haynes & Co. Ltd.

Dedication
To the Midland line over the Peak, the men who worked it and the photographers who recorded it.

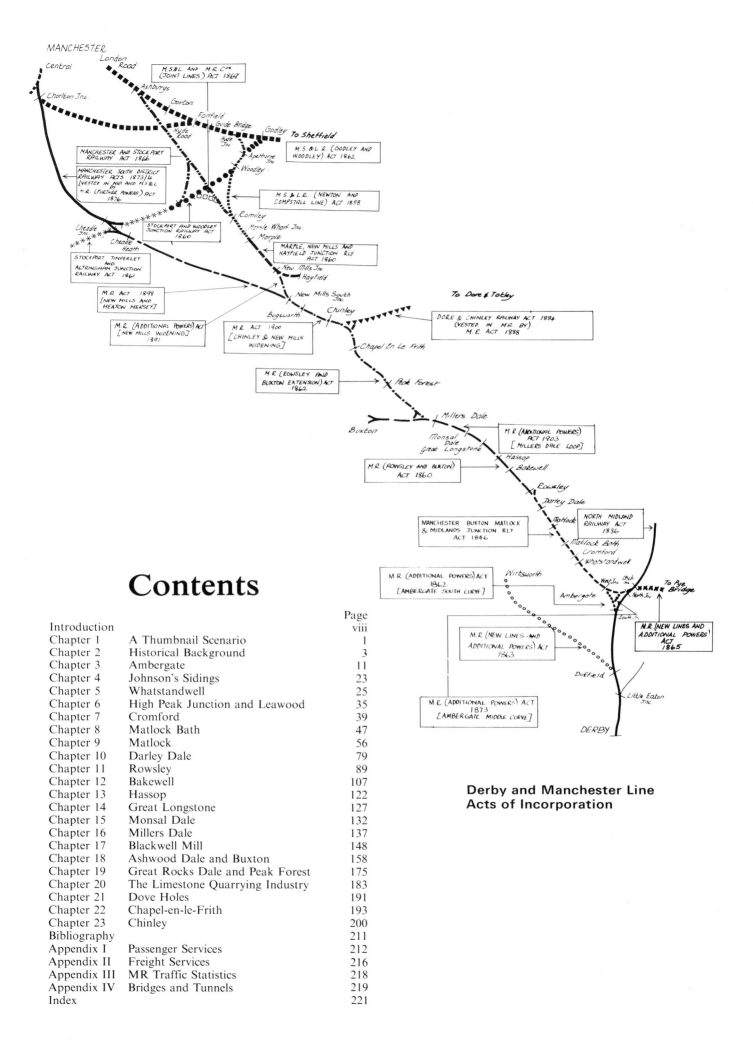

MANCHESTER
Central
London Road
Chorlton Jnc.

M S & L AND M R Cos
(JOINT LINES) ACT 1867?

Ashburys
Gorton
Fairfield
Guide Bridge
Hyde Road
Godley
To Sheffield

MANCHESTER AND STOCKPORT
RAILWAY ACT 1866

M.S.& L.R. (GODLEY AND
WOODLEY) ACT 1862

MANCHESTER SOUTH DISTRICT
RAILWAY ACTS 1873/4
(VESTED IN MID. AND M S & L
BY
M.R. (FURTHER POWERS) ACT
1876

Apethorne Jnc.
Hyde Jnc.
Woodley

M.S.& L.R. (NEWTON AND
COMPSTALL LINE) ACT 1858

Cheadle Jnc.
Cheadle Heath

STOCKPORT AND WOODLEY
JUNCTION RAILWAY ACT
1860

Romiley
Marple Wharf Jnc.
Marple

MARPLE, NEW MILLS AND
HAYFIELD JUNCTION RLY
ACT 1860

STOCKPORT TIMPERLEY
AND
ALTRINGHAM JUNCTION
RAILWAY ACT 1861

New Mills Jnc.
Hayfield

M.R. ACT 1898
[NEW MILLS AND
HEATON MERSEY]

New Mills South Jnc.

To Dore & Totley

M.R. (ADDITIONAL POWERS) ACT
[NEW MILLS WIDENING]
1891

Bugsworth
Chinley

M.R. ACT 1900
[CHINLEY & NEW MILLS
WIDENING]

DORE & CHINLEY RAILWAY ACT 1884
(VESTED IN M.R. BY)
M.R. ACT 1888

Chapel En Le Frith

M.R. (ROWSLEY AND
BUXTON EXTENSION) ACT
1862

Peak Forest

Millers Dale

Buxton

Monsal Dale
Great Longstone

M.R. (ADDITIONAL POWERS)
ACT 1903
[MILLERS DALE LOOP]

Hassop
Bakewell

M.R. (ROWSLEY AND BUXTON)
ACT 1860

Rowsley
Darley Dale

MANCHESTER BUXTON MATLOCK
& MIDLANDS JUNCTION RLY
ACT 1846

Matlock

NORTH MIDLAND
RAILWAY ACT
1836

Matlock Bath
Cromford
Whatstandwell

M.R. (ADDITIONAL POWERS) ACT
1862
[AMBERGATE SOUTH CURVE]

Wirksworth

West Jnc. Chch
North Jnc.
To Pye Bridge

M.R. (NEW LINES AND
ADDITIONAL POWERS) ACT
1863

Ambergate

South Jnc.

M.R. (NEW LINES AND
ADDITIONAL POWERS)
ACT
1865

Duffield

Little Eaton
Jnc.

M.R. (ADDITIONAL POWERS) ACT
1873
[AMBERGATE MIDDLE CURVE]

DERBY

**Derby and Manchester Line
Acts of Incorporation**

Contents

List of Drawings

Introduction

Hamilton Ellis said that the Midland was a magnificent railway – and who am I to argue? It was magnificent in its locomotives and its rolling stock and in the lines it built. Few railway routes can truly claim to pass through areas of outstanding natural beauty, but the MR had two, the Settle-Carlisle and the Derby-Manchester. While the former fights it way dramatically over the roof of England, the latter had a more intimate magic as it threaded through the limestone dales of the Peak District.

Known to railwaymen as the 'Manchester Bank', the line climbed steadily from Derby to Rowsley following closely the course of the River Derwent. At Rowsley the route turned sharply westwards into the valley of the Wye and began to climb in earnest on a gradient of 1 in 100. Near Bakewell the line left the river and passed close to Hassop and Great Longstone before bursting back into the Wye Valley at the northern portal of Headstone Tunnel. Crossing the river five times, and passing through five tunnels the line climbed through Monsal Dale, Millers Dale and Chee Dale, before dividing at Millers Dale Junction.

The left hand fork took the line through Ashwood Dale to Buxton, from where the MR could gain access to the LNWR routes to Ashbourne, Cheshire, and Lancashire. The right hand fork took the line on a final three mile climb at 1 in 90 to Peak Forest Summit, 980 feet above sea level. Passing through the infamous Dove Holes Tunnel the line ran downhill to Chinley and New Mills. Here it split again, the original route running through Marple, first via Hyde and Guide Bridge to Manchester London Road, then later via Romley, Stockport Tiviot Dale and Heaton Mersey to Manchester Central. The left hand route at New Mills South Junction took the railway via the quicker new line, opened in 1902, through Disley Tunnel and Cheadle Heath to rejoin the old route at Heaton Mersey Station Junction.

Almost from the opening of the route throughout to Manchester, in 1867, both passenger and freight traffic was heavy, for it was the Midland's trunk route from London and the Midlands to the North West. It was also the main outlet from the coalfields of Derbyshire and Nottinghamshire to the industry and ports west of the Pennines, and an artery to the South for industrial production and imports.

Although the line is still open from Ambergate and Matlock, for local passenger services and from Buxton to Manchester and Cheshire for mineral traffic, the remainder of this magnificent route closed in 1968. No doubt this closure would have given great satisfaction to Ruskin, who condemned this line above all others, but valiant efforts are now being made by the Peak Railway Society to reopen the line from Matlock to Buxton, as both a tourist attraction and a commercial enterprise.

My attraction to the line came with teenage cycling, but it was not until I became a serious railway modeller, about 1970, that I realised I was hooked on the Peak District and I began to collect information for possible modelling projects. At the time I was living in Yorkshire and it was some years before my attention was turned fully to the Derby-Manchester line. By then the route had been closed several years and much had disappeared. Ambergate and Whatstandwell stations had been demolished, together with most of Millers Dale and many smaller buildings, and much of the line north of Chinley had been devastated. Bearing in mind the level of detail I wished to study, the lack of official records and the physical disappearance of the route, it rapidly became clear that my study would have to be limited to part of the line only. The obvious part was the 'mountain' section from Ambergate to Chinley.

In carrying out research into local history one experiences moments of elation, balanced more commonly by periods of disappointment for part of the story almost always proves elusive. For example, there are many private owner wagons from the Peak District which were never recorded and there are no known pre-war photographs of Rowsley or Gowhole sidings. As a bonus, however, one comes into contact with a number of incredibly helpful and knowledgeable people. It is a pleasure to record their assistance, but the devil's own job to decide where to start!

Without pictorial records research would be virtually impossible and I am deeply grateful to the sadly departed 'threesome' from Buxton, the late E.R. Morten, Dr S.T. Cowan and H. Townley, together with M.A. King, for considerable freedom in access to their collections. A formidable list of other photographic sources has been used and acknowledgement is given in the picture captions. To supplement the photographs there are over 100 line drawings of track plans, buildings and private owner wagons. Many of the drawings have been prepared from on-site measurements by the author, with the ever present Ann usually holding the other end of the tape. However the standard of this work is eclipsed by those drawings prepared by Martin Critchley, an architect whom the author had the pleasure of meeting at the L.M.S. Society Teach-in at Dillington House in 1976. I am also honoured to include the drawing of the up waiting shelter at Cromford, prepared by J.W. Tiernam as part of his R.I.B.A. final examinations. For access to track plans I must thank R.J. Coon, Chief Civil Engineer, British Rail London Midland Region and his staff.

For factual and historical data I must thank the Keeper of Public Records, Kew for access to minute books etc. I must also sincerely thank T. Griffin and J.B. Arnold for detailed help and advice on Cromford, the Matlock area and the limestone industry. To Frank Lomas I owe a special thank you for so generously giving from his immense knowledge of Bakewell. To Laurence Knighton, Glynn Waite and Chris Crofts I owe a great debt of gratitude for not only allowing me access to their extensive collections, but for proof reading the whole book and offering advice and encouragement throughout its preparation. I am also grateful to Stan Roberts for giving me free access to his extensive knowledge and drawings of Bakewell, Rowsley and Cromford.

In addition to the foregoing I must also thank the following who are primarily present or retired railwaymen, businessmen or enthusiasts: B.W. Ault (British Rail Engineering), B. Bowker (Severn Trent Water Authority), M. Bentley, Miss. M. Carey (Clerk to Bakewell Town Council), Miss Joyce Critchlow, J. Edgington, J. Ellis, the late S. Farrow, R.D. Fawkes, the late F. Frith, J.A. Fox, P.B. Garland (Standard Railway Wagon Co. Ltd), the late E. Gilbert, D.L.F. Gilbert, R. Gregory, C.R. Goodwin (Stancliffe Stone Ltd), H.G. Hall, D.G. Halliday, H. Heaven, M.T. Heyes (National Farmers' Union), Mrs Eveline Heyworth, D.J. Hopton, E.V. Hunt, M.D. Key (Via Gellia Colour Co. Ltd), S. Marshall (Gloucester Railway Carriage and Wagon Co. Ltd), J. Merritt, J.D. Rushton (ICI Mond Division), Miss Joan Sinar (Archivist, Derbyshire County Council), L. Smith, the late J. Turner, Mrs D. Wales (Sheffield City Polytechnic), H. Wardman, P. Weston, S. Willcox (Peakstone Lime), J.S. Wyatt (Regional Architect, British Rail).

I must also thank publicly Richard and Marilyn Morton (Sheffield City Polytechnic), who undertook the onerous task of preparing the index and Miss P. Kellett who typed the manuscript with commendable efficiency, as usual. At the end of the day, however, the responsibility for the content and its accuracy lies with the author. Omissions I am aware of, errors I am sure there will be. For these one can only apologise in advance and invite correction via the publishers. The compilation of this book has given the author many years of pleasure. It is hoped that some of this can now be shared with the reader.

Last but by no means least I must thank Ann and my two sons Richard and James who have developed an ability to live with my garden, my modelling and my writing.

Bill Hudson
South Wingfield, Derbyshire.

Chapter 1

A Thumbnail Scenario

Lying almost in the centre of England and extending some 55 miles from north to south, and about 35 miles at its broadest, Derbyshire forms the southern limit of the Pennines. It is a county of contrasts, almost equally divided into upland and lowland, and is surrounded on three sides by the industrial areas of Lancashire, the Potteries and the Yorks/Derbys/Notts coalfield. Today over 17 million people live within 50 miles of the Peak District National Park, yet in part its solitude can be frightening, even dangerous.

The southern and eastern parts of the county are unmistakably a part of the rolling farmland landscape of the Midlands, but in part this pastoral dream is interspersed with the surface installations of the mining industry, the associated spoil tipping and the austere pit villages. Yet to the west of the Exeter-Leeds trunk road and north of Derby the scenery changes to upland, becoming higher and wilder until it culminates in the north west in the peat bogs of Kinder Scout, a little over 2,000 feet above sea level.

The commonly accepted title of the 'Peak District' is somewhat of a misnomer for this upland area, for there are very few distinct heights, unlike North Wales or the Lake District. The name is actually derived from a tribal group of seventh century settlers called the Pecsaetans, 'the hill dwellers'.

The Peak must have been a desolate place at that time, and the local populace had more to worry about than develop an appreciation for the wild, natural beauty that today we take for granted. In fact it was to be some time before outsiders began to observe the area in detail, but in 1662 an opinion was expressed by Edward Browne, a native of East Anglia, that the Peak was a "strange mountainous, misty, moorish, rocky, wild country". To a point he may have been right, but the district is far from always misty, nor entirely wild, and its major attractions stem partially from its grandeur, and perhaps more so from its variety.

It was this variety which so impressed the late Sir John Betjeman, who wrote that within the Peak "stone never seems far below the surface, and stone of such variety, colour and quality as is found nowhere else in England". To understand the landscape, and the problems and opportunities this presented to the railway engineers, one must understand this stone.

The geological structure of the county dates predominantly from the carboniferous age, and the bulk of the rocks were laid down as three distinct strata. At the base is carboniferous limestone, some 1,600 feet thick. Above this are the shales and gritstones of the millstone grit series, approximately 2,200 feet in thickness. Finally the surface layer comprises the coal measures about 2,900 feet thick. Primeval earth movements folded these rocks and forced them upwards. Subsequent weathering and erosion removed the top two layers from the crests of the folds, to leave the limestone exposed in the 'Derbyshire Dome', and produce the 'edges' of shale and gritstone, which are such a prominent feature of the landscape to the east of the Derwent Valley and on the Derbyshire/Staffordshire border. In the extreme north of the area the gritstones proved more resistant and remain today as the Kinder plateau. An extension of these rocks runs southwards to the west of Buxton, and the joining plane between the gritstone and limestone was to present severe difficulties during the driving of Dove Holes Tunnel.

The higher parts of the county in the north and west naturally received the highest levels of precipitation, and the impervious nature of the rocks caused considerable run off, which in turn led to concentrated erosion and the formation of valleys. Where the softer shales of the Edale or Yoredale series were met, as in the Derwent Valley, erosion was more rapid and a wider valley was formed. Over the limestone the initial denudation was equally rapid, and by the time the harder rock was encountered the rivers were set on their downward course.

Thus although slowed down, the incision of the waters continued, and assisted by vertical splitting of the rock, narrow, steep sided valleys were formed by the rivers Wye and Dove. Chee Dale and Water-cum-Jolly on the Wye are perfect examples, but the most spectacular and widely known example of such weathering is in the Matlock Gorge, which interestingly still poses unanswered questions for the geologist.

North of Matlock the river has cut a relatively wide, straight course through the shales, but immediately below Matlock Bridge the waters turn sharply to the west into the limestone, abandoning what would have been a much easier course towards Tansley and the south. A major school of thought argues that the river was cutting down through the gritstones, and was sufficiently set in its course when it met the limestone to continue oblivious of the extra effort required. A secondary opinion, supported by the abruptness with which the river changes direction, is that its original course was blocked by ice coming in from the east, forcing the waters onto a south westerly course. Suffice it to say that having planned his railway up the valley to Cromford, Stephenson was offered a natural route to the north through the gorge.

While the Peak District is predominantly limestone and gritstone, other rocks and minerals are present in isolated areas and among the former, marble, basalt and chert have been worked at various times. Of the minerals, lead and copper were once extracted, and more recently the gangue or secondary minerals comprising fluorspar, barytes and calcite have assumed great importance. All of these natural deposits have been of value, at one time or another, and much of the wealth of the settlements and ducal estates was based on the extraction of lead, but it is the extraction of limestone for agricultural, construction and industrial purposes that has increasingly ruled much of the economy of the Derbyshire hills since the beginning of the 19th century.

The county is second only to Yorkshire in the proliferation of limestone quarries, many of which have been worked since Roman times. While the Wirksworth and Matlock areas have seen much quarrying, it is the land to the south west of Buxton, around Grin and Harpurhill, and to the east from Millers Dale to Dove Holes, that has produced the bulk of the output and suffered the greatest despolation. The latter area contains the largest limestone quarry in Europe, with a face 1¼ miles long and 200ft high, at Tunstead.

It is ironical indeed that the canals and railways which were built largely because the roads were unable to handle the bulk carriage of such minerals as limestone, have now been abandoned in the southerly direction, forcing the transport of vastly increased amounts of stone back on to the roads, which have remained virtually unchanged since the railways were built.

In addition to its rocks and minerals the Peak has another great natural resource in its rivers, and it is considered by many that the industrial revolution in the cotton industry began in Derbyshire when Sir Richard Arkwright built his first water powered mills at Cromford in 1771 and 1777. The successful use of such power encouraged him to build further mills at Cressbrook (1779) and Bakewell (1782). These ventures gave him confidence to tackle the fast flowing waters of the Derwent, and his Masson Mill, a six-storey structure in uncharacteristic red brick, built in 1783, remains in business today, and forms a familiar landmark to travellers approaching Matlock Bath from the south, on the main road from Derby.

Apart from cotton and textile mills, other industries including colour grinding, wire-drawing, timber, and various facets of engineering have come and gone, and many will be referred to in more detail later.

While natural resources, and later industrial development, have played their part, it cannot be forgotten that agriculture has been, and still is, a major element in the Peak District economy.

In the past, as now, altitude, climate, soil fertility and water supply posed problems, but the agricultural practices, and the resultant landscape are the product of developments in farming over the last 200 years. Although now primarily grassland, it is thought that much of the limestone was once given over to arable farming, but from the 14th century onwards there was a very gradual change to stock rearing. This was due in part to labour shortages and increasing wage bills, and to satisfy the escalating demands of the country's wool trade. This change eventually saw the breaking down of common lands into smaller fields, but it was not until the Enclosure Acts of the mid 18th century that the now familiar geometric pattern of limestone walls became established. Along with the enclosures came many new farm houses and associated buildings, which not only affected the landscape, but also called for a considerable increase in the output of quarried stone.

From the 1870s onwards there was a more marked decline in arable farming, and while a very limited amount of rye, oats, barley and wheat may have left the area by the newly opened railways, it was the increase in livestock farming that brought them much welcome traffic. Sheep farming had long been a tradition on the uplands, but following enclosure of the lower slopes, cattle breeding and dairying became an important activity, increasing markedly as the urban population surrounding the Peak District grew. Much of the dairy produce was previously disposed of in the form of cheese, but the rapid transportation offered by the railways allowed fresh milk to be delivered to the surrounding towns and cities. At first sales were made direct from farmers to small dealers, but later, there was a tendency more towards centralisation, and much of the milk was sent to the Co-operative Societies in the Manchester area. Later still a modern dairy was built at Rowsley and from the early 1930s milk was dispatched daily to Cricklewood, for the London market.

In addition to the carriage of milk by passenger trains, which usually called for some smart working by porters, the railways benefited by the transport of livestock, animal feedstuffs, fertilizers etc, and almost every station had the cattle dock so beloved of modellers.

Long before railways even became an idea in the mind of the entrepreneurs, communications had become clearly established, and the Peak District has been familiar to travellers for at least 2,000 years, with many clearly cut footpaths being established over the heights, avoiding the dangers and difficulties of the valleys below. By the time of the Romans a multitude of routes had been developed, and several of these, together with some new ones, particularly to Buxton (Aquae Arnemetiae), which became a bathing settlement, were surfaced as roads. Through the Norman era and the Mediaeval period the disappearance of such creatures as wolves and an increasingly more peaceful attitude among man led to the development of routes along the valleys, rather than over the hills, and by the 18th century, with the exception of the Bakewell-Buxton turnpike opened circa 1815, virtually all the communication and settlement pattern we know today had been established. The widespread surfacing of roads, and the great improvements following the 18th century Turnpike Acts consolidated this pattern. The opening of the Cromford Canal in February 1792, and the Peak Forest Canal some eight years later, greatly enhanced the outward shipment of minerals and agricultural produce, and the inward transportation of coal and manufactured goods.

The coming of the railways rapidly drew traffic away from the roads and canals, and by an act of Parliament in 1878, the status of Turnpike was nullified and the term 'main road' crept into use, their care and maintenance becoming the responsibility of the County Council on its formation in 1888.

By this time the urban pattern was developed, the agricultural economy was on a sound footing, and the extraction of minerals was rapidly growing, The railways across the Peak were able to expand their services and from their inception were to form a vital part of the economic and social life of the Peak District for well over a hundred years.

Plate 1 An up Manchester-St Pancras express nears bridge 8A south of Whatstandwell, behind Compound No. 1092, about 1927. The leading coach is an ex-LNWR 57ft cove roof corridor brake composite, still in LNWR livery. Behind this is a MR clerestory corridor brake third and two twelve-wheel dining cars, probably the 'twinned' kitchen/first plus open third.

(Railways Yesteryear)

2

Historical Background

The seeds of a railway from Derby to Manchester were sown with the opening of the first section of the North Midland Railway from Derby to Rotherham via Ambergate, and Chesterfield on 11th May 1840. The second phase began shortly afterwards, in the fertile mind of George Hudson and his thoughts eventually led to the incorporation of the 'Manchester, Buxton, Matlock & Midlands Junction Railway', some six years later.

In drawing up proposals for the route, under the guidance of George Stephenson, who had been appointed as the engineer, the Matlock company threw up one of the great 'might have beens' in railway history. The route to Rowsley was quite obvious, but northwards from there it presented a choice of the Wye or the Derwent valleys. Eventually Stephenson proposed that the line should follow the Wye Valley to Bakewell, passing through the estate of the Duke of Rutland. The company accepted his advice and in 1845 deposited its plans with Parliament, whose subsequent approval led to the Act of Incorporation on 16th July 1846. At that time the 'Manchester & Birmingham Railway' was anxious to secure an alternative route to the south and were more than pleased to support the Matlock company, morally and financially. However, before any substantial progress was made the M&BR amalgamated with three other companies to form the London & North Western Railway, the desire for another southerly route evaporated and support turned into alienation.

In the meantime the Duke of Rutland had expressed opposition to a line through the Wye Valley, thus forcing the MBM & MJR to look once again to the route through the Derwent Valley and the Duke of Devonshire's Chatsworth estate. The company had strong ties with the Cavendish family, through its chairman, George Henry Cavendish, MP and one of its directors, Joseph Paxton who was the sixth Duke's agent. In addition the Duke himself was strongly committed to a railway through the county and the change to the new route was not difficult to establish. In August 1846 Cavendish wrote that Stephenson had procured a route which would pass through Chatsworth Park without intruding upon the vista from the house. This new line was to have a station for Baslow and Edensor, and one near the site of the latter day Hassop station to serve Bakewell.

As these proposals became public the residents of Bakewell began to reflect upon the future of their town without a railway station and they approached the Duke of Rutland for assistance. The Duke was receptive to this concern and was able to induce the House of Lords to turn down the Chatsworth proposals. Indeed, evidence would tend to suggest that he was not so violently opposed to a railway through his own estate as historians would have us believe. However, the Matlock company was now firmly in favour of the route through the Derwent Valley, and put forward plans for an entirely new route from Rowsley to Whaley Bridge via Baslow, Grindleford Bridge, Hope and Edale. The proposals also included a branch from Chapel-en-le-Frith to Buxton and one from Rowsley to Bakewell. The plans for these new routes were submitted to Parliament in November 1847.

By this time the Duke of Rutland was openly in support of a railway across his estate, but on his terms, and in May 1848 revised proposals were put forward for a branch from Baslow to Bakewell to replace that originally proposed from Rowsley. The Act for the new line, and the Baslow to Bakewell branch, received its Royal Assent on 31st August 1848, but by then the railway mania bubble had burst and financial implications took preference over routeing considerations. So severe was the general lack of money that George Cavendish expressed the view that construction of the railway might not even begin, but in November 1848 a bold decision was taken and construction work was put in hand from Ambergate to Rowsley.

The line was officially opened on 4th June 1849, and from the outset became dependent on the Midland Railway, who not only provided the outlet to the south, but also provided the locomotives and rolling stock to work the line. This was not just a display of cordial relationships but was indicative of the Midland's desire to expand its empire to the north west.

The LNWR however, had inherited an interest in the line from the M&B, and on 1st July 1852 the MR were forced to agree to a joint lease of the line for a period of 19 years. With the signing of the lease the Midland thought it had secured a foundation for its desired route to Manchester; the North Western were convinced they had blocked the way. Indeed, with this in mind, the latter encouraged proposals put forward the following year for a line from its own metals at Stockport, to Whaley Bridge, via Disley. The Midland were naturally opposed to this line, as any route into the Peak District would conflict with its own proposals, but it was refused a hearing on the grounds that it had no right to intervene.

Three years later, in 1856, the MR approached the LNWR with a suggestion that the original proposals of the Matlock company should be resurrected, and that a through line across the Peak should be constructed. It was willing to start the ball rolling by putting up £200,000. The Duke of Devonshire was willing to contribute £50,000 and allow the line to pass through his Chatsworth estate. The North Western replied that while it thought provision should be made for local traffic, it could not recommend to its shareholders that they should become party to the expense of a through line for express traffic.

Meanwhile, and clearly demonstrative of the intense rivalry that existed among the railway companies at the time, the LNWR, which had previously assured the MR and the Manchester, Sheffield and Lincolnshire Railway that it had no intention of trying to reach Buxton, quietly backed a proposed extension of the line from Whaley Bridge to Buxton. The suggested route was sinuous and steeply graded, and when the proposals were made public, the MR clearly saw this as an attempt to prevent fast through running should they ever succeed in getting to Buxton themselves. Having attempted to promote a route to Manchester on friendly terms with the LNWR, and having failed, the Midland directors decided to press ahead alone, and on 25th May 1860, they were authorised to construct a line 15 miles in length from Rowsley to Buxton. The LNWR was not at all pleased, and although it could not block the proposals, it made it quite clear that it would not agree to through running. It also persuaded the MSLR to take any necessary steps to prevent a through route being established.

Thus temporarily thwarted the Midland looked to an alternative route to Lancashire and it was concluded that by heading north it could make a junction with the Lancashire & Yorkshire Railway, and so gain access to Manchester from the east. Accordingly an agreement was reached with this company in February 1861, but a few months later someone suddenly recalled that in 1850 the LYR, LNWR and the MSLR had drawn up the "Triple Agreement" by which they undertook to exclude all other companies from the traffic they carried. The Midland had lost again!

Having now been trying to reach Manchester for twelve years a lesser company might have accepted defeat, but not so the Midland, and they settled on the only course of action left open – build an independent line. To secure this the general manager and the chief engineer were ordered to find a suitable route for an extension of the Buxton line then nearing completion. The search began at once and according to F.S. Williams one fortuitous autumn morning the same year, the Midland chairman, Mr Beale, the deputy chairman, Mr Hutchinson, and James Allport, the general manager were visiting the area north east of Buxton. The land had already been surveyed and they were carrying plans on which various routes were sketched. While driving down a narrow lane, they came face to face with another dog cart carrying three gentlemen, who turned out to be a director and two officers of the MSLR. "What are you doing here?" the latter enquired. "We will show you," came the reply. The Midland party then explained that they were endeavouring to find a route for a new line to Manchester. Now the MSL also had its sights on the Peak District, and had recently received approval for the construction of the "Marple, New Mills & Hayfield Junction Railway", which would connect with previously authorised routes from Hyde, on their main line. They certainly had no wish to see a parallel line competing with their own, and must have immediately seen friendship with the MR as their best defence.

To pursue this they suggested that the two groups should spend the day together, and later, no doubt after dining at some local hostelry, where the liquid refreshment would have broken down the barriers further, the MSL director suggested that the Midland may wish to have use of his line from New Mills to Manchester. They of course leapt at the chance and it was soon agreed that a formal meeting would be arranged with the Sheffield company board, who had recently fallen out with the LNWR. It is a matter of history that this meeting was successful, and in 1862 the Midland's "Rowsley and Buxton Extension" line was promoted to run from Blackwell Mill (near Millers Dale) to New Mills.

The LNWR was at first furious, and then panic-stricken, and offered the MR facilities over its proposed Buxton line, via Disley and Stockport. The Midland was not to be fooled, and at the parliamentary hearing it made it quite clear that it understood the North Western's interpretation of the word 'facilities' to mean 'not a lot'. The LNWR still thought it could stop the line, for it felt that it had a serious objection in that gouty patients, travelling to take the waters at Buxton, would have to change trains at Blackwell Mill. Commendable as was the company's interest in the less fortunate members of society, it was faced with support for the new line from every land owner on the route, Manchester Corporation, Manchester Chamber of Trade and many of the city's leading business men and manufacturers. Needless to say the line was authorised by Parliament and as the Rowsley and Buxton line was nearing completion, work on the extension began.

A foretaste of the problems to be faced was gained from the fact that the line from Rowsley had taken over three years to build. Apart from the collapse of Haddon Tunnel, with tragic results and the consequent delay, the construction of the line as far as Great Longstone was comparatively rapid. From that point the engineers had to drive seven tunnels, totalling a little over 2,000 yards, erect two major viaducts and build eleven other bridges in 5½ miles. In due course, however, the work was completed and the line was carried up Ashwood Dale and into Buxton.

The official opening was celebrated by a special train from Derby and a luncheon in Buxton at 2.00pm on 30th May, 1863. The LNWR did not give in easily, and ran their official 'opening' train from Manchester on the same day, with their luncheon an hour later. The Midland line was opened for traffic the following day, but the line from Disley was not ready for public traffic until 15th June 1863.

It speaks volumes for the influence of the Duke of Devonshire and Sir Joseph Paxton, that after all the animosity the LNWR were eventually persuaded to build a fascia for their station identical to that of the Midland, in the interests of architectural unity. This must have been one of the earliest examples of the railways becoming involved in Town Planning.

Meanwhile, as the Directors and their guests were feasting in Buxton, the engineers and navvies were flogging away over the hill to the east. Some three years earlier, William Barlow, the chief engineer had already made up his mind about the route and while the line could be carried quite easily, albeit on a gradient of 1 in 90, from Blackwell Mill to Peak Dale, it then had to pierce the hill known as Cow Low. While this was the lowest pass through the Peak it was to prove extremely difficult to tunnel, with the south side of the hill being of limestone, which dipped steeply to the west, leaving the north side at its surface overlain by red sandstone and shales.

Near the south end of what was to become Dove Holes Tunnel, was a well known spot called the 'swallow hole' where a substantial brook rising in the vicinity of Buxton simply vanished underground. This puzzled the contractors, and further investigations in the nearby quarries revealed an underground stream running from the general direction of the

swallow hole. This in turn alerted the contractors, Messrs Echerley and Bayliss of Westminster, to the geological nature of the area, and fearful of the problems they might encounter, they refused to continue work, except on terms which the Midland found unacceptable. This was something of a set-back, but after much deliberation the railway company simply said, "We will build our own tunnel", and Mr. James Campbell was appointed to see the project through, under the guidance of the chief engineer.

The first essential operation was to divert the stream and prevent it flowing underground until it was out of harm's way. A channel was cut from the vicinity of the swallow hole towards Great Rocks Dale, and the water was diverted, only to rapidly disappear again about half a mile south of the tunnel. After some six months or so the water suddenly reappeared at the same point, and having, it was assumed, filled up a gigantic underground cavern, it resumed its course along the channel cut for it, until finally vanishing in another fissure near the site of Peak Forest station.

Once the stream had been taken care of, the actual work of tunnelling began, but the hardness of the rock at the northern end, and the vast quantities of water encountered in the limestone at the southern end, resulted in over three years being expended on the works. The completed tunnel was 2,860 yards long and at the time it was the biggest engineering operation the Midland Railway had undertaken.

With completion of the tunnel, progress with the remainder of the works was rapid and the line was completed to New Mills, and thus Manchester, in October 1866, and shortly afterwards opened for goods traffic.

The autumn of that year was marked by torrential rain over much of the country and drivers had hardly learnt the new route when a gigantic landslip occurred at Bugsworth, south of New Mills. No less than 16 acres of land, comprised of shales and clay, slipped downhill over the underlying sandstone, taking with it a road bridge and a neighbouring farm. Just south of the bridge was a curved viaduct, and this was straightened out by the force of the slip. Work was put in hand at once to rebuild the line, and some 400 men worked night and day for ten weeks. The line was deviated to the east of Bugsworth station, which was thus turned back to front. The total length of the diversion was about ½ mile and included the construction of a timber viaduct, two skew bridges, an embankment and a deep rock cutting. Later, in 1885, a new embankment was built and the remains of the original masonry viaduct and the temporary timber viaduct were removed.

The line was re-opened for both goods and passenger traffic on 1st February 1867 and the Midland began running express trains from London King's Cross to Manchester London Road, 18 years after its trains had first run north westwards from Ambergate. Meanwhile, at the opposite end of the system the company had been building its London extension and on 1st October 1868, St Pancras station was opened for traffic. Shortly afterwards two expresses a day were introduced each way between London and Manchester, on a five hour schedule, which equalled the best times by both the LNWR and GN/MSL routes, in spite of the climbs over Sharnbrook and Peak Forest. It was clear to the latter companies that a formidable competitor had arrived on the scene, but these expresses, plus local trains between Manchester, Buxton and Derby, were only the beginning of the Midland's subjugation of Lancashire and Cheshire.

Having allowed their competitor to use their line from New Mills to Manchester, with great advantage, the MSL quickly came to the conclusion that running and maintenance costs should be shared. The Midland could not argue, and in June 1869 an Act was passed by Parliament vesting the line from Hayfield to Hyde Junction in the "Sheffield and Midland Joint Committee", each company having an equal number of members on the Board. As part of the agreement the Midland undertook to take over the unfinished 'Manchester & Stockport Railway', which had been supported by the MSL and which was planned to run from Ashburys to Romiley. Although this implied a contribution towards the cost of the line, it also meant a more direct route to Manchester than the congested line via Guide Bridge. At the same time it was agreed to build a short line, known as the 'Marple Curve', between Romiley Junction and Bredbury Junction, on the Cheshire Lines Committee's Woodley-Stockport route. The Midland, which had become the third partner in the CLC three years earlier, certainly had no objections to being given facilities to run their trains directly to Stockport and Liverpool.

The two expresses of 1868 quickly grew into a more regular service, but the real value of the line was as a freight artery, with a vast flow of coal going north from the Derbyshire and Nottinghamshire pits to the domestic and industrial consumers in the North West, and manufactured goods and Liverpool's imports coming south. Such was the growth of traffic that as early as 1870 a huge goods depot, covering 70 acres, was opened at Ancoats, in Manchester, at the then astronomic sum of £1½ million.

Just as traffic was settling down, and income was proving that the venture had been worthwhile, the Midland had to return to the negotiating table, for as readers will recall, 1871 marked the end of the lease of the line from Ambergate to Rowsley. In anticipation of this event, and realising that the fight to agree amicable terms with the MBM & MJ would be a difficult one, the Midland had already opened part of an alternative route. This took the form of a branch leaving the main line at Duffield, between Derby and Belper, and running to Wirksworth. From here it would have been possible to tunnel under the Heights of Abraham at Matlock Bath, and run up the western side of the valley through Darley Dale to Rowsley. Negotiations came so close to deadlock that a detailed survey was put in hand for this extension, but at the last minute the heads of terms were agreed with the Matlock directors, and the Midland took over the line and the Cromford canal, "with all the liabilities and obligations thereon".

In 1874 the Midland took advantage of its holding in the CLC and began to work a combined St Pancras, Liverpool and Manchester service. At first the Liverpool coaches had to be worked into London Road and then out via Woodley to gain the route for Liverpool, but this changed with the opening of the 'Marple Curve' in April 1875. From that date the trains were split, or joined, at Marple, which had been enlarged in anticipation of this new traffic.

By this time the growth in Midland traffic at London Road, together with the increase in MSL trains, was giving rise to severe congestion, and the latter gave the MR three years notice to quit. It was indeed fortunate that the CLC had recently been authorised to construct a new terminus, to be known as Manchester Central, and being a partner, the Midland were naturally anxious to gain access to the new station. All they had to do was find a route. Fate was certainly on their side, for in 1873 the 'Manchester South District Railway' had been authorised as a line from Manchester to Alderley, which included a line from Heaton Mersey on the Godley-Liverpool line, to Throstle Nest Junction on the Manchester-Liverpool line.

Construction had not gone ahead for the GNR were going through a period of poor relations with the CLC, and refused to give support, and the MSL could not make up its mind. In characteristic fashion the Midland stepped in and adopted the proposals as its own, opening the line on 1st January 1880.

While this line had been under construction the new Central station had been rising, and with a roof having a clear span of 210 feet, some 90 feet above rail level, it turned out at first sight to be very much a twin of St Pancras, even to the extent of having similar warehousing facilities below the platforms. Where it differed however was on the frontage. Here temporary wooden office accommodation was meant to be developed as a hotel, but it never was, and remained in use up to the closure of the station. The Midland did eventually get its proposed hotel, in 1903, but on a separate site.

The station opened on 1st July 1880, and principal services from St Pancras and the south were immediately transferred from London Road. For a time the Liverpool trains were worked via Central, but this proved to be slower, and a reversion was made to splitting at Marple.

While developments to the passenger services had been going on around Manchester, the expansion of freight traffic had continued unabated and in the early 1870s the problems of congestion and operation had to be faced. In searching for solutions two important considerations emerged. First, it had become clear that to increase efficiency, and to prevent delays to express passenger trains, freight loadings over the severe gradients up to Peak Forest had to be reduced. Secondly, to ease the chronic congestion at the northern end of the line, some earlier sorting of traffic for Buxton, Manchester, Liverpool, and other north western destinations had to be carried out. Attention was therefore turned to finding a suitable site for a marshalling yard, and it was not long before the answer became obvious – Rowsley. Here there was not only an existing engine shed, albeit only for one locomotive, but much more important, there was land available for development.

Thus plans were drawn up for the laying out of sidings, and under the MR (Additional Powers) Act 1874, the company was authorised to acquire the necessary land. It is officially recorded that new up and down goods lines were brought into use on 19th March 1877, and this is generally accepted as the opening date of Rowsley Yard. The opening of the sidings was following by the completion of a new three road engine shed and associated facilities adjoining the old existing shed in 1879.

By the late 1880s the Midland had well developed services to Manchester, Liverpool, Stockport, Warrington, Chester and Southport, but it was still not satisfied with its grip on the North West. In 1889, a very short but important line, known as the Midland Curve, was opened to link Ashburys to the LYR at Ancoats Junction, thereby giving access to Manchester Victoria. It soon became possible to provide through coaches from St Pancras to Victoria and on to Bolton and Blackburn, again detaching these coaches at Marple. Having abolished 2nd class, and uprated 3rd class by the provision of upholstered seats some 14 years earlier, (to the horror of other railway companies) the Midland soon captured a sizeable proportion of the traffic from these Lancashire towns.

Although the company had arrived comparatively late in the North West, the MR enjoyed the rapid growth experienced by all the railways during the 1890s, but this led to problems of congestion yet again, and nowhere was this worse than between Chinley and Heaton Mersey. The opening of the Dore and Chinley line from Sheffield in 1894, which joined the Derby line at Chinley North Junction, was probably the last straw. In addition to the sheer volume of traffic which included Great Central and CLC trains, it should be recalled that the line from New Mills to Manchester was built in eight different stages, and with sharp curves, gradients and many junctions it was quite unsuitable for express running. Once more the Midland faced up to the problem and sought permission for a new line, suitable for high speed running, from New Mills to Heaton Mersey. This was authorised in 1898 and shortly afterwards approval was given for the quadrupling of the line from New Mills South Junction, where the 'new line' joined the Marple route, to Chinley North Junction, the construction of a new station at Chinley, and the laying out of sidings at Gowhole just west of Bugsworth. The latter were necessary to further refine the sorting carried out at Rowsley, and to deal with heavy traffic, particularly coal, coming via the Dore and Chinley line.

All this newly approved work commenced at once, but with the volume of engineering work involved in building a six platform station, opening out Bugsworth Tunnel, and driving a new tunnel, well over two miles long, at Disley, it was not until the summer of 1902 that the new facilities were brought into use. Chinley at once supplanted Marple as the hub of the Midland system in the North West, and saw considerable activity in the marshalling of express passenger trains, and the interchange of passengers on local services. With the opening of the 'new line' the timings of the St Pancras–Central trains was cut to 3 hours 50 minutes, and cut again by a further 15 minutes in 1904, keeping them in line with those of the LNWR and GCR. A far cry indeed from the five hours of 1868, and demonstrative of the track improvements and rapid developments in operating practices and motive power over the last three decades of the 19th century.

This period of expansion was also marked by the drawing up of proposals for a new engine shed at Rowsley, and by major quadrupling works, including a new viaduct, at Millers Dale.

The opening years of the 20th century saw the heyday of all the railway companies of Great Britain, but as the first decade closed the development of the petrol engine and political uncertainty in Europe produced ominous rumblings. The storm broke in 1914 with the outbreak of World War I, and the railways were immediately taken under Government control. As the war progressed matters went from bad to worse with skilled staff leaving for the forces, either voluntarily or later under conscription, workshops given over to munitions manufacture and rolling stock sent all over Europe for military transportation. At the same time the railways were called upon to handle unprecedented volumes of special traffic, while still maintaining at least a semblance of normal services. By 1917, however, savage cuts had been made in express passenger services and many of the through coaches had been withdrawn, some never to be restored.

During the war maintenance of track, buildings and rolling stock had been reduced to essential or emergency work, and with the cessation of hostilities the railways were thoroughly run down, physically, financially and in staff morale. Nevertheless, some companies had fared slightly better than others, and it became obvious that some sort of unification, with the stronger supporting the weaker, was the only way forward. Total state control, known lovingly as National-isation, was anathema to the Government of the day, and a compromise was reached by drawing the various companies into four large groups. Thus, at one minute past midnight on 1st January 1923, the London, Midland and Scottish Railway Company was formed, and those old adversaries, the MR and LNWR found themselves uneasy stablemates.

In spite of the rivalries railwaymen at all levels were optimistic of a return to pre-war standards, but alas this was not to be. In an attempt to give priority to military traffic the Government tried to restrict private travel by imposing a 50% fare increase on 1st January 1917. It also cancelled all excursion trains from the same date. After the war the railways remained under Government control and as a result of the inevitable post war inflation, fares (and goods rates) were again raised on 6th August 1920 to 75% above pre-war levels. On the day it was formed, 1st January 1923, the LMS reduced fares to the 1917 level, but the damage had been done. The increased charges had driven away traffic and the situation had not been helped by the Government selling off cheaply vast numbers of army surplus vehicles, many of which were snapped up by ex-servicemen who then set up in business as road hauliers. By 1923 the number of goods road vehicles had grown to over 160,000, double the pre-war total, while the ownership of private cars was gradually increasing and the omnibus companies were becoming established.

In facing up to competition from the roads the LMS had to increase efficiency and shortly after Grouping operating problems at Rowsley became the centre of attention. As far back as 1898 a totally new engine shed had been considered, and the following year a site at Darley Dale was selected, but in uncharacteristic fashion the Midland proceeded no further. It therefore fell to the LMS to build the new shed, and when it opened in 1926 it was probably the most modern and well equipped motive power depot in the country. Shortly afterwards congestion in the sidings was eased by expansion of facilities on the down side.

By this time problems were arising on the North Midland line between Derby and Ambergate. From the former, northwards to Duffield there were four tracks, but from there to Ambergate the original dual line remained, and with Sheffield and Manchester trains competing for line space, considerable congestion occurred regularly. The major constraints to widening this stretch of line lay at Belper, where much of the line was in cutting, passing through the heart of the built up area, and while this problem must have been discussed, it was decided to tackle the problem from the northern end. Accordingly plans were drawn up and eventually approved by Parliament, to widen the 1½ miles from Ambergate South Junction to Broadholme. The work began in May 1930, and involved a new viaduct crossing the Derwent, widening of the embankment to the south, the opening out of Longland Tunnel and a second new river crossing at Dunge. This was the last major engineering job to be carried out on the

Plate 2 Everything forward and trust in the Lord. The driver leans nonchalantly on the cabside as 4F No. 4019 climbs away from Rowsley with a down mineral train for Buxton on 2nd July 1938. This engine was one of the last MR built 4Fs and was one of only fourteen (Nos 4013–4026) which did not have a beaded cabside, just a plain strip between the upper and lower panels. It is seen here with a Fowler chimney, piston tail rod guides removed and a Johnson 3,500 gallon riveted tender.

(E.R. Morten)

Derby-Manchester line, and the works to the tunnel involved the removal of no less than 1,000,000 cubic yards of rock, to leave a steep sided cutting. It is a tribute to the skill of the engineers and operating staff that normal train services were maintained for much of the time the contract was in hand. The implementation of this scheme certainly eased some of the congestion, but with hindsight one questions its value, for the remaining dual track section to Duffield, and the need for up trains from Manchester to cross the down line to Sheffield, at Ambergate, still caused potential delay.

Nevertheless the work which was carried out must have provided some welcome employment in the locality, at a time when Britain was reaching the climax of the economic crisis into which it had been drifting for some years. There was widespread and severe depression in every aspect of trade and commerce, with manufacturing industry being hit particularly hard. This of course led to a drastic reduction in the demand for coal, huge quantities of which had previously been hauled over the Peak to fuel the factories of Lancashire and the North West. Passenger receipts naturally fell as fewer businessmen, and even fewer private travellers used the railways. Gradually, however, the country pulled itself together, and by the mid 1930s considerable recovery had been made.

At this time the demand for increased efficiency from the LMS chairman, Sir Josiah Stamp, was at its height and a major programme of motive power depot re-organisation was put in hand, which included modernisation of the facilities at Buxton. Up to then the sheds built by the MR and LNWR had remained in use, each serving their own stations and yards, although some intermixing of shunting duties took place, but such duplication was really unnecessary. The cramped site of the Midland shed, and its tortuous access, presented no scope for alteration, but the North Western shed, opened in 1892, had ample space available. Mechanical coaling and ash plants were installed, along with a new turntable and additional storage roads, and the engines and men were transferred up the hill from the Midland shed, which was closed in 1935.

Elsewhere on the line, particularly from Chinley northwards, local services had retained much of their custom, as more and more people moved out of the Manchester conurbation to live in the attractive villages on the western fringes of the Peak District. By 1938 all traces, if not the memories, of the slump had gone and holiday and tourist traffic was again important, with the summer timetable showing many extra trains. There was for example a daily fast train from Nottingham and Derby to Southport, via Marple and the CLC. An even more interesting service was the 11.32pm (Friday only) from Manchester Victoria to Yarmouth via Chinley, Ambergate, Nottingham, Melton Mowbray and South Lynn. This was balanced by two return workings from Yarmouth at 8.00am and 9.15am on Saturday.

Just as the railways were settling down, and the LMS was looking to the future with a modernised locomotive and rolling stock fleet, a certain gentleman in Europe threw the world into chaos, and on 3rd September 1939, Great Britain once again found itself at war with Germany. In repetition of events some 25 years earlier, the railways were immediately placed under Government control. Since 1914 great advances, if one can call them such, had been made in the machinery of warfare and Britain prepared itself for a spate of aerial bombardment. Drastic cuts were made to passenger services, (although later there were some restorations) along with a deceleration of all trains, and a maximum speed limit of 60mph was introduced. Blackout precautions were imposed from the start, and apart from the reduction in lighting at stations, goods yards, etc., engines had their cab windows painted out and carriage lighting was reduced. At an early date all signposts were removed, and on the railways most station nameboards were taken down, so as not to assist the enemy should an invasion occur. It was at this period that many Midland stations lost the well known angled nameboards so beloved of modellers. The bombing did not come, which was doubly fortunate, for in January 1940, the country was hit by the most severe weather since the great storms of 1916. The worst affected area was a belt from Derbyshire northwards to the Glasgow area and the line through the Peak was completely blocked by snow drifts

for several days, and badly disrupted for a good deal longer.

While the cuts in services led to fewer passenger trains between St Pancras and Manchester, the flows of freight traffic were considerably increased. Output from the collieries was maintained and often accelerated, with many men fighting the natural desire to enlist for their country, and remaining in a 'preferred' occupation, of which mining was one. With factories everywhere given over to munitions and other war time production, as much coal as possible was carried from the pits of Derbyshire and Nottinghamshire to the industrial towns in Lancashire. In the reverse direction came not only the produce of these factories, bound for the south coast, and thence the forces in Europe, but also a high proportion of the food, fuel, and armaments brought into the Irish sea ports by the great convoys of ships from America. Gowhole and Rowsley sidings bore the brunt of this traffic, and the latter, together with the associated engine shed saw the beginning of its busiest period ever. As the war progressed much of the line fortunately escaped bombing, but serious disruption to services did occur with the heavy night bombardment of Manchester in 1941.

Just as in the First World War maintenance of track and rolling stock took a low priority, but with the heroic effort of all staff the railways struggled on and finally when peace came in 1945, they were able to relax slightly, and perhaps even spare a thought for the future.

The future, however, was to be far different, for with the election of a Labour Government the same year, and memories of the reorganisation necessary to save the railways after the last war, it became ominously clear that Nationalisation would follow. For a time ordinary staff had other things to worry about, for as late as the autumn of 1946 the LMS was still running approximately 550 troop trains, and 300 special freight trains for the forces, every week, and some of this traffic ran over the Peak.

Hardly had this special traffic begun to subside when staff resources took another hammering from the weather, and early in February 1947 the Peak District was struck by snow storms which made those of 1940 pale into insignificance.

At this time considerable acrimonious debate was taking place in Parliament over the Transport Bill, but even though all and sundry knew that state control was inevitable, the LMS was still bravely looking to the future. The summer of 1947 saw continual reference to the speed by which the American railways were turning to diesel traction, and H.G. Ivatt, the Chief Mechanical Engineer decided upon an analysis of the economics of steam versus diesel power. To fulfil this experiment two diesel-electric locomotives of 1,600hp were ordered from the English Electric Company, and the first, No. 10000 entered service in December proudly lettered on its side LMS. It was intended that these engines would run in tandem against the 'Duchess' class on the West Coast Main Line, and singly against the 'Black 5s' on the Midland. Moreover, it was the St Pancras-Manchester services which saw the bulk of the Midland routes experimentation, and while the schedules laid down did not demand anything like maximum output from the steam locomotives, it was clear that on the gradients up to Peak Forest, the diesels were superior.

While the final days of 1947 saw the second strange motive power on the line (the first had been Ljüngstrom's turbine tested by the LMS in 1927), 1948 was to see further unusual visitors, as the route was one of those chosen to participate in the historic locomotive exchanges of that year. These trials were carried out by the infant British Railways, created on 1st January 1948, supposedly to plan its future locomotive fleet, based on the best of the existing designs. It was only natural that hill climbing should be an important part of the tests and the Derby-Manchester line was admirably suited for the trials with mixed traffic locomotives. To represent these engines four types were chosen, an LMS Class 5, a GWR 'Hall', an LNER B1 and an SR 'West Country'. The latter two, No. 61251 *Oliver Bury* and No. 34005 *Barnstaple* were used on the Peak line.

While these tests were of very great interest to railway enthusiasts and photographers, O.S. Nock has expressed doubts that they were of any real technical value. There was no common standard of coal supply or driving, nor any uniformity in the standards of 'conducting', for each engine was driven by men familiar with the machine but not the route, and pilots were carried at all times. It all seemed rather pointless for Riddles, the new CME, and his team had already decided upon a range of new standard locomotive designs based very much on Stanier's engines for the LMS.

Apart from these trials, and the appearance of locomotives and rolling stock in new liveries, the first physical change was the appearance at stations of the familiar enamel signs for the station name, 'Way Out', 'Waiting Room' etc. On the London Midland Region these signs were maroon, with white letters, and unlike the MR and LMS practice, the station name was carried in small totems on lamps, roof pillars etc., in addition to the large name at the platform ends, giving a much higher level of information.

The years following the war saw shortages in almost every facet of life, and it was not until the early 1950s that the overhaul of rolling stock and permanent way was sufficiently advanced to permit the restoration of something like pre-war services. By this time it was beginning to be too late, for considerable traffic had been lost forever to the roads, and with over one million goods vehicles on the roads at the end of 1952, and cheap motor cars becoming rapidly available, the railways were deteriorating. In 1955 British Railways made its first deficit and the policy of reducing costs by closing little used stations and lines was born.

It was rapidly becoming clear that if railways were to remain an efficient and competitive force in the country's transportation system, then a major overhaul of their infrastructure and stock was necessary. Thus in 1955 the Government introduced its Modernisation Plan. The main proposals of the plan were to eliminate steam power and turn to diesel traction as an interim measure leading to electrification; to update passenger vehicles and drastically reduce the huge fleet of low capacity freight wagons.

Although the Modernisation Plan was put in hand without delay, with some beneficial results, it did not prevent the overall downward trend in the fortunes of the railways, and by 1962 the annual loss had reached the then staggering figure of £104m. At the end of that year reorganisation of the administrative structure saw the disappearance of the British Transport Commission and the Railway Executive and their replacement by the British Railways Board. The first chairman

of this new body was Dr Richard Beeching, who did for railways what Count Dracula did for camping holidays in Transylvania. The following year saw the publication of his first report, "The reshaping of British Railways", which has subsequently become known by all as the "Beeching Report". Interestingly this did not call for the closure of the Derby–Manchester route.

In pure economic terms much of the report rang true. Many of the lightly used passenger and freight services ran at such a loss as to nullify the profitability of the busier lines, and many of the suburban services in and around the major towns and cities ran practically empty for the greater part of the day. On the freight side, in spite of road competition the railways had continued to concentrate on small consignments, rather than setting their sights on the bulk haulage to which they were eminently suited. The remedies were obvious: close down the unprofitable parts of the network, make the commuter pay for his needs, and concentrate on bulk freight haulage. Lest it go down in history that Beeching was nothing more than a hatchet man, it should be remembered that in his follow up report, "The Development of the Major Trunk Routes", he put forward the concept of concentrating traffic on *certain* lines, and made out a sound case for investment. In plain English his view was that the railways should devote themselves to the tasks for which they were technically best qualified. However, we digress!

Two aspects of the Modernisation Plan were of direct consequence to the Derby–Manchester line. The first was the introduction of the "Blue Pullmans". These were the brainchild of H.P. Barker, a part time member of the British Transport Commission, who argued passionately for the introduction of high speed, luxury trains aimed primarily at the businessman, and based on the trans-European express trains then being developed to compete with air travel. The idea of the Pullman principle of meals at every seat, and multiple unit construction allowing high stock utilisation and quick turnaround, proved attractive and the Commission set up a small team to develop it.

To begin with the operating authorities were not keen on the idea, and in particular the London Midland Region, who must have known that the forthcoming electrification of the West Coast Main Line would cause severe disruption to its London–Manchester services, said that they could only diagram the units for one daily trip from Derby to St Pancras and back. Fortunately the Committee studying the matter were quickly able to disprove this and show that paths could be found for a morning train from Manchester Central to St Pancras, with an evening return, and a fill in turn to Leicester, and later Nottingham, during the day.

Plate 3 LNER B1 No. 61251 *Oliver Bury* leaves Millers Dale with a London-Manchester express in June 1948 during the locomotive exchanges.

(E.R. Morten)

The New **MIDLAND PULLMAN**

First Class de luxe travel — Supplementary fares

8.50 am	Manchester Central ↑	9.21 pm	Mondays to Fridays from 4th July	12.45 pm	St. Pancras ↑	4.00 pm
9.04 am	Cheadle Heath	9.07 pm			Leicester	
12.03 pm ↓	St. Pancras	6.10 pm		2.10 pm ↓	London Road	2.33 pm

The last word in rail comfort. Limited accommodation, book in advance

Plate 4 One of the most colourful posters produced by British Railways London Midland Region, was that designed to advertise the introduction of the "Midland Pullman", which entered service on 4th July 1960.

(Author's collection)

Plate 5 In recognition of its status as 'capital' of the Peak District, Buxton enjoyed a service of through carriages to St Pancras. In this view 3F 0-6-0, No. 43329 awaits departure for Millers Dale at 9.30am on 15th October 1957, where the carriage will be attached to the 9.00am Manchester Central-St Pancras. To the right of the engine is the cattle dock erected in 1866.

(E.R. Morten)

Thus the trains, which it was hoped would pioneer a new concept of inter-city travel, were introduced on 4th July 1960 and with their high speed and good food became, for a time, very popular with the executives who used them. But despite the use of the Schlieren bogie, designed and used with great success under lightweight coaches in Switzerland, bad riding and vibration from the motors soon gave rise to criticism. While the units provided an acceptable alternative to the temporary chaos on the Euston–Manchester services, they quickly lost popularity when the electrification was completed in 1966, and they were quickly withdrawn, after half-hearted utilisation on the Western Region.

The second, and by no means so welcome feature of the plan, was the rationalisation of the freight business. With vast amounts of small consignment traffic, and much mineral distribution, having been lost to the roads, and with less and less coal being burned as a prime fuel by both domestic and industrial consumers, the necessity for the sorting and marshalling of freight trains fell dramatically. As a result activities at Rowsley yard were scaled down, and complete closure of the sidings came on 27th April 1964.

By this time the widespread introduction of diesel power and the general reduction in the loading of freight trains enabled the operating authorities to look at the costs of banking north of Rowsley. It was suggested that additional catch points be put in at selected locations, to deal with runaways, and that banking engines be dispensed with. However, the intransigence of the trade unions led to the diversion of the remaining freight traffic between Derby and the North West over the relatively easy route via Chesterfield and the Dore and Chinley line. With the sidings closed and no requirements for banking engines, Rowsley shed closed shortly afterwards. In two years 248 men had been made redundant and life on the railway became something to recall over a pint or two. Even today, people in Darley Dale and Rowsley speak lovingly about the 'old days' with memories so clear the listener would think they had just finished a turn of duty.

Although these events had a dramatic effect on the local railway community, it was the proposed withdrawal of passenger services which caught the wider public eye, and after the introduction of the new high speed services from Euston to Manchester Piccadilly (as London Road had been renamed after its rebuilding), the routes in the Peak District came under renewed scrutiny. Among the lines put forward for closure were the LNWR route to Buxton, the MR branch to Buxton, the Cheadle Heath route and the Hope Valley line. In addition all local trains were to be withdrawn between Derby and Manchester, but it was recommended that a semi-fast service should remain, calling at Chinley, New Mills, Marple and stations to Piccadilly.

It goes without saying that there was a great public outcry against these proposals, and while it was accepted that economies had to be made, it was widely thought that Dr Beeching had gone much too far. Fortunately closure of railway lines is not that simple, for on Nationalisation the Transport Users Consultative Committee (TUCC) was set up as an early form of consumer protection body. Although objections to closures could only be made to the Committee on the grounds of hardships, it was better than nothing.

When the notices were posted late in 1963, announcing the withdrawal of all passenger services to Buxton via the remaining routes (the Ashbourne line having lost its passenger services in 1954), the TUCC was swamped with objections. British Railways had made a poor choice for a test case, as many commuters used the railway, particularly the LNWR route to Manchester, and they put forward a strong case. It could not be disputed that the A6 road was heavily congested and along with all other roads into the town was badly affected, and sometimes closed by heavy snows in winter. At the end of a long and bitter campaign even the anti-rail Minister of Transport, Ernest Marples, had to admit defeat and refuse to give his consent to the closure.

In the meantime the level of car ownership was increasing daily, and passenger traffic on the main lines through the Peak continued to fall. As a result BR again proposed the closure of the Millers Dale-Buxton branch, and the withdrawal of all stopping services between Derby and Manchester. Predictably another fight was put up, but this time the Minister, then Mrs Barbara Castle, agreed to the proposals. Closure came in two stages, with stations between Cheadle Heath and Stockport Tiviot Dale, and all traffic round the Marple Curve ceasing to run on 2nd January 1967. Two months later stopping services from Chinley to Matlock, and on the Buxton branch, were withdrawn.

The local service from Derby to Matlock remained although Matlock Bath and Nottingham Road stations were closed. A prime factor in the retention of this route was that the County Council had moved its headquarters from Derby to Smedley's Hydro at Matlock, but many staff preferred to keep their homes in Derby. It was not unduly difficult to prove that genuine hardship would result from loss of the rapid travel facilities provided by the railway.

Main line trains continued to run from St Pancras to Manchester Central via Millers Dale and Cheadle Heath, but with much quicker timings and more modern rolling stock on the Euston–Manchester services, it was only the intermediate towns such as Leicester, Nottingham and Derby which still derived a benefit from the Midland route. These trains still called at Chinley to connect with a new semi-fast service which had been introduced between Sheffield and Manchester Piccadilly via the Dore and Chinley line. However, with no local passenger traffic and no through freight trains it was argued that the cost of maintaining the line over Peak Forest, with its many tunnels and bridges, and the ever present problem of water seepage in Dove Holes Tunnel, for a few express trains, was excessive. On 1st July 1968 these trains were diverted on to the Dore and Chinley line and the Midland's great route through the Peak was closed. Today, the remaining bridges and tunnels are in remarkably good order and the section through Dove Holes Tunnel to Buxton is still open for the considerable limestone traffic from Hindlow, Tunstead and Peak Forest.

As a prelude to this final closure expresses had been re-routed to terminate at Manchester Piccadilly, no doubt disturbing a few ghosts in the process. In May 1969, Manchester Central was closed, but it was not demolished and after many years' use as a car park it has now been converted into a major exhibition centre. For a while the last vestige of the old order lingered at Chinley, where the remaining Nottingham and St Pancras trains called, almost from force of habit, but it was no longer a junction for anywhere. Early in 1972 the Sheffield local trains were extended beyond Chinley to terminate at New Mills, where local services from Manchester Piccadilly terminated. In May 1972 the St Pancras–Manchester service was reduced to two trains each way daily and the Chinley stop was omitted. At the same time several of the Sheffield–Manchester expresses were re-timed to stop and connect with the locals at New Mills, which thus became the hub of the remaining Midland line services to Lancashire. It was not to be long before the remaining London trains were allowed to fade into obscurity and St Pancras finally lost all direct connection with Manchester.

All but one of the buildings and the footbridge at Chinley, have been demolished and the platforms reduced to two. Although a few trains still call today it is no more than a semi-derelict halt, occasionally enlivened by the steam specials which run on the Dore and Chinley line from time to time.

While the Midland Railway had battled for 31 years to get its trains from Derby to its own terminus in Manchester, British Railways succeeded in closing the route in under five. Not only did this cause hardship to the towns and villages along the line, but it also denied the traveller the pleasure of passing over one of the most scenic railway lines in Britain.

Trains, even steam hauled, may return to this route under the control of the Peak Railway Society, but in the meantime it is with the scenic section of the route, from Ambergate to Chinley, that this book is now concerned.

Chapter 3

Ambergate

Before the North Midland Railway opened on 5th July 1840, Ambergate was no more than a group of cottages near the confluence of the rivers Derwent and Amber. It was also the junction of the turnpike from Nottingham with that from Belper to Cromford, opened on 1st July 1818. Some six miles north along the latter, lay the Matlocks, which within the limits of pre-railway travel had already become established as a tourist centre. At that time the civic leaders, who were quick to appreciate the advantages of the new-fangled railway, could not foresee a line through their own town and so brought pressure to bear on the North Midland Board to build a 'First class station' at Ambergate, to serve their townsfolk and visitors. This potential source of traffic and the meeting of established roads from surrounding towns and villages was sufficient to convince the railway company that a station was desirable.

As the NMR approached Ambergate from the south it pierced a low ridge by Longland Tunnel, crossed the River Derwent and pierced a second spur of higher land, by Toadmoor Tunnel, as it curved gently eastwards into the Amber Valley. Spoil from these two tunnels was laid out north of the second and the first station was built on this site, conveniently served by the original road to Ripley which had become a minor loop when the turnpike was opened. Minor that is except for the fact that it gave access to the Thatched House Inn which was to cater for the bodily needs of travellers for some years to come. The facilities at the station consisted of a main building on the northbound platform with a shelter on the opposite side, a small goods shed and a station house.

The main building was designed by Francis Thompson in a symmetrical Jacobean style, with an elaborate square central porch on the platform side. It is probable that the goods shed and house were built at about the same time but it is uncertain if Thompson had a hand in their design.

In 1846 George Stephenson was appointed engineer to the Manchester, Buxton, Matlock and Midland Junction Railway, a position he already held with the NMR. In drawing up plans for the Matlock line, it is believed two curves were proposed at Ambergate to join the main line, one south towards Derby, the other north towards Leeds. Logic suggests that the south curve should have been built at the time, but it was the north one which was eventually put in, presumably with a view to joining

up with the Ambergate, Nottingham and Boston and Eastern Junction Railway which was authorised on the same day as the MBM & MJ. This must have been considered as very important for the centre line of the curve passed straight through the station house, which was dismantled and re-erected close to the northern portal of Toadmoor Tunnel. The North Junction and associated sidings gave access for freight traffic, while a line running off the outside of the curve towards the rear of the existing station served a new platform for passenger trains. A turntable and basic coaling and watering facilities were provided for locomotives. The line opened between Ambergate and Rowsley for passengers on 4th June 1849, for coal on 20th August 1849 and general goods by the end of 1849.

Although by no means ideal these arrangements could cope with the traffic to Rowsley, but when plans were being formulated for the extension from Rowsley to Buxton and Manchester it became clear that the layout would require complete revision. Parliamentary powers were thus sought to build a new line from a point south of Toadmoor Tunnel to join the existing branch, thereby allowing through running from Derby and the south. The new track curved sharply away from the main line immediately north of the Derwent bridge but the severity of the curve later gave cause for concern. In July 1875 a plan was approved to widen the Derwent bridge over its last 45ft on the down side and the curve was eased by moving the junction slightly to the south. From the junction the line curved round Thacker's Chase, where considerable fill, supported by a massive retaining wall, was required. The route then crossed Heage Road (now Newbridge Road) and curved westwards over Chesterfield Road to join the original Rowsley line at the Amber Viaduct, which was widened to accommodate the new junction.

A contract for this work was let in 1862 and by 1st April 1863 the engineer was able to report to the construction committee that the retaining wall was complete and that work on bridge Nos 1 and 2 was well in hand. It was decided at this meeting that the platforms for the new station to be opened at the South Junction could advantageously be erected by the current contractor, Mr Thompson. Work proceeded rapidly and following inspection by the Board of Trade the line was

Plate 6 In 1875 the bridge over the River Derwent at Ambergate was widened at its north western corner, to ease the curve on to the Manchester line, as clearly seen in this view of 15th June 1911, taken from the signal box steps.

(British Railways)

opened on 1st June 1863 for passenger traffic, temporary waiting shelters having been erected on the new platforms. On 3rd June it was resolved that "the engineer be requested to confer with Mr Paxton on the spot, as to the plans for the new station at the junction". A few weeks later Joseph Paxton advised the committee to continue with the temporary accommodation for the present before deciding upon plans for the new station, in order that the requirements be better ascertained.

Thus matters rested, but in September 1863 the General Manager drew the attention of the Traffic Committee to the "serious inconvenience caused by the want of a proper station at the new Ambergate Junction". The matter was passed to the Way and Works Committee and after due consideration it was resolved that the old station buildings be removed to the new station and rebuilt on the vacant space between the branch and the main line. Drawings and estimates were submitted to the Chairman's Committee in March 1864, but they were rejected as too expensive. The plans were revised and a contract was eventually awarded to J.E. Hall, in July 1864, for the sum of £2,790. It is generally accepted that the work involved the dismantling of Thompson's original building and its reconstruction, in a much less ornate, but greatly enlarged style, in the form of a letter 'A'.

The opening of the new line involved two new junctions and these were controlled by Ambergate South Junction and Ambergate West Junction signal boxes respectively. Historians are fortunate that as the result of an accident at the south junction in the early 1890s the original signal box was photographed.

The opening of the new station provided more than adequate passenger facilities for the locality but this was a time

Plate 7 (above) The original signal box at the South Junction, photographed as the scene of an accident about 1890.

(R.C. Betts Collection)

Plate 8 (below) Late in 1864 Thomson's original station was dismantled and rebuilt in enlarged form at the South Junction. The main building was later used as a plan store, and is seen here a few years before demolition.

(R.T.B. Price)

of change. Less than ten years later, at the end of May 1872, the Traffic Committee, on their annual tour of inspection resolved that at Ambergate "this place will require remodelling preparatory to the opening of the Pye Bridge and Ambergate line". While the company's solicitors set in motion the process which was to lead to the Midland Railway (Additional Powers) Act, 1873 (Ambergate Middle Curve), the engineers set about preparing plans for the new station. The general principle was to move the station to the west junction and put in a new curve to cater for the Derby-Sheffield local trains. The original NMR route was left in situ for use by express passenger and freight trains. The first plans were submitted to the Way and Works Committee on 1st October 1872, with estimated costs of £18,300 for the line and works, £15,000 for station buildings and £5,000 for land acquisition. This was referred to the General Purposes Committee but was rejected on the grounds of excessive cost. A second plan was put forward in February 1873, with a total cost of £22,000, and

following some further revisions, a contract was finally let in November of that year. This was for erecting and widening the necessary bridges for the new middle curve and platforms. In the meantime it had been resolved to purchase all the land within the triangle from Mr F. Hurt.

The first contract involved the widening of the two bridges over Chesterfield Road and the filling of additional land near the goods yard to carry the new curve. This in itself required a new underbridge to maintain access to the goods yard. It is not surprising, therefore, that it was not until May 1875 that a contract was let, to Messrs W. & H. Harris, for the construction of platforms and station buildings. In purchasing the land for the new station the Midland had acquired the Thatched House Inn, and mindful of the additional staffing requirements for the station, the company concluded that the building would be of more value to them as staff accommodation. A plan and estimate of £300 for conversion to three cottages was approved in October 1875, and Messrs Harris

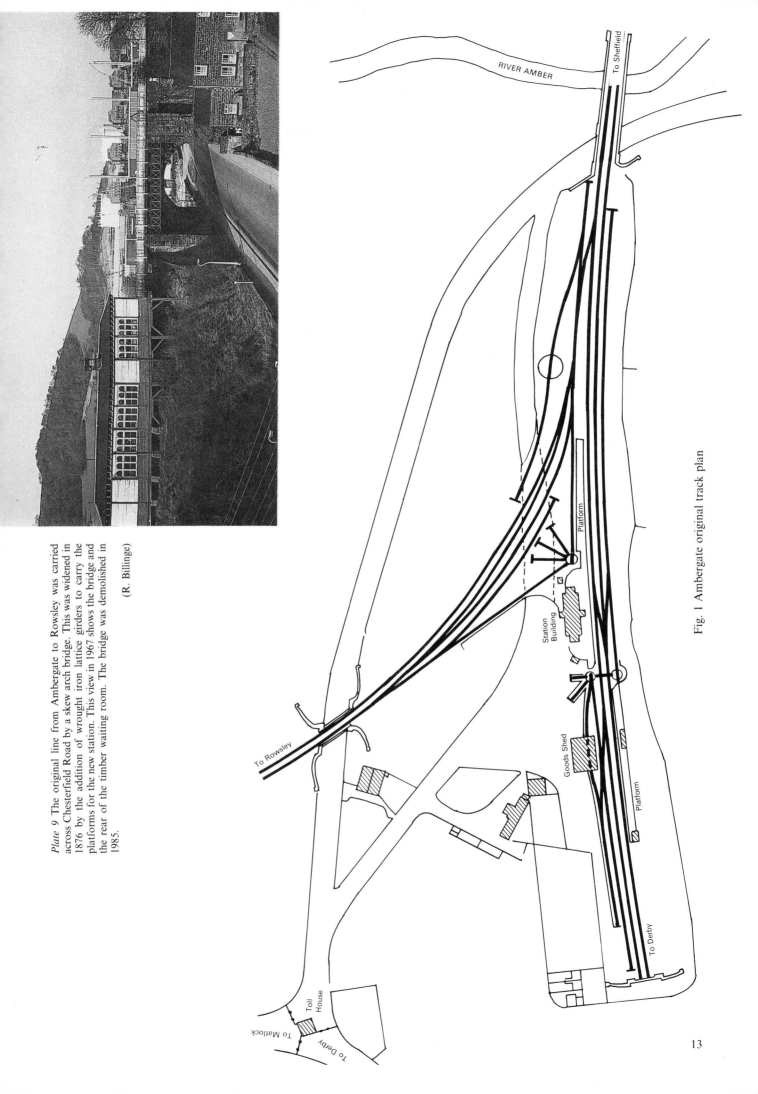

Plate 9 The original line from Ambergate to Rowsley was carried across Chesterfield Road by a skew arch bridge. This was widened in 1876 by the addition of wrought iron lattice girders to carry the platforms for the new station. This view in 1967 shows the bridge and the rear of the timber waiting room. The bridge was demolished in 1985.

(R. Billinge)

Fig. 1 Ambergate original track plan

RIVER AMBER

To Sheffield

To Rowsley

Station Building

Platform

Goods Shed

Platform

To Derby

Toll House

To Matlock

To Derby

13

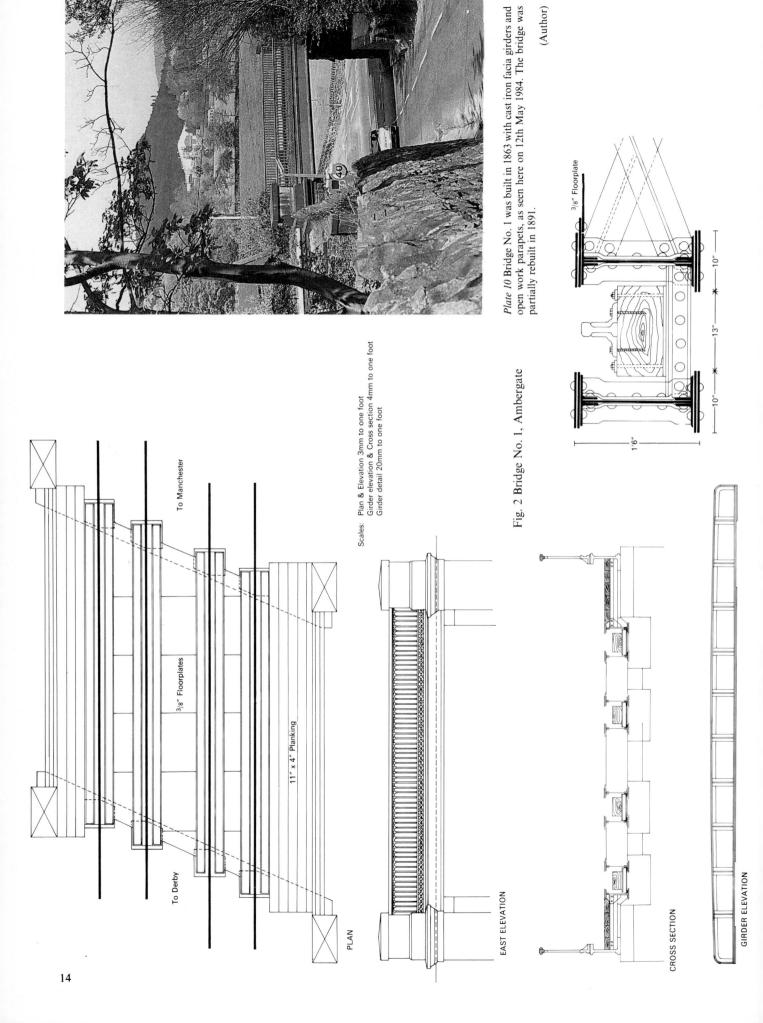

Plate 10 Bridge No. 1 was built in 1863 with cast iron facia girders and open work parapets, as seen here on 12th May 1984. The bridge was partially rebuilt in 1891.

(Author)

Fig. 2 Bridge No. 1, Ambergate

Scales: Plan & Elevation 3mm to one foot
Girder elevation & Cross section 4mm to one foot
Girder detail 20mm to one foot

To Manchester

³⁄₈" Floorplates

11" x 4" Planking

To Derby

PLAN

EAST ELEVATION

CROSS SECTION

GIRDER ELEVATION

³⁄₈" Floorplate

10"   13"   10"

1'6"

Fig. 3 Ambergate Final MR track plan

Plate 11 Ambergate 20th May 1911. In the right distance can be seen Longland Tunnel, the Derwent bridge and the South Junction. Beyond the station bridge and the South Junction. Beyond the station from left to right can be seen the North Midlands goods shed, the former Thatched House Inn, the five cottages built in 1894, and the station master's house, dismantled and rebuilt on its new site about 1847. In the station stands a west country express, with a GWR through coach second from the engine, and the Pye Bridge local train, the rear coach of which is standing on Chesterfield Road bridge. To the extreme right of the station can be seen part of the Amber Viaduct, just beyond which is the Hurt Arms Hotel.

(N.R.M.)

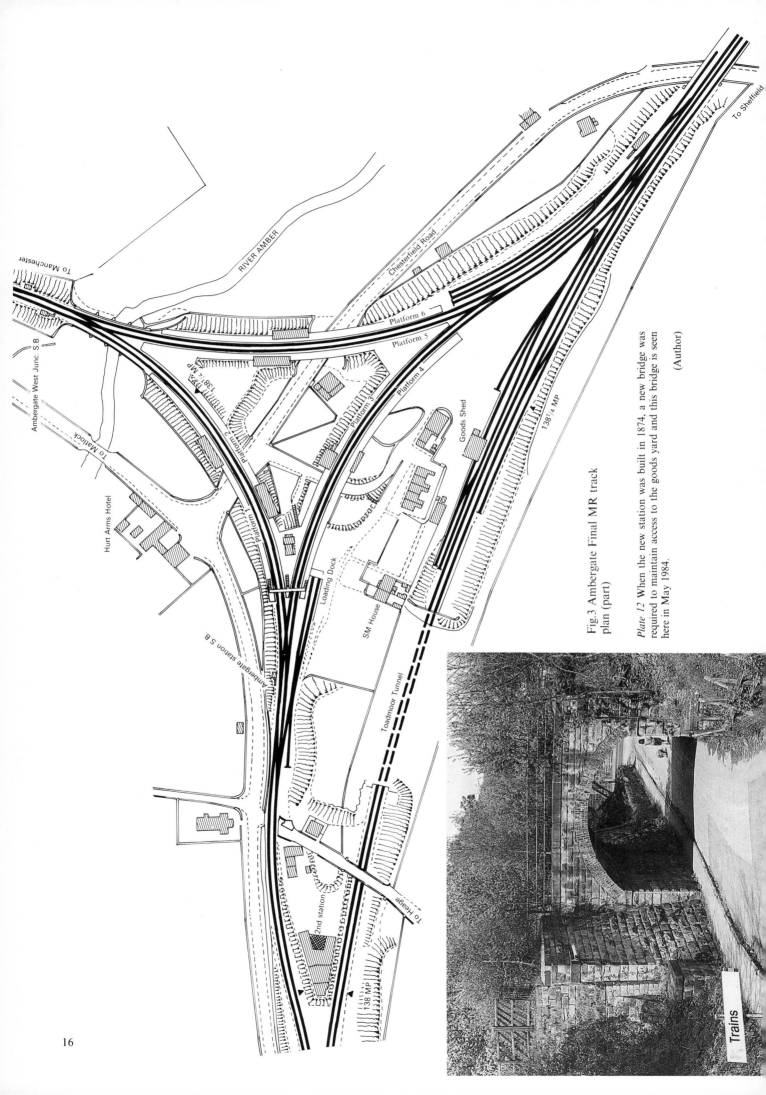

To Manchester

RIVER AMBER

Chesterfield Road

Platform 6

Platform 5

Platform 4

Ambergate West Junc. S.B

To Matlock

138½ MP

Platform 3

Platform 2

Platform 1

Goods Shed

138¾ MP

Hurt Arms Hotel

Ambergate station S.B

Loading Dock

SM House

Toadmoor Tunnel

To Heage

2nd station

138 MP

Fig.3 Ambergate Final **MR** track plan (part)

Plate 12 When the new station was built in 1874, a new bridge was required to maintain access to the goods yard and this bridge is seen here in May 1984.

(Author)

Trains

16

Plate 13 On the same day, the view from above Toadmoor Tunnel shows the Amber Viaduct and the embankment carrying the line northwards into the Derwent Valley. To the right rise the slopes of Crich Chase, the limestone outcrop separating the Amber and Derwent valleys. The 'scar' on the hillside to the right is the tramway bringing limestone down from the quarries at Crich to the lime works at Bullbridge.

(N.R.M.)

were employed to carry out the work at their schedule of prices for the main contract. When Francis Hurt was considering the sale of his land to the railway company he must have foreseen that the Thatched House would not survive as a viable inn, and he began construction of a new hostelry, just to the west of the Belper turnpike. Today the Hurts Arms Hotel stands as a familiar landmark to travellers on the A6 trunk road.

The new station was brought into use on 10th December 1876, and the old one was closed, but being only 13 years old it was not demolished and in 1882 it was recommended to the General Purposes Committee that the buildings be repaired and converted into a book and plan store for the Way and Works Committee. This was agreed and the building was to remain in a similar use until it was dismantled in the 1960s. The completion of the station and the opening of the middle curve also saw the opening of a new signal box, Ambergate Station Junction, and the renumbering of the bridges within the station limits, to give those numbers shown in *fig. 3*.

During the last quarter of the 19th century the railways saw a rapid rise in the number of passengers carried and the number of trains operating. With this intensification of services came a growing awareness of safety which was reflected in one way by the increasing provision of footbridges or subways at many stations. Although the term 'standard Midland footbridge' has been used for many years, this really is a misnomer and as we shall see, there was considerable variety in the design of such structures. Messrs Anderson & Fox *(A Pictorial Record of LMS Architecture,* OPC) are of the opinion that the Midland was never quite satisfied with basic designs, and this, coupled with the fact that the erection of footbridges was contracted out, just like other building work, probably explains the multiplicity of designs.

The footbridge at Ambergate was ordered in December 1883 at the request of the Traffic Committee, and the plans and estimate of £600 were approved the following month. The design could be described as 'lightweight' to say the least, and was probably produced because the end pillars and staircase were very close to the top of the embankment. The contract for the supply of ironwork was let to Smedley Bros on 17th April 1884, in the sum of £379 1s 2d (£379.06).

With the erection of the footbridge the initial development of the station was complete, but in 1893 the signal boxes at the South, Station and West junctions were renewed at a total cost of £734. At that time the box at the Station Junction was less than 20 years old, but its replacement was to stand for well over 70 years until the station closed as a junction in 1967.

As the traffic increased in the 1890s so did the railway staff and in terms of efficiency it was in the company's interest to house its employees close to the job. With this in mind it was decided to erect a block of cottages near the station. It was originally proposed to put up ten dwellings, but the plan was subsequently modified to include only five and these were built by J. Walker & Sons in 1894. Shortly after their completion a petition was submitted from the tenants, (this also included those tenants of the company's dwellings at Edale and Grindleford), begging a reduction in the rents, then 4s (20p) per week. This was rejected out of hand, for while the Midland may have shown a genuine concern for the welfare of its staff, it was not a charitable institution.

Rail travellers of the last 20 or 30 years may, at times, have questioned the maintenance policy of railway property, but on the Midland Railway it was a different picture. Stations, cottages and other buildings were cleaned and repainted on a regular basis and as with actual construction this work was put out to competitive tender. Ambergate was repainted in 1887, 1897, 1908 and 1914, each time by a different contractor. Most of the stations in the Derby District were again painted in 1922 and came into LMS ownership in pristine condition. They were treated again in 1928/29 and in the mid 1930s, but the outbreak of war put an end to the pattern and Nationalisation came before the LMS had recovered sufficiently to indulge in spring cleaning. The author has little knowledge regarding British Railways' maintenance policy, but with the first few years spent in 'settling down', the austerity years of the early 1950s, and then the search for economies, it is doubtful if the station was repainted more than twice between the war and demolition of the last remaining buildings in 1970.

For painting buildings the Midland used chocolate and cream, with maroon doors. The ironwork to doors was painted black, but that for roof and awnings was cream, except for chocolate dado to columns. Signal boxes were Venetian red and lemon chrome. These colours continued in use until the mid-1930s, when the LMS finally decided on an 'official' colour schedule. The colours designated for station painting then became middle brown, Venetian red, mid-Brunswick green, deep cream and Portland stone, with one dark colour paired with one light colour. From 1931 the painting of signal boxes was standardised using light stone, dark brown and white. Doors, guttering, water pipes, fascia boards, barge boards and staircase were brown, window frames and sash bars white and the rest of the woodwork light stone. From 1933 the corner posts, bottom sills, window cleaning stage and closet, if on the ground, were painted brown. Within the limits set down in the above schedule, variations did occur as much of the fine detail was left to the foreman concerned. There could also be subtle differences in the colours, the paint being mixed on site from the various raw materials, and while a standard specification was set down, the final colour matching often depended on the 'eye' of the foreman. This schedule remained in force until changed by British Railways in 1951. The same pattern of maintenance was broadly repeated at the remaining stations to Chinley and it is deemed unnecessary to raise the matter again.

Following the construction of the cottages in 1894 no significant development was mooted at Ambergate until 18th December 1929, when the Chief General Superintendent recommended that the line from Broadholme signal box, north of Belper, to Ambergate South Junction be widened from two tracks to four, at an estimated cost of £148,750. This would greatly improve the working of trains and would save an estimated £4,000 per annum in operating costs. One strongly suspects that the scheme was put forward at this time to take advantage of the Development (loan guarantees and grants) Act, 1929, which had just reached the statute books. This legislation would provide a grant of £124,370 towards the work. The Traffic Committee was quick to seize the chance and a contract for the earthworks was let to Shanks & McEwan Ltd at the end of May 1930, in the sum of £69,264 11s 11d (£69,264.60). At the same time a contract was let to the Motherwell Bridge and Engineering Co. for the supply of ironwork for bridges, in the sum of £28,779 5s (£28,779.25).

This scheme was one of major civil engineering exercises carried out by the LMS and involved a new viaduct over the River Derwent at Dunge, widening the embankment and an underbridge, opening out Longland Tunnel and a second new viaduct at Ambergate. The junction at Ambergate was moved to the south side of the river and the Manchester line was straightened, necessitating further landfill, the moving of the main road to the west, and a further major retaining wall, all clearly seen in *plate 15*, taken shortly after the work was completed in 1932. The scheme also included the construction of new signal boxes at Broadholme and Ambergate South Junction, the roof of the latter being just visible at the bottom of the picture. These two boxes were among the earliest to be erected to the new LMS standard design, introduced by H.E. Morgan soon after he became signals assistant to the Divisional Engineer, Crewe, in 1927. It had been decided that a modified form of MR locking frame would be used in new boxes and Morgan favoured the continued use of a MR style cabin. He was persuaded, however, that the use of a brick base, as used by the LNWR would be more durable, avoiding the rotting of wooden corner posts at ground level. The upper storey retained its Midland appearance, although the hipped roof was superseded by flat gables to simplify erection on site, which also reduced costs. Broadholme box was built on an embankment and an all-timber structure had to be erected, the end product looking very much like the MR 'Period III' type, except for the roof.

From 1872 onwards the Midland Railway maintained precise records of traffic at all its stations, but although the LMS continued the practice, the records are thought to have been accidentally destroyed, with just the occasional stray document having survived. The compilation of these records was resumed after the war, but the author has been unable to locate the whereabouts of these records. Thus while full statistics are only available up to 1922, this information does give a valuable insight into the volume of traffic and perhaps

Plate 14 The severity of the west curve through the station is clearly seen in this view as LMS built 4F, No. 4407, carrying express head lamps, runs into the station in the early 1930s. The station nameboard probably carries black letters on a yellow background and makes an interesting comparison with the one shown in *plate 30*.

E.R. Morten

Plate 15 *(above)* The remodelled layout of the South Junction was completed in 1932 and is seen here from the hillside above the signal box, the roof of which can just be seen in the left foreground.

(Railways Yesteryear)

Plate 16 *(below)* The new signal box at Ambergate South Junction is believed to have been the first LMS standard *composite* box, using a timber upper floor, based on MR practice, and a brick base of LNWR design. The nameboard, located above the end windows, had been removed when it was photographed in the late 1960s.

(V.R. Anderson)

more importantly allows comparison to be made between stations. These records were used extensively by David Jenkinson in his detailed socio-economic study of the Settle-Carlisle railway, *Rails in the Fells* (Peco Publications), but in the present work the author has only tried to give a broad indication of the type and volume of traffic. Thus it was decided to take the figures at ten-yearly intervals, starting in 1872, which allowed the figures for 1922, the final year of Midland activity, to be included. While all six sets of data have been used to discuss the build-up of traffic on the line, the publication of all the figures would seem unnecessary, but those for 1872, 1902 and 1922 are given in Appendix III.

Before the opening of the railways, travel for the mass of the population was restricted to a journey on foot to the next village, but as the railway network expanded, so did industrial development and output. Together with the easier and therefore cheaper, distribution of food and household goods, social conditions began to improve and personal incomes started to show a small surplus. Under these conditions the desire to travel became stronger. By the 1860s even annual holidays had become a reality, at least for the middle classes, although it was to be another 30 years or so before this was to become a widespread institution. With this increased mobility also came the habit of working in the town and living in the country and by the 1890s daily residential travelling had been born.

Although Ambergate may have been opened as a station for Matlock, it rapidly became the main line station, for both passengers and freight for Ripley, some 3½ miles to the east. In 1872, 28,297 passengers purchased tickets at Ambergate, paying an average fare of 1s 4½d (7p), which would have taken the third class traveller on a round trip of approximately eight miles. If one arbitrarily accepts that no more than 5% of the week's bookings were made on Sundays, then this would give a weekday average of 86 passengers. The opening of the

Plate 17 (above) The lightweight construction of the footbridge is clearly shown in this view, as LMS built Compound No. 1063 runs into the station with a down local train in September 1932.

(E.R. Morten)

Plate 18 (below) A little over 50 years later the view from the same spot, as a Derby bound dmu leaves on 12th May 1984, shows how nature has almost taken over.

(Author)

Pye Bridge line and the general increase in traffic took the number of bookings to over 56,000 by 1882 and up to 63,637, or 194 per weekday in 1892. Growth then continued at a reduced rate, but notwithstanding war time fluctuations, bookings had risen to 90,157 by 1922. The average fare at that time, with rates having risen from 1d (0.4p) per mile in 1917 to 1³/₄d (0.7p) per mile in 1922, was 1s 10d (9p), giving a round trip of about 6¹/₄ miles, hardly a significant change over 50 years.

On the other hand a marked change did take place with regard to season tickets, which came into widespread use on the MR in the 1880s. In 1892, 17 seasons were issued at Ambergate making the station second in importance to Matlock Bridge for this class of traffic. Little change took place before World War I, with 89 such tickets being issued in 1912, but by 1922 the total at Ambergate had shot up to 371, making it easily the most important station for this traffic in our study area. While this no doubt reflected an increase in commuter traffic to Derby it may also have been a way of absorbing the 75% increase in fares since 1912, at least for the regular traveller. On the assumption that the majority of season ticket holders would travel on a normal weekday, the final years of MR operation saw a weekday average of some 645 passengers, but whereas passenger profits had been over £1,800 at the turn of the century, they had fallen to only £62 in 1922. This was due quite simply to the tremendous increase in wage costs following World War I. It was claimed that the cost of living rose by 120% between 1914 and 1919 and the National Union of General Workers asked for wages to be at least 100% above pre-war levels. This pressure led to a wages spiral and by mid 1921 wages had risen by 120% while fare increases had been limited to 75%. Coupled with this came the introduction of the 8-hour day on the railways on 1st February 1919, with the consequent increase in overtime which was only counteracted by the appointment of additional staff!

In 1922 Ambergate was served on the Manchester line by nine down and eleven up trains. In the down direction six of the trains ran through to Manchester, the first being an express, the 4.25am ex St Pancras. On the up line only two trains had come through from Manchester, the majority of the remainder were locals to Derby, from Chinley, Buxton, Bakewell and Matlock. One train started from Ambergate, the 7.10am to Derby, which was worked empty stock from Derby. One through train regularly used the north curve, the 4.25pm Manchester Central-Nottingham, although this curve was often used by excursion trains to and from the Peak District. In addition to the Manchester line trains the station was served by semi-fast and local trains between Derby, Chesterfield and Sheffield, and by a local shuttle service to Pye Bridge, on the Erewash Valley line. Space precludes a full discussion of these services, but relevant connecting trains are shown in the timetables in Appendix I.

The 1920s and early 30s were marked by alternate periods of industrial boom and depression, but by the mid point of the LMS period the economy was growing stronger, and the 1935 summer timetable saw 17 down and 21 up trains stopping at Ambergate on the Manchester line, almost double the Midland total. Of these, ten down and six up trains connected with services on the Sheffield line, and several connected with the Pye Bridge service, which by then had been extended to Mansfield. On Saturday afternoons one train ran through from Mansfield to Rowsley, giving passengers approximately

five hours to visit Chatsworth House or Haddon Hall, before returning at 8.05pm. The expansion of the timetable primarily consisted of a more varied local service between Derby and Matlock, Darley Dale, Rowsley, Buxton and Chinley. One additional regular train using the north curve was the Saturday only 4.05pm Manchester Victoria to Nottingham.

The general curtailment of passenger trains following the outbreak of World War II saw the timetable cut back below the final Midland level, to ten down and eight up trains. The Derby-Manchester semi-fasts were reduced to 'all-stations' and the through Derby-Buxton trains were cancelled altogether. However, in an attempt to uplift public spirits the 1943 summer timetable included Saturday through trains from Leicester and Derby to Blackpool North, at 7.25am and 8.55am respectively. The cessation of hostilities was followed by a period of austerity gradually changing to one of growth, but the number of road vehicles in the country had increased from 650,000 in 1920 to 4,409,000 in 1950, and the railways stood no chance of regaining their pre-war passenger levels. In fact by 1954 the service at Ambergate had shrunk to eight up and eight down Manchester line trains, the cutbacks mainly being on the local trains. Contrary to popular opinion, the service improved in the 1960s and by 1968 one semi-fast in each direction between Derby and Manchester had been reinstated, together with an early morning train from Derby to Buxton.

To give a full analysis of the freight traffic on the line would not only take up far too much space, but would also drive the reader to despair, and the author has taken just one period to discuss goods traffic.

If one accepts that the war years saw an abnormal disruption to the normal daily carriage of freight, then it is fair to assume that the early 1930s were the mid point of the LMS regime. Even though the nation's economy was at a low ebb, 1932 saw approximately 100 freight trains passing through Ambergate West Junction on weekdays. This flow was comprised of an almost equal number of up and down trains, dominated by coal traffic in the down direction and corresponding empty wagons in the up. The heaviest flow of coal traffic came over the Pye Bridge line from Kirkby,

Plate 19 Johnson rebuilt 4-4-0, No. 331, gets away smartly from Ambergate with a down local train about 1927.

(Railways Yesteryear)

21

Plate 20 Class 2F 0-6-0, No. 3479 and an unidentified Kirtley 0-6-0 make a magnificent sight as they take the Rowsley line at Ambergate North Junction with a coal train from the Butterley area pits, probably on the same day as the previous plate.

(Railways Yesteryear)

Nottingham and Toton. While the loaded/empty mineral flows to and from the Chesterfield direction were almost equally balanced, there were eight loaded mineral trains from Chaddesden or Derby St Marys to Rowsley, but there were no booked empty return workings. Such wagons could have gone back to the collieries via Toton, back to Derby on an 'as required' basis, or be sent on one of the four daily empty workings from Rowsley to Ambergate, for sorting and onward dispatch.

Virtually all the limestone from the Peak District to the South and East was sorted at Chaddesden and empty wagons were sent back on three daily trains to High Peak Junction, Rowsley and Peak Forest respectively. In addition to the mineral traffic there was a considerable flow of merchandise of every description between the South, the Midlands and the North West, or vice versa. This movement was handled by seven through freight trains in each direction plus seven down and eight up express freights, which normally ran during the night.

For compilation of its annual statistical return the Midland broke goods traffic down into four classes: livestock; coal, coke, lime and limestone; merchandise, and minerals. These classes will be used as a basis for the discussion of local traffic patterns at each station on our journey.

Livestock rearing and milk production were fundamental aspects of the Peak District agriculture, and both activities were once highly dependent on rail transport. While milk production was very much a day to day activity, the carriage of livestock was usually confined to peaks associated with weekly or fortnightly cattle markets and annual fairs. Thus while the total traffic, expressed by the MR in truck loads, may appear to be insignificant, it gave rise to some hectic activity from time to time. Ambergate was not the most important station for this traffic but it nevertheless saw a moderate trade, which grew steadily in overall terms from 57 truck loads in 1882 to 152 loads in 1922.

The main traffic out of the station was probably lime, the local production of which began about 1780 with the burning of stone from Hilts Quarry, Crich, which was brought down by tramway to Bull Bridge just north of Ambergate. These kilns, taken over by the Butterley Co. and operated until the early 1930s, were overshadowed, in terms of output, by a bank of 20 kilns completed by George Stephenson in 1841. Stone for these was obtained from Crich Cliff Quarry and was burnt using

slack from Stephenson's collieries at Clay Cross. While much of the output was used in the blast furnaces at Clay Cross, some was sold on the open market and later led to the wide travels of the company's wagons (in addition to their use for the carriage of coal). Coal came into the station for both the domestic and industrial market. In the 1920s and 30s the latter primarily consisted of Ambergate Gas Co., the lime works, Glossops brickworks and Stevenson's dye works. At that time the goods yard served about 3,000 people locally, plus perhaps 50% of Ripley, giving a total around 10,000 people served. Annual domestic coal consumption during that period was near enough one ton per head, and with an average wagon load of 8½ tons, this would bring in 10,000-10,500 tons of coal per annum, or 23-25 wagon loads weekly. As far as the author is aware there was only one local coal dealer around 1930, Mr A. Naylor, but eleven dealers from Ripley used the station. However, none of these appear to have operated their own wagons, and supplies would have arrived in railway owned wagons, or in colliery owned vehicles from local pits of the Butterley group, or from Pentrich, Wingfield Manor or Swanwick collieries.

The merchandise class of traffic covered almost every conceivable item of household and commercial goods. In the early 1920s some 17,000 tons of this traffic were handled annually, and at an average of three tons per vehicle would have called for 19 or 20 open wagons or vans daily. In terms of mineral class traffic the station was second only to Matlock, as far as the author's study area is concerned, at the close of the Midland period. In 1922 the station handled over 33,000 tons of minerals, consisting primarily of gritstone from quarries in Shining Cliff Woods, bricks and refractory materials from Glossop's brickworks and output from Swarkestone Sand and Gravels Ltd. In addition to this traffic Pratts Anglo-American Oil Co. would have brought tank wagons into the yard on a regular basis.

Johnson's Sidings

Plate 21 (top) Bridge No. 6, Poyser's bridge.

(Author)

Plate 22 (above) Among the first generation of BR diesels were the Metrovicks and No. D5701 of that class is seen here approaching Hay's Wharf bridge on 28th March 1959 with the 4.00pm Derby-Manchester stopping train.

(R.J. Buckley)

Plate 23 (below) Bridge No. 7, Hay's Wharf bridge.

(Author)

From Ambergate West Junction the line ran north westwards on a low embankment, crossed Poysers Bridge, (No.6) and passed onto the western flank of Crich Chase. Exactly 1/4 mile from the junction the Cromford Canal came in from the east, at Hays Wharf, and the line passed under bridge No.7, built to maintain access to the canal. From this point the line curved slightly to the north and running parallel to the canal passed under bridge No.8, built to connect Mold's Wharf to the Cromford turnpike, and approached Johnson's sidings.

The wire rod rolling and wire drawing works of Messrs Johnson Nephew & Co Ltd were established in 1876, on the site of a former ironworks operated by John and Charles Mold. These works were in operation in the 1760s, and Mold's Wharf was opened to serve them when the Cromford Canal was constructed. The company later looked to the railway for transportation facilities and in December 1853 the Way and Works Committee agreed to the provision of a siding for Messrs Mold and Co., the applicants to pay 10% of the cost. Originally known as Alderwasley Siding this was put in close to the Cromford road, now the A6, and served a pair of North Eastern Railway style coal drops, shown in *plate 26*. Messrs Johnson and Nephew may well have used this siding but as their business became established the facilities proved inadequate, and in January 1883 the Midland agreed to lay in new sidings. These were laid out in what had become the traditional MR manner, and basically comprised a loop connected to the down main line by a trailing point, and to the up by a trailing point and a single slip point. On one arm of the loop the wireworks company built a large shed, in random stone, to

23

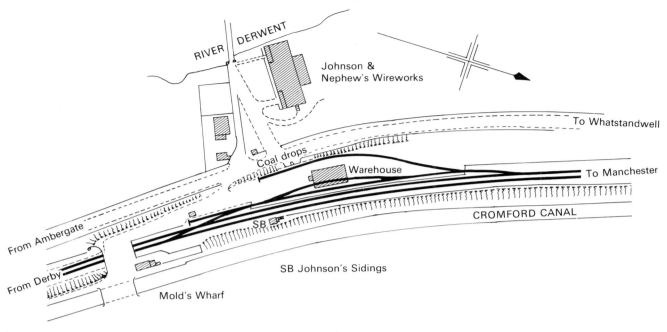

RIVER DERWENT

Johnson &
Nephew's Wireworks

To Whatstandwell

Coal drops

Warehouse

To Manchester

From Ambergate

CROMFORD CANAL

SB

From Derby

SB Johnson's Sidings

Mold's Wharf

Scale 1″ = 198 ft

Fig. 4 Johnsons Sidings track plan

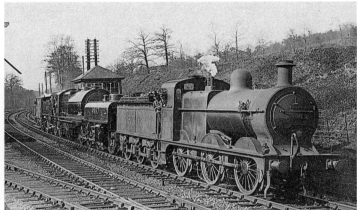

Plate 24 (above) Bridge No. 8, Mold's Wharf bridge. This was similar to No. 7 but much wider, with an angular, rather than round-edged, string course. In addition the arch was in ashlar stone, whereas on No. 7 the arch was deeply tooled.

(Author)

provide storage and covered loading facilities. The sidings were controlled by a new signal box called Johnson's Sidings. This was a 15 ft box, partially visible in *plate 25*, from which it is apparent that it had been replaced by a standard 'Period III' design, but the date of renewal is not recorded in the minutes. By the early 1930s the company was making increased use of road transport, and the lower levels of rail-borne traffic, improvements in track circuiting and the LMS economy drive led to closure of the box. This took place on 20th April 1933, with the connection to the up main line being taken out on the same day. A ground frame was installed to cover access from the down line, and control of the appropriate signals was transferred to Ambergate West Junction signal box.

Inward traffic to the sidings consisted of coal from local collieries, steel bar and rod, and lime, the latter being important in the wire drawing process. Outward traffic comprised various gauges of wire, either straight or coiled, normally loaded in low-sided wagons. After World War II the company became increasingly inclined to road transport, and the sidings were eventually closed, although the loading shed remains in use today for storage.

Plate 25 (above right) The crew of 3F 0-6-0, No. 3308 pose for the camera at Johnsons sidings signal box while hauling brand new Beyer-Garratt, No. 4997, from the builders to Toton shed, in 1927.

(Railways Yesteryear)

Plate 26 (above) The warehouse and coal drops seen from the A6 road in February 1985.

(Author)

Chapter 5

Whatstandwell

Plate 27 Stanier 8F. No. 48379 storms round the curve towards bridge No. 8A at Whatstandwell with a mineral train from Kirkby to Rowsley on 24th May 1952.

(E. R. Morten)

Plate 28 (above) Bridge 8A, Chase bridge.

(Author)

Plate 29 (below) Just south of Whatstandwell the river, road and railway run parallel through a sharp curve, with a high retaining wall supporting the railway. The wall can just be made out above the second coach in this view as rebuilt Johnson 4-4-0, No. 347 rounds the curve with a down relief express about 1930.

(Railways Yesteryear)

From Johnson's Sidings the line ran straight for a short distance, curved gently westward, then eastwards before passing under Chase Bridge, No.8A. The line was originally crossed at this point by a level crossing, protected by a small crossing keeper's cabin and on 6th December 1881 it was ordered that plans be prepared for the erection of a cottage for the gate keeper. However before these were ready, the engineer presented a report listing the places on the Matlock line where, in his opinion, the curves were capable of improvement at moderate cost to contribute to much easier running of the trains. The places were:

1. Hay's Wharf and 1 mile from Ambergate   £800
2. Chase crossing – bridge to be built.   £1,200
3. Whatstandwell station and sidings.   £500
4. Cromford curves.   £4,000
5. Matlock Bath.   £300

These proposals were accepted by the Way and Works Committee, approved by the full Midland Board in October 1882 and put in hand without delay. The bridge was completed the following year but was raised in 1912, at which time the wooden parapet walls were fitted. These lasted until the 1960s when British Rail made a rather unsuccessful attempt to match the original stonework by rebuilding the parapets in artificial stone and concrete. This was in connection with the building of the Severn-Trent pumping station to the east of the line.

North of the bridge the line ran straight for a short distance and then entered a long curve to the west, at the end of which it curved northwards and arrived at Whatstandwell station, 1 mile 67 chains from Ambergate West Junction.

The origins of the settlement at Whatstandwell are somewhat obscure, but it is generally accepted that it grew up around a ford across the River Derwent, where the ancient route from South Wingfield and Crich to Wirksworth crossed the river. The present bridge was constructed in the 15th century and subsequently widened, when the Cromford Turnpike was built in 1818. In planning the railway the directors of the MBM & MJR saw no reason to build a station at this point, but later, the success of the line, plus pressure from local residents, induced a change of heart. In building the Cromford Canal it was necessary to tunnel through a spur of higher land which came down to the east of the river and the railway also had to pierce this ridge. The amount of land available between the river and the canal was extremely limited, such that at the northern portal of the tunnel the bank of the canal had to be cut away and be replaced by a massive retaining wall. The spoil from this work, plus that from the tunnel was spread to form a low shelf above the river to carry the railway. It was on this shelf, immediately north of the tunnel, that the first wooden station, known as Whatstandwell Bridge, was opened towards the end of 1852.

Readers will recall from Chapter 2 that from 1852 to 1871 the line from Ambergate to Rowsley was owned by the MBM & MJR, leased by the MR and LNWR, and operated by the MR. Under the circumstances it is not surprising that the records of these early years, when it is believed that the line was administered by both a joint committee and various MR committees, are somewhat confused, and for the historian, rather frustrating. Events at Whatstandwell are a prime example of where it has only been possible to trace part of the history, and the author can only hope that more knowledgeable students can complete the story.

Fig. 5 Whatstandwell station track plan

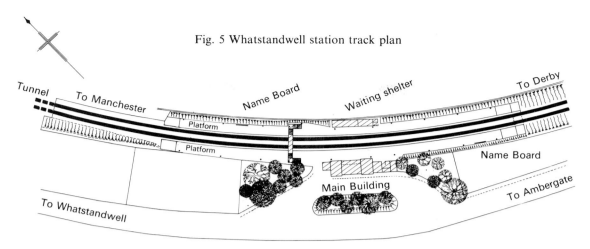

On 17th March 1857 it was reported to the MR Way and Works Committee that a suggestion had been made through the traffic department that the old wooden stations at Matlock Bath and Matlock Bridge should be removed to Darley and Whatstandwell Bridge. It was resolved that 'the matter be referred back to the General Manager, this committee expressing an opinion that should the work be considered necessary then the Ambergate and Rowsley company should be called upon to do it'. What happened next is not clear, for while it is known that the station at Whatstandwell Bridge was opened for traffic in 1852 the only other reference which has come to light regarding the old wooden stations is that on 17th April 1866 a contract was awarded to E. Dustanoy for removing and refixing the old station and building a new lamp room at Matlock Bridge. As far as is known there was never a wooden station at Darly Dale, and it seems most likely that a temporary structure was erected at Whatstandwell Bridge, until the building was removed from Matlock Bridge.

In January 1860 Francis Hurt approached the MR and requested permission to put up a drinking fountain on the platform. This proposal was accepted and the fountain, often

Plate 30 Class 3F 0-6-0, No. 3332 drifts through Whatstandwell station with an up empty mineral train from Rowsley to Westhouses in 1937. The straight nameboard, based on the standard MR angled board, appears to have white letters on a black background, cream posts and brown support brackets.

(E.R. Morten)

wrongly referred to as a well, can still be seen in the retaining wall just north of the tunnel. The basic elements of this structure were adopted by the Midland as their standard drinking fountain.

While the provision of passenger facilities at Whatstandwell may have been an afterthought, goods traffic was important almost from the start. Quarrying of gritstone in Shining Cliff Woods, to the south, and on both sides of the valley to the north was underway long before the railway opened. As early as January 1855 the MR made an agreement with Mr S. Simms whereby in consideration of a payment of £20, the company was granted permission for seven years, to take away for ballast any quantity of the small stone and rubble from the heaps belonging to him on the east side of the canal. With the transport opportunities afforded by the railway the quarrying industry rapidly expanded, and in 1867 a new stone wharf was constructed on the up side of the line, north of the station, after the trustees of the then late Mr Simms had agreed to construct a road so that the wharf could be used by the general public. Stone from the area soon found itself all over the country and abroad, for use in major public works. A measure of the rapid increase in this traffic can be gauged from the fact that a 6 ton crane was provided at the wharf when it was built, followed by a 5 ton crane in 1883, and the moving of the 10 ton crane from Ambergate to Whatstandwell two years later.

In the meantime, passenger traffic had not been overlooked and after the lengthening of the platforms early in 1868, the Traffic Committee, following their tour of inspection at the

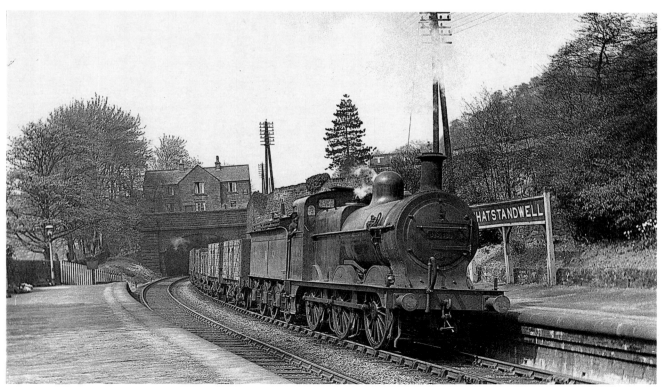

27

Plate 31 The drinking fountain erected on the up platform of the original station in 1861.

(R.T.B. Price)

end of May 1872, resolved that the station was inadequate for the traffic of the area and ordered that plans be prepared for a new station. Why this instruction was not acted upon may never be known, but it was almost 20 years before plans and an estimate of £3,590 were put before the committee, in March 1892. Even then it was almost two years to the tender stage, with a contract eventually being awarded to C.W. Hardy for erection of the station buildings. This was two weeks after a contract had been awarded to Messrs Handyside & Co. for erection of a footbridge, but two months before the land agent reported that he had purchased the land for the station from A.F. Hurt, for £105. In contractual terms the Midland seemed to be living dangerously!

The main building, on the down side of the line, was built in the twin pavilion style, with one end projecting as the porters' room, W.C.s and coal store, and the recess on the platform side was roofed in to form an open-fronted shelter. It is interesting to note that the same basic design was used for Higham Ferrers station, built at about the same time, but at Whatstandwell a delightful wooden shelter was added to the north end of the building. One suspects that this may have been added later, but the author has no documentary evidence to this effect. The up platform building was a long, low structure dominated by a tall chimney stack, as on the main building, and contained a general waiting room, ladies' room and urinals. The access to the station was formed by a short loop off the main road and the island so formed was planted with trees to hide the station from Alderwasley Hall, the home of A.F. Hurt, some 3/4 mile distant across the valley. Further planting of deciduous species was carried out on both sides of the railway, but much of that on the up side was later felled and replaced by coniferous trees.

The new station was opened at 12 noon on 11th November 1894 and was also called Whatstandwell Bridge until the name was shortened in July 1896. It was located a little over 300 yards south of the original, and this extra distance for virtually every passenger walking to and from the station eventually led to a request to ease the situation. In December 1897 the Traffic Committee received a letter from Crich Parish Council and a petition from the residents of Crich Carr, to the east of the railway, requesting the company to provide a footbridge over the canal. The latter further stated that the landowners involved had agreed to dedicate the necessary land for continuing the footpath to the main road and the Parish Council were willing to construct and maintain the footpath. On the engineer's recommendation the request was declined, but Derbyshire folk are not dissuaded easily and the matter was taken up by the more powerful Belper R.D.C. who themselves agreed to build and maintain the footpath. This time the request was not ignored and the construction of the footbridge, to link directly with the station footbridge, was agreed on 8th August 1901. The work was carried out shortly afterwards, with the MR erecting the bridge itself.

Following this episode Whatstandwell settled down as a rural outpost, but it was to come to the management's attention once more. On 16th November 1922 it was reported to the Way and Works Committee that there were 90 stations on the MR, apart from those in large towns, which did not have a Station Master's house. At 59 of these the company owned sufficient land upon which such accommodation could be built, at an estimated cost of £700 per dwelling. Included in these 59 were Whatstandwell, Matlock Bath and Chapel-en-le-Frith. The report was referred to the General Purposes Committee who approved the proposals on 14th December 1922, and subsequently passed on the consequences to the LMS. The matter was progressed quickly and a contract for the erection of a house at Whatstandwell was awarded to F.A. Roberts on 30th April 1924, in the sum of £808 17s (£808.85).

Passenger levels at the station reflected its more rural location and some 9,793 people, or approximately 30 on the average weekday, began their journey at this location, in 1872, paying an average fare of 11d (4½p). The volume of traffic increased in almost the same manner as that at Ambergate, and by 1922 annual bookings had risen to 25,517, or 78 per weekday. By this time the average fare had risen to 1s 9d (9p) representing a return journey of about six miles each way. One suspects that the main bookings were to Matlock or Belper, with a significant number of daily travellers to Derby. The number of season ticket holders, excluded from the above figures, increased from 5 in 1892 to 108 in 1922, an almost identical growth rate to that at Ambergate.

The passenger service at Whatstandwell was compatible with the catchment population, but with fewer trains stopping the expansions and contractions of the timetable over the years were less marked than at its larger neighbour. At the close of the Midland period there were seven stopping trains each way on weekdays. In the down direction four of these were through trains to Manchester Central, but there was no direct return service, passengers having to change at Chinley or Millers Dale. By 1935 the service had been extended to ten down and nine up trains. Two of the down trains ran to Manchester, but there was still no up return. The wartime cutback only saw the loss of two trains each way, but the principle of making a few trains serve as many stations as possible gave Whatstandwell three trains to Manchester and three back. The early British Railways period saw a comparable service, but by 1967 a drastic change had taken place. While five down trains stopped, only the two early morning locals from Darley Dale and Bakewell, and the 7.45am Manchester Central-Derby called. One can only assume that trains were run to carry commuters to Derby in the morning, and return them in the evening. Why trains called to take up passengers for stations to Buxton and Manchester without a return service can only be put down to the mysteries of timetable planning. In practice the station closed at 6.15pm from 15th July 1963 and passengers for the vicinity would have to alight at Cromford or Ambergate.

Local freight traffic was varied although it was never really significant and in broad terms it declined after the turn of the century. While the surrounding area was just as agriculturally productive as at Ambergate the levels of livestock shipped through Whatstandwell were much less and fell from some 56

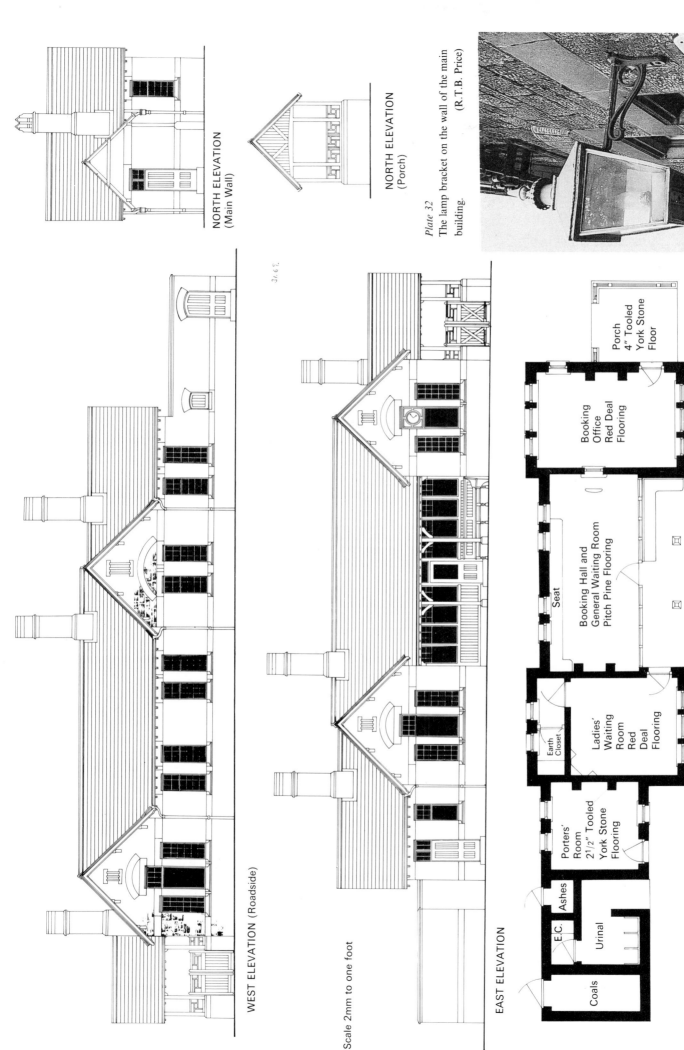

NORTH ELEVATION
(Main Wall)

NORTH ELEVATION
(Porch)

Plate 32
The lamp bracket on the wall of the main
building. (R.T.B. Price)

WEST ELEVATION (Roadside)

Scale 2mm to one foot

EAST ELEVATION

Porch
4" Tooled York Stone
Floor

Booking
Office
Red Deal
Flooring

Booking Hall and
General Waiting Room
Pitch Pine Flooring

Seat

Ladies'
Waiting
Room
Red
Deal
Flooring

Earth
Closet

Porters'
Room
2½" Tooled
York Stone
Flooring

Ashes

E.C.

Urinal

Coals

PLAN

Fig. 6 Whatstandwell station main building

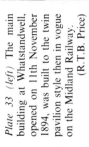

Plate 33 (left) The main building at Whatstandwell, opened on 11th November 1894, was built to the twin pavilion style then in vogue on the Midland Railway.
(R.T.B. Price)

Plate 34 (right) The roadside elevation of the main building, clearly showing the tooled stone-work and the ashlar string courses at window sill and lintel levels. (R.T.B. Price)

Plate 35 (left) The up plat-form shelter. (R.T.B. Price)

Plate 36 (right) The station master's house built by the LMS, just south of the station in 1924. The conservatory and front porch are modern additions. (Author)

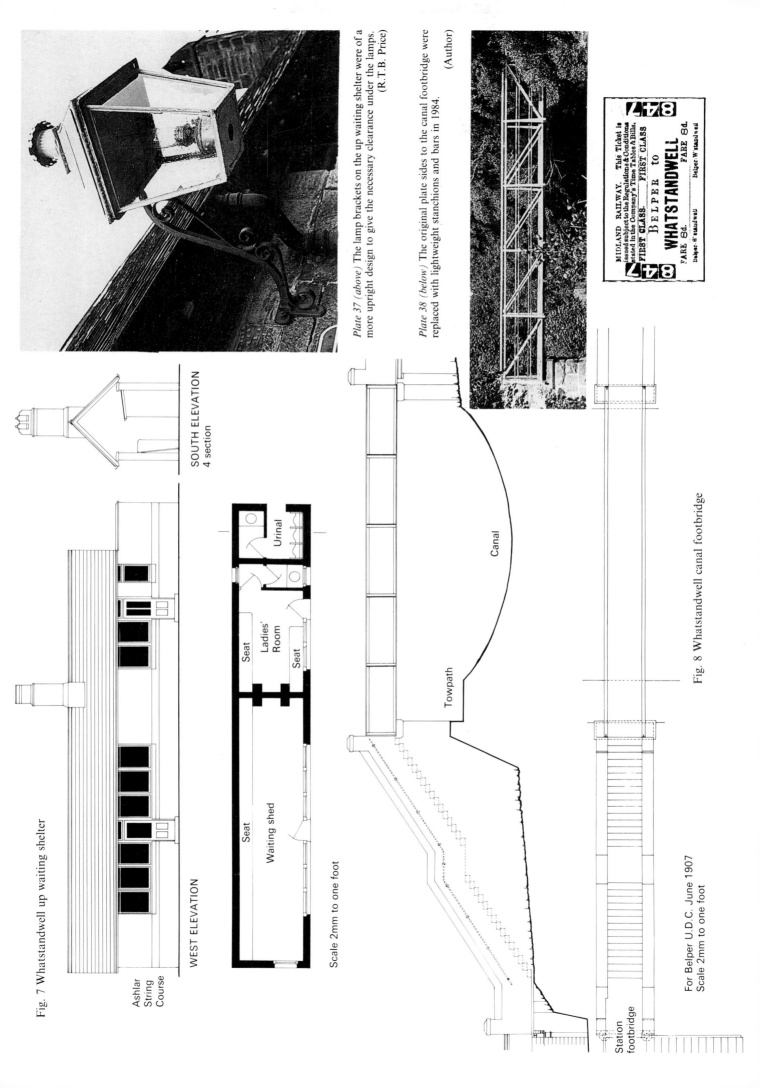

Fig. 7 Whatstandwell up waiting shelter

Ashlar
String
Course

WEST ELEVATION

SOUTH ELEVATION
4 section

Seat

Seat

Ladies'
Room

Seat

Urinal

Waiting shed

Scale 2mm to one foot

Plate 37 (above) The lamp brackets on the up waiting shelter were of a more upright design to give the necessary clearance under the lamps.
(R.T.B. Price)

Plate 38 (below) The original plate sides to the canal footbridge were replaced with lightweight stanchions and bars in 1984.
(Author)

Canal

Towpath

Station
footbridge

Fig. 8 Whatstandwell canal footbridge

For Belper U.D.C. June 1907
Scale 2mm to one foot

MIDLAND RAILWAY. This Ticket is
issued subject to the Regulations & Conditions
stated in the Company's Time Tables & Bills.
FIRST CLASS.   FIRST CLASS
BELPER   to
WHATSTANDWELL
FARE 8d.   FARE 8d.
Belper-W'standwell   Belper-W'standwell

Plate 39 Detail of footbridge stanchion with the steps up to the canal footbridge behind. (Author)

Plate 40 Whatstandwell footbridge. (Author)

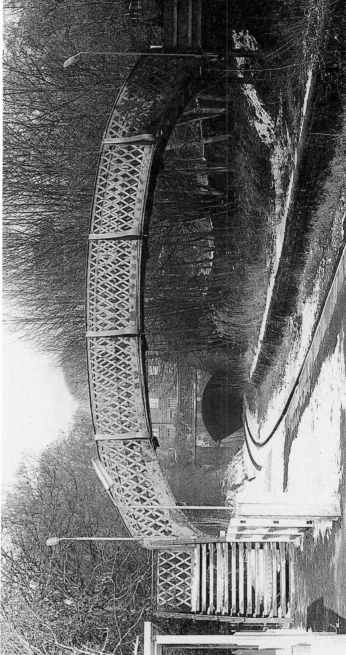

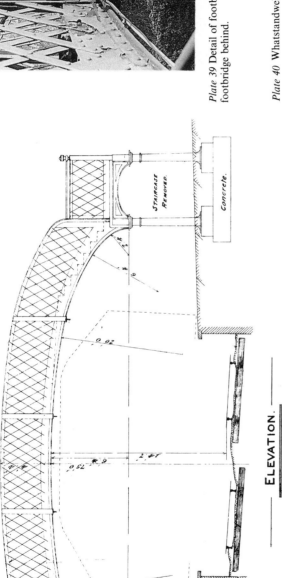

STAIRCASE REMOVED.

Concrete.

— ELEVATION. —

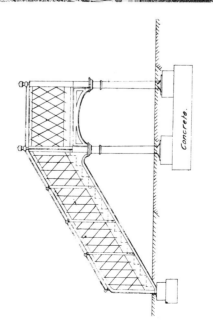

Concrete

— SIDE ELEVATION. —

Fig. 9 Whatstandwell station footbridge
Scale 3mm to one foot

32

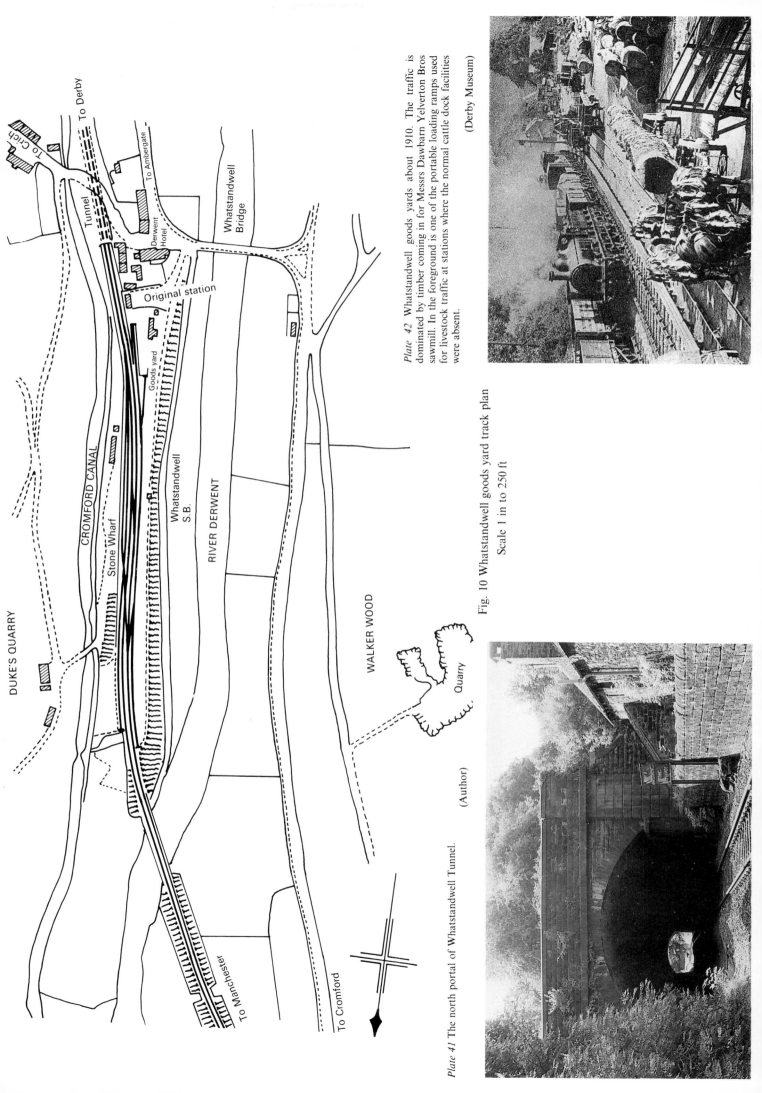

DUKE'S QUARRY

To Crich

To Derby

Tunnel

To Ambergate

Derwent Hotel

Original station

Goods yard

CROMFORD CANAL

Stone Wharf

Whatstandwell S.B.

Whatstandwell Bridge

RIVER DERWENT

WALKER WOOD

Quarry

To Manchester

To Cromford

Plate 41 The north portal of Whatstandwell Tunnel.

(Author)

Plate 42 Whatstandwell goods yards about 1910. The traffic is dominated by timber coming in for Messrs Dawbarn Yelverton Bros sawmill. In the foreground is one of the portable loading ramps used for livestock traffic at stations where the normal cattle dock facilities were absent.

(Derby Museum)

Fig. 10 Whatstandwell goods yard track plan
Scale 1 to 250 ft

Plate 43 Stanier 2-8-0, No. 48765, of Sheffield (Grimesthorpe) runs past the original station on 24th May 1952 with a very short empty wagon train. Taken from above the tunnel mouth, the view shows how the land supporting the canal, on the right, was cut back and replaced by the retaining wall. Just in front of the engine can be seen the drinking fountain set in the wall, which was isolated when the up platform was removed during the easing of the curve in 1882. On the left is the original station, in a remarkably good state of preservation and, omitting the train and upper quadrant signal at the end of the wall, the view has not changed since the Midland days.

(E.R. Morten)

truck loads in 1902 to just one such load in 1922. This may possibly have been because the Midland requested local farmers to send such traffic through Ambergate, for administrative convenience. There was no working of limestone within the local area and the coal class traffic primarily consisted of incoming coal and coke for both domestic and industrial use. At various times during the 1920s and '30s there were five coal merchants at the goods yard: Messrs Bowmers, Eite, Jackson, Rackstraw and Snow, but none of these are thought to have operated their own wagons. In terms of coal traffic the station had a catchment population of about 4,000 in the mid 1930s and this would bring in eight or nine coal wagons each week. These would have been railway company vehicles, some local colliery wagons, and the occasional colliery agent such as Nathaniel Atrill or W.N. Toft. Industrial supplies would primarily have been for the Lea Mills textile complex and the lead smelting works at Lea, which remained in use well into the 1930s and were reputedly the largest in Derbyshire, processing much of the output from Mill Close mine at Darley Dale (although some historians disagree on this point). It may also have been that coal supplies to the nearby water softening works were included in the Whatstandwell returns.

General merchandise traffic was not considered of sufficient level to warrant the construction of a goods shed and much of the traffic for the locality was probably handled at Ambergate. It is the author's opinion that much of the tonnage shown in Appendix III was composed of rough and finished timber to and from Messrs Dawbarn Yelverton Bros joinery works, just to the east of bridge No.10 and *plate 42* leaves no doubt as to the importance of this trade.

By far the most important traffic to pass through the yard was gritstone, although this declined in the early years of the century as the era of major public works drew to a close. Dukes Quarries in Oxhay Woods to the east of the station, Oakhill Quarry in Walker Wood to the west, together with Birchwood Quarry and the Meerbrook Quarries a little further north, all shipped out stone to a multitude of home and foreign destinations. From the 1880s up to World War I some 50-70 wagon loads of gritstone left the station every week. A small proportion of the annual mineral class tonnage comprised lead ore coming in from Darley Dale to the smelter at Lea, but it is not clear whether the outgoing lead pigs would have been classed as merchandise or mineral.

To deal with this goods traffic the yard was shunted twice daily in the 1930s, by the 9.00am stopping freight from Derby St Marys to Rowsley and the 12.20pm from Rowsley to Chaddesden.

The up platform shelter was dismantled in the spring of 1970; in the same year the main building was painted and the windows boarded up, but the Property Board's attempts to lease or rent the property failed with the result that the building was pulled down in January 1976, the stone being acquired by the Midland Railway Trust. The intention to rebuild the station elsewhere regrettably never materialised. For local passengers a small bus type shelter was provided but has become prone to vandalism and it is now proposed to erect a more substantial stone shelter similar to those in the Manchester area. The access to the station from the A6 which is substandard is to be improved, the southernmost part of the loop road being stopped up.

Chapter 6

High Peak Junction and Leawood

Plate 44 The densely wooded slopes contrast sharply with the open nature of the valley floor, as Midland 4F No. 3875 crosses the River Derwent bridge just north of Whatstandwell, with a down mineral about 1930.

(W.A. Camwell Collection)

From Whatstandwell station the line curved to the east, passed through the tunnel and continued north for a short distance before turning gently west to cross the river for the first time by Derwent Viaduct, No. 10. This bridge, just north of which was a favourite vantage point of the photographer, H. Gordon Tidey, was rebuilt in 1891, by J. Butler & Co., at a cost of £3,747 15s (£3747.75). After the bridge the line continued to curve, on a low embankment and crossed Meerbrook cattle creep before straightening. It then passed over Homesford cattle creep, and under Homesford bridge before arriving at High Peak Junction, 2 miles 78 chains from Ambergate West Junction.

The junction was the point at which a single track spur left the main line on the down side, to join up with the Cromford and High Peak Railway at Cromford Goods. Opened on 21st February 1853, this link and its associated exchange sidings alongside the main line, was the first assault on the dominance of the Cromford Canal, for it allowed through running of freight traffic onto the MR. As the output from the limestone quarries on the C&HPR increased in the 1890s, the link and the sidings at the junction became progressively more important.

As late as 1955 they still handled over 170,000 tons of limestone per annum. This was sent to many destinations but was dominated by steel works at Barrow Hill, Corby, Kettering and Sheepbridge, and glass works at Knottingley and Plumstead.

In 1873 a siding was put in on the down side, just south of Holmesford bridge, for Mr Jefferies, a local quarry owner and late in 1875 a lie by for 35 wagons was put in on the up side, immediately north of the bridge. The sidings were controlled by High Peak Junction signal box, which was erected on the up side of the line, eight chains north of Holmesford bridge. The box was renewed early in 1901.

A little prior to this date Mr Jefferies' siding has been taken over by the Simms family and it changed hands again in 1902, when it was acquired by the Ilkeston and Heanor Water Board, to serve its new pumping station, then being built on the opposite side of the line. In the latter part of the 19th century rapid population growth in the area around Ilkeston and Heanor forced the respective councils to search for adequate public water supplies. Although various local schemes were tried no satisfactory results were obtained and in 1900 both authorities consulted the civil engineers, Messrs George and F.W. Hodson. This company also failed to find an adequate local water supply and suggested that the two councils should form a joint committee and expand the area of search. This was done and after considering wide areas of the north Nottinghamshire sandstone, the moorlands around Ashover and the Meerbrook Sough near Whatstandwell, the engineers recommended that the latter be purchased in view of its exceptional purity and its average daily flow of 17m gallons. Set against the predicted demand of 2m gallons per day by 1941, this source was more than sufficient.

The sough was a series of tunnels over five miles in length, commenced in 1722, to drain the lead mines around Wirksworth. The main tunnel was driven through both millstone grit and limestone and the natural outflow of water was thus too hard for direct consumption. It was therefore necessary to build a plant which would not only soften the water, but which would pump the resultant flow into a storage reservoir from which controlled supplies could be provided to the consumers. Water was passed from a sluice on the sough,

Plate 45 Bridge 14, Homesford bridge, 28th August 1984.

(Author)

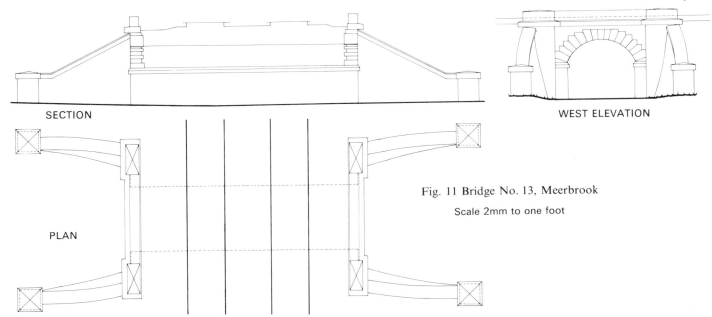

SECTION

WEST ELEVATION

To Derby

PLAN

Fig. 11 Bridge No. 13, Meerbrook

Scale 2mm to one foot

through a culvert constructed under Homesford cattle creep, into the plant which was designed to supply 1m gallons per ten hour working day. To do this required almost a ton of lime and 10 to 15 tons of coal. In addition the spent lime had to be disposed of and the transport facilities of the railway were vital to the whole operation.

The precipitated lime from the softening tanks, in the form of calcium carbonate, emerged in a semi-liquid form and ran by gravity to the settling beds from which it was wheeled by barrow to an adjacent tip. Within a few years however, the tip was rapidly becoming filled and alternative methods of disposal had to be investigated. Samples were sent to farmers and agricultural colleges with a view to ascertaining its value as a fertiliser. The lime was given and loaded into railway wagons, free of charge, the consignee paying the carriage. Over 1,500 tons were sent away in this manner, but the Midland eventually stopped the traffic on the grounds that the lime, still in a wet condition, ran out of the wagons, making the trackbed slippery and dangerous for permanent way staff. The water board was forced to concede that the track was indeed white for several miles. Estimates were obtained for the construction of water-tight wagons but it was realised that the cost of sufficient vehicles would be prohibitive.

Various experiments were carried out to find a method of drying the lime so that it could be carried in ordinary wagons and eventually it was decided to build a fire-heated drying floor, in a covered shed near the settling tanks. Between this shed and the railway siding a similar building was erected to house grinding and bagging machinery. The drying floor could cope with three tons of lime per day, consuming approximately 1¼ tons of mixed coal and coke in the process. The bagged lime left the works in both covered vans and sheeted open

Plate 46 Bridge 13. Homesford cattle creep. For many years a narrow gauge tramway ran through the bridge carrying coal and lime into the waterworks from the adjacent main line siding. The pipes carrying the inflow of water from Meerbrook sough run under the roadway.

(Author)

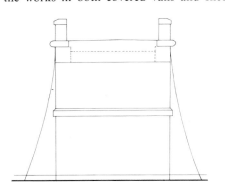

Fig. 12 Bridge No. 14, High Peak Junction

Scales Elevation &
Plan   1mm to one foot
Section   2mm to one foot

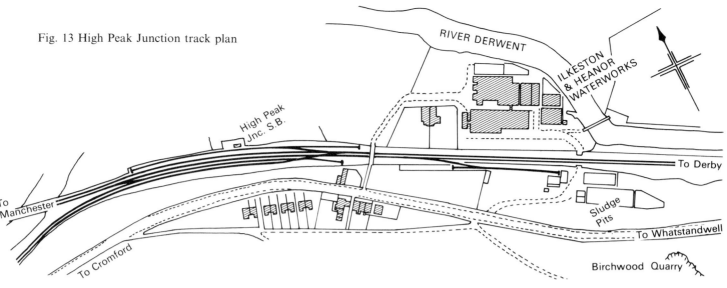

Fig. 13 High Peak Junction track plan

wagons and was used by many water companies to prevent plumbo solvency in moorland waters. It was also sold to face, toilet, tooth and polishing powder manufacturers, paper and glass works, the Ministry of Munitions and many others.

To bring in coal supplies the water board originally relied entirely on the railway company, but eventually they purchased a number of wagons, at least two of which were 1923 standard 12 ton vehicles, painted royal blue, with white letters shaded red.

With considerable limestone traffic off the C&HPR and coal, plus small amounts of merchandise in the reverse direction, together with the water works traffic, High Peak Junction was shunted several times daily in the 1930s. Loaded coal and empty limestone wagons came in on the 6.40am mineral from Westhouses, with a similar flow coming from Chaddesden on the 9.00am stopping freight. Loaded limestone and empties for the south or the Nottinghamshire pits were taken out by the 12.20pm stopping freight from Rowsley to Chaddesden, while similar traffic for north Derbyshire and south Yorkshire was taken on the 2.15pm mineral from Rowsley to Avenue.

From High Peak Junction the line continued on an embankment, crossed the river by High Peak bridge, No. 15, passed under the Cromford Canal and entered Lea Wood Tunnel. It was origjnally intended to skirt this bluff, but the sharp curvature, and the proximity of the road, river and canal made it clear that a short tunnel was a better option. The tunnel, 308 yards in length, curved gently northwards, and as the line emerged it passed under the Lea branch of the canal, opened in 1802 to serve the Lea lead smelter and Nightingale's

Plate 47 The view north from Bridge No. 14, about 1930, with the exchange sidings to the left and High Peak Junction signal box on the right.

(Author's Collection)

mills, and recrossed the river by Leawood bridge, No. 19.

Bridge No.15 was strengthened in 1878 by Messrs Handyside and then rebuilt completely by Richards & Sons in 1886/7. It remained in that state until 1933, when the Chief Civil Engineer recommended that extensive repair and modification be carried out, a contract for the work being subsequently awarded to Messrs Braithwaite & Co. on 26th April 1933. Upon completion of works to this bridge in 1878, Messrs Handyside moved their gang round the hill and carried out almost identical works to bridge No. 19. In a repeat

Plate 48 This view of High Peak bridge was probably taken for record purposes early in 1886, just before rebuilding began.   (N.R.M.)

performance this bridge was rebuilt by Eastwood, Swingler & Co. in 1888. Lest historians may question the quality of Messrs Handyside's workmanship it should be made clear that these rebuilding projects were necessary in view of developments in Midland motive power. Quite simply, heavier engines need stronger bridges. The aqueduct just south of bridge No. 19 was partially rebuilt in 1922, following the collapse of one of the parapet walls, which were removed and replaced by light-weight cast iron balustrading. Today the structure serves as a footbridge over the railway.

From this river crossing the line ran across a low embankment, pierced by Leawood cattle creep, which was filled in 1931 and then passed under Brown's bridge, a footbridge built in 1883 in conjunction with development of

Plates 49, 50 & 51 (above, right and below) were taken at Leawood in 1888. *Plate 49* shows the original bridge, while *Plate 50* shows construction work on the new bridge, with Leawood aqueduct and the tunnel mouth behind. *Plate 51* shows the new bridge, a much more substantial structure than the old one, the clear span allowing a free flow for the river.

(Author's Collection)

the adjacent land as a sewage works for Matlock U.D.C. A few years ago the cattle creep was re-opened and repaired as a link between two parts of the sewage farm and Brown's bridge was rebuilt early in 1986. For approximately 1,000 yards from this point the railway had to be squeezed into a very narrow strip of land between the canal and the river. In places this strip was no more than 50 yards wide and construction of the line called for great skill as the land supporting the canal was cut back and replaced by a long retaining wall. With the constraints of topography, and the proximity of the river and canal one finds it difficult to imagine that further development could be envisaged. It certainly was however, for on 3rd June, 1898 the Traffic Committee received a letter from the Clerk to Dethick, Lea and Holloway Parish Council, requesting that the company receive a deputation from the Council to discuss the provision of a station for goods and passengers at Leawood. The Assistant General Manager reported that in his opinion such a station would be unremunerative. It was then resolved that "the Council be informed that it was not necessary to

trouble a deputation to wait upon the company", a rather nice way to say "get lost"!

Leawood has been witness to three mishaps. The first and most spectacular occurred between Leawood Tunnel and Brown's bridge where the canal and C&HPR run to the south west of and some feet above the MR. The Sheep Pasture incline of the C&HPR begins at this point and in 1888 a brake van and a loaded wagon broke away on the incline and somersaulted over the canal and the Midland Railway, just missing an express. In the second, the Cromford Canal burst its banks, about 175 yards east of bridge No.16, on 21st February 1920. It was repaired and re-opened for traffic on 20th April, but at that time the canal was still carrying approximately 1,000 tons of coal, coke and limestone per month and the breach caused considerable inconvenience. A bigger, although shorter lived headache, was caused to the traffic department on 27th May 1930, when a mineral train left the road just north of the tunnel breaking 1,867 chairs and 20 sleepers with two bridges damaged.

Chapter 7
Cromford

Plate 52 Cromford station about 1930.
(Brookside Photographic Services)

North of Leawood the valley became much broader, as a result of the river meeting an area of softer rock, and the line entered a long curve towards the north, passing Cromford sidings on the down side of the line. As traffic increased in the 1880s congestion at Rowsley resulted in more and more freight trains being held on the main line while awaiting entry to the yard. To relieve the situation the Traffic Committee requested the provision of an additional block post and sidings at Cromford, where down freight trains could be held without delaying passenger traffic. When the curves at Cromford had been eased in 1883, the embankment and culvert No.21 had been extended to the east and the sidings were laid out on the site of the original route in 1892/93. There were three sidings, situated about 1,000 yards south of Cromford station. They had a capacity of 152 wagons and were controlled by Cromford Sidings signal box which was on the up side of the line. In addition to holding Rowsley traffic they were also used as a 'bolt hole' for High Peak Junction at times of congestion, a shunting tail lamp being kept at the junction for use when wagons were worked from that point to the sidings. Cromford Sidings signal box was taken out of use on 19th December 1965, together wth Matlock Bath, leaving one block section from High Peak Junction to Matlock station.

From the sidings the line continued to curve, on a low embankment over 'Cromford Meadows' and passed over a farm occupation bridge, Arkwright's bridge. It then curved to the west and straightened before crossing the river once more by Cromford Viaduct to arrive at Cromford station, 4 miles 64 chains from Ambergate West Junction.

The story of Richard Arkwright's application of water power to the production of cotton goods is too well known to warrant repetition but his wide ownership of land and his strong financial interest in the Cromford Canal are of interest to the present narrative. After his death in 1792 Arkwright's estate passed to his sons Richard and Peter and it was with the latter that the railway company had to negotiate. In purchasing the land for the railway the MBM & MJR agreed to build a 'First Class' station at Cromford, ie one served by all trains, at the south end of Cromford Meadows, where the line swung away from the river. It was further agreed that a new road would be built to link the station with the Cromford

turnpike, and that a new canal wharf would be built at the station. In the following year, 1847, the agreement was revised, and Arkwright was authorised to build a private siding from the site of the proposed station to the existing wharf at the head of the canal. Shortly afterwards the canal was deviated in preparation of the site for the new station and this work involved the demolition of the pump house used to replenish the canal with water from the River Derwent. A new pump house, known as Leawood Pump, with a Watt type single acting beam engine, was built just north of Wigwell aqueduct, by which the canal crossed the river at Lea Wood, and this remained in use until the canal was abandoned in 1944. Fortunately the building was not demolished and the engine was restored to working order in the mid 1970s by the Cromford Canal Society.

Just how far work progressed with the plans for the station is not clear, but failure to agree with Arkwright led to the opening of a 'temporary' station in the cutting approaching Willersley Tunnel. Simple wooden shelters were erected on short platforms which ran right up to the tunnel mouth, and a short, steep access road was built parallel to the down line. In 1850 a deputation from Cromford tradespeople expressed their concern to the railway company regarding the lack of parcels and goods facilities at the station, but to protect his interests in the canal Arkwright insisted that the station be restricted to passengers only. A little later he relented slightly and agreed to the station handling parcels traffic for Lea. This traffic was to develop almost exclusively as outgoing parcels from John Smedley's Lea Mills (formerly Nightingale's) and remained important to the railway until the 1960s. 1850 was also the year in which Peter Arkwright abandoned his plans for a station, but the railway management were to hear from him again, for in 1854 he submitted a claim for compensation for damage by fire to one of his cottages near Cromford, allegedly caused by cinders from a Midland engine. At the same time the tenant, a Mr Brown, submitted a claim for damage to his furniture, but while Arkwright's claim was settled within three weeks, there is no record of any payment to the unfortunate tenant. There is no indication in the minutes as to the location of this cottage.

The author has already noted that the records of the early

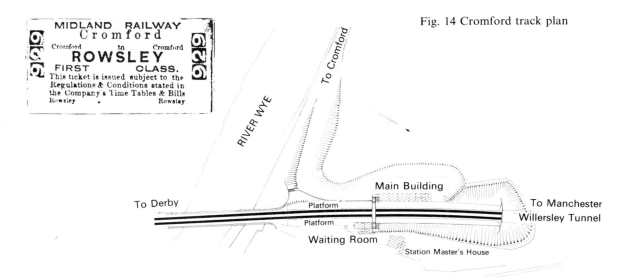

Fig. 14 Cromford track plan

RIVER WYE

To Cromford

To Derby

Platform

Platform

Main Building

Waiting Room

Station Master's House

To Manchester
Willersley Tunnel

years are incomplete, but it is generally accepted that the station house at Cromford was built about 1855 to a design by G.H. Stokes, Paxton's son-in-law. At that time Stokes was strongly under the influence of French architecture, for between 1853 and 1859 he worked with Paxton, on Ferrières Chateaux for Baron Rothschild, while his sketch book of French styles is dated 1853-6. But with only simple wooden buildings for passengers one is led to question why such an ornate building should be erected for staff purposes. Marc Girouard in *Spirit of the Age* said "The explanation for its fanciful appearance is that it acted as a kind of railway entrance lodge for the family that lived at Willersley Castle". His theory, but probably correct. With such an imbalance between the elegance of the house and the spartan nature of the passenger accommodation it is only natural that steps were taken to correct the situation. There was very little room on the down side of the line, within the company's ownership, but access across the line was easy, and it is the opinion of Trevor Griffin, a noted local historian, that what later became the up waiting room was in fact erected as the main station building, probably about 1860. Almost certainly designed by Stokes, the building has a clock tower – unusual for a 'secondary' building, and it originally had three rooms. During recent renovation work an old cable was discovered, suggesting that it once had a telegraph, again pointing to it being the main building.

In the late summer of 1865 the platforms were extended to the standard length of 300ft, the access road being moved over slightly to accommodate the down platform extension. The following year a contract for cleaning and repainting the station house was awarded to George Wood, in the sum of

Fig. 15 Ilkeston & Heanor Water Board wagon livery

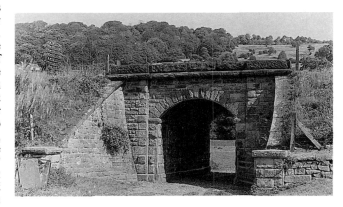

Plate 53 (above) Bridge No. 22, Arkwright's bridge.

(Author)

Plate 54 (below) The station house, Cromford. The original building was heavily influenced by Stokes' stay in France, but the symmetry of the design was destroyed by the extension at the rear added in 1911.

(Author)

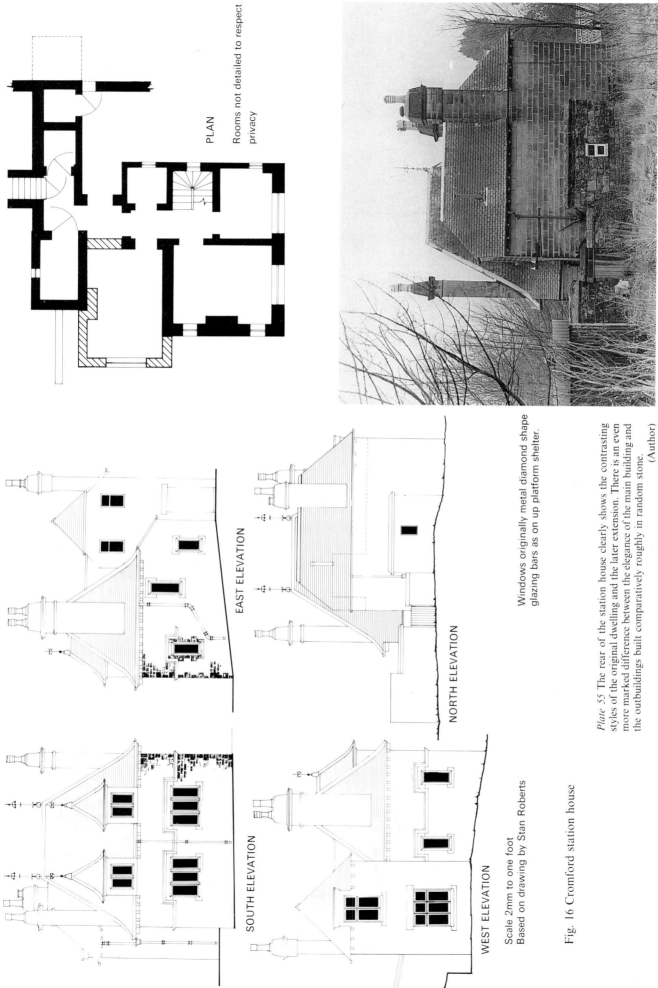

PLAN

Rooms not detailed to respect privacy

EAST ELEVATION

NORTH ELEVATION

Windows originally metal diamond shape glazing bars as on up platform shelter.

SOUTH ELEVATION

WEST ELEVATION

Scale 2mm to one foot
Based on drawing by Stan Roberts

Fig. 16 Cromford station house

Plate 55 The rear of the station house clearly shows the contrasting styles of the original dwelling and the later extension. There is an even more marked difference between the elegance of the main building and the outbuildings built comparatively roughly in random stone.

(Author)

41

Plate 56 (above) The up waiting shelter seen here a few years ago before renovation works were put in hand. The tall chimneys, seen in *plate 52*, were removed by British Railways who considered them to be unsafe.

(Author)

Plate 57 (left) The toilet facilities to the shelter were provided in a small extension to the rear, the ladies having access from inside, while gentlemen had to walk round the back.

(Author)

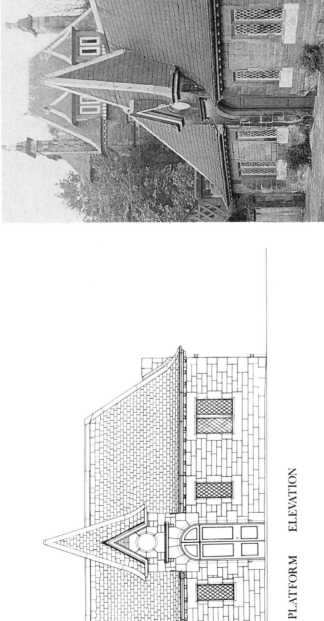

PLATFORM ELEVATION

Scale 3mm to one ft

PLAN

Note: Walls actually bowed as drawn

Ladies' w.c.

Coal Store

Gentlemen's toilet

Ladies' waiting room

General waiting room

Fig. 17 Cromford up waiting shelter

MIDLAND RAILWAY. This Ticket is issued subject to the Regulations & Conditions stated in the Company's Time Tables & Bills.

FIRST CLASS.

CROMFORD to

CHESTERFIELD

Via Ambergate

FARE 2s. 6d.   FARE 2s. 6d.
Cromford Chesterfield   Cromford Chesterfield

AUG 8 97

401

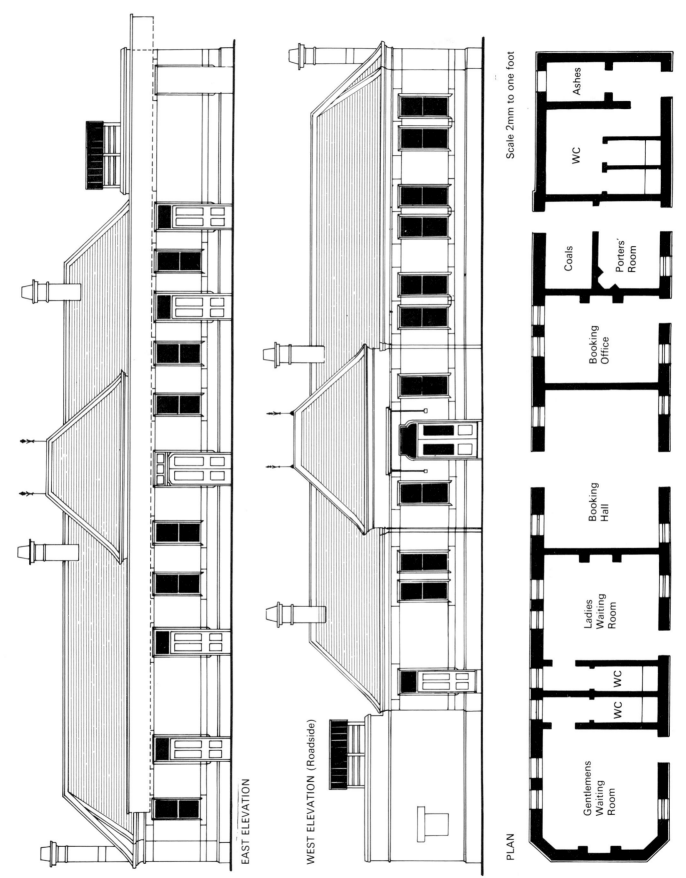

EAST ELEVATION

WEST ELEVATION (Roadside)

PLAN

Scale 2mm to one foot

Ashes WC

Coals **Porters' Room**

Booking Office

Booking Hall

Ladies Waiting Room

WC WC

Gentlemens Waiting Room

Fig. 18 Cromford main building

43

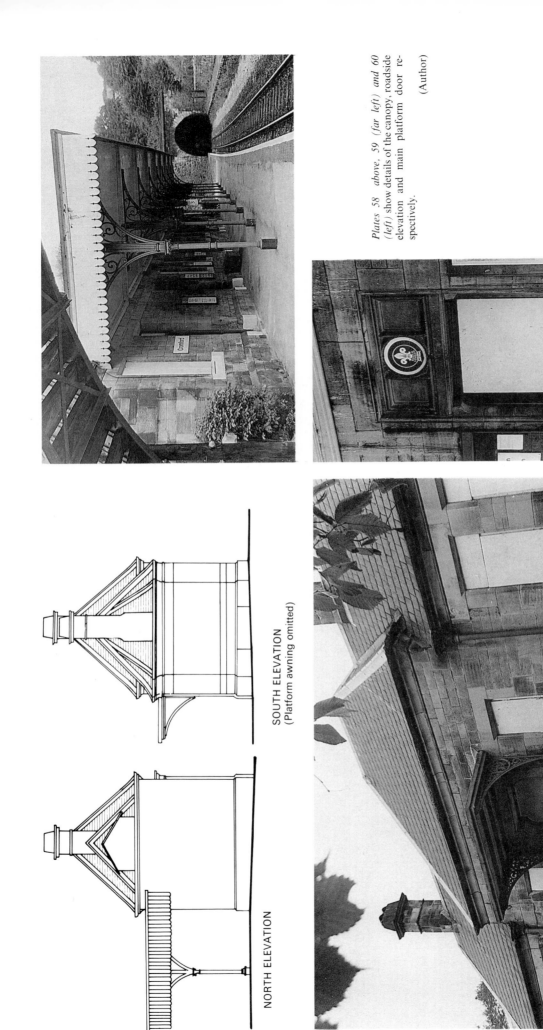

Plates 58 above, 59 (far left) and 60 (left) show details of the canopy, roadside elevation and main platform door respectively.

(Author)

SOUTH ELEVATION
(Platform awning omitted)

NORTH ELEVATION

44

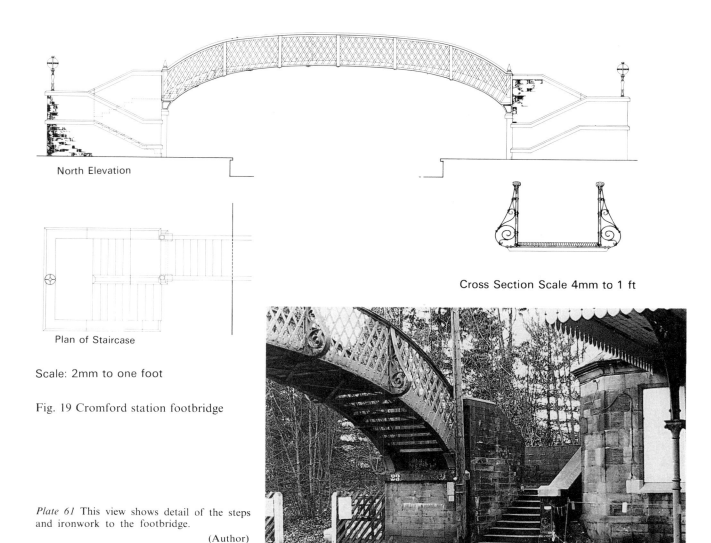

North Elevation

Plan of Staircase

Scale: 2mm to one foot

Fig. 19 Cromford station footbridge

Cross Section Scale 4mm to 1 ft

Plate 61 This view shows detail of the steps and ironwork to the footbridge.

(Author)

£6 18s (£6.90). As it was normal practice to paint structures every 8-10 years or so, this contract helps to date the erection of the house.

When the Midland took over full control of the Ambergate-Rowsley line in 1871, it quickly set about improving it. Among those facilities considered inadequate were the structures at Cromford and in 1872 it was ordered that plans be prepared for erecting new station buildings, served by a new access road. These plans, at an estimated cost of £2,960, were approved on 18th June 1872, but it proved impossible to acquire additional land by agreement from S. Smith and another and it was necessary to obtain an additional powers act. This was duly achieved and a contract for the erection of the new station building was finally awarded to Joseph Berresford and Sons on 4th August 1874. It is interesting to note that while early plans show two small buildings on the platforms, the plans accompanying the new act show three. It is just possible that the building removed from Matlock Bath circa 1860 was in fact re-erected at Cromford. It is also worthy of note that the indenture of 1873 between S. Smith, etc and the MR includes the following words: "the said piece of land ... shall be used only for the purpose of a station for passengers, carriages, horses and parcels and as an approach road thereto and not for the purpose of a goods station or any other purpose whatsoever." A little over ten years after the new building was completed a contract for the erection of a footbridge was awarded to the Butterley Co. in May 1885.

Towards the end of the 1880s the Midland began to question the need of retaining the Cromford Canal, which was carrying traffic that could equally well be moved by rail and they sought the opinion of the company's solicitors, Messrs Beale & Co., as to the prospects for closure. In January 1890 they reported

that in their view the canal must remain open as long as there was a public demand for traffic. The idea of closure must still have been alive when the Traffic Committee's tour of inspection on 21st March 1894 took them to Cromford for they ordered that plans be prepared for the construction of a branch line to the wharf at the head of the canal and the provision there of a goods shed. However, when the plans and estimate of £10,188 were put to the committee in July 1894 the matter was promptly forgotten. The superior facilities offered by the railway gradually drew traffic away from the canal but notwithstanding the collapse of the Butterley Tunnel in 1908, the wharf remained open until 30th September 1921.

Apart from an extension to the station house in 1911, Cromford was quiet until the end of 1925, when the engineer reported that the land at the south end of the tunnel, which had moved slightly at the end of May, had slipped more seriously. The cutting had moved once before, in 1862, but this time more drastic works were required. Additional land was acquired and the cutting was graded back around the tunnel mouth to ease the slope. As an added precaution the retaining wall behind the up platform was raised and a channel was put behind it to take away water from land above the tunnel and the cutting slope.

The catchment area of Cromford station included parts of Lea and Holloway, Cromford itself, Bonsall, Middleton and at least for northbound traffic, Wirksworth. These areas gave a population of around 7,000 in the 1920s and 30s. In 1872 some 24,141 tickets, or approximately 74 per weekday, were purchased at the station, with an average fare of 1s 3½d (7½p). Unlike many stations on the line, the annual number of bookings did not increase markedly and by 1892 they had only risen to a little under 34,000. At the close of the Midland

period the figure had fallen to 20,884, but the average fare had only risen slightly to 2s 3½d (11½p) representing a return journey of a little over seven miles, virtually unchanged from 1872. In general terms the train service was similar to that at Whatstandwell.

With these fares, a very heavy parcels traffic from Lea Mills and no goods yard to maintain, the station made a profit of £2,841 in 1922 and the books were handed over to the LMS in a respectable condition. The station stands today much as the Midland left it, and forms part of the Cromford Conservation area, with the buildings and footbridge individually protected as 'listed buildings'. In 1973 the main building was leased by the Scout County of Greater London South and converted into an Activity Centre for Venture Scouts, the Bernard Sunley Activity Centre. The exterior of the building has not been altered and railway features have been restored. The platform canopy remains in BR ownership and has recently been repaired with new woodwork throughout. The station is served by the Derby-Matlock trains and hikers still use the facilities as they have done for well over 100 years.

Plate 62 LMS built 4F 0-6-0, No. 4050 brings a long through freight past the station in August 1934. The bi-directional signal, used extensively on the MR, had by this time been fitted with upper quadrant arms. The cleanliness of the engine is worthy of note.

(E.R. Morten)

Plate 63 Class 150 'Sprinter' dmu, No. 002, one of the 3-car prototypes, leaves Cromford with the 9.13am Matlock-Derby train on 15th March 1985.

(Author)

Chapter 8
Matlock Bath

Previous page: Plate 64 Class 5XP, No. 45649 *Hawkins* storms through Matlock Bath as it accelerates away from the Matlock stop with the 4.00pm Manchester Central-St Pancras express on 24th May 1952.
(E.R. Morten)

Plate 65 This view of Matlock Bath was taken about 1888/89 to show the new footbridge, and records the station as it was before the signal box was renewed on a site to the south of the up platform, and the gable to the main building cut back. Points of interest include the inside keyed track, the length of the platforms and the rockery at the side of the signal box. Under the awning are a proliferation of timetables which include those of the Midland, Lancashire & Yorkshire, North British and North Eastern Railways.

(N.R.M.)

As a matter of principle Stephenson used the Matlock Gorge to carry his line to the north, but he could not, of course, follow the sharp bends of the river. By swinging the route to the east, at the south end of Cromford Meadows, he was able to drive a straight tunnel, 746 yards long, through the ridge and emerge on the eastern, undeveloped side of the river at Matlock Bath. Here, a shallow valley coming down from the east afforded a site for a station, 5 miles 47 chains from Ambergate West Junction.

Although a bridge had been built across the river at Matlock in the 15th century, giving access to Derwent Gorge, the latter remained one of the most secluded places in Derbyshire, but the beginnings of change occurred in 1698 with the discovery of a thermal spring below Masson Hill. A little over 30 years later the Old Bath Hotel had become established on the site. By the early years of the 18th century two more hotels and a number of lodging houses provided accommodation for some 400 visitors. The town had by then become a fashionable resort and remained so, in spite of the cutting of a gap through Scarthin Nick at Cromford in 1818, to allow the construction of a turnpike from the south, which in turn allowed the introduction of a daily coach service from Manchester to Nottingham and Derby. The arrival of the railway in 1849, however, was to have a far different effect, for it suddenly brought the resort within the reach of the day tripper from the Midland cities. With the new visitors came the 'wide boys', anxious to relieve their fellows of any spare cash and the resultant commercialism would leave today's entrepreneurs speechless. The class conscious Victorian gentry did not care for these hordes of city folk, and Matlock Bath rapidly declined as a 'high class' resort, during the second part of the 19th century.

When the railway was under construction, spoil from Willersley Tunnel was laid out to the north to form the level site for a station, and a road bridge was built across the river to provide access. In true Midland fashion this bridge was later given a number, 24B, and a distance from St Pancras, 143

miles 67 chains. In those early years the railway company was still conscious of the fashionable image of the resort and in 1853 an application from Messrs Rains and Green for a siding to serve their stone quarry was turned down on the grounds that the site was objectionable.

The author is not aware of any records covering the design and date of the main station building but as Paxton was heavily involved in the design of many of the original structures on the MBM & MJ it is logical to assume that he had some influence at Matlock Bath. As the Duke of Devonshire's agent he lived near Chatsworth and he would have been familiar with the comment that Matlock Bath was the 'Switzerland of England'. Hence the station buildings were designed in the style of Swiss chalets, with a low profile and massively overhung eaves.

Although it is only an opinion that the main building was erected ready for the opening of the line, it is a known fact that the first alterations occurred in 1859. In May of that year it was ordered that the refreshment room and larder be converted to waiting room and WCs, following which the station was repainted by G.W. Harrison, Derby. In 1861 orders were given to lengthen the platforms and put in sidings for excursion traffic, followed two years later by an instruction to provide a goods shed and sidings. It appears that none of this work was carried out, for in January 1865 a similar instruction was issued again. This time the trackwork was put in, but still the goods shed was forgotten.

By the time the Midland took full control annual passenger bookings at the station were approaching 45,000, freight traffic was growing strongly and again urgent improvements were put in hand. In April 1872 plans were approved for re-arranging the sidings, followed soon afterwards by the provision of a water crane and an order that a new waiting shelter be erected on each platform. It is not clear what design was put forward for these structures, but the tenders were opened on 18th February 1873 and were given to Mr Crossley, the engineer, to report thereon, the lowest tender being that of

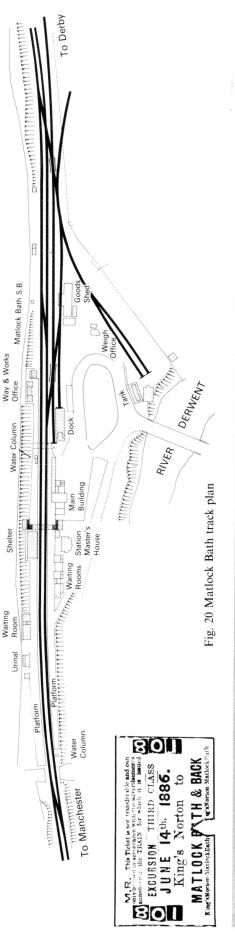

Fig. 20 Matlock Bath track plan

MATLOCK BATH

Musical Festival

FRIDAY and SATURDAY,
JUNE 10th and 11th, 1932.

CHEAP TICKETS

(FIRST AND THIRD CLASS)

will be issued by the

London Midland & Scottish Railway Co.

TO

MATLOCK BATH

AT ABOUT

SINGLE FARE

(Plus fractions of a 1d.)

FOR THE DOUBLE JOURNEY

from Stations within a radius of 60 miles, available by any
train on the day of issue.

CHILDREN under three years of age, free; three years and under fourteen, half fare.

CONDITIONS OF ISSUE OF EXCURSION TICKETS & OTHER REDUCED FARE TICKETS.
Excursion tickets and tickets issued at fares less than the ordinary fares are issued subject
to the Notices and Conditions shown in the Company's Current Time Table.

DAY AND HALF-DAY EXCURSION TICKETS.—Tickets are issued day or holiday

Plate 66 (above) Handbill to promote the Musical Festival of June
1932.

(G. Waite Collection)

Plate 67 This general view of the station and goods yard was taken
from above Willersley Tunnel around the turn of the century as a
Johnson 4-4-0 runs through with an up express.

(Railway Revivals)

49

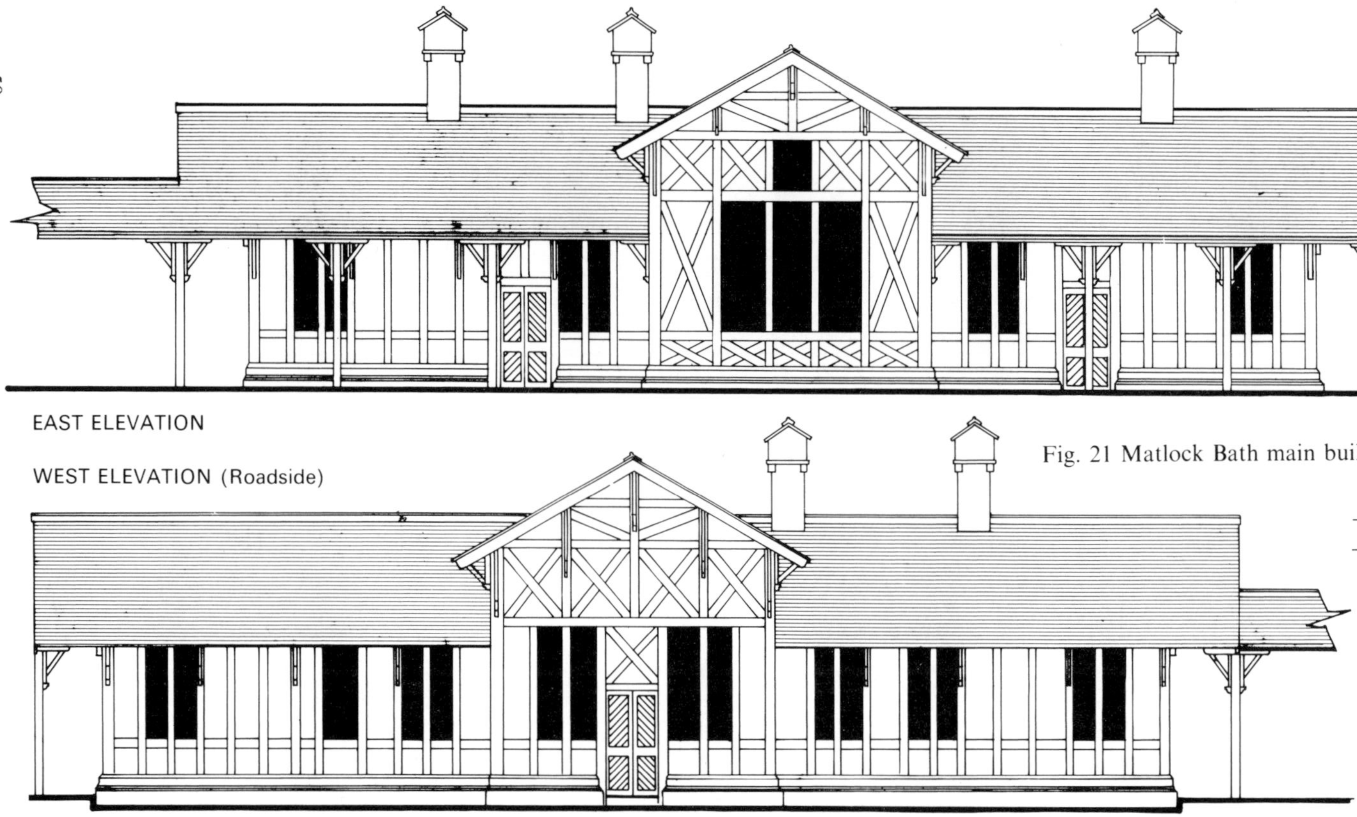

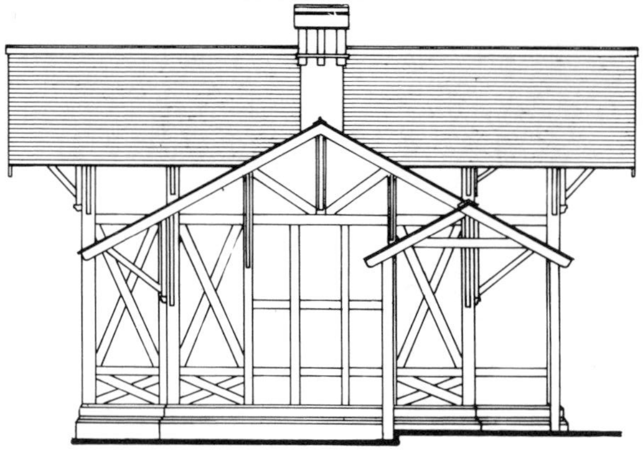

SOUTH ELEVATION

Scale 2mm to one foot

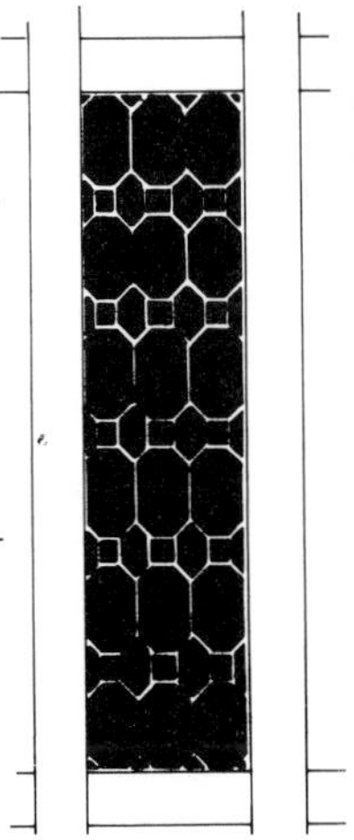

Plate 69 Window detail of main building.   (Author)

Window detail
(not to scale)

Plate 68 (left) This view shows the main building from the yard about
1968/69, and sadly shows the attitude at that time towards the
maintenance of British Railways' historic buildings. Fortunately times
have changed and plans are now afoot to restore the building,
although this work had not been started at the time of writing.
(HMRS)

Fig. 21 Matlock Bath main building

EAST ELEVATION

WEST ELEVATION (Roadside)

PLATFORM ELE. Fig. 22 Matlock Bath down waiting rooms NORTH ELE.

ROADSIDE ELE. Scale 2mm to one foot SOUTH ELE.

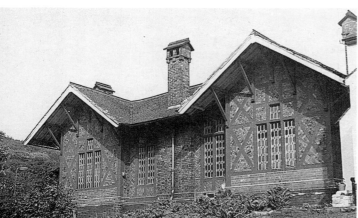

Plate 70 (left) Rear elevation of down waiting rooms.

(Author)

Plate 71 (below left) This view around 1900 is the only photograph known to the author which includes the up waiting rooms erected in 1875.

(Lens of Sutton)

Plate 72 (below) As late as 1965 British Rail was still encouraging use of the line to Buxton.

(Author's Collection)

RAMBLES in Derbyshire
also
MATLOCK BATH ILLUMINATIONS
and
FIREWORKS DISPLAY
Excursions

to AMBERGATE CROMFORD
MATLOCK BATH MATLOCK
DARLEY DALE ROWSLEY
BAKEWELL MILLER'S DALE
and BUXTON

Bank Holiday Monday
30th August 1965

51

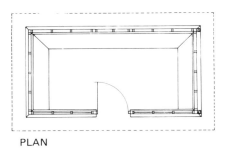

| PLATFORM ELEVATION | END ELEVATION | REAR ELEVATION |

PLAN

Scale 3mm to one ft

Fig. 23 Matlock Bath British Rail shelter

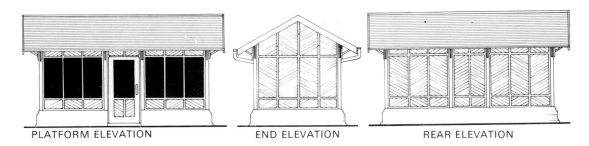

BRITISH RAILWAYS (E) (S.T. 113-?)
SCENIC HALF-DAY EXCURSION
31st MAY, 1959
Lincoln (St. Marks) to
MATLOCK BATH & RETURN
Whole ticket to be collected at
LINCOLN (St. Marks) on return
SECOND CLASS

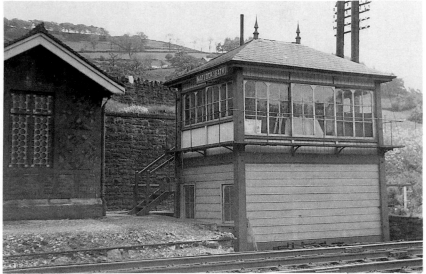

Plate 73 (above) The new waiting shelter designed by Fiona Mann and erected in 1984.

(Author)

Plate 74 (left) The signal box at Matlock Bath was renewed about 1890/91 and was a standard period II structure 15ft x 10ft, but with a relatively unusual rear staircase. The adjacent waiting shelter was erected in 1873 and while following the design of the original building it had a much less pronounced roof overhang and different windows.

(M.A. King)

C. Cash at £2,012 17s 11d (£2,012.90). A few weeks later it was agreed that Mr Cash put in the foundations at the rates in his tender, but that a new design be submitted for the buildings. On 6th May a revised drawing was put before the Way and Works Committee, with an estimated cost of £1,725. It was then resolved to erect the buildings in accordance with the original design, that "being more in character with the building now in existence". This little exercise demonstrates that the management gave a lot of thought to the design and appearance of buildings, a concern which was eventually to be expressed at this location much nearer our own times.

Along with re-arrangement of the sidings the general question of freight traffic arose again and in February 1874 the committee opened tenders for the construction of a goods shed. Of the eleven bids received the lowest was from J. & E.

Woods, at £1,327 7s 4d (£1,327.36½p) and a contract was let accordingly. We have already noted that the MR was not averse to changing its mind and the contract was subsequently cancelled, possibly on the grounds that someone had made an error in assessing the size of building required. With passenger traffic still growing, a further waiting shelter was added at the north end of the up platform in 1875, and on 14th March 1882 the Way and Works Committee raised a familiar subject. As a result a contract for the erection of a goods shed was awarded to James Salt in June of that year, with the building being completed early in 1883, at a cost of £405 18s 7d (£405.93) somewhat cheaper than the proposal of 1874, and much more in scale with the character of the station and its traffic.

Following erection of the footbridge by W. Thomas Woodall in 1887 and the renewal of the signal box in 1890, a

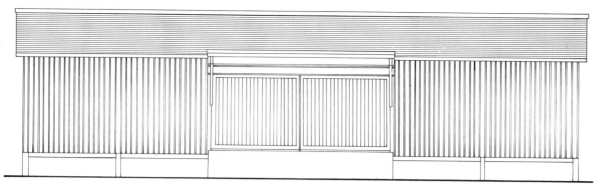

WEST ELEVATION
(Road)

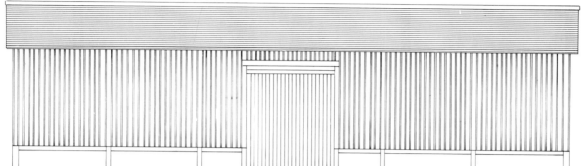

EAST ELEVATION
(Rail)

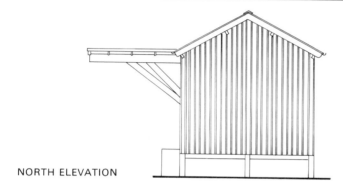

NORTH ELEVATION

Fig. 24 Matlock Bath Goods Shed
Scale 2mm to one foot

Plate 75 (below) This view shows the roadside elevation of the goods shed, which was painted buff with chocolate brown corner posts and doors, until repainted black in the 1960s.

(Author's Collection)

Plate 76 (bottom) Very late in LMS days a pre-cast concrete store, raised on concrete piles, was provided adjacent to the goods shed, for use as an animal feed and corn store.

(Author's Collection)

siding was put in to serve Station Quarry, being developed by Messrs Shaw Bros on the down side of the line immediately north of Willersley Tunnel. The opening of this quarry saw a sudden jump in limestone being shipped from the station, but the tonnage fell sharply again shortly afterwards when two quarries almost in the heart of the town, just opposite the station entrance, closed down. Matlock Bath seemed to suffer a jinx over proposed alterations, for while the Traffic Committee requested an awning over part of the up platform in July 1894, it was not until 5th November 1897 that a contract was awarded to Messrs Groom & Co. The awning, which was erected immediately north of the footbridge was a 'standard' ridge and furrow structure, with a sloping front face.

In 1902 the Traffic Committee received a petition from the residents of Wirksworth requesting that the Wirksworth branch be extended to join the main line near Matlock Bath. The communication was dealt with in classic 'committee' fashion, with the secretary being requested to inform the petitioners that the company must decline the suggestion while the engineer was requested to prepare an estimate of the costs. Where the junction could have been without cutting across the goods yard the author knows not, but the question is purely academic for the matter was never heard of again.

The final works carried out by the MR at Matlock Bath comprised the extension and covering of the loading dock at the southern end of the down platform, in 1908, and the removal of that part of the original building which projected on the platform side, in 1907. This was presumably done on safety grounds as the platform at that point was quite narrow. Strangely the LMS rating plan, circa 1932, still shows this projection, but omits the awning from the northern section of the building, which remained until closure. The LMS left its mark at the station by the erection of the Station Master's house very early in 1924 and by the provision of a pre-cast concrete warehouse, adjacent to the original MR goods shed, either just before or just after World War II.

Throughout much of its history this station was the destination of many special and excursion trains, and thousands of words must have been written by the railway companies extolling the virtues of the town as a resort. Of this prose, little, if any can surpass that of the LMS publication, *The Track of the Twenty Fives,* published c1930, which describing the area said, "There is the river, brilliant, smooth, subtle, inscrutable as a jade amulet, the dazzling limestone cliff, tricked out with yew and ivy, as awesome as stage properties. It is scenic scenery – a perfect background for the holiday-maker with his switchbacks and all his reckless panoply of make-believe". After the war this popularity did not change, but the means of access did and to the detriment of the resident population, and the railway, visitors arrived by road in ever increasing numbers. With relatively few regular travellers and on the assumption that Matlock station could adequately cover the area, British Railways were able to close the station when through local services to Manchester were withdrawn north of Matlock in March 1967. The up platform buildings were all demolished by the end of the same year, with the footbridge being removed early in 1968. At the same time the platform eaves of the main down side building were cut back and the building leased to a furniture/antique business, after which it became a café, with part of the goods yard being used for car parking.

Local businessmen were convinced that a serious mistake had been made. Strenuous efforts by the Chamber of Trade, the Illuminations and Venetian Nights Committee and Derbyshire County Council, whose combined efforts raised sufficient finance to counter several years of neglect, resulted in the station being re-opened on 27th May 1972. Since that time the summer timetable has seen an increasing number of excursion trains, the popularity of which was boosted in 1984 by the opening of the Heights of Abraham cable car service across the gorge. This starts from a point just north of the station from which there is direct access via a pedestrian crossing and fenced path along the remains of the up platform. With increased usage British Rail recently looked at the facilities for passengers and in 1984 a new waiting shelter was

Plate 77 Modern day British Rail poster.

(Author's Collection)

erected adjacent to the main building. The shelter was designed by Fiona Mann, a student member of the Regional Architect's staff and perfectly encapsulates the character of its older neighbour. It was built by Edward Wood and Sons of Derby, with a base in Butterley Cathedrals wire-cut rustic bricks and softwood walls coated in Sadolins teak preservative. The roof, supported on delicate eaves brackets is finished with Blue Brindle Rosemary clay tiles.

The goods shed was demolished early in 1984 and in 1986 ownership of the goods yard and station buildings passed to West Derbyshire District Council. Within days of the new ownership the windows were smashed and badly damaged and upon British Rail's advice were boarded up by the Council.

The station served Matlock Bath and Starkholmes, a small settlement to the east, with a combined resident population of around 2,000 at the turn of the century. One can only conclude that the relatively high number of passenger bookings at the station may have included tourists using the railway to visit other localities during their stay. In 1872, 44,078 tickets were purchased, an average of 125 per weekday at an average fare of 2s (10p), which would have taken the ordinary third class traveller to Monsal Dale and back. This figure increased to well over 60,000 in the next decade, but then fell steadily until at the end of the MR period it was almost back to the 1872 level, with an average fare of 3s 3d (16½p) representing a slightly shorter journey than 50 years previously. The timetable reflected the importance of the station and was broadly similar to that at Ambergate, although before 1904 the station was marginally better served than Matlock Bridge.

In terms of freight traffic the yard also served Cromford and surrounding areas, but certainly in LMS days it always worked in the shadow of its much larger neighbour at Matlock. Nevertheless an interesting and varied traffic once passed through the yard. The coal class traffic included the output of limestone from Messrs Shaw Bros and incoming coal and coke for both domestic and industrial consumption. While coal merchants from Matlock no doubt shared the market, much of the local demand was satisfied by Nathaniel Wheatcroft & Son, who became established at Cromford shortly after the canal opened, and reputedly became one of the largest carriers and general merchants in the Midlands, if not in England. The company made much use of the canal system and the C&HPR, but on the opening of the railway they began to concentrate on coal, corn and building materials, but the headquarters of the business always remained at Cromford Canal Head Wharf. An idea of the material which came in barges to Cromford, and later in railway wagons to Matlock Bath can be obtained from a reprint of a booklet entitled *The Matlocks and Bakewell* recently published by the Arkwright Society. This publication, essential reading for the historian of the area, informs us that the company dealt in corn, bran, pollard, meals, hay, straw, cotton, linseed cake, well seasoned timber, slates, bricks, tiles, sanitary pipes, chimney pots, lime, sand, cement, coal and coke. When the wharf closed in 1921, much of the business in Cromford and Matlock Bath was transferred to the railway, although the company continued to use the canal and C&HPR for many years. Fortunately many records of the firm have survived and *fig. 25,* selected at random, shows the coal account at Matlock Bath for July 1938. Coal in that month came from various collieries in the Butterley group and from Pentrich Colliery, while coke came from Grassmoor Colliery. As far as the author is aware Messrs Wheatcroft never owned their own railway wagons and of those used in the sample month, 24 belonged to collieries, four were LMS and one each

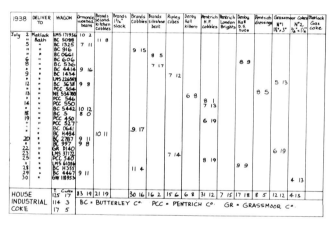

Fig. 25 N. Wheatcroft & Son Coal Account, July 1938

(Author)

came from the GWR and LNER. The LMS wagons comprised a 12 ton ex-GSWR, an ex-LNWR and two ex-MR vehicles. The LNER wagon was an ex-GCR vehicle.

For some considerable time the largest single industrial consumer of coal was probably the Matlock Bath and Scarthin Nick Gas Co. It is believed that the works were in use when the railway was opened for access was by an occupation bridge at the north end of the station, appropriately named Gas House bridge. Some time later the company was acquired by Bakewell R.D.C. and on 1st April 1924, when the parishes of Tansley and Cromford were removed from Bakewell R.D.C., ownership passed to the Matlocks U.D.C., which was formed by the amalgamation of these two parishes and the former Matlock and Matlock Bath Urban District Councils. From 1924 until 1926 virtually all coal was obtained from Rothervale Collieries Ltd but for the next four years or so Nathaniel Atrill or Newton Chambers and Co. were the main suppliers. By the early 1930s the Rotherham and District Collieries Association had been formed and Rothervale and Tinsley Park Collieries dominated supplies. Towards the end of 1932 the Matlock Gas Co. made an offer to purchase the works, at almost the same time as Clay Cross Co. made an offer to supply coke oven gas to the gas holder at the works. The gas company was asked to increase its offer, while Clay Cross Co. was asked for its lowest price for gas, and was invited to make an offer for purchase. After considerable argument a preference for the local involvement emerged and the works were sold to Matlock Gas Co. in August 1933.

Shortly afterwards this company was itself taken over by the Sheffield Gas Co., who almost immediately put in new mains from the Matlock works to the Matlock Bath area and closed down the now redundant works. The paper, textile and paint mills at Cromford, Lea and the Via Gellia were all significant users of coal for heating, power or manufacturing purposes. Together with shops and other business establishments these mills provided much valuable general merchandise carriage to the railway, amounting to some 8,000–9,000 tons per annum in the 1920s, or 4–6 wagon loads daily.

The minerals of Derbyshire have long been ground for use in the paint industry and one of the best known manufacturers in the country, Joseph Mason, who supplied paint to both the MR and the LMS, was established in Derby in 1800. Several concerns actually processed minerals, but one of the most important was the Via Gellia Paint and Colour Company, who

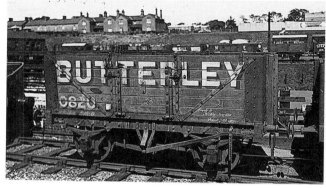

Plate 78 A 10 ton vehicle, built by E. Eastwood, 15ft 6in x 7ft 6in, with five 7in and one 9in planks, painted grey with black corner plates, white letters, black shading.

(Lens of Sutton)

Plate 79 A 10 ton wagon from a batch numbered 150–179, built in March 1916. It was 15ft 6in x 7ft 6in x 3ft 9in, with one 9in, four 7in and one 9in planks. The base colour was red, with one black plank, white letters, black shading.

(Author's Collection)

had several mills at Ashford, Cromford and Matlock Bath. The latter works are still in operation today, just north of the station on a narrow strip of land between the railway and the river, in premises that were built as a lead mill in 1769 and rebuilt after a fire in 1896. The company supplied all manner of oils, paints and pigments, which left the station in a variety of cans, barrels, boxes and drums, not only to firms such as Mason's, but to many other destinations at home and abroad. Not all the minerals used were obtained locally and among the more unusual goods traffic to come into the yard was Persian Red Oxide, from the island of Abamusa. For a long period between the wars 1,000–2,000 tons per annum arrived, bagged and carried in sheeted open wagons. At an average load of 8 tons this traffic would bring in five or six wagons weekly, and with the odd burst bag must have added a little colour to the goods yard!

The Matlock & Bonsall Basalt Co. and the Peak Mining Co.'s spar quarry provided additional outgoing mineral traffic, while the establishment of a spirit store in the yard by Shell Mex Ltd in 1922 brought tank wagons into the station.

Chapter 9

Matlock

Plate 80 Class 4F 0-6-0 No. 3982 runs out of High Tor No. 1 Tunnel with an up goods train about 1935. The down signal has been fitted with upper quadrant arms, but the up home remains in original condition. It is carried on a short post on the outside of the curve so as to be visible as drivers come through the tunnel.

(D. Ibbotson)

Plate 81 MR 4-4-0 Compound No. 1028 just north of High Tor No. 2 Tunnel with a Derby-Manchester Central local train in August 1934. This photograph is of considerable value in providing the only known illustration of coke wagons operated by ICI (Lime) Ltd. Wagon No. 9385 appears to be a standard 1907 10 ton vehicle, 16ft x 7ft 6in, with seven planks, side and end doors, brakes either side, Ellis pattern axleboxes and removable coke rails. The adjacent wagon belongs to Meadows, Stockport. The words Heaton Norris are written on the second plank up to the left of the door. It is a 10 ton wagon, 16ft x 7ft 6in and is painted red with white letters and black shading.

(E.R. Morten)

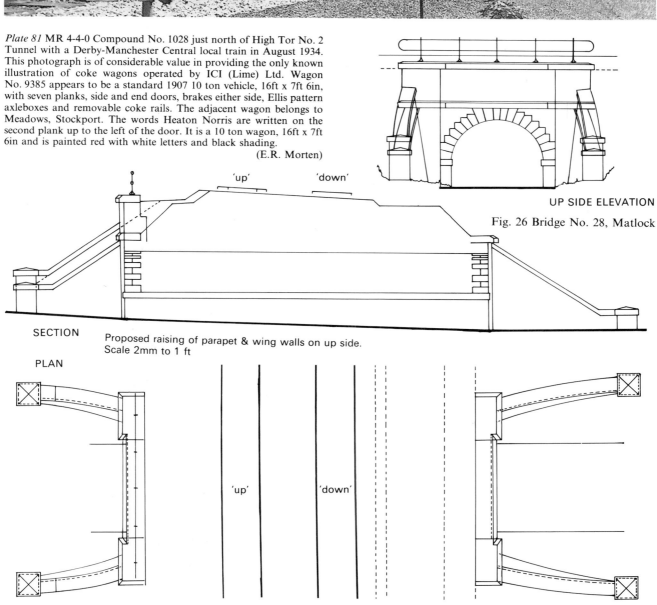

UP SIDE ELEVATION

Fig. 26 Bridge No. 28, Matlock

SECTION

Proposed raising of parapet & wing walls on up side.
Scale 2mm to 1 ft

PLAN

'up'   'down'

Immediately north of Matlock Bath station the limestone bluff of High Tor rises vertically some 480ft above the river, and the railway pierces this, on a gentle eastwards curve, by two closely spaced tunnels. The first, High Tor No.1, begins eight chains north of Gas House bridge and runs for 321 yards. Originally there was a gap of four chains before the line entered High Tor No.2 (378 yards), but following repeated falls of rock in the gap the engineer recommended that the gap should be arched over in brick to protect the line. This work was approved in April 1893 and comprised a 30ft extension to No.1 tunnel, and then a covered way.

From the northern portal of the second tunnel the line curved westwards on a low embankment, crossed Lime Tree Lane by a small occupation bridge and then crossed the river and road by Boat House bridge. This crossing comprised an attractive three arch stone bridge over the river, followed by an austere plate girder structure over the road. The latter was rebuilt by Eastwood Swingler & Co in July 1891 and its design was necessary to achieve the newly required clearance standards over the road. Just north of this bridge the line passed under Green Lane bridge (now demolished) and entered Holt Lane Tunnel. After 126 yards daylight was regained and running through a short cutting the line passed under Holt Lane bridge to arrive at Matlock station, 6 miles 54 chains from Ambergate West Junction and exactly 145 miles from St Pancras.

Matlock, which is an amalgam of eight separate townships, is one of the oldest settlements in the Peak District, the original core of the town, around the Parish church at Matlock Green, being mentioned in the Domesday Book in relation to lead mining. By the end of the 18th century Matlock Bridge had become established around the crossing of the river, where five turnpikes converged. At that time Buxton was developing under the paternal oversight of the Dukes of Devonshire and in a very similar way it was the influence of the eccentric industrialist, John Smedley, which was to guide the development of Matlock.

Towards the middle of the 19th century Smedley had modernised the hosiery mills at Lea, which his father, Thomas, had taken over from the Nightingale family, but it was his health and the opening of the railway that was to shape the future of the town. In 1849 he took the 'water treatment' at Ben Rhydding, the West Riding spa near Ilkley, and with recovery from a serious illness he saw hydropathic treatment as the panacea for all ills. He immediately introduced this therapy for his workers at Lea and contrived to get himself appointed as voluntary – and unqualified – medical adviser to a hydro which had been opened at Matlock Bank, high on the eastern side of the valley. He quickly made his mark and by 1853 he had become the owner and he gradually expanded the complex until his dark gritstone empire came to dominate the hillside. In less than 20 years ten similar establishments had been set up as Matlock Bank spread down the hillside, to merge with the expanding shopping and commercial area of Matlock Bridge, thus forming the basis of the modern town. The railway, which had driven away the early Victorian gentry from Matlock Bath, was the life-line to Smedley's Hydro and by the turn of the century was bringing in some 3,000 of the self-same gentry each year for treatment.

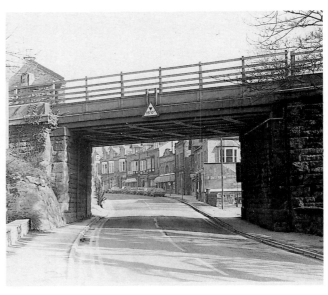

Plate 82 (above) The down side of bridge 28, Lime Tree Lane bridge.
Plate 83 (below) Class 150 'Sprinter' dmu crosses bridge 29, Boat House bridge, with the 11.03am to Derby on 16th February 1985.
(Author)

Plate 84 (above) Bridge 29A, part of Boat House bridge, carries the line over the A6 road at Matlock.

(Author)

Plate 85 (above) The prototype Stanier 8F, No. 48000, heads smartly across Boat House bridge with an up through freight early in 1953. Just beyond the houses on the right can be seen Green Lane bridge, No. 30, which gave access to Holt Lane quarries and which was demolished about 1960.

(E.D. Bruton)

Plate 86 (right) The southern portal of Holt Lane Tunnel, which was immediately north of Green Lane bridge.

(Author)

With such traffic it is not surprising that other businessmen were keen to join in. In 1862 Job Smith, of Matlock, happened to be in the United States where he came across the San Francisco cable tramway. He considered that the same principle could be applied to Matlock Bank and on his return to England in 1868 he approached John Smedley, his former employer, but he was unable to help with such an enterprise. However about 15 years later an Australian engineer friend of Smith proposed a tramway from Crown Square to Smedley Street, Rutland Street being too narrow to go any further. Prior to this Smith had become Chairman of the Local Board and although the Board gave its consent to the scheme the matter did not proceed, perhaps due to the fact that the proposed line was only 600 yards long. So the idea was shelved once more, only to be revived yet again in Smith's mind in 1890 when he read a report on the Lynton and Lynmouth Cliff Railway, which had opened on 1st April. Later that year

Smith's ideas came to the notice of Mr G. Croydon Marks, the engineer to the Lynton railway and to Mr George Newnes, M.P., a native of Matlock Bath, who having conferred with Marks eventually agreed to finance the project, if local business men would form a company. Thus the Matlock Tramway Company was formed and work began in 1891 on the depot and engine house which still stands at the corner of Rutland and Wellington Streets. The tramway, just 1/2 mile in length, was finally opened on 28th March 1893 and in its first nine months it carried 252,163 passengers, many of whom arrived in Matlock by regular or excursion trains.

Power was originally provided by two high-pressure horizontal steam engines installed by Dick Kerr and Co. Ltd, with boilers supplied by Sinclair of Leith. These were fired with steam coal, which was principally Pinxton Low Main supplied by Tom Wright. In 1898 Sir George Newnes gave the tramway to the Urban District Council but it began to lose

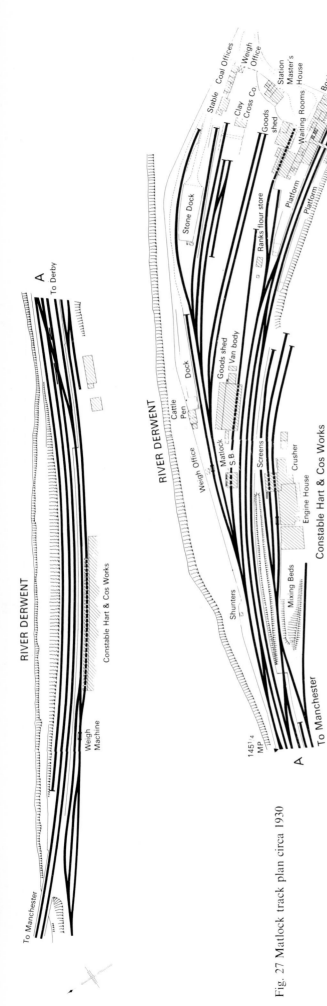

RIVER DERWENT

To Manchester

A
To Derby

Weigh
Machine

Constable Hart & Cos Works

RIVER DERWENT

Stable   Coal Offices   Weigh
                        Office
                 Clay
Stone Dock   Cross Co.   Station
                             Master's
Cattle   Goods   House
Pen   Dock   shed   Booking Hall
          Goods shed   Waiting Rooms   To Derby
Weigh Office   Van body   Platform
          Matlock   Ranks Flour store   Waiting
          S.B   Room
Shunters   Platform   Ladies
          Screens   Room
          Engine House
          Crusher
Mixing Beds

145¼
MP

A
To Manchester

Constable Hart & Cos Works

Fig. 27 Matlock track plan circa 1930

Plate 87 Beyer-Garratt No. 47989 runs through Matlock station with a down mineral train on 16th July 1951. These engines were a common sight on the line as far as Rowsley until their withdrawal in the mid 1950s.   (R.J. Buckley)

60

Plate 88 This general view looking north shows the station about 1905. The roof to the original booking hall on the right had the pronounced overhang on all four sides, very much as at the old station at Rowsley seen in *plate 139*. The overhang on the northern end and the roadside was removed in 1888 when the building was extended and the canopy erected. That at the south end was removed early in British Railways days, when the front edge was also cut back to counteract the deteriorating woodwork.

(M.L. Knighton Collection)

Plate 89 *(below)* During the last few months of steam operation Class 7 Pacific No. 70013 *Oliver Cromwell* ran many excursion trains over the London Midland Region of British Railways and is seen here at Matlock on 10th June 1968 with the last steam-hauled passenger train to run over the line.

(Author's Collection)

money and the effects of World War I plus the ensuing inflation placed it in serious deficit. In 1921 suction gas engines were installed, fed on anthracite, primarily from Gellyceidrim Colliery *(plate 226 Private Owner Wagons from the Gloucester Railway Carriage and Wagon Company Ltd, K. Montague, OPC)*, supplied by Tom Wright or H.C. Rackstraw. In spite of these modifications the venture continued to lose money and closure became scheduled for 30th September 1927. On 23rd September a strand in the cable broke and was not repaired. Anyone who has walked up Matlock Bank must long for some form of rapid transit system. If operating today the tramway would not only be a major tourist attraction but useful to townsfolk, visitors and county council employees alike.

After World War I the popularity of hydropathic treatment gradually faded but Smedley's Hydro struggled on with a declining clientele until 1956, when it was bought by Derbyshire County Council, who then transferred their administrative offices from Derby to Matlock. This move revitalised an almost dying town and with Matlock Bath's continued importance as a holiday resort, has secured Matlock's future as the urban and administration heart of West Derbyshire.

When the railway arrived, at what was then known as Matlock Bridge, temporary wooden accommodation was provided, but a few months later, in 1850, two stone buildings were brought into use. The southerly of the two, which originally comprised the booking hall and booking office, stands today as the Peak Rail Society bookshop. This structure has often been referred to as Paxton's original station, but as we shall see later it is now considerably altered from its original design. Shortly after the station was opened, what became the Station Master's house was erected. This building, designed by Paxton, was put up at the expense of the MBM & MJR following a request from the Midland in May 1853 that the former "construct one or more cottages near the goods warehouse at Matlock Bridge, as some protection to the warehouse, the same having been several times broken open".

Little overall change occurred in the early years, but in 1865 the platforms were extended and waiting rooms were erected on the down side, while two years later Josiah Glossop built a stable for four horses. The following year the same man was given a contract for the erection of a weighing machine office. In the absence of evidence to the contrary it is the author's opinion that this contract was extended to cover the construction of a block of four coal offices *(plate 112)*. By now readers will be well aware that when the Midland took full control of the line development was rapid and in April 1872 a plan and estimate of £6,000 was approved for remodelling the goods yard. By any standards this was a major job and included not only relaying the sidings, but also the construction of a new goods shed. The growth of freight traffic was by then accelerating and in 1874 authority was given for the provision of two travelling cranes.

Along with this growth in goods traffic came a rapid increase in passenger bookings and Matlock Bridge was the first station between Ambergate and Chinley to receive a footbridge. The contract for its erection was awarded to Messrs Lees & Co in July 1875, in the sum of £331 5s 10d (£331.29). With continued growth in passenger traffic the existing facilities became inadequate and in 1887 the Traffic Committee requested the provision of additional accommodation. This was approved and the work was put in hand by W. Walkerdine in August 1888. Fortunately the 'existing' and 'proposed' ground plans have survived and from these it has been possible to see what alterations were made. The northerly of the two buildings, which comprised the waiting and porters' rooms, appears to have been completely rebuilt, such is the difference between the two plans. The original booking hall was extended, on the road side, by the addition of a stone gable and a glass and timber verandah. Internally the building was divided into booking hall, booking and parcels office, station master's office and coal store. Later the station master's office was given its own entrance by converting the window on the platform side into a door. The contract also included the erection of the two ridge canopy adjacent to the building and the reconstruction of the southerly of the two shelters on the

down platform. To complete the improvements to the station the footbridge was covered in, late in 1889, at a cost of £174 10s (£174.50).

Continued growth in freight traffic saw the provision of an up lie by to the north of the station and the erection of an awning on the loading dock adjoining the old goods shed, in 1890, followed some twelve months later by the addition of a wooden office to the large goods shed. In the summer of 1895 the welfare of passengers again came to the fore with the erection of a standard ridge and furrow awning outside the up waiting rooms.

As the layout at Matlock Bridge developed the control of trains came under two signal boxes, Matlock Bridge North and South. The latter was just north of the station, set well back from the line actually in the goods yard, and can just be made out on the original photograph of *plate 88*, just below the far corner of the up platform awning. The north box was also on the up side, 11 chains from its partner. In September 1899 the engineer recommended the renewal of these two boxes, south box being renewed on 3rd December 1899 to be followed by north box on 7th January 1900.

Economics and the introduction of track circuiting resulted in the two block posts being replaced by a single one on 27th February 1910, known simply as Matlock following the shortening of the station name on 1st July 1905. Due to severe

Plate 90 A handbill for stations from Derby to Bakewell, 1934.

(G. Waite Collection)

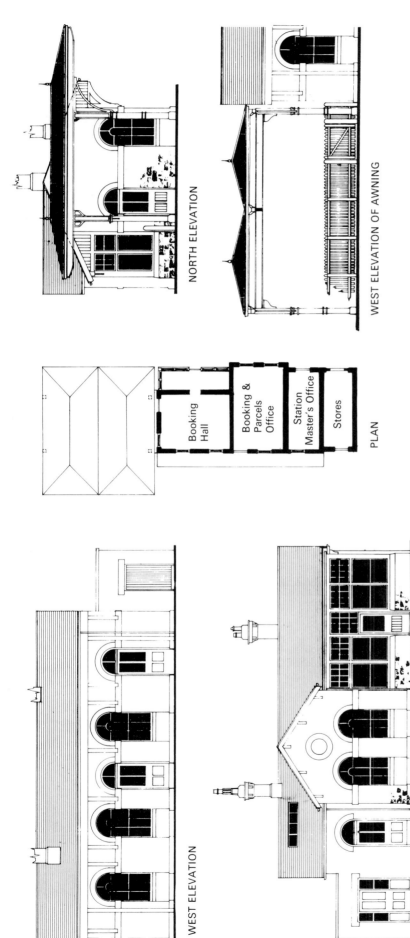

NORTH ELEVATION

WEST ELEVATION OF AWNING

PLAN

Booking Hall

Booking & Parcels Office

Station Master's Office

Stores

WEST ELEVATION

EAST ELEVATION (Roadside)

Scales Elevations 2mm to one foot
Plan 1mm to one foot

Fig. 28 Matlock booking hall, etc.

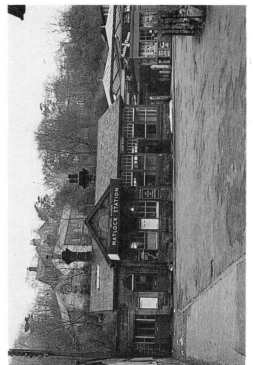

Plate 91 (right) The roadside elevation of the booking hall. To the right is W.H. Smith's bookstall, opened on 22nd May 1905.

(M.A. King)

Plate 92 (far right) The platform side of the original booking hall, seen here about 1971, clearly shows how the roof was cut back to ease maintenance.

(Author)

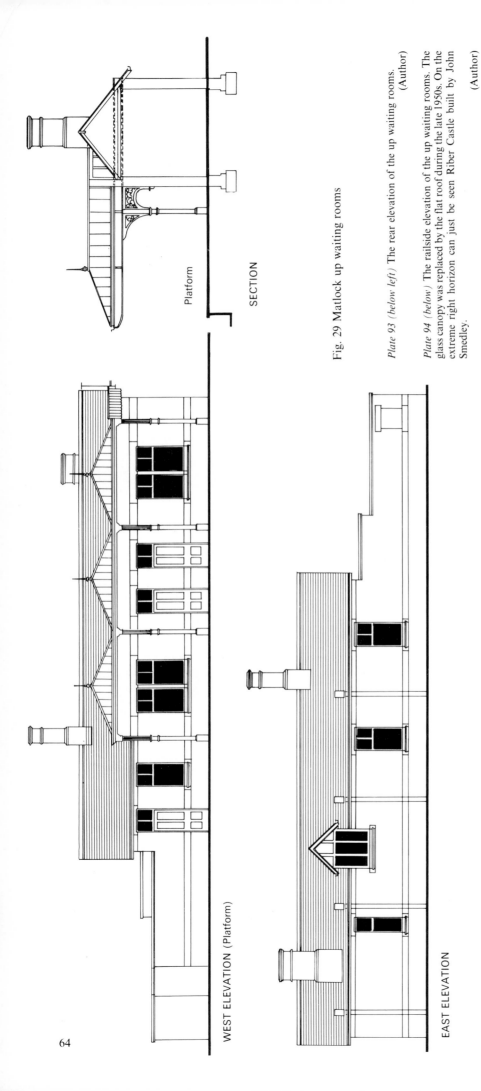

Platform

SECTION

WEST ELEVATION (Platform)

EAST ELEVATION

Fig. 29 Matlock up waiting rooms

Plate 93 (below left) The rear elevation of the up waiting rooms.
(Author)

Plate 94 (below) The railside elevation of the up waiting rooms. The glass canopy was replaced by the flat roof during the late 1950s. On the extreme right horizon can just be seen Riber Castle built by John Smedley. (Author)

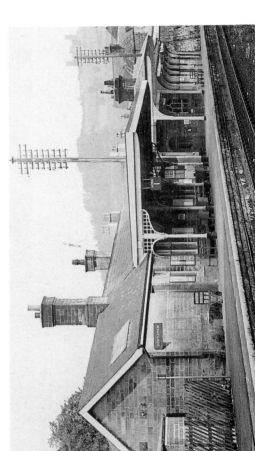

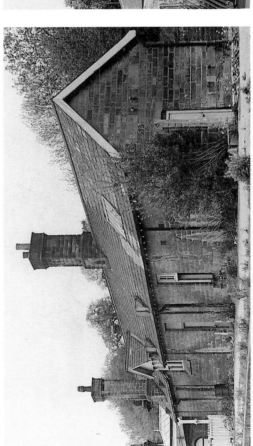

Plate 95 (above) The signal box at Matlock was renewed in 1910 and although a standard 30ft later period III cabin was provided, this was elevated above the goods shed approach track. Access to the box was via a flight of steps up to the top of the frame and then a second flight up to the door which was at the rear. A chemical closet was situated on the frame, but coal was stored in a traditional sleeper-built bin at ground level.

(M.A. King)

Plate 96 (below) Class 4F 0-6-0 No. 44515 passes the box with an up freight on 15th March 1952.

(E.R. Morten)

Plate 97 Stanier Class 5, No. 45285, one of the batch built by Armstrong-Whitworth in 1936, drifts into the station with the 1.45pm Manchester Central-St Pancras, again on 15th March 1952. Most of the open land visible between the goods shed and the gas works on the extreme left has since been developed for new housing.

(E.R. Morten)

constraints on space the new box was an unusual elevated structure sited at a point almost exactly midway between the earlier boxes. In 1911 the original station building was again extended, on the road side, by moving out the walls of the station master's office and the coal store to a point in line with the front of the verandah.

Matlock almost achieved notoriety, as the first station on the LMS to suffer a major accident, for on 16th February 1923, the 4.25pm passenger train from Manchester Central to Nottingham came into collision with a wagon which had been derailed in the goods yard and had come to rest fouling the up main line. The footboards on one side of the passenger train were completely stripped off. The derailment of the wagon was held to be the joint responsibility of the guard and shunter in charge of shunting operations and they were both suspended three days for their carelessness.

The restrictive layout at Matlock and lack of opportunity for land purchase resulted in a 'hotchpotch' of buildings, extension and new works resulting in a somewhat tatty appearance. The passenger on a slow train for Rowsley, Bakewell or beyond, held in the loop at Darley Dale for a late running express to pass, often wished that Matlock's layout had included a loop and the station facilities a refreshment room.

Subsequent to the demise of activities north of Matlock the line was singled between Ambergate and Matlock on 11th May 1969 and 'One Train Working' brought into operation. Initially the former down line became the single line, the colour light inner distant signal at Matlock being replaced by a fixed semaphore arm as a marker on the same post. A start was soon made recovering parts of the up line but on 6th July 1969 the single line was severed at Ambergate and slewed into the former up line which was then used as far as the site of Johnson's Sidings ground frame. At that point the line was slewed back into the original down line.

For some months the single line terminated in the former down platform at Matlock and all passengers were inconvenienced by having to use the footbridge. Matters were put right on 26th October 1969 when the single line was slewed into the former up line north of Matlock Bath station. By

December of that year the down side platform buildings and footbridge at Matlock had been dismantled. Track recovery did not take place immediately north of Matlock for on 7th February 1971 the line was brought back into use for a short time, as a Research Department test track.

In terms of potential passenger traffic Matlock had a catchment population of about 9,000 in the 1930s and was easily the most important station on our journey. When the MR took control of the line Matlock Bridge was second to Buxton, with 47,245 passengers buying tickets in 1872, paying an average fare of 1s 7d (8p), representing a return journey of 9½ miles. Within ten years the number of bookings had overtaken those at Buxton, and by the turn of the century well over 100,000 passengers per annum were starting their journey from Matlock Bridge. At the close of the MR period bookings were in excess of 134,000 and the average fare had risen to 3s 6d (17½p), being a return journey of 12 miles. This was roughly the distance to Derby and coupled with the growth in season ticket holders from 18 in 1902 to 204 in 1922 reinforces the previous arguments regarding the growth of commuter traffic. At that time the expenses of the station, which would have included the goods yard, were less than 25% of the income from passenger traffic alone.

The train service at Matlock was relative to its importance and in addition to the local and semi-fast trains we have already mentioned several express trains stopped. The Midland in its final years ran a London-Manchester service of eleven down and ten up trains, of which five down, but only one up, the 9.55am ex Manchester Central, stopped at Matlock. While the LMS slightly reduced the overall service they did redress this imbalance somewhat and of the ten down and eight up expresses six and four respectively called at Matlock. With the outbreak of war the service was cut dramatically and in 1943 five down and four up trains ran between the two cities, all stopping for Matlock passengers. After the war this level of service was basically retained, but from April 1966 a more frequent service of semi-fasts ran between Manchester and Nottingham with three down and five up trains on weekdays, replacing certain London expresses. This was a prelude to closure.

MANCHESTER, BUXTON, MATLOCK & MIDLAND JUNC. RLY. GOODS SHED

AST ELE.

NORTH ELE.

'A'

EST ELE.

SOUTH ELE.

Scale 2mm to one foot

office

DETAIL OF GATE AT 'A'

Twice scale of main drawing

DETAIL OF OFFICE

AN

Fig. 30 Matlock original goods shed

Plate 98 (below) The original goods shed built about 1850 at the request of the MBM & MJR is seen here in 1974 before restoration work was started by the Peak Railway Society. This building is almost identical to the North Midland goods shed at Ambergate.

(Author)

Plate 99 (below right) A tiny wooden office was provided inside the goods shed, but sadly this was removed during restoration of the main building.

(Author)

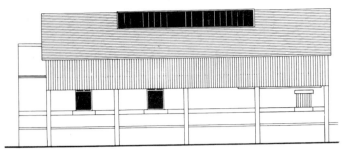

EAST ELEVATION

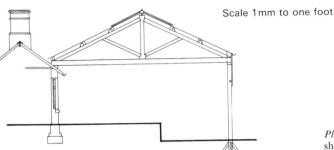

SECTION

Scale 1mm to one foot

Fig. 31 Matlock loading dock awning

Plate 100 (below) In 1890 the loading dock adjacent to the old goods shed was roofed over to provide covered unloading space for cement, animal feedstuffs, corn etc. If not immediately delivered this produce was stored in the old goods shed, and this storage accommodation was augmented by the LMS which provided the grounded CCT body seen on the left.

(M.A. King)

Plates 101 and 102 (bottom) show two consignment notes for goods traffic in 1854. *Plate 101* dates from 26th October and covers a bundle of plants from James Smith's nursery at Tansley, to Rowsley. *Plate 102* from 18th October shows candlewick yarn being sent to Birmingham, Yarm (County Durham), Neath and Hull.

Of the local trains two are worthy of note. In the mid 1930s an early train left Buxton at 6.05am, calling at all stations to Matlock, except Monsal Dale and Hassop. On arrival the engine ran round and 16 minutes later, at 7.10am the train returned to Buxton. These trains were primarily workmen's services, with the down train connecting with the 8.10am Buxton to Manchester Central express. During the same period the 3.05pm Derby-Matlock local carried a through carriage off the 12.25pm St Pancras-Manchester. Only five minutes was allowed for detaching at Derby, and equally smart working was called for at Matlock, where the train was turned prior to return to Derby at 3.46pm six minutes after arrival. The through coach would have returned to London by the most convenient express from Derby.

Today the station is the northern terminus of the line, and enjoys a regular daily service to and from Derby together with a number of excursion trains on summer weekends. The line was chosen for the in-service evaluation of British Rail's new Class 150 'Sprinter' diesel multiple units introduced late in 1984, and now rapidly replacing the ageing fleet of original dmus in the East Midlands and North Wales. While the two prototypes were 3-car units, the production models came out as 2-car sets, with a passenger capacity of 387 (138 seated). Each power car has a Cummins diesel engine providing 570 hp per train, which not only gives exceptional fuel economy by the high power to weight ratio, but also rapid acceleration, thus reducing overall journey times. Indeed, during trials one of the units covered the trip from Derby to Matlock non-stop in 21 minutes, and regular services have been cut from 34 minutes to 31.

Freight traffic was heavy and varied, but in terms of annual tonnage it was dominated by coal and limestone. Few records of the former have come to light prior to 1863, but the first two weeks of October that year saw 147 tons 18 cwt arrive in 23 wagons, an average of 6 tons 8 cwt per wagon, which indicates a surprisingly high number of 10 ton vehicles, at a time when 6 or 8 ton was the normal capacity. Private ownership of wagons was in its infancy during the 1860s and 19 of the wagons belonged to railway companies. The coal merchants involved as consignees were Messrs Blackwell, Garton, Marsden and Woodhouse. Allowing for the seasonal variation in demand and the level of consumption at the time, the traffic over this fortnight would indicate an annual tonnage of about 2,000-2,500 tons, or 310-390 wagon loads. By the middle of the LMS period demand for domestic coal would have grown to the order of 8,000-10,000 tons per annum, or 18-23 wagons per week. In the 1930s the coal merchants at Matlock station included W. Birch, Clay Cross Co. Ltd., Derwent Valley Co-operative Society, A.E. Hawley & Sons, H.C. Rackstraw, Messrs Swift Bros and Tom Wright. The latter and Clay Cross Co. are known to have operated their own wagons, while the other traders received much of their stock in colliery owned vehicles.

The largest single consumer was the gas industry and although the 1880 ordnance survey shows two gas works on the Bakewell road, one opposite Cawdor Quarry, the other about 400 yards to the north, it was the southerly one which prospered and became registered on the Stock Exchange in 1887 as the Matlock & District Gas Company. Until the widespread growth in motor transport during the 1930s all raw material into the works and almost all by-products and waste were carted to and from the station yard. The flow of raw material into the works primarily consisted of coal and iron oxide, as fuel and purifying agents respectively. Products emanating from the works, other than gas, included coke, clinker, spent oxide, tar and ammonia liquor. While the latter was occasionally bought by the Sheffield Chemical Co., who were regular buyers of the spend oxide, it was more often passed into the River Derwent as effluent. Tar was produced in large quantities and while some was sold locally, a considerable proportion was purchased by Stanton Iron and Coal Co. Thus in addition to mineral wagons the goods yard saw both cylindrical and rectangular tank wagons on a regular basis.

The exact dates of the opening of the two gas works are not known by the author, but there exists a mineral invoice dated 6th July 1865, showing 15 tons 11 cwt of coal consigned to the "Gas Co" from Dunston & Barlow sidings (Chesterfield). Comprehensive records of coal supplies to the Matlock and District Gas Co. begin in May 1899, when the following contracts were made for the year ending 30th June 1900:

J. Brown and Co. Ltd	800 tons @	13s 1d per ton
Grassmoor Colliery Co.	1,000 tons @	10s 5d per ton
J. & G. Wells Ltd.	500 tons @	12s per ton
Tom Wright (Hardwick Coal)	500 tons @	10s 11d per ton
Tom Wright (Cannel)	500 tons @	12s 1d per ton
Total	3,300 tons	

The first three suppliers were colliery companies, while Tom Wright was a local merchant and civic dignitary. He was a director of several local companies and was elected to the board of Matlock Gas Co. in 1901. For the next ten years the above suppliers, together with Nunnery Colliery Co. provided the bulk of the coal, with intermittent amounts coming from Barrow Haematite Colliery Co., Sheepbridge Coal & Iron Co., and Rothervale Colliery Co. By 1910 the annual requirement had risen to 6,300 tons and Tom Wright was supplying over half of this from Ashgate, Hardwick, New Hucknall, Swanwick and Tinsley Park collieries.

In 1911 he was elected Chairman of the gas company and had it not been for the incidence of the war, and the disturbed nature of the mining industry which followed, there is little doubt that he would have dominated the coal supply earlier than he did. In the event he supplied 6,500 tons out of the 9,000 tons used at the works in 1921. At that time the 12 ton wagon was appearing in increasing numbers and the average wagon load had crept up to about 8 tons. Thus some 22 to 24 wagons per week would arrive with gas coal. The period following World War I was a troubled time for the mining industry with both output and demand fluctuating markedly and many gas managers were forced to obtain their coal supplies as best they could. Over this period the goods yard at Matlock must have been colourful indeed with private owner wagons appearing from many sources, including:

J. C. Abbott, Birmingham.	Lowell, Baldwin Ltd, Bristol.
N. Atrill, Chesterfield.	
Babbington Colliery, Nottingham.	Renwick, Wilton Ltd, Torquay.
T. Cash & Co., Birmingham.	Spencer Whatley Ltd, London.
Clay Cross Co., Clay Cross.	Staveley Coal & Iron Co. Staveley.
Wm. Cory Ltd, London.	Stephenson Clarke Ltd, London.
Dalton Main Colliery, Rotherham.	
J. Longbotham & Sons, Sheffield.	Albert Usher Ltd, London. Wingfield Manor Colliery Co., S.Wingfield.

As an aside it is interesting to note that the coal trade was in such a confused state that in June 1925 the LMS had over 16 miles of sidings filled with empty private owner wagons awaiting routeing instructions. What a time to have been out with a camera! Following the General Strike the coal trade settled down and supplies were once more being received regularly from those collieries normally used before the war. There seems to be no reason why this pattern should have changed markedly until after 1939, when pooling resulted in private owner wagons running anywhere. Apart from the gas company coal was of course brought in for other industries, but the only unusual supply known to the author was slack from New Lount Colliery, in Leicestershire, to Messrs Paton & Baldwin, hosiery manufacturers.

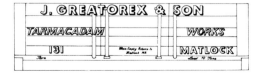

Fig. 32 J. Greatorex & Son wagon livery

Limestone had been worked on a small scale in the Matlock area for a considerable time before the railway arrived, but the opening of the line provided the initial impetus for the commercial expansion of the industry. In October 1857 it was agreed to put in a siding for the stone traffic of Messrs Thomas Wakely and John Weston, 20 chains north of the station. This siding took the form of a loop off the down main line and marked the beginning of Cawdor Quarry. As further quarries opened, both limestone and gritstone, the railway responded to the demand for transportation facilities by building a loading dock in the goods yard in 1876, to serve those workings away from the railway. The construction of this dock provided the stimulus for Messrs Job & A. J. Greatorex to open Harvey Dale Quarry at the northern end of the Matlock Gorge. By the 1870s the use of tarred stone for road surfacing was emerging and the modern development of limestone extraction at Matlock can be attributed to W.E. Constable, who was coating gravel with crude tar, at Mitcham in Surrey, in 1878. In 1895 he moved north and acquired Cawdor Quarry, which by then is believed to have become the Matlock Limestone Company. Shortly afterwards the Shaw Brothers, whom we have already noted at Matlock Bath, expanded their activities by opening Station Quarry at Matlock Bridge some ten chains south of Cawdor Quarry.

Plate 103 This view is the only known photograph of Thomas Shaw's wagons.

(Author's Collection)

A little after the turn of the century W.E. Constable appears to have gone into partnership for on 23rd November 1905 two rectangular tank wagons, Nos 4 and 5, were ordered from Charles Roberts & Co. These were 15ft x 7ft 1in x 3ft 4in on a 9ft wheelbase with oil 111 axleboxes and were painted red. They bore cast iron plates on the solebars lettered:

CONSTABLE HART & Co. LTD
MATLOCK BRIDGE MR

The development of a considerable fleet of wagons was soon in hand and *fig. 33* shows a 10 ton wagon registered by the MR in 1910. In the summer of 1915 a further 200 wagons, 16ft x 7ft 6in x 2ft 11in and numbered 201-400 were built by Wm. Rigley, followed soon afterwards by Nos 401–450 from S.J. Claye and Nos 451–500 from Wm. Rigley. At least one more batch of wagons was acquired. These were Railway Clearing House (RCH) standard 12 ton vehicles, built in 1927 and numbered 1000-1099.

About 1906 Josiah Smart & Sons purchased Station Quarry from the Shaw brothers, and it would appear that Thomas Shaw used his share of the proceeds to open Holt Quarries immediately north of Harvey Dale Quarry. Like Greatorex, Shaw operated his own fleet of wagons from the dock in the goods yard and while very little is known about these vehicles, *plate 103* offers a tantalising glimpse as to their appearance. It is known that two secondhand wagons were hired from the Birmingham Railway Carriage and Wagon Co. in June 1912,

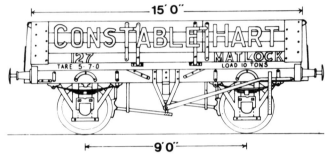

Fig. 33 Constable Hart wagon livery

Plate 104 This 12 ton wagon appears to be 16ft 6in x 7ft 11in and is fitted with round bottom Ellis axleboxes. It is painted black with plain white letters. The small lettering on the door reads 'Empty to Hopton Quarries High Peak Junction'.

(Author's Collection)

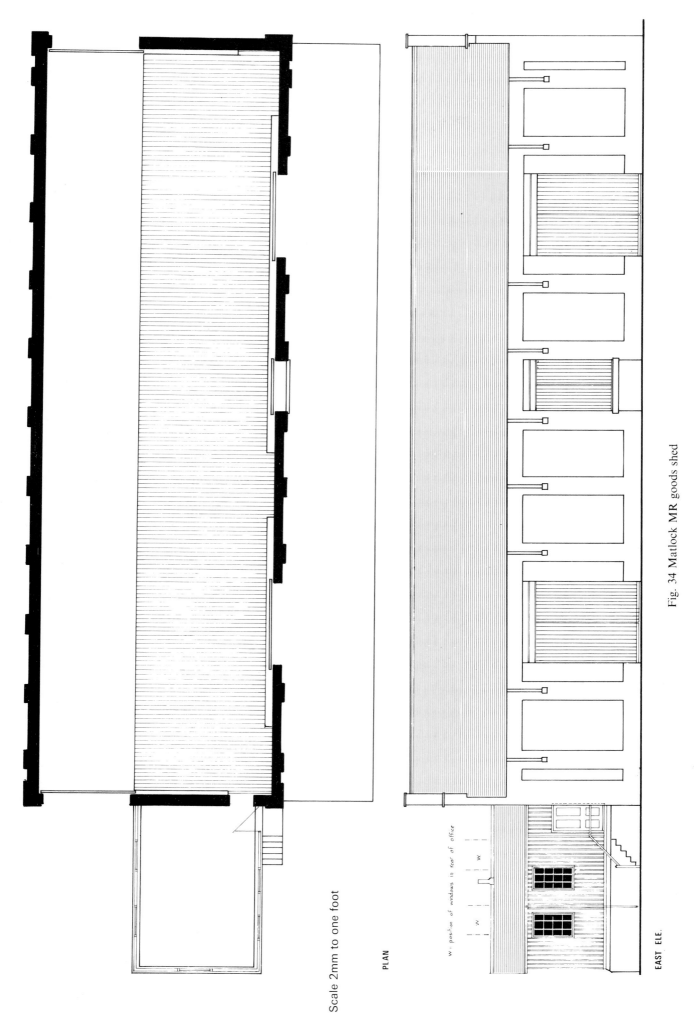

Scale 2mm to one foot

PLAN

w: position of windows in rear of office

EAST ELE.

Fig. 34 Matlock MR goods shed

71

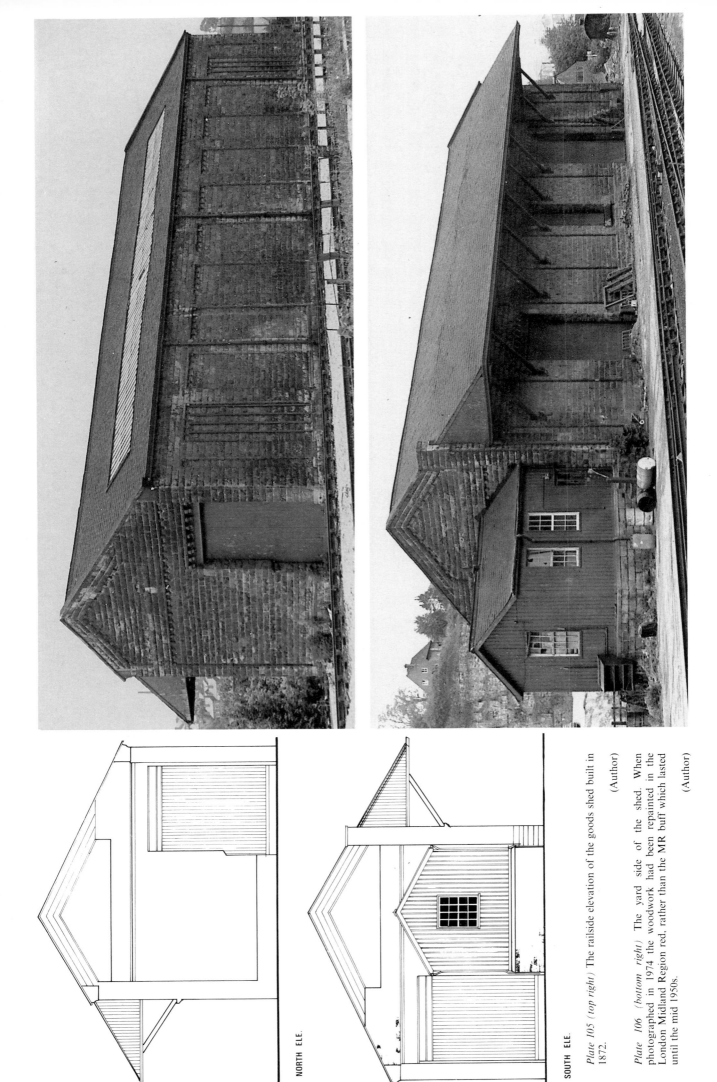

NORTH ELE.

SOUTH ELE.

Plate 105 (top right) The railside elevation of the goods shed built in 1872.

(Author)

Plate 106 (bottom right) The yard side of the shed. When photographed in 1974 the woodwork had been repainted in the London Midland Region red, rather than the MR buff which lasted until the mid 1950s.

(Author)

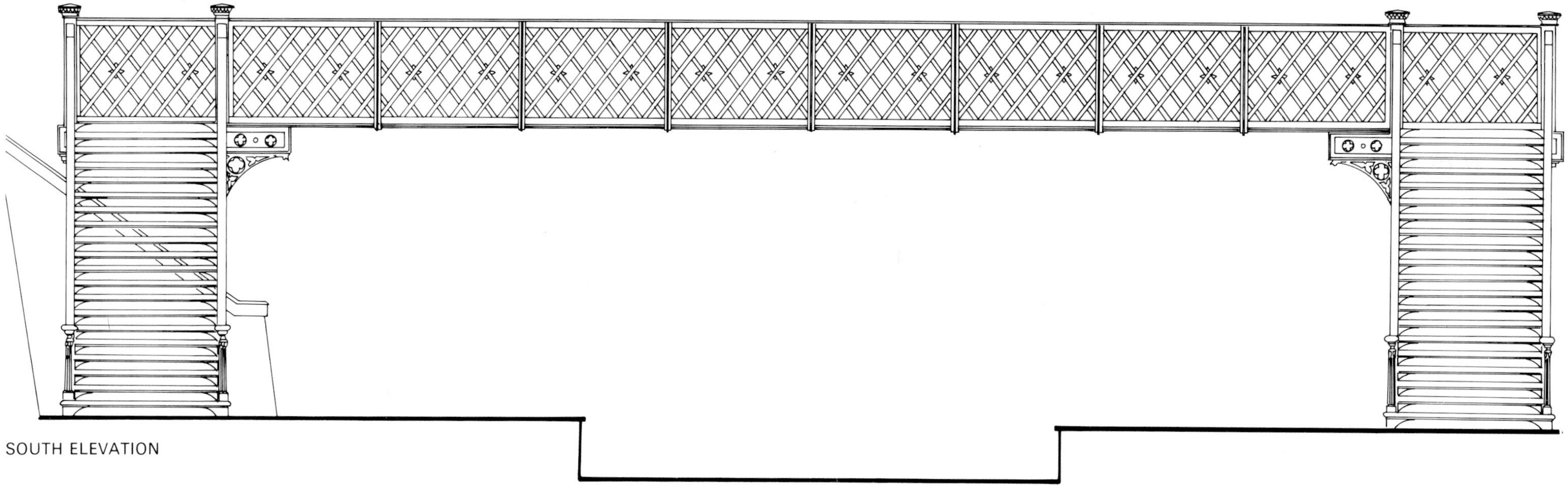

SOUTH ELEVATION

Note: New smokeplates fitted 7 September 1919

Plate 107 This view shows the wooden cladding to the footbridge added in 1889. It is interesting to note that the bridge carries a LNWR number plate, several of which were used in the Matlock area, but the author cannot explain why. The view also shows clearly the construction of the glass canopy.

(M.A. King)

WEST ELEVATION

Fig. 35 Matlock original station footbridge

Scale 4 mm to 1 ft

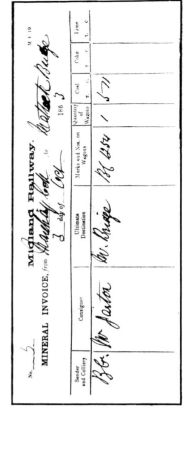

Plate 109 (above) During the late 1930s a second asbestos warehouse was provided this time on a brick and timber base. Shown in *fig. 36*, this building was photographed about 1976, by which time the earlier structure had disappeared.

Plate 108 (left) In the early 1930s the LMS introduced a standard warehouse comprising a wooden frame with asbestos cladding normally set on concrete piles or earthenware pipes. Such a building, used at Matlock as a flour store is on the left of this view taken in October 1960. The ex-MR square panelled clerestory coach was also used for storage purposes and probably appeared during the late 1930s.

(H. Townley)

Plate 110 (below) A mineral invoice showing 5 tons 11 cwt of coal delivered from Marehay Colliery to Matlock Bridge, in Butterley Company wagon No. 1254, on 3rd October 1863, for Mr Grafton.

(Author's Collection)

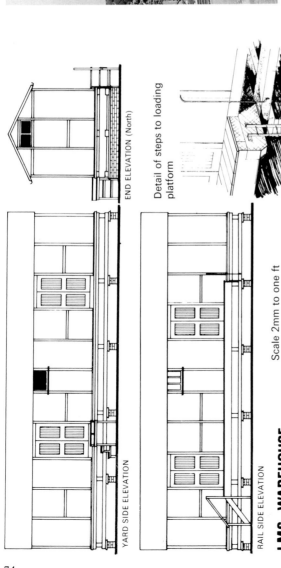

YARD SIDE ELEVATION

RAIL SIDE ELEVATION

LMS WAREHOUSE
(Rank's Flour Store)

END ELEVATION (North)

Detail of steps to loading platform

VIEW OF PLATFORM END

Scale 2mm to one ft

Fig. 36 Matlock standard asbestos warehouse

FRONT ELE.

ROADSIDE ELE.

REAR ELE.

NORTH ELE.

STATION MASTERS HOUSE Scale 2mm to one foot

Fig. 37 Matlock station house

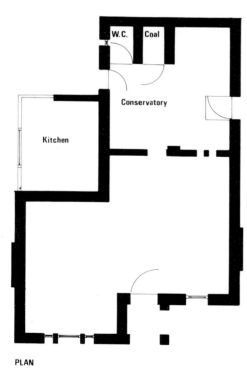

W.C.   Coal

Conservatory

Kitchen

PLAN

Plate 111 The station master's house at Matlock was erected about 1853/54 and bears all the hallmarks of Paxton's design. The low pitched roof, round topped windows and corbelled window sills are typical features of his work. The original iron fencing erected in 1865 can still be seen in this view, taken on 16th February 1985, behind the modern chain link fencing.

(Author)

these being 8 ton side door vehicles, numbered 40 and 45 and painted grey with one bright red plank. This is indiscernible on the photograph but was probably the second plank up, which bore the words LIMESTONE & TARMACADAM MERCHANT. Two further wagons, Nos 30 and 50, 16ft x 7ft 6in x 2ft 9in were built by the same company early in 1914. Josiah Smart did not remain long at Station Quarry for he sold out to Constable Hart and while the date of the sale has not been ascertained it may well have been shortly before Hart's took delivery of the new wagons from Wm Rigley in 1915. In repetition of the events of 1906 Josiah Smart used his income from the sale of Station Quarry to buy Shaw's quarry at Matlock Bath.

At the end of World War I the business of J. Greatorex and Son was purchased by the Ragusa Asphalte Paving Co., and along with other non rail connected quarrying concerns prospered to the effect that the MR agreed to construct a second stone loading dock in the goods yard, at an estimated cost of £3,100. It was submitted that Messrs Greatorex, who would be the major user, would give an undertaking that if during the first ten years the total obtained from the tolls to be charged for use of the dock in any one year was less than 10% of the cost of providing the dock, they would make up the deficiency. As it transpired the tolls exceeded the capital cost within eight years, by which time over 45,000 tons of stone were being sent out annually and from the end of 1932 Greatorex's liability was limited to the payment of an annual maintenance charge of £30, with other users paying a toll of 3d (2½p) per ton.

At the beginning of 1935 Derbyshire limestone producers were in an unhappy situation, with lack of demand holding down prices and serious competition for the limited markets. To remedy the position a bold merger of five major companies took place and Derbyshire Stone Ltd came into being on 1st January 1936. The companies involved were Constable Hart, Hopton Wood Stone Firms, J. Greatorex and Sons, The Hartington Quarries Ltd and John Hadfield & Sons. All the members of the group bought their own wagons into the merger, and these were gradually repainted in the new livery, although with a considerable number of vehicles to treat it was probably several years before the job was completed. A large proportion of the wagons were sold off during the late 1930s to finance the purchase of lorries, but many ran well into the British Railways period. At least one, wagon No. 2220, was still in main line service in 1958, at which time almost 60,000 tons of limestone was still being sent out of Matlock by rail. In 1968 Derbyshire Stone Ltd became part of the Tarmac group, the same year that the railway, which had brought about the development of the quarries, became a thing of the past.

Matlock was the most important station between Ambergate and Chinley in terms of merchandise traffic which grew from 11,791 tons in 1872 to 32,776 tons in 1912. After World War I competition from road haulage began to bite, but over 25,000 tons passed through the yard in 1922, requiring 25-30 wagons per weekday. In the 1920s there were over 100 shops and small businesses in the town and a huge variety of goods was handled by the railway, much of this being of interest to both the historian and the modeller. Several grocers and provision merchants were established, among whom were

Burgons Ltd, who were also tea blenders and would have received a steady supply of the well known wooden tea chests. George Drabble, English timber merchant, would have received all manner of sawn timber, plywood and veneers, while Poysers Patents Ltd, agricultural engineers would no doubt have required the occasional Lowmac for the delivery of new farm machinery. Flour came in regularly for the Derwent Valley Co-operative Society's bakery on Smedley Street, mainly in covered vans, while imported grain arrived, in vans or sheeted wagons, for E.H. Bailey's mill at Matlock Green. Earles cement and Silcocks animal feedstuffs also came in regularly, and all these bagged items were unloaded at the covered dock adjacent to the old goods shed. The latter, together with an adjacent CCT van body, was used for storage of these goods, particularly the animal feed. Fruit of all descriptions arrived for the greengrocery trade but the most interesting was banana traffic. Two or three times a week the 4.30am through freight Rowsley to Mansfield would put off two banana vans, which had come over earlier from Garston Docks, for Messrs Edge Brothers. It was standard practice after unloading the green bananas to sweep out the vans, wearing heavy boots and the trouser legs well tied up with string, and burn the straw immediately where it lay. On the odd occasion however a bag or two of the straw would find its way out of the yard, sometimes accompanied by a sub-tropical guest of the arachnid class!

Among the heavier materials to be dealt with was bleach, in metal barrels weighing 6 or 7 cwt, which came in from ICI at Winnington for Messrs Drabble's bleach works. These came in open wagons and it was back-breaking work to manhandle them from wagon to delivery lorry. Steel girders of various sizes from Dorman Long, Middlesbrough for Wm Twigg, iron and steel merchants, were even heavier, but could at least be handled by the yard cranes, as could similar bulky items such as telegraph poles, bales of raw wool and cotton etc. Spent hops, bagged and sheeted down in open wagons regularly came in from Burton-on-Trent, for James Smith at Scotland Nurseries, Tansley. Tank wagons, to be seen almost daily in the yard, included rectangular tanks from Ellison and Mitchell, Kilnhurst, bringing tar for the production of tarmacadam at the quarries, and cylindrical tanks of Shell Mex and BP, carrying oils and petroleum spirits.

Outgoing goods were equally varied and included large bales of wadding from Drabbles, bales of waste wool from Paton & Baldwin's and the occasional load of scrap from Wm Twigg or R. Lane & Co. Trees, shrubs and plants of all description were regularly sent out from Scotland Nurseries, these being brought down to the yard by J. Slack, whose single horse and cart has today developed into a thriving coach hauliers business. A business which must have been a contender for that being nearest to any goods yard on the LMS was Curtis Cultivators, who produced lawnmowers about 30 yards from the goods yard gates. The majority of their output was sent away by rail, in wooden crates and boxes, until the business ceased about 1938, following a serious fire.

The traffic which has proved most troublesome to the author was lead, for considerable disagreement exists among local historians as to how this traffic was handled. Mr Harold

YARD ELEVATION

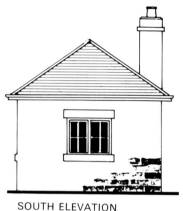

SOUTH ELEVATION

| H. C. RACKSTRAW | W. BIRCH | T. WRIGHT | DERWENT VALLEY Co-op Soc | WEIGH OFFICE |

Scales: Elevations   3mm to 1 ft
          Plan   2mm to 1 ft

Fig. 38 Matlock coal offices

Plate 112 (below) The coal offices at Matlock provided accommodation for four merchants, with a weigh office at the right hand end. The building is thought to date from around 1868 and was demolished a few weeks after it was photographed and measured by the author in 1974.

(Author)

Wardman, who worked in the yard during the late 1930s categorically states that lead ore, known locally as 'blend', was brought from Millclose Mine in Sentinel steam waggons, by a Mr F. Toplis. This was loaded at the New Dock into mineral wagons, with the joints packed with rags and paper, sheeted down, and sent out mainly to Avonmouth, for export. Much of this was sent to Germany, even up to the summer of 1940. The recipients expressed their gratitude by throwing it back at us rather faster than they had received it!

Mineral class traffic, although including a certain amount of general building materials was primarily composed of gritstone and tarmacadam, the former declining in importance after World War I, while the latter rapidly increased in value. The gritstone of Derbyshire has long been recognised as a superior building stone, and that found to the east of the Derwent between Matlock and Rowsley, and generally referred to as 'Darley Dale sandstone grit', was held in very

high esteem. Around the turn of the century three companies were engaged in the working of this stone at Matlock, the dominant one being Messrs T. C. Drabble. This concern was reputedly the largest stone producer in the county and worked Farley Quarry, to the north of the town and Old Bentley Brook Quarry to the east, which was in operation at the end of the 17th century. The company specialised in the production of fine building stone which was used, among others in the Savoy Hotel, London, Nottingham Law Courts and Smedley's Hydro. A considerable amount of dressed stone blocks of all sizes, and carved stone such as columns, capitals, sills, lintels, etc., etc., was sent out by rail, usually in low sided vehicles, the stone being securely packed with timber and straw.

Thomas Beck was established as a stone merchant about 1840 and specialised in the production of millstones, the majority of which were exported to Norway and the United States for the production of woodpulp. The third producer was George Boden, the owner of Poor Lots Quarry a little over two miles to the east of Matlock, near Tansley. Building stone of all types was produced, but the quarry was best known for its grindstones of all shapes and sizes, these enjoying a wide market both at home and abroad. The main works and storage yard of the company was in the goods yard at Matlock Bridge, but these closed down shortly after World War I. The buildings were later cleared and the site was used for construction of the new stone dock referred to earlier. Limited production of grindstones continued at the quarry and the occasional wagon load was still being sent out in the late 1930s.

To deal with all this traffic the goods yard staff, in the mid-1930s, comprised a working foreman, two goods checkers, two goods porters, weighbridge clerk, junior number taker and five lorry drivers. There was generally one merchandise wagon daily from Sheffield Wicker or Queens Road, Derby St Marys, Lawley Street, Somers Town and Ancoats. These would be rough shunted into the yard during the night by the appropriate train. Some coal wagons would also be put in by down mineral trains. The yard had its own shunting engine which came up from Rowsley about 6.00am, with more wagons for the yard and empties for the quarries. The first task was to sort out the wagons which had been set down during the night. Small loads were put inside the goods shed, full wagons loads for one consignee were put down the yard, animal feedstuffs, flour and cement were put in the covered dock. Coal, cattle and any special wagons were put into the appropriate siding. The engine would then move across to the quarries to start sorting again. The goods porters and the number taker came on duty at 7.00am. The latter's first job was to make and light fires in the goods office, weigh office and mess room. He then had to go round the yard making a note of all wagon numbers, and the names of any private owner wagons. Once the shunting engine had sorted out the yard he had to go around again to take stock of all the wagons, sheets and ropes. This information was then entered on the daily return and telephoned through to control, at which time a request would be made for any empty wagons required for outgoing traffic which could not be supplied from those in the yard due to be unloaded during the day. More often than not goods invoices would be in a waterproof bag behind the wagon label, and as the porters prepared to unload each wagon the goods checker would remove the invoices, enter the details in the ledger and check that each wagon actually carried its specified load. He would also attend to the necessary paper work as goods were loaded on to the lorries for delivery. Small consignments dealt with in the goods shed were stacked in certain parts of the building according to their destination, each lorry driver knowing which pile to put on his lorry for his own regular delivery run.

In the late 1930s the road vehicle fleet at Matlock comprised two Dennis 'Lancets', two Karrier 'Cab-over-engine-style', one Scammell mechanical horse and a Jowett van at the station for parcel deliveries. In the afternoon the lorries would be returning to the yard with goods collected for despatch, and private hauliers would be bringing in their own goods. These would be sorted, loaded as appropriate and wagon labels made out. Towards the end of the day's work the number taker would go round again noting those wagons unloaded, those awaiting attention and those ready for despatch, entering the details on the daily return once more.

Meanwhile the shunter would have sorted out Constable Hart's wagons, putting loaded wagons for the south either in the quarry exit sidings, or in the up lie-by, or both. Loaded wagons for the north were brought across to the yard, and put in a siding while merchandise wagons and empty minerals were picked up, coupled to the limestone traffic and taken back to Rowsley for marshalling and despatch. The engine could well have been at work for twelve hours by this stage, having had a change of crew at 11.00am. The men engaged on shunting duties worked two shifts of 5.00am – 1.00pm, 1.00pm – 9.00pm. A mess room, in the form of a six-wheel coach body was located immediately north of the goods shed, but even in the mid 1930s there was no organised meal break. However the men were allowed a 20 minute rest, at a convenient lull in traffic between the third and fifth hour of a shift.

WEST ELEVATION   SOUTH ELEVATION

Scales: Building   2mm to 1 ft
         Wagon   4mm to 1 ft

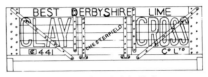

Livery: Red, black ironwork, unshaded white letters

Fig. 39 Matlock Clay Cross Co. office

Plate 113 Clay Cross Co. was big enough to warrant its own office at Matlock and erected this two storey building in the yard. The ground floor provided stabling for a horse, and later garaging for a motor lorry. The date of construction is unknown but may well have been in the 1880s.

(Author)

Southbound stone traffic was taken out to Chaddesden, for sorting, at 10.35pm and it was quite common to see this train double-headed with up to 80 wagons. In addition to this, and the trains already mentioned, the yard was serviced by the 1.30am mineral Derby to Matlock, two down stopping freights, and the 1.20pm mineral Chaddesden to Rowsley which set down cattle wagons on Tuesday and Friday. In the up direction the 6.55am stopping freight, Rowsley to Matlock Bath, and the 3.22pm mineral on the same run, both served the yard.

Plate 114 (above) Stanier 5XP, No. 45618 *New Hebrides* climbs away from Matlock with a St Pancras-Manchester express early in 1953. The open nature of the valley north of the town is clearly shown in this view, which also shows Cawdor Quarry on the extreme right and Riber Castle above the second carriage.

(E.D. Bruton)

Plate 115 (below) Taken on the same day as the previous plate this view shows Stanier 8F, No. 48655, a few hundred yards further north with a Toton-Rowsley mineral train. At this point the valley assumes an almost parkland setting as a result of tree planting by Sir Joseph Whitworth at the close of the 19th century.

(E.D. Bruton)

From Matlock the line curved gently westwards, then turned northwards, crossing Cawdor cattle creep, which was blocked up in 1883 as the adjacent quarry was being developed, and crossed the Derwent for the sixth time by Cawdor bridge (No. 35). The bridge was strengthened in 1879 by Messrs Handyside and was completely rebuilt in 1886/87 by the Darlington Wagon & Engineering Co., who had won the contract with a bid of £4,107 8s 5d (£4,107.42). Towards the end of the job the company submitted a request for a grant on the grounds that the work was proving more costly than had been anticipated. This request was refused in May 1887 – the Midland did not suffer fools lightly! North of the bridge the valley broadens considerably, as the underlying rock changes from limestone to the much softer shales. The railway, keeping more or less to the centre of the valley, on a low embankment,

pursued a relatively straight course to the north west, crossed three occupation bridges, passed under Warney Lane bridge, over a culvert and ran into Darley Dale station, 8 miles 68 chains from Ambergate West Junction.

The area hereabouts is thought to have first been settled around the 8th century, as the Mercian kingdom expanded from the Midlands into the Peak District, along the Derwent Valley. It is generally accepted that the original settlements were Wensley, in the west, Darley and Rowsley, in the valley and Farley, to the east. As Winster became an important lead mining centre, a pack horse route was established through Wensley, across the Derwent, up the Sydnope Valley and across the gritstone moorland to Chesterfield. This route was later developed to become the Toadhole Turnpike, crossing the River Derwent at Darley Bridge. Further scattered settlement took place along the east side of the valley, well above the flood plain, at Darley Hillside, Two Dales and Upper Hackney, but the bulk of the ribbon development seen today along the A6 road has occurred during the last 100 years, under the influence of Sir Joseph Whitworth, Stancliffe Estates, Matlock Urban District Council, and of course the Midland Railway.

The first station at Darley, as it was known officially until 1st October 1890, was south of what is now Station Road, and the main building, almost certainly designed by Paxton, stands today, in use as transit residential accommodation by West Derbyshire District Council. The building is set back a considerable distance from the site of the running lines and must have been independent of the platforms. Why such an arrangement was followed is quite unknown, but in the now familiar manner the MR were not happy with the situation and on 20th February 1872 the Way and Works Committee ordered that plans be prepared for a new station and additional sidings. A contract for erection of the station was subsequently awarded to Joseph Glossop and the work was completed early in 1874, at a final cost of £2,247 17s (2,247.85). Constructed in local stone, in a neo-gothic style the work consisted of a single main building on the down platform, and a smaller, matching waiting room on the up side. At that time the station was served from the west by a road from Warney Lane/Church Lane, which was the original turnpike from Matlock to Bakewell.

Shortly before the new station was built Sir Joseph Whitworth, the distinguished engineer, had moved from Stockport to Darley Dale, taking up residence in Stancliffe Hall and becoming owner of the adjacent gritstone quarries. By that time Stancliffe stone had become much admired as a building stone, being used for example in the construction of St George's Hall, Liverpool, to where it had been transported by pack mule. Many readers will in fact be familiar with the wearing properties of this stone as Trafalgar Square is still paved with it. As a philanthropist Sir Joseph was quick to use his wealth for the benefit of the local populace and in the early 1880s he constructed New Road (the present A6) through the fields to shorten the circuitous route via Warney Lane and Church Lane. At the same time he built Station Road from New Road westwards to the station, and in 1882 a contract was let by the MR to G.H. Lees for the installation of level crossing gates operated from the signal box.

Almost from the opening of the line the despatch of stone and timber became important at Darley Dale and in 1894 additional sidings were constructed in the goods yard to cope with growing traffic. At the same time a siding was put in for Joseph Hodson's stone traffic which was brought by road from his quarry near Farley. This siding was eleven chains south of the station, on the down side of the line and was taken over a few years later by the Darley Dale Stone Company. The original rail facilities for Stancliffe quarries comprised a siding and a crane two chains north of Church Lane level crossing. Following the death of Sir Joseph Whitworth production was continued by the Stancliffe Estates Co. Ltd, and as output increased the company asked the Midland to provide additional sidings. These were constructed in 1900 to the south of the crossing on the up side of the main line. From the sidings a private standard gauge track curved across the fields and passed under New Road into the stone yard, beyond which it crossed Whitworth Road and ran into Stancliffe Quarry. From here a second line switchbacked across the eastern slope of the valley to Halldale Quarry, overlooking Two Dales. To operate this system two 0-4-0 saddle tanks were used, named *Sir Joseph Whitworth* and *Henry Dawson*.

Very soon after the new sidings had been laid increasing traffic generally led to the provision of slow lines between Darley Dale station and Church Lane crossing, the up slow being brought into use on 12th May 1901 and the down slow on 18th August 1901.

The district no doubt fell under the influence of Matlock as far as merchandise traffic was concerned and the MR never deemed it necessary to provide a traditional goods shed. A small sleeper-built platform originally catered for this traffic but this was extended in 1906, when a 25 cwt crane, portable weighing machine and goods checker's office were provided. A 10 ton outside framed van body was later placed on the platform as a rudimentary store and a standard asbestos warehouse was erected near the cattle dock in the 1930s.

Darley Dale was the penultimate station on our journey to receive footbridges, for it was not until October 1910 that a contract was awarded to Messrs Cross & Cross to erect these at the two level crossings. The work was carried out between April and June the following year, with the footpath between Warney Lane and Church Lane being constructed at the same time.

Passenger traffic was relatively healthy at Darley Dale, growing steadily from 12,888 bookings, or some 40 per weekday, in 1872, to 43,320, in 1902. This total climbed rapidly after the war to a little under 65,000, almost 200 per weekday. While the majority of journeys were probably local, either to Matlock or Bakewell, an increasing number of passengers travelled regularly to Derby from the early 1920s, with 96

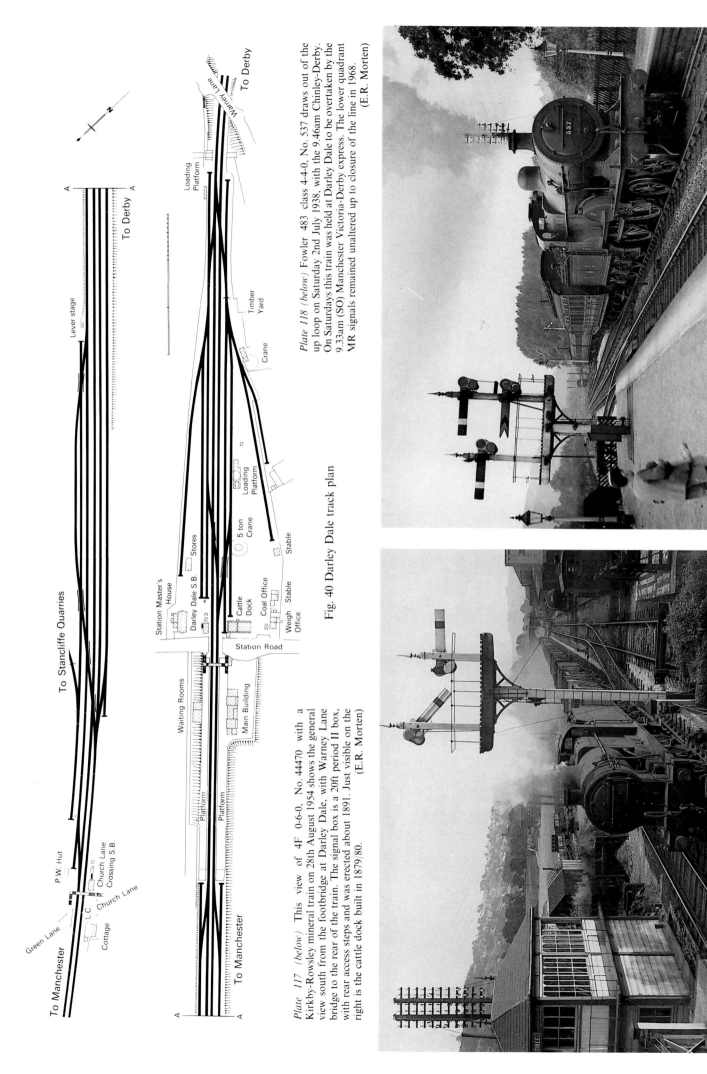

To Manchester

To Stancliffe Quarries

Green Lane

P.W. Hut

Cottage

L.C.

Church Lane

Church Lane Crossing S.B

A

Lever stage

To Derby

A

N

A

Station Master's House

Waiting Rooms

Platform

Platform

Main Building

Station Road

Darley Dale S.B.

Stores

5 ton Crane

Cattle Dock

Coal Office

Weigh Office

Stable Office

Stable

Loading Platform

Crane

Timber Yard

Loading Platform

Warney Lane

To Derby

To Manchester

Fig. 40 Darley Dale track plan

Plate 117 (below) This view of 4F 0-6-0, No. 44470 with a Kirkby-Rowsley mineral train on 28th August 1954 shows the general view south from the footbridge at Darley Dale, with Warney Lane bridge to the rear of the train. The signal box is a 20ft period II box, with rear access steps and was erected about 1891. Just visible on the right is the cattle dock built in 1879/80.

(E.R. Morten)

Plate 118 (below) Fowler 483 class 4-4-0, No. 537 draws out of the up loop on Saturday 2nd July 1938, with the 9.46am Chinley-Derby. On Saturdays this train was held at Darley Dale to be overtaken by the 9.33am (SO) Manchester Victoria-Derby express. The lower quadrant MR signals remained unaltered up to closure of the line in 1968.

(E.R. Morten)

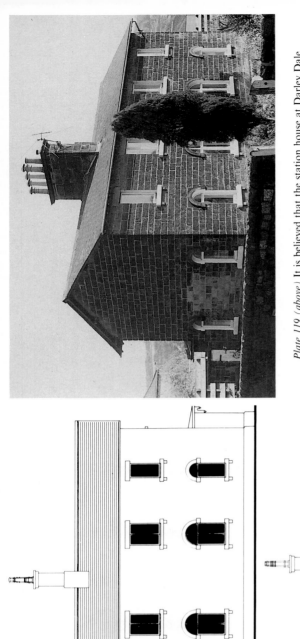

Plate 119 (above) It is believed that the station house at Darley Dale was the original station opened in 1849, as a combined station and station master's house. This view shows the west and north elevations, the latter bearing clear indication where the original passenger doorway was removed sometime after the mid 1930s. The building clearly shows the design features of Sir Joseph Paxton.   (Author)

Plate 120 The south and east elevations, showing the remaining doorway and outbuildings.   (Author)

WEST ELE.

EAST ELE.

NORTH ELE.

SOUTH ELE.

Scale 2mm to one foot

Darley Dale
Station Master's House

Fig. 41 Darley Dale station house

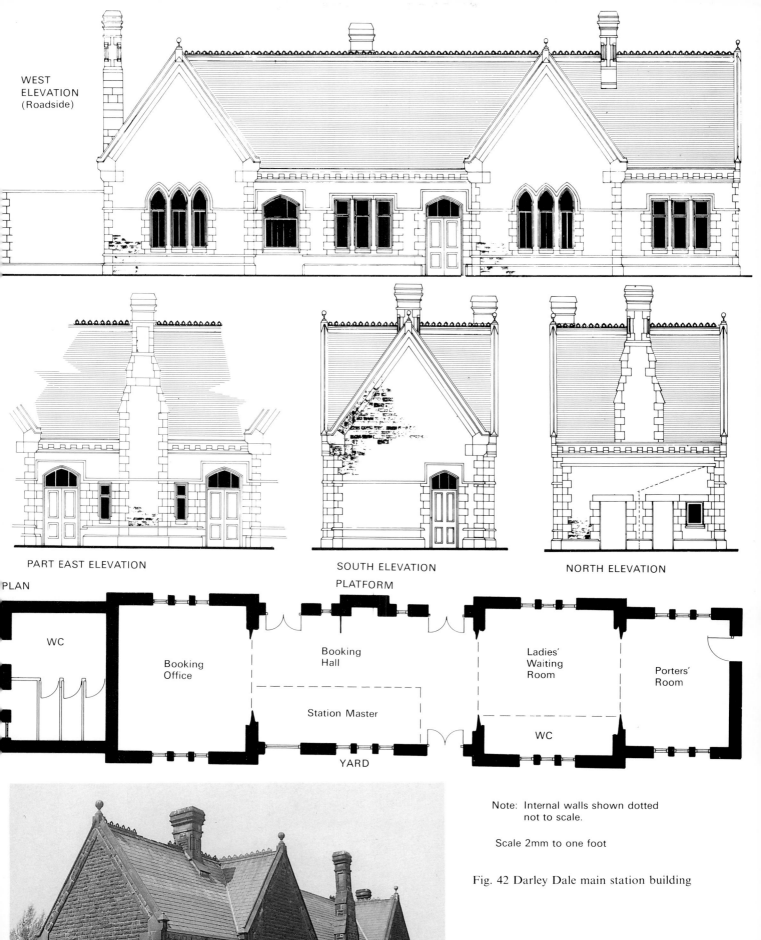

WEST
ELEVATION
(Roadside)

PART EAST ELEVATION

SOUTH ELEVATION

PLATFORM

NORTH ELEVATION

PLAN

WC						
Booking Office	Booking Hall		Ladies' Waiting Room	Porters' Room
	Station Master			
			WC	

YARD

Note: Internal walls shown dotted not to scale.

Scale 2mm to one foot

Fig. 42 Darley Dale main station building

Plate 121 (left) The new station erected at Darley Dale in 1873/74 was arguably the most impressive station on the line, and its neo-Gothic style was a far cry from the twin pavilioned style then being adopted by the MR as its 'standard' station building.

(Author)

FRONT ELEVATION   END ELEVATION

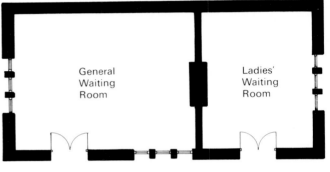

General
Waiting
Room

Ladies'
Waiting
Room

PLAN   Fig. 43 Darley Dale up waiting shelter

Plate 122 (left) The driver of MR 4F 0-6-0, No. 3864, conveniently stops to have a word with an acquaintance on the down platform, on 20th May 1933 and allows the photographer to capture the engine in front of the up waiting shelter. The photographer's bag left by the seat reflects a different age from the one we know now.

(E.R. Morten)

Plates 123 (left), 124 (centre) and 125 (right) show the window detail. *Plate 123* shows how the northerly of the two original doors on the roadside elevation was converted to a window when the station master's office was enlarged in 1897.

(Author)

Fig. 44 Darley Dale station footbridge

EAST ELEVATION

Platform

SOUTH ELEVATION

Scale 2mm to one foot

Plate 126 MR 4F 0-6-0 No. 3886, of Hasland shed, waits for the road on a murky day in the late 1920s. The view shows the painted nameboard moved a few yards down the platform when the footbridge was erected.

(G.W. Wright)

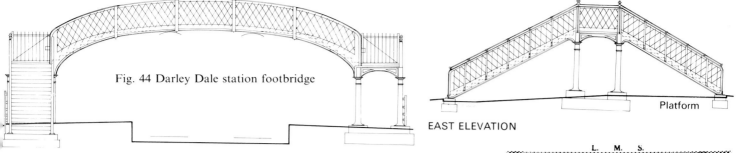

Plate 127 One of the many handbills published to attract visitors to Belle Vue Zoological Gardens during the 1930s.

(Author's Collection)

people holding season tickets in 1922. The train service was broadly similar to that at Whatstandwell or Cromford, but a steady decline in the more local services was apparent from LMS days through to closure. In 1935 ten down and eleven up trains called, two in each direction being Derby-Manchester services. This pattern was cut to eight down and six up trains during the war, with three each way being Derby-Manchester. At closure only eleven trains in total called on weekdays, but three each way ran between the two cities, with an additional Manchester-Nottingham service in the evening.

Although Darley Dale was only a small station, freight traffic was surprisingly heavy and varied, but was dominated by the coal and mineral classes. Unlike many other locations, where business fortunes ebbed and flowed, the coal trade at Darley Dale station was for many years in the hands of two dealers, Tom Wright, whom we have already met at Matlock, and Thomas Smith & Sons.

The first company was set up in the early 1850s by Matthew Wright who at the time was also the Station Master. When eventually asked by the Midland if he wanted to be a station master or a coal merchant he promptly told them which job paid best and left their employ. In May 1888 the business passed to his nephew Tom whose acumen and personality soon brought him the directorship of several companies, including Pinxton Colliery. It was not long before he became their sole agent for sales between Ambergate and Manchester; and at a royalty of 3d (1¼p) for every ton of coal he sold this proved most profitable. In addition to this coal, Wright supplied from several other collieries in Derbyshire, Nottinghamshire and Staffordshire, plus smith's and malting coal from South Wales.

As his trade expanded, so did his wagon fleet, which eventually grew to about 20 vehicles. While full details of all the wagons have not yet been ascertained by the author, it is known that Nos 17, 18 and 19, were acquired from the Butterley Company in April 1924. These were standard 12 ton vehicles, with side, end and bottom doors. They were painted red, with white letters shaded black, as per *fig. 45*. In addition to supplying domestic coal to the immediate locality, Tom Wright also delivered to scattered settlements and farms as far west as Newhaven and Friden, on the Buxton-Ashbourne road, eastwards towards Kelstedge and Ashover, and to Chatsworth House. He also supplied coal to Stancliffe Quarries and Millclose mine for powering machinery and smelting ore.

As a person Tom Wright is remembered as a gentleman in all respects, never being seen in public without his grey homburg and a buttonhole. He was also the first man in Matlock to own a Rolls-Royce, chauffeur driven of course! When he died in the early 1930s his business was taken over by his nephew Alfred Smith, who retained the company name and wagon livery unaltered.

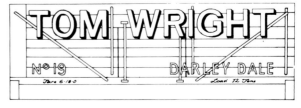

Fig. 45 Tom Wright wagon livery

85

FRONT ELEVATION

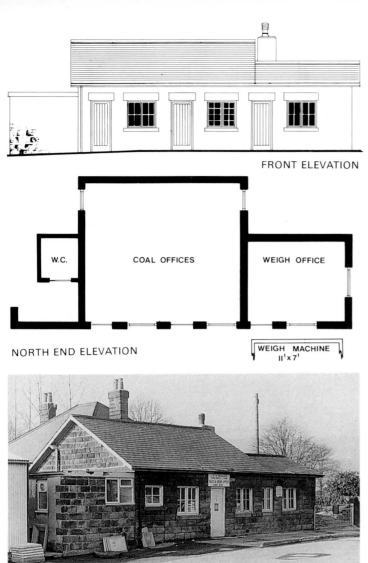

Scale 2mm to 1 ft

Fig. 46
Darley Dale coal offices

NORTH END ELEVATION

| WEIGH MACHINE |
| 11' x 7' |

Plate 128 (left) shows the coal offices and weigh office built during the 1870s. The main office was originally occupied by Tom Wright and was enlarged by building on to the rear and re-roofing about 1901. At that time the small window at the left end of the main building was put in, in place of a previous door. The extension on the left is of modern origin.

(Author)

Plate 129 (above) When Thomas Smith set up his business this was his head office and remained so until Tom Wright moved from the coal office into his own property close by, in the early years of the century. T. Smith then took up tenancy of the coal offices but continued to use the hut as a yard office.

(Author)

Plate 130 (below) This view shows the stables erected by T. Smith in the early 1890s, somewhat run down but still used for storage in 1981.

(Author)

Plate 131 (bottom) A coal consignment note from November 1897, showing coal at 9s 6d (47½p) per ton.

(L. Smith)

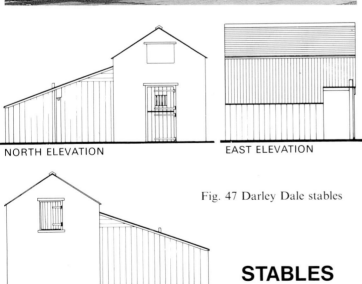

NORTH ELEVATION

EAST ELEVATION

Fig. 47 Darley Dale stables

STABLES

Scale 2mm to 1 ft

SOUTH ELEVATION

Scale 3mm to 1 ft   Fig. 48 Darley Dale T. Smith's office

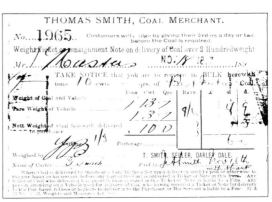

The second coal business at the station was set up by Thomas Smith in September 1888. This later became T. Smith and Sons, with the founder's grandsons, Lewis and Ted, taking control in the late 1920s. The company eventually took over the interests of Tom Wright, on 1st April 1950, and the Smith family finally gave up the coal trade in 1972 when the business was sold to British Fuels Ltd. Lewis Smith recalls that the wagon fleet comprised eight vehicles, Nos 1-7 and 9. One of these was a 12 tonner, with a hinged top plank, the remainder were 10 ton, 5-plank wagons with full height side doors and rounded ends. While one cannot expect memory of these details to be exact, it is known that at one time Nos 2 and 3 were secondhand 8 ton 'converted' wagons acquired from Birmingham R.C. & W. Co. in January 1916. The company's livery was black, with plain white letters and *fig. 49* has been prepared from Mr Smith's description.

Coal was normally purchased either directly from Denby and Pentrich collieries, or from the Barber Walker group's Moorgreen and Watnall collieries, through their agent, Nathaniel Attrill. When so required anthracite was usually purchased from Cynheidre Colliery, Llanelly. Domestic coal was supplied mainly to Darley Dale, Wensley, Winster and Birchover, with small amounts to customers in Matlock and Rowsley.

Fig. 49 T. Smith wagon livery

The company had two horses and a tipping cart for delivery, with one horse pulling the cart outwards and the other following 'light engine' in readiness for the return journey. Shortly after World War I the proprietors were able to expand their business with the purchase of a surplus Fiat lorry from the Italian army. This vehicle soon became a familiar sight in the area, and it is recalled with some pride that when it was eventually withdrawn its big brass radiator cover was acquired by the Fiat Museum in Milan. By the early 1930s the business had expanded somewhat and T. Smith & Sons could then have been best described as 'Coal, coke, hay, straw, builders and general merchants'. The latter side of the business soon became important enough for the LMS to provide an ex-MR, six-wheel coach body, supported on earthenware pipes filled with concrete, to serve as a cement store. Such a diversification of interests was very common among coal merchants, as the lower demand for fuel in summer, gave an opportunity to use the wagons to bring in bricks, pipes, tiles, slates, sand, cement etc, at a time when the construction industry was at its peak. This period also presented the best opportunity to look at the wagon fleet and although Smiths' had a repair and maintenance contract with Wagon Repairs Ltd, they treated the floors of their vehicles, as the opportunity arose. The wagons were carefully swept out and the floor was given a thick coating of tar onto which was sprinkled gravel. This gave a surface not dissimilar to tarmac and considerably eased the job of shovelling out the coal.

While both merchants supplied lime as required, one can safely assume that the tonnages shown in the coal class traffic did indeed represent primarily coal and coke. The steady rise in this traffic, from a little over 5,000 tons in 1872 to over 19,000 tons in 1922, reflected the growth in the resident population and the expansion of industrial consumption. At that time, about 9,000 tons per annum, or some 20-22 wagons per week, came in for the domestic market.

Of the remainder, by far the largest tonnage arrived for use at Millclose lead mine. This enterprise was opened by the London Lead Co. in the 1720s, closed about 50 years later and then reopened in 1859. By the late 1920s it had become one of the richest lead mines in the world, producing 600-1,000 tons

of lead and 200-300 tons of zinc sulphide per week. It was unfortunately also taking in some 30 million gallons of water over the same period. In an attempt to control this influx the mine had a number of pumps, powered by a Cornish beam engine. It was stated in the previous section that there is some argument as to which station dealt with the lead traffic, but Lewis Smith, who was in his office at the goods yard virtually every day, is adamant that it was dealt with at Darley Dale. Lead ore was reputedly sent to the Continent, while quantities of lead slag were sent to the Manchester area for reprocessing. Some finished ingots were also despatched, presumably in covered vans for security purposes. The transport of coal to the mine, and minerals to the station was handled for many years by a small fleet of Sentinel and Foden steam lorries, which were fed exclusively on anthracite from Werfa Dare Colliery, Glamorgan, supplied by the indomitable Mr. Wright.

The Darley Dale Stone Co., referred to earlier, closed down in the early 1900s and the site was taken over by A. & P. Hill as a furniture factory. After a few years the site was acquired by the Damard Lacquer Co. and was taken over again about 1925 by Mouldensite Ltd. This company manufactured bakelite, a forerunner of today's plastics, using heat and pressure to combine phenol, formaldehyde and a fibrous filler. To provide the heat and power for the presses, Thomas Smith supplied Denby washed doubles, a high quality steam coal, while the sawdust for use as filler, and timber for pattern making was provided by the adjacent timber yard. Just after World War II the company moved to Birmingham and the land was taken over by S. & E. Johnson who still produce cattle and poultry food today.

The timber yard and bone grinding mill was established by John Gregory in the 1890s and for a considerable period the company relied heavily on rail transport. Indeed, the value of the traffic was such that in the 1930s the Station Master, John Sanger, called round personally every morning to ascertain what wagons would be required for the day's work. Timber was purchased over a wide area of the north Midlands and the trees were felled by travelling gangs of men who were billeted in farm buildings together with their horses and vehicles. These gangs would transport the timber to the nearest station where it would be loaded on to bolster wagons by railway staff, to be sent to Darley Dale for seasoning and ultimately cutting. Sawn timber for local markets was delivered by horse and cart, but anything over nine miles, which was the maximum distance a horse could deliver and return in one day, was sent by rail, either in bolster or open merchandise wagons, according to size. Apart from joiners and builders the company supplied to collieries over a wide area and to wagon builders including W.H. Davis, Wm Rigley and Charles Roberts. Much of the stock and several buildings were destroyed in a serious fire in 1939, but while Mr Ralph Gregory, who had succeeded his father, came to his own conclusions, the cause of the fire was never established. However, all agreed that a northbound express stormed past the yard a short time before the flames were spotted.

Fig. 50 Werfa Dare wagon livery

Whether or not it was micro-climate, soil, business acumen or some combination of these factors is not certain, but in the 1920s there were no less than seven nurserymen and market gardeners in and around Darley Dale, all of whom made use of the railway. Foremost among these concerns were James Smith & Son who supplied a huge variety of plants to landscape architects and gardeners all over the country. A speciality of this firm was the cultivation of heathers, and the hybrid *Erica darleyensis* was developed at their nursery. One unusual activity was the growing of heathers specifically for use in the packing of iron pipes for safe transit and large quantities were sent to Stanton Iron Works, in sheeted open wagons. Thomas Smith & Sons also enjoyed part of this market, sending out wild heather gathered on the surrounding moorland. With such activity in the area it comes as no surprise that wagon loads of spent hops regularly came into the yard from various breweries, for composting and use as a fertiliser. From the 1920s onwards Shell Mex and BP tank wagons came into the yard on a regular basis.

The yard was serviced by the 6.55am stopping freight from Rowsley to Matlock Bath and the 3.55pm from Rowsley. The engine of this train shunted the yard and returned with the 5.40pm freight to Rowsley.

Plate 132 (above) This view taken about 1908 shows a magnificent piece of oak which has come in by rail and has been loaded on to a heavy duty cart for the short journey round to John Gregory's saw mill. Behind stands Blackwell Colliery Company wagon, No. 897.

(R. Gregory)

Plate 133 (below) Rebuilt Johnson 0-4-4T, No. 1429, in the 1936 block style livery, leaves Darley Dale with a Derby-Bakewell local about 1937. The leading coach is an ex-LNWR elliptical roofed brake third. These carriages were built in 1920 and remained in service until the mid 1950s.

(E.R. Morten)

Plate 134 One of the final MR built 4F 0-6-0s, No. 44013, fitted with the plain splashers used on the later LMS engines, makes a splendid sight as it passes Church Lane crossing, north of Darley Dale with an up stopping freight on 14th September 1957.

(E.R. Morten)

From Darley Dale station the line ran straight, towards the north west, but at Church Lane crossing it entered a long curve to the east, and keeping more or less at natural ground level it passed through a narrow gap between the river and the Bakewell road. At this point it crossed a bridle road, Derwent Lane, by a level crossing from where it kept close to the Bakewell road for about ³/4 mile before swinging sharply to the west into Rowsley station, 11 miles 10 chains from Ambergate West Junction.

Rowsley was once the terminus of the line, with the original route running northwards under the Bakewell road to a terminus which stands today, preserved as a listed building, in the middle of a civil engineer's yard. Very little is known about the early history of Rowsley, other than that the station, together with a number of cottages close by, were designed by Sir Joseph Paxton and that it saw the first fatal accident on the line. On New Year's Eve 1859, a sheep was killed on the railway and the company secretary was instructed to settle the owner's claim for £1 10s (£1.50) compensation on the best terms he could effect.

From 1849 until the autumn of 1860 Rowsley remained a quiet branch line terminus, serving a small community of little more than 400-500 residents, but then Messrs Thompson & Co. moved in to begin construction of the line to Buxton. This line left the original route 28 chains south of the station, at what then became known as 'Goods and Engine Shed Branch Junction' and curved to the west on a gradient of 1 in 102. The new line was engineered by William Barlow and his plans for the new station, which were drawn up by his friend, Edward Walters, a Manchester architect, were approved on 4th

December 1861, along with those for the stations at Bakewell and Hassop, which were almost identical. The contract for construction of all three stations was awarded to John Wood of Derby, on 4th February 1862, with the onerous condition that the work must be completed by 10th June 1862, on penalty of liquidated damages of £10 per day for each station not finished.

The main station building was a long single storey structure, built in local gritstone under a hipped roof, surmounted by four huge chimney stacks. The roof had a wide overhang, at each end and on the road side, supported on attractive wooden eaves brackets. At the road side the centrally placed door and the windows each side, illuminating the booking hall and booking office, had segmentally arched openings, while the remaining rooms had plain sash windows. The small portico over the door, to provide shelter while unloading luggage, was added to the design at the request of the Traffic Committee. On the rail side the main wall was carried up in the form of a parapet, with chamfered ends, to provide support for a ridge and furrow awning in glass and iron. The theme of arched and plain openings was repeated on this side of the building, under six false arches, the central pair of which each had an arched door and window opening, one to the booking hall, one to the booking office. Between each of these doors and windows was a semi-circular column, with a decorative capital, above which was a simulated coat-of-arms. A challenge indeed to the model maker!

With the opening of the line to Hassop and then Buxton the original station and yard was given over to goods traffic. The traffic of the time must still have been relatively light for it seems there was only one horse employed in the yard. However the poor animal certainly did not have an easy life, for on 4th July 1865 the General Manager requested that the stable accommodation be enlarged, as there was not enough room for the horse to lie down. The work was approved but it was

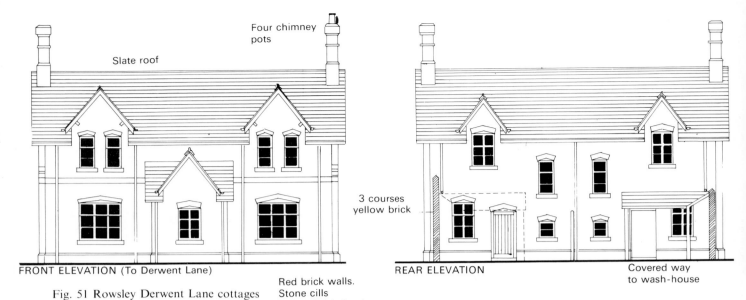

Four chimney pots

Slate roof

FRONT ELEVATION (To Derwent Lane)

REAR ELEVATION

3 courses yellow brick

Covered way to wash-house

Fig. 51 Rowsley Derwent Lane cottages

Red brick walls.
Stone cills
Yellow brick lintels

Scale: Front & Rear elevations cottages   2mm to one foot
End elevations and rear of outbuildings   1mm to one foot

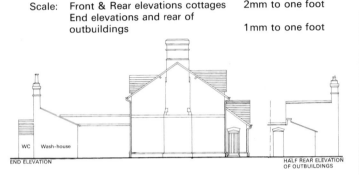

WC   Wash-house

END ELEVATION

HALF REAR ELEVATION OF OUTBUILDINGS

Plate 135 (right) This view, taken in 1984, shows the pair of cottages built at Derwent Lane in 1873.

(Author)

well into the autumn before it was carried out, by adding the adjacent empty coal office to the stable. The original facilities for motive power comprised a turntable, with three stabling roads, one of which was covered to provide shelter for one engine. When the line was opened throughout to Manchester the traffic increased to the extent that assisting engines were required to Peak Forest and following a minor extension in 1869, the depot was considerably enlarged in 1878. This work included a new shed over three tracks and the provision of what has become known as a standard Midland ramped coaling stage. A retired driver proudly informed the author that he could get five wagons into this stage by rushing up the hump, pushing the wagons hard against the stop ends until the buffer springs were fully compressed, and letting his fireman pin the brakes fully down, before releasing the engine.

This general increase in traffic meant more use of the level crossing at Derwent Lane (later Rowsley South Junction) and early in 1873 a pair of cottages were erected close by for staff accommodation. It is interesting to note that the drawings had only just been filed when cottages were required at Selside on the Settle-Carlisle line, so they were used again, but the material was changed from brick to stone. Just under ten years later a second pair of cottages, of similar design, were erected by Solomon Fox, on a site about 100 yards south of Derwent Lane.

As freight traffic expanded in the early 1870s, some preliminary sorting, before the climb over the Peak, became desirable and Rowsley was the most suitable place. It is not known exactly when the first sidings were laid in, but on 4th March 1873 it was ordered that "tenders be obtained for the erection of a wooden hut at Rowsley sidings for the use of yardsmen". This was followed two months later by an instruction that "steps be taken to acquire the necessary land for additional sidings". Early the following year the committee asked for an estimate to be prepared for the construction of new sidings. This was submitted on 3rd March 1874, in the sum of £998 and must have been a minor extension, for twelve months later a request was made for plans to be drawn up for the provision of sorting sidings. The estimate of £27,944 was put before the Way and Works Committee on 1st June 1875, and following approval by the General Purposes Committee the work was put in hand. The sidings were opened for traffic in March 1877, and as they became established there was a marked increase in the number of men employed there. To cater for their needs a contract was awarded to Joseph Glossop on 18th December 1877 for the erection of lamp room, mess rooms and foreman's office.

A well-cared-for workforce is an efficient workforce and with this very much in mind, in the summer of 1886, the GP Committee asked the land agent, Mr Gratton, to "report upon the best site for company houses at Rowsley and to prepare plans and estimates for building in stone". Six weeks later he reported that the Duke of Rutland had agreed to sell two acres of land, for £800, on condition that he be allowed to approve the plans. It was resolved to continue negotiations. The Duke subsequently agreed to the designs but changed his mind on a

90

Plate 136 (above) Fowler class 4-4-0, No. 513 and a Compound 4-4-0 double head a down express past Rowsley South Junction in August 1935.

(E.R. Morten)

Plate 137 (below) After the passage of the express class G1 0-8-0 No. 9217, makes a spirited start from Rowsley yard with an up freight. The line of trees was probably planted by the MR to screen the yard from the main Bakewell road.

(E.R. Morten)

sale of the land and asked for a perpetual rent charge of £32 per annum. This was agreed in December 1886 and a contract for construction of the dwellings was awarded to W.J. Salt in the sum of £5205 19s 6d (£5,205.97¹/₂p), the cottages to be built in three blocks. It then transpired that the Duke of Rutland was only a limited owner of the land and thus had no authority to dispose of it by a lease. After protracted negotiations the Midland's solicitors, Messrs Beale, Marigold and Beale, were able to report that they had "induced the Duke of Rutland's advise to waive the requirement of a perpetual annual rent charge" and that purchase of the land had been completed in the original sum of £800. Work finally began on the cottages late in 1887.

Such was the growth in freight traffic at this period that in a little over ten years problems of congestion in the sidings were arising and in January 1889 a scheme for providing a new arrival line and an additional siding for crippled wagons was authorised, at an estimated cost of £1,550. This new down coal road was brought into use in August 1889, and was followed later the same year, by renewal of the signal box at Rowsley North Junction, with further alterations to the sidings following early in 1891. At the same time strengthening of the culvert carrying Hoe Brook under the sidings and construction of a subway at the station was put in hand, the contracts being awarded on 6th February 1891 to the Cleveland Bridge & Engineering Co. and Eastwood Swingler & Co. respectively.

By the mid 1890s the need for additional staff accommodation had become manifest and on 2nd March 1896 it was ordered that plans be made for erecting a further 31 cottages. After approval of the plans the contract for their construction was awarded to W. Forrest on 6th August 1896, in the sum of £6,732 8s 8d (£6,732.43p). It is a sobering thought that in ten years the cost of housing had only risen from £208 to £217 per dwelling. These cottages were built in five blocks, one on the road frontage to the south of the earlier ones and four to the rear. Finally, in 1898, a block of four cottages was built for train examiners, again on the Chatsworth road frontage. The influence of the railways on settlement patterns is superbly illustrated by these cottages, the construction of which increased the housing stock at Rowsley by almost 50% in less than 12 years. It also reminds one of the high standards demanded in those times to see these dwellings today, albeit reroofed and modernised, but with many years life ahead of them.

As traffic in the sidings continued to grow, the demand for train, pilot, and shunting engines increased and it became apparent to both men and management that the cramped facilities at the engine shed were rapidly becoming intolerable. The actual date of the decision to build a new motive power depot has been lost in the mists of time, but in 1898 the MR found itself on what was to prove a very long road. On 21st July of that year the land agent reported that an area of 7 acres 1 rood and 29 perches, at Darley Dale, had been offered to the company for £1,500. He recommended that the land should be purchased as a site for an engine shed and cottages for the company's servants. This was agreed and by January 1899 the land had been purchased from Stancliffe Estates Co., but in the meantime internal communications seem to have broken down, for on 16th November of that year the Way and Works Committee were read minute No. 6216 of the Locomotive Committee requesting the purchase of land at Rowsley for the site of a proposed engine shed.

The agent re-opened negotiations with Stancliffe Estates on a further 5a 3r 10p of land, but while they were quite willing to give up this land they suggested that the railway company should purchase a further area of a little over three acres in their ownership. In August 1900 it was agreed to buy the whole of the land on offer, a few weeks after the committee had accepted an estimate of £28,938 for the construction of the new depot. There the matter rested until 3rd October 1902 when a revised estimate of £22,030 was submitted and approved. Still no action was taken and apart from minor changes in the old yard, the raising of one of the platforms and moving the water crane at the station, no significant development took place in respect to Rowsley, until 14th May 1914, when the Way and Works Committee accepted an estimate of £21,430 for the

construction of a new engine shed. This estimate was submitted by the Traffic Committee, but before it could be acted upon, World War I broke out and the luxury of a new engine shed was out of the question. Almost by coincidence Rowsley South Junction signal box, which was then on the down side of the line, came up for renewal at this time and the new box was erected on the up side of the line to allow for the access tracks to the proposed engine shed. The new box, which was reputedly the busiest between Derby and Manchester, was opened at 8.30am on 20th June 1915.

The period following the war was one of steady recovery for the railways but the Midland was determined to get its new motive power depot at Rowsley and with a final flourish a contract for the work was let on 14th December 1922, to E. Wood & Sons in the sum of £22,205 11s 8d (£22,205.58). It is not known if the first sod was turned before the end of the month but from February 1923 the Chief Engineer began to make regular reports to the LMS Works Committee on expenditure on the project. The total estimated cost of the works, including track and sidings for a civil engineer's depot was £41,753, of which a little over £28,500 had been paid out by the end of 1924. By this time the engineer's depot must have been in operation for plans were approved in May 1925 to extend the stocking ground, provide additional sidings and a 2 ton derrick crane. It is believed that the main shed building was completed late in 1924 but the depot was not formally brought into use until July 1926, at which time the old shed was closed. The new coaling plant, however, was not completed and light engines were taken four at a time to the old shed for coaling until October of that year.

With locomotive servicing taken care of, attention was turned to the yard and in July 1927 the Chief General Superintendent reported that the existing down marshalling sidings at Rowsley were inadequate to enable the wagons passing through to be satisfactorily handled. The position was aggravated by the lack of siding accommodation at Buxton for dealing with traffic from the Midland Division to the Western Division, which necessitated wagons being held back at Rowsley. It was resolved to accept a proposal for the provision of new sidings which would provide standing room for an extra 193 wagons, together with accommodation for an extra 33 crippled wagons. This would allow a greater proportion of the vehicles then being sorted at Buxton to be made up into through trains at Rowsley. These new sidings were brought into use early in 1929.

This work was part of the general drive towards more efficient working and was followed late in 1930 by proposals to extend the permanent way depot by the provision of additional sidings and a wagon weighing machine. By re-arranging the track layout it was estimated that one shunting engine could be dispensed with at an annual saving of £1,075. As work proceeded authority was given, in July 1931, to put in a larger weighbridge than that originally proposed, which would weigh 60ft rails at one attempt. *Fig. 63* shows that this was achieved by installing three standard weighing machines in line, balanced and working in unison. It was also intended to provide a travelling crane for the depot, but it was later decided that the crane allocated to Derby could cover the work in the Rowsley district.

Plate 138 LMS identification card.

(Courtesy: H. Wardman)

Fig. 52 Rowsley Sidings track plan

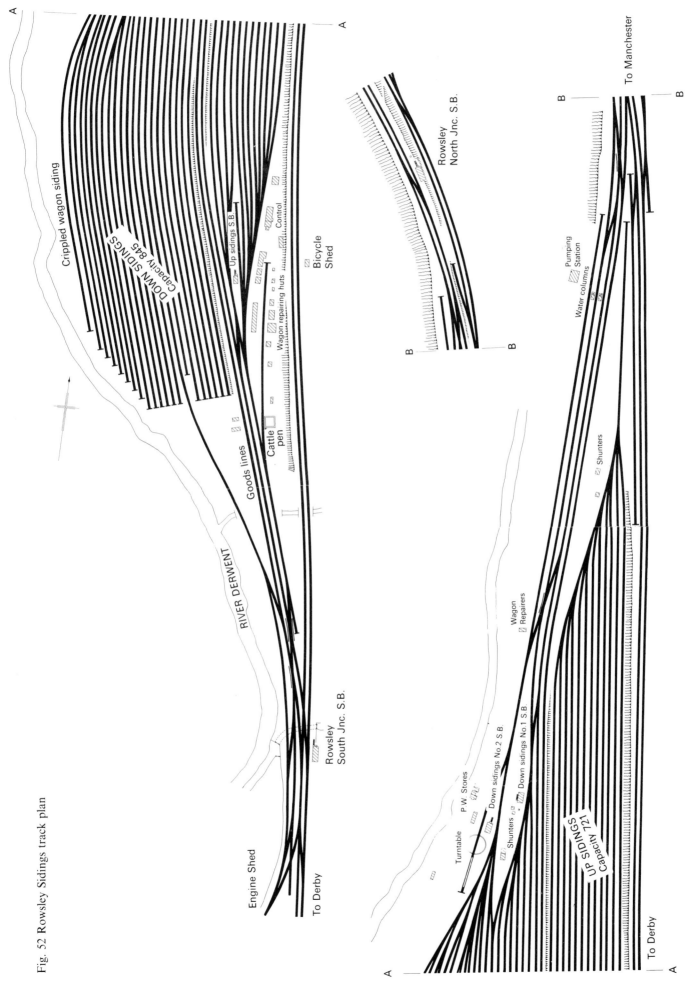

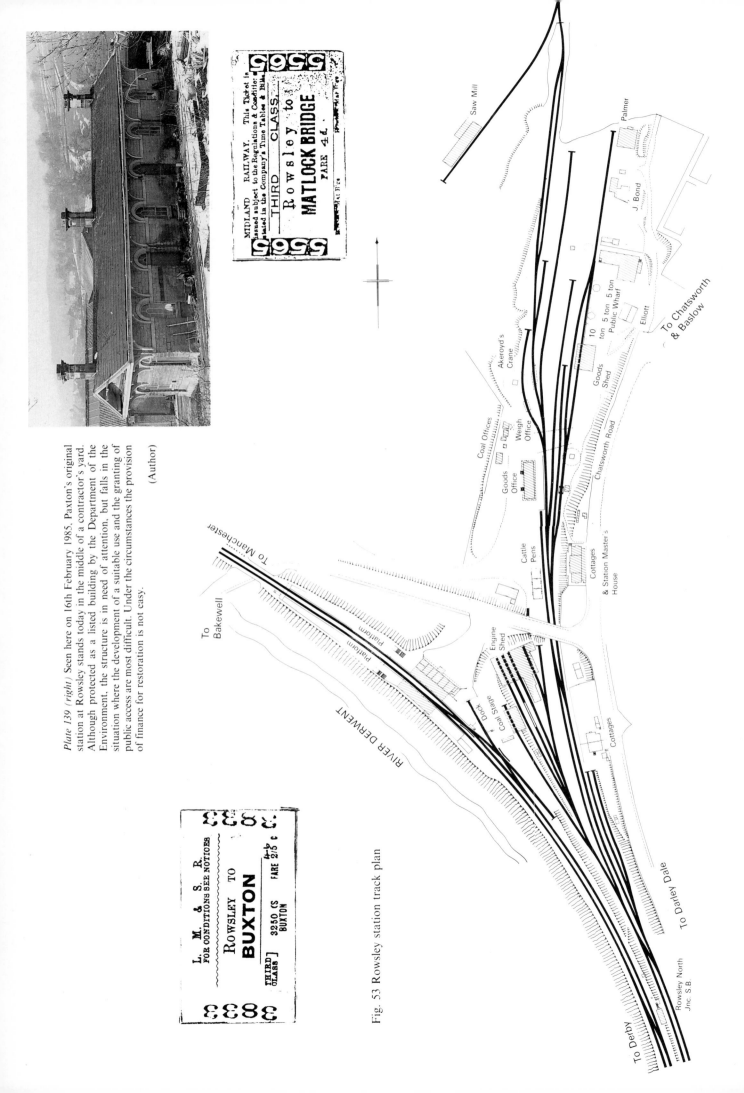

Plate 139 (right) Seen here on 16th February 1985, Paxton's original station at Rowsley stands today in the middle of a contractor's yard. Although protected as a listed building by the Department of the Environment, the structure is in need of attention, but falls in the situation where the development of a suitable use and the granting of public access are most difficult. Under the circumstances the provision of finance for restoration is not easy.

(Author)

MIDLAND RAILWAY. This Ticket is
Issued subject to the Regulations & Condition
stated in the Company's Time Tables & Bills.
THIRD CLASS.
Rowsley to
MATLOCK BRIDGE.
FARE 4d.

L. M. & S. R.
FOR CONDITIONS SEE NOTICES
ROWSLEY TO
BUXTON
THIRD CLASS   FARE 2/5 c
3250 CS
BUXTON

3833

Fig. 53 Rowsley station track plan

To Manchester

To Bakewell

Platform

Platform

RIVER DERWENT

Dock

Coal Stage

Engine Shed

Saw Mill

Akeroyd's Crane

Coal Offices

Goods Office

Weigh Office

Cattle Pens

Cottages

& Station Master's House

Goods Shed

10 ton   5 ton   5 ton
Public Wharf

Elliott

Palmer

J. Bond

To Chatsworth & Baslow

Chatsworth Road

Cottages

To Darley Dale

To Derby

Rowsley North Jnc. S.B.

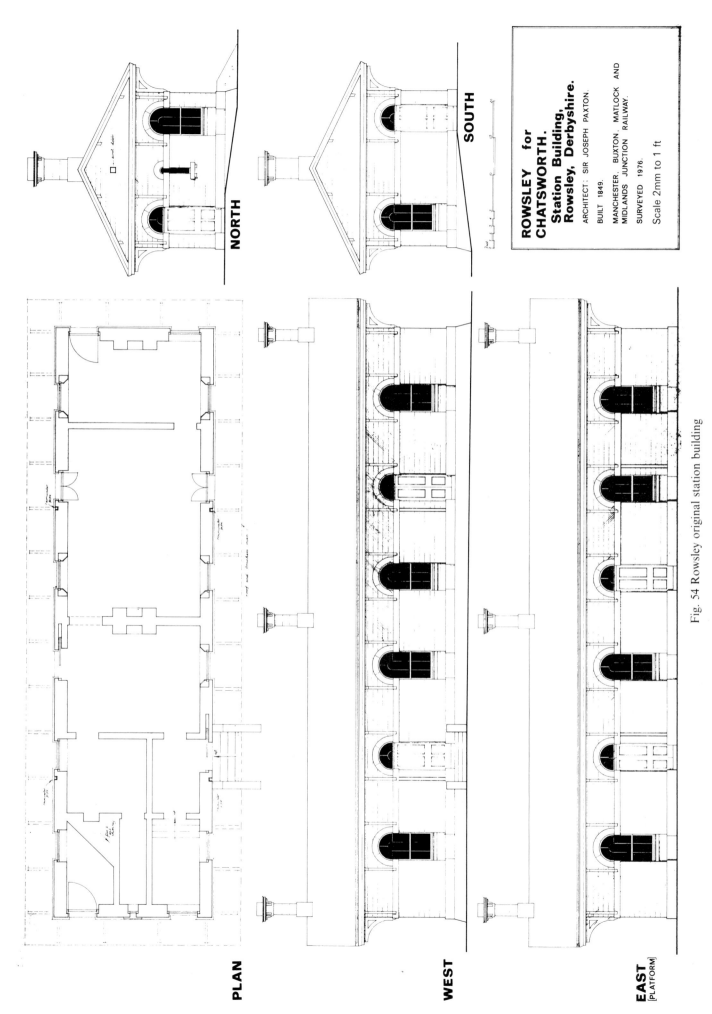

NORTH

SOUTH

**ROWSLEY for CHATSWORTH.
Station Building, Rowsley, Derbyshire.**

ARCHITECT: SIR JOSEPH PAXTON.

BUILT 1849.

MANCHESTER, BUXTON, MATLOCK AND MIDLANDS JUNCTION RAILWAY.

SURVEYED 1976.

Scale 2mm to 1 ft

PLAN

WEST

EAST
[PLATFORM]

Fig. 54 Rowsley original station building

Plate 140 To the author's eye this view of the old goods yard on 8th August 1953, is the most evocative plate in the book and perfectly captures Rowsley's former status as a branch line terminus.

(H. Townley)

EAST ELEVATION

Scale 2mm to 1 ft

Fig. 55 Rowsley goods shed

Plate 141 (bottom left) A parcels cart bill of 6th August 1910 showing that the morning cart from Chatsworth carried a parcel for Manchester, a box for Sheffield and a basket for London.
(Author's Collection)

Plate 142 To augment storage during the late **MR**/early LMS period four 12 ton van bodies, set on earthenware pipes, were provided close to the goods shed, two of which remained at least up to 1953.
(H. Townley)

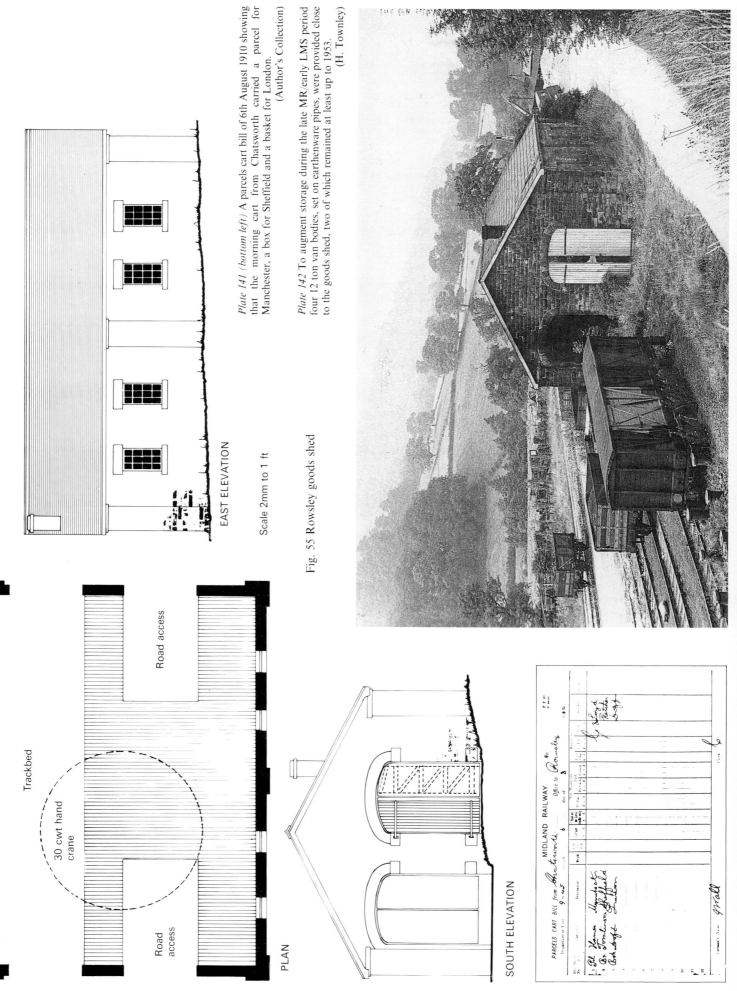

Trackbed

30 cwt hand crane

Road access

Road access

PLAN

SOUTH ELEVATION

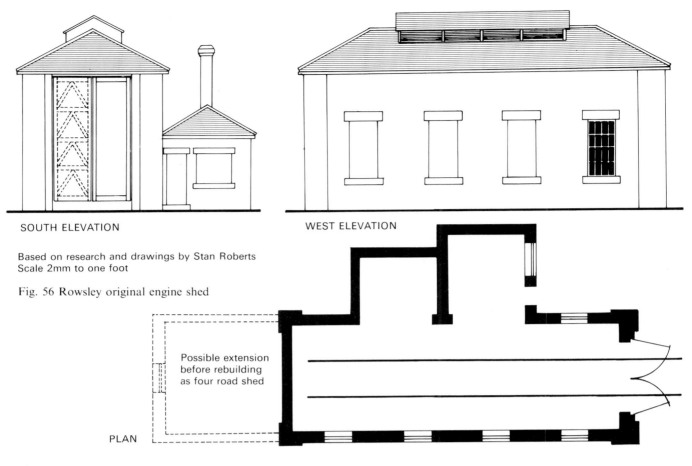

SOUTH ELEVATION

WEST ELEVATION

Based on research and drawings by Stan Roberts
Scale 2mm to one foot

Fig. 56 Rowsley original engine shed

Possible extension
before rebuilding
as four road shed

PLAN

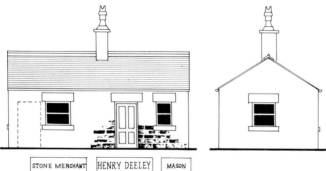

STONE MERCHANT   HENRY DEELEY   MASON

Fig. 57 Rowsley H. Deeley's office   Scale 2mm to 1 ft

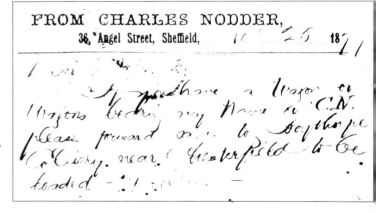

FROM CHARLES NODDER,
36, Angel Street, Sheffield,

Plate 143 "Please sir, I've lost my wagon!"

(Author's Collection)

Plate 144 (below) This view taken on 5th August 1945 shows the two cranes on the dock immediately north of the goods shed. In the background can be seen stocks of timber cut for the war effort.

(N.R.M.)

Fig. 58 Rowsley weigh office   Scale 2mm to 1 ft

Fig. 59 Rowsley goods yard office   Scale 2mm to 1 ft

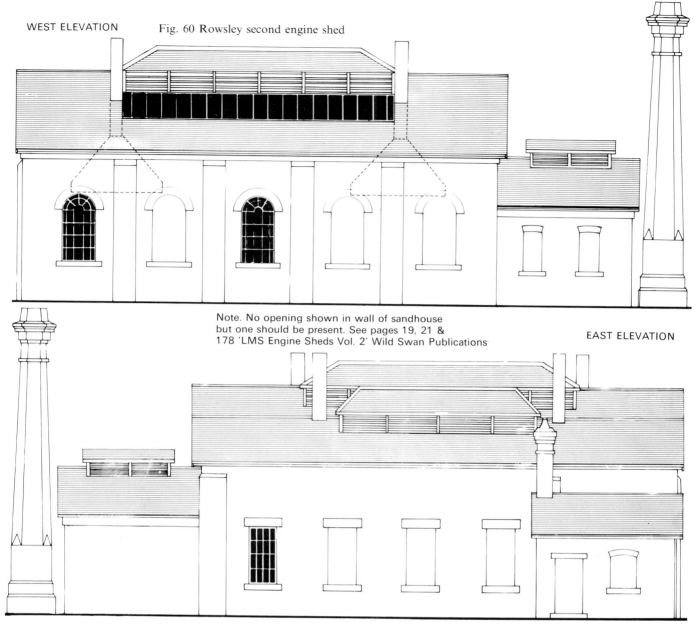

WEST ELEVATION   Fig. 60 Rowsley second engine shed

Note. No opening shown in wall of sandhouse
but one should be present. See pages 19, 21 &
178 'LMS Engine Sheds Vol. 2' Wild Swan Publications

EAST ELEVATION

Plate 145 The original engine shed was the small building seen here just to the right of the tall chimney. The bulk of the shed buildings and the coaling stage were added in 1878. By the early years of the century congestion had become so acute that the down line into the old goods yard had to be used for stabling locomotives, but it was to be many years before the problems were eased.   (Author's Collection)

NORTH ELEVATION

Note Position of windows is correct but shape is conjectural based on study of all MR straight sheds.

Base of chimney conjectural

Scale 2mm to one foot

SOUTH ELEVATION

Although the new engine shed had been opened in 1926 it was not until the end of 1934 that proposals were drawn up to deal with the original depot. On 28th November the Chief Operational Manager recommended that action taken to clear the various buildings be confirmed. The structures, which were in a dilapidated condition, had been removed by a demolition contractor who had paid £75 for the materials, some of which were subsequently used to build a bungalow which is still occupied today. The trackwork consisted of five sidings, one of which served the Express Dairy, opened in June 1933 on an adjacent site. It was agreed that the four remaining sidings be retained temporarily for holding those wagons of locomotive coal for Rowsley and Buxton which were received in excess of the accommodation at those sheds. At the same meeting the Chief Commercial Manager recommended that a 99 year lease be granted to the Express Dairy Co. on approximately 2,538 sq yards of land upon which the company had already erected a milk cooling depot, spray, pond condenser and filter plant. This seems a rather strange method of estate management and certainly an odd way to set up a business, but on being informed that in the twelve months to the end of May 1934 the carriage value of milk forwarded from Rowsley was £16,886, the committee retrospectively granted the lease. Milk tanks were normally attached to the 5.18pm local to Derby, for Cricklewood, or the 10.15pm express freight to Brent. With the completion of works to modernise Buxton motive power depot the four sidings used for storage became obsolete and were removed in 1936.

By the 1930s Rowsley had become one of the most important locations on the LMS, for with the West Coast Main Line passenger services at their zenith, much of the freight from the Midlands and the South East to the North West, or vice versa, was sent over the Peak. This traffic, together with a considerable flow of coal and the corresponding empties, resulted in something in the order of 17,000 wagons per week passing through the yard. To deal with this the LMS continued the Midland practice of sorting loaded minerals on the down side and empties on the up, during the day, and merchandise, etc, on both sides during the night. The only goods trains which did not enter the yard were the Toton-Gowhole coal trains, the block iron ore trains from Northamptonshire to Glazebrook, Garston shipping traffic and empty vans from Bristol and Birmingham to Manchester, and Brent to Liverpool, together with certain fitted freights.

In addition to sorting wagons for many destinations, a principal objective on the down side was to make up trains suitable for the climb to Peak Forest or Buxton, to either of which strict loading schedules were applied. A Class 4 engine could take 29 loaded mineral wagons unassisted to Peak Forest or 26 to Buxton. Over this number a banking engine was required and trains in excess of 45 wagons to Peak Forest called for a pilot engine as well (40 wagons was the maximum load to Buxton due to limitations in track capacity at that point). Until the early 1960s about ten 2F or 3F 0-6-0 tender engines were kept for banking purposes, but from 1962 Stanier and Fowler tank engines were utilised. Through trains

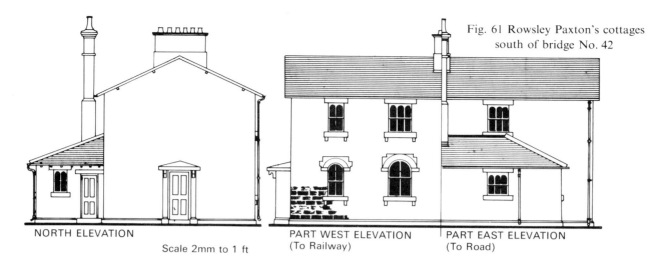

Fig. 61 Rowsley Paxton's cottages
south of bridge No. 42

NORTH ELEVATION

Scale 2mm to 1 ft

PART WEST ELEVATION
(To Railway)

PART EAST ELEVATION
(To Road)

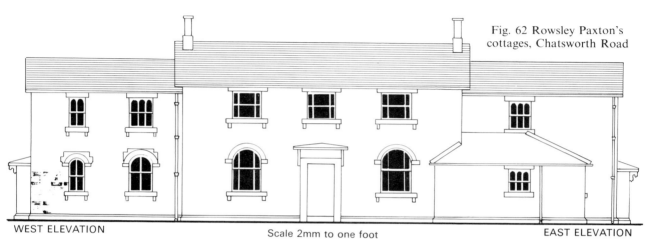

Fig. 62 Rowsley Paxton's
cottages, Chatsworth Road

WEST ELEVATION

Scale 2mm to one foot

EAST ELEVATION

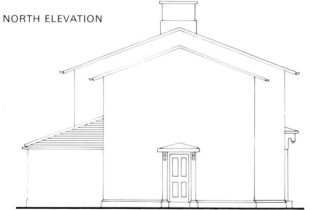

NORTH ELEVATION

Plate 146 (right) Among the cottages built at Rowsley about 1850 was this block of three just north of bridge 42, in Chatsworth Road. Almost certainly by Paxton the block contains a foreman grade's house, flanked each side by a smaller dwelling.

(Author)

Plate 147 (below) The western elevation of the same block. Apart from new windows and the modern extension on the right the buildings remain virtually as built.

(Author)

Plate 149 (below) The three blocks of cottages built on Chatsworth Road in 1887/88 are seen here in 1984.

(Author)

Plate 148 (above) This view south from bridge 42, taken on 8th August 1953, shows the pair of platelayers' cottages illustrated in fig. 61, the original line into the old station and on the extreme right, the embankment carrying the main line to Manchester. The line of trees to the right of the splitting signal is the northern end of the line seen in plate 137.

(H. Townley)

ready to start the sequence again. The first diesel to work from Rowsley towards Peak Forest was another 'Peak', No. D73, with the 9.16pm to Ancoats on 13th February 1962.

By this time however, the yard was only a shadow of its former self and the general fall in freight traffic led to the closure of the sidings on 27th April, 1964. The depot remained open as a banking and relieving point but on 3rd October 1966 all freight trains were diverted from the Peak line. The men were kept on and used to 'best advantage' until 17th October the bi-monthly traincrew transfer day when the depot finally closed.

Passenger traffic at Rowsley may have been insignificant in comparison with the volume of freight passing through the yard, but it was nevertheless important in terms of revenue. Before 1900 passenger bookings were much higher than at Darley Dale, and before the Midland's accelerations of 1904 a number of expresses stopped, but the more rapid residential development of Darley Dale coupled with the steady pull of Derby as a commuter town reversed the figures. Indeed by 1922 the number of bookings had fallen to 42,770 as compared with 64,835 at Darley Dale, and were below the level of 1872. In general terms the train service was similar to that at the neighbouring station, with one exception. Within a few miles of Rowsley stood Chatsworth House, Haddon Hall and Stanton Woodhouse, the residence of the Duke of Devonshire, the Duke of Rutland and the Marquess of Granby, respectively. As such the station was often an advance request stop for express trains, particularly to and from London and from time to time was host to even more important passengers, for members of the Royal Family were not infrequent visitors to Chatsworth.

Although only a small, rural community, Rowsley enjoyed a heavy local freight traffic, the tonnage of which is somewhat difficult to explain. There was a significant trade in livestock, the station ranking third in our area of study for this traffic, after Bakewell and Matlock. This may possibly be explained by the proximity of the large estates and their agricultural interests. The goods yard served Rowsley, Beeley, Northwood, Birchover, Stanton-in-Peak and Youlgreave, together with the large houses mentioned earlier. There was very little traffic in lime or limestone and the bulk of the coal class traffic comprised such fuel, the majority of which was for the domestic market. During the 1920s and 1930s the trade was dominated by Clay Cross Co. Ltd, E.A. Willgoose & Son and Derwent Valley Co-operative Society. The latter did not own any wagons, but may well have been responsible for bringing in the Butterley, Pentrich and Swanwick wagons which are recalled as being frequent visitors to the goods yard. E.A. Willgoose did operate his own wagons, but the author has been unable to trace any details other than that two

requiring assistance picked up a banker at the south junction, where engines stood just inside the permanent way yard, or a pilot engine at the north junction.

The yard could never have operated on the level it did without the modern engine shed. This was designed to accommodate 60 locomotives and was fully equipped with office, stores, fitters and mess accommodation. For the men it was almost like moving to a luxury hotel, compared with the old shed, (unless one had to walk from Chatsworth Road!). The depot was laid out such that engines could move to and from the yard without using the main line, and rapid turn round times were achieved daily. The shed had a small number of 4-4-0 passenger engines for the Bakewell and Darley Dale local workings, but was primarily a freight depot and while its allocation included a high proportion of ex-Midland and LMS 0-6-0 tender engines, many interesting visitors appeared regularly. These included ex-L&Y 'A' class 0-6-0s from Walton and Aintree plus ex-LNWR 0-8-0s from Speke Junction. In the late 1930s two of the surviving LNWR 'Claughtons', No. 5906 *Ralph Brocklebank* and No. 6023 *Sir Charles Cust* were frequent visitors. When they were introduced the Beyer-Garratts were tried on the line, but while they could climb easily enough they had insufficient brake power to hold trains back coming down the bank. They were, however, regular performers from Toton and Westhouses to Rowsley, and on the Hope Valley route through Chinley right up to their withdrawal in the mid 1950s. With the advent of modernisation diesels began to appear on the line and the first working from Rowsley was of 'Peak' No. D74, in the hands of Driver Tom House, on the 10.45pm class C freight to London on 11th September 1961. The engine then worked an express to Nottingham and a local passenger thence to Darley Dale, secondhand 8 ton vehicles were purchased from Birmingham R.C.&W. Co. in June 1912. In addition to the coal supplied by Tom Wright to Chatsworth House, some came direct from the collieries and Tinsley Park wagons were regularly seen on this duty.

General merchandise traffic was something of a mystery, for while the catchment population of the station was no more than 3,500-4,500, the volume of this traffic placed the station third after Matlock and Ambergate. The annual tonnage grew from 10,287 in 1872 to over 20,000 by 1912 and following the general fall during the war it had recovered to almost 14,000 tons by 1922, over 50% greater than that being dealt with at Buxton during the same year.

Among this traffic was that to and from Rowsley corn mill. This was owned by the Haddon Estate but had been run by Messrs Caudwell as a flour mill since about 1870. The original power was by an undershot waterwheel which was replaced by turbines around 1920. Apart from flour milling, considerable

quantities of maize and barley were ground principally for animal feedstuffs. Two drays were continuously at work carrying grain from the goods yard and returning with bagged produce which was despatched over a wide area, in both covered vans and sheeted open wagons. Today Caudwell's mill is a working museum.

For a period after World War I there was a heavy traffic in timber from the sawmills established by the Canadian Forestry Corps. In January 1919 the MR agreed to lay in sidings to serve these mills, as a joint venture with the Government, the latter paying for sleepers and crossing timbers and taking care of diverting a footpath which crossed the site. The Government must soon have lost interest in the project for in November 1920 the railway company was allowed to purchase the sidings for £150. The works were set up to help post war recovery and several hundred acres of hardwood, particularly oak, were cut from Lindup Wood and Lees Moor Wood, a mile or so to the north on the Chatsworth Estate. To reach this

Plate 150 (above) The LNWR Royal train is seen here arriving at Rowsley on Thursday 6th July 1933 on the occasion of the visit to Chatsworth by Their Majesties King George V and Queen Mary. The train worked wrong line into the station to obviate the need for the Royal party to pass through the subway. Hauled by 5XP 'Patriot', No. 5996, the train was made up as follows: 1st brake No. 10071, Saloon No. 10508, HM Queen's Saloon, HM King's Saloon, Dining Saloon No. 10400, Saloon No. 10507, Dining Saloon No. 10411 and 1st Brake No. 10070. Driver F.C. Bishop of Camden was in charge from Euston to Northampton where A.G. Tidsbury of Kentish Town took over. Fireman H. Banting worked throughout. The engine was serviced at Rowsley, where it received the personal attention of the foreman cleaner from Buxton.

(E.R. Morten)

Plate 151 (below) A Midland telegram from 12th September 1910 requesting that the 10.20am Manchester Central-St Pancras be stopped at Rowsley to pick up the Duke of Rutland.

(Author's Collection)

Plate 152 (right) A more mundane, but nevertheless important traffic, was the excursion train, for which promotional handbills were produced in a great variety of styles. This particular example from May 1891 shows the verbose style in vogue at the time.

(H.N. Twells Collection)

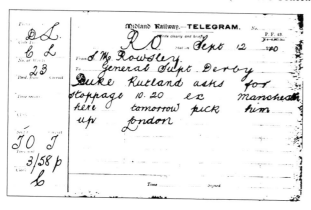

MIDLAND & LANCASHIRE & YORKSHIRE RAILWAYS.
COOK'S WHITSUNTIDE EXCURSIONS.
Manchester Miniature Volunteers' Camp of Instruction at Matlock Bridge. May 22 & 23.
ON WHIT FRIDAY AND SATURDAY
May 22 and 23, 1891,
COOK'S CHEAP EXCURSION TRAIN TO
ROWSLEY, MATLOCK,
DERBY & NOTTINGHAM

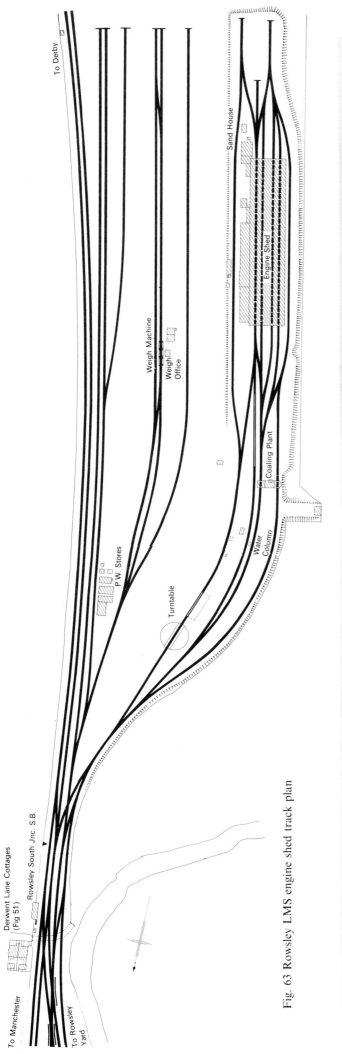

To Manchester

To Rowsley Yard

Derwent Lane Cottages (Fig 51)

Rowsley South Jnc. S.B.

To Derby

Weigh Machine

Weigh Office

P.W. Stores

Turntable

Water Column

Sand House

Coaling Plant

Engine Shed

Fig. 63 Rowsley LMS engine shed track plan

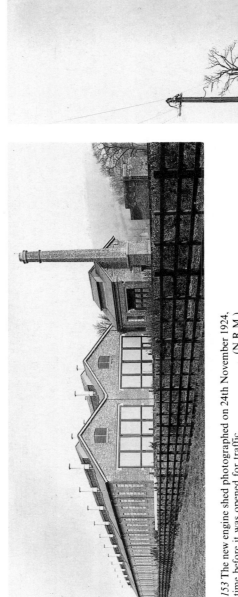

Plate 153 The new engine shed photographed on 24th November 1924, some time before it was opened for traffic. (N.R.M.)

Plate 154 The new coaling plant at Rowsley, brought into use about three months after the shed was opened, was a lightweight structure with little storage capacity. Coal was tipped into a pit and carried aloft by a small tub, for discharge direct into locomotive tenders. Control of the mechanism was from the ubiquitous asbestos lamp hut. (N.R.M.)

woodland a temporary bridge was built across the Derwent and a 2ft gauge light railway was built. After clearance the woods were replanted with conifers which were cut down, mainly for pit props, during World War II. Ralph Gregory, Darley Dale, was one of the timber merchants involved in this second cutting and it is interesting to note that during the war he paid £50 an acre for the timber, which fetches over £1,300 an acre today.

In terms of annual tonnage by far the most important traffic at Rowsley was stone, and no fewer than seven stone merchants were operating in the vicinity at the close of the Midland period. One of the earliest to take advantage of the railway was William Boden, for whom a siding was constructed in the goods yard in 1871. The business had passed to his son John J. Boden by the 1890s and he supplied many types of random building stone and self-faced, tooled or polished flags, together with a great variety of troughs, cisterns etc, from Birchover, Beeley Moor and New Stanton quarries. He also supplied alabaster, tufa, limestone and Derbyshire spar. In addition he produced millstones, described by a contemporary writer as "thoroughly even in temper, well-set, and altogether as perfect as it is possible to procure them". In addition to the stone trade this merchant used the railways to bring in coal, and by the turn of the century he had built up a sizeable business in this field.

Boden was soon joined in quarrying by Henry Deeley, who owned Burntwood Quarry to the east of Rowsley, Darley Dale quarries and Stanton Woodhouse Quarry. If anything his was a bigger concern and he operated his own railway wagons, but no details whatsoever regarding these vehicles have come to light. The main output of the quarries was again building stone, which was used, for example, in the Royal Arsenal, Woolwich; Prestwood Asylum; the MR arches into Manchester Central and the masonry of the Manchester Ship Canal. He also supplied considerable quantities of grindstones to the major steel processing areas of Yorkshire and the West Midlands.

After World War I the use of natural stone as a building material went into decline, as architectural tastes changed and rising labour costs forced developers to use more functional designs and cheaper materials. By the 1930s only three stone merchants, Messrs Ackroyd, Bond and Palmer retained private wharves at the goods yard, although a public wharf was still available. Annual traffic had fallen from around 26,000 tons at the turn of the century to well under 10,000 tons by the mid 1920s, but nevertheless eight cranes still stood in the yard in the 1930s.

Situated so close to Rowsley sidings the goods yard was serviced by daily trip workings.

Plate 155 (above) The down waiting shelter, erected in 1894, was a simple wooden structure on a brick base, with a standard open-fronted ridge and furrow awning. Short intermediate wooden partitions gave some protection from the wind.

(M.A. King)

Plate 156 (right) A Staff Association Raffle ticket sold on the occasion of the outing to Epsom on 5th June 1946.

(H. Wardman)

FOR MEMBERS ONLY.

THE DERBY SWEEPSTAKE

RUN WEDNESDAY, JUNE 5th, 1946.
ROWSLEY L.M.S. AREA STAFF OUTING.

— PRIZES VALUE —

1st—£20.   2nd—£10.   3rd—£5.

4th—£2.   Last Horse—£1/10/-

Other Runners—£1.

Promoters—Committee of the above.

Winners notified.

Tickets 6d. each.

Book of 22—10/-   N°. 90

Plate 157 (above) This general view looking south soon after the turn of the century, dominated by Copy Wood on the eastern slope of the Derwent Valley, shows the station and the roof of the engine shed on the left. The nameboard, which has white letters on an ultramarine blue background, is of particular interest as it appears to have a full stop after the name, a very unusual feature. Just beyond the down shelter lies the station signal box which was removed when the station and North Junction boxes were amalgamated and renewed in 1910. The station has the vertical-paled fencing which was expensive to maintain (it needed painting) and was eventually replaced by the now-familiar diagonal fencing.

(British Railways)

Plate 158 (right) Among the most popular cheap day excursions were trips to football matches as shown by this 1934 handbill for principal stations from Buxton to Derby.

(Author's Collection)

Plate 159 (below) This view of the station, taken during an SLS visit to the line in the mid 1960s, shows where one of the canopy columns on the up platform was removed to allow Royal visitors to walk straight from the carriage door to the station exit.

(W.A. Camwell)

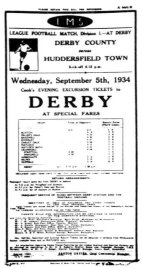

Chapter 12
Bakewell

Plate 160 (top) One of the most attractive bridges on the line was No. 45, Dukes Private Road bridge, carrying the line over the footpath from Rowsley to Calton Lees and Chatsworth. At the time of writing the structure was under threat of demolition due to lack of maintenance. Such action would be a serious setback to the proposed re-opening of the line.

(Author)

Plate 161 (above) Class 3F 0-6-0, No. 3612 climbs away from Rowsley with a mineral train for the Manchester area on 2nd July 1938. This engine was one of two 3Fs kept at Trafford Park specifically for the Rowsley freights. The splitting signal is the distant for Rowsley North Junction and by this time had been fitted with LMS upper quadrant arms.

(E.R. Morten)

Plate 162 (left) The southern portal of Haddon Tunnel.

(D. Ibbotson)

From Rowsley station the line continued its sharp curve to the west, on a low embankment, crossing Bakewell Road, the River Derwent for the last time, the bridle path to Calton Lees and the main street of Great Rowsley, all in under 400 yards. It then followed natural ground level for a short distance as it ran due west into the Wye Valley, assumed embankment once more, passed over Park Lane and then entered a long curve to the north towards Haddon Tunnel. It has already been noted that the Duke of Rutland laid down stringent conditions in granting permission for the railway to cross his land, the chief one being that the line should not be visible from Haddon Hall. Although part of the line was in true tunnel towards the centre, this was extended at either end by the 'cut and cover' principle. Despite the tragic collapse of the works during construction, on 2nd July 1861, when four men were instantaneously killed, with a fifth passing away on the following morning, the whole 1,050 yards were completed in 16 months.

Emerging from the tunnel the line curved northwards and passed Haddon signal box, which was opened on 15th December 1889, together with a down lie-by for 33 wagons, to break up the long section between Rowsley station and Bakewell station block posts. North of this point the route crossed Greaves bridge and passed through a shallow cutting before turning westwards on an embankment to cross Combs Lane Viaduct. This bridge, known locally as the 'Arches', carried the railway over the original road from Rowsley to Bakewell, which prior to the opening of what is now the A6, just after the Napoleonic wars, had passed north from Great Rowsley and through the valley below Manners Wood. From Combs Lane the railway kept to its westward curve across the

flanks of Calton Pastures, passed under Outrake bridge and turned north once more as it passed under Station Road bridge, No. 52, and arrived at Bakewell station, 14 miles and 38 chains from Ambergate West Junction.

Bakewell is thought to have been developed as a military outpost by Edward the Elder in the years around 920 AD and historians generally agree that a community of some local importance had grown up on the west bank of the Wye, by the time of the Norman Conquest. The earliest record of a market appears in 1254, with the granting of a weekly market and a fifteen day fair, to the Lord of the Manor, William Gernon. The granting of these rights and the construction of a bridge over the river about 1300 suggests that the settlement had by this time developed as an important focus of regional traffic in the southern Pennines. The construction of a bath house over the tepid chalybeate baths, by the Duke of Rutland in 1697, in an attempt to promote Bakewell as a spa town, the exploitation of marble and chert, and later the construction of various mills along the river had established the town as a market and commercial centre well before the railway arrived in 1863. By 1900 the population had grown to a little over 3,000 and today the town is the administrative, shopping and tourist heart of the Peak District National Park.

The original plans for a station at Bakewell were submitted to the Rowsley and Buxton Construction Committee on 5th February 1861 but these were rejected and the engineer was asked to submit a revised plan. This he did, on 4th December of that year when he submitted drawings for Rowsley, Bakewell and Buxton stations. Although it is minuted that the proposals were approved at that meeting further consideration must have been given to the matter, for in practice the final

decision on Buxton was deferred, while it was decided to use the Rowsley and Bakewell design for Hassop, the proposals for which had not previously been considered.

The MR must have been pleased with the workmanship on the station for a few months after it was completed, they appointed the same builder to erect goods sheds at both Bakewell and Hassop, at a cost of £500 each. Shortly after the line was opened a contract for the erection of three coal offices, which still stand just outside the station yard, was awarded to Wm Ward and this was followed in 1866 by the construction of a small stone wharf, which had been removed by the early 1920s. As the town grew so did goods traffic and alterations were made to the siding layout in 1866, 1870 and 1873, while both rail and road weighbridges and offices were built in 1882. The following year the shelter and urinals were built on the up platform behind the awning wall. Passenger facilities again came under scrutiny in 1892, when a contract was awarded to the Butterley Co. for the erection of a footbridge, prior to which passengers had used steps down from the road bridge. In November 1900 a petition was received from the residents of Bakewell requesting that the footbridge be covered. The company replied that although it could not agree to this the directors would look at the matter the next time they were in the district, but no action was ever taken.

It would appear that up to the turn of the century shunting of the yard involved the use of the down main line, but the growth of traffic finally rendered this intolerable and in 1904 land was purchased for the construction of a headshunt, which was put in soon afterwards. Early in 1907 improved accommodation was provided for the goods clerk by the construction of a wooden office on the southern end of the goods shed. Apart from repainting the station in the same year and again in 1912, together with the provision of a bathroom at the Station Master's house late in 1914, no further works were carried out at Bakewell until 1920, when five additional ground signals were installed in connection with renewal of the signal box, which was brought into use on 16th January 1921.

For longer distance journeys the station served Ashford, Bakewell, Baslow, Hassop, Over Haddon, Pilsley and Youlgreave and in terms of passenger traffic the station ranked fifth between Ambergate and Chinley. Annual passenger bookings rose from 34,395 in 1872, passed the 50,000 mark around 1900, finally reaching a peak of 70,126 in 1920. Two years later this figure had fallen to just under 47,500 which can only be attributed to the remarkable growth in competition from the new motor omnibus services then springing up. There was no longer any need to walk up Station hill for local services.

In the final years of MR ownership ten down and nine up trains called at Bakewell, of which five down were Manchester trains and three up were from Manchester to Derby. One up train started from Bakewell, for Derby, at 7.24am and was balanced by the 5.48pm return. At many stations on the line the service increased markedly under LMS control, but at Bakewell only three additional weekday trains had been added by 1935, all in the up direction. The early train to Derby, which had become known locally as the 'Joe Wright', after a long serving and popular guard, was retimed to leave at 7.32am and the through services became more equal with three trains in each direction between Derby and Manchester. The wartime cutbacks fell mainly on local services and Bakewell suffered severely, with the timetable decimated to five down and four up trains, of which three each way continued to run between Derby and Manchester. The morning local to Derby was retained but the 5.48pm return from Derby was extended to Chinley and a late train left Derby for Bakewell at 9.42pm. After the war services improved slightly and by 1954 six down and seven up trains called. Of the down trains three were Derby to Manchester and one was from Nottingham to Liverpool. In the up direction, three were Manchester to Derby, one Manchester–Nottingham and one Liverpool–Nottingham. The early train to Derby still ran but strangely the return was brought forward to 5.05pm, which would have been inconvenient for some office workers. This general pattern was retained up to closure, although by 1967 the Nottingham–Liverpool service had been cancelled and the evening train from Derby had been put back to 5.55pm.

As with the Matlocks many excursion trains ran to Bakewell, but nothing could compare with activity on 'Show Day'. The first Thursday after August Bank Holiday Monday marked the Bakewell Agricultural and Horticultural Show – sometimes referred to as the 'little Royal', which until it recently became a two day event was acknowledged as the largest one day show in England. Normal freight traffic was suspended and excursions arrived from Derby, Buxton, Ashby and Burton, Walsall and Wolverhampton, Manchester, Rotherham and Sheffield, Nottingham, Long Eaton, Hinckley

Plate 165 (above) This view from the signal box, about 1957, shows the general design of the station and the traditional MR track layout of trailing turnout and a single slip giving access to the yard. The pre-cast concrete cattle pens are a modern replacement for the original wooden type. The bus in the yard is one of the Sheffield Transport fleet and is waiting at the station prior to its return to Sheffield. No services were routed via the station but the yard provided ample parking space, which was very scarce in the town centre. It is understood that the station master's house, seen on the left, was a public house in the 1860s, with the rather strange name of the Three Flying Childers.

(British Railways)

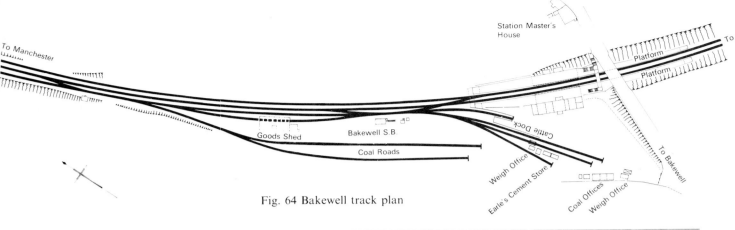

Fig. 64 Bakewell track plan

Plate 166 (above) The roadside elevation of the main building shows the symmetrical design, with the arched windows to the booking hall and the four plain openings either side. Taken after closure the view also shows coal merchants' stock delivered to the station by road!

(Author)

Plate 167 The railside of the building was dominated by the wall carried up as a parapet to form a basis for the awning. The two outer sections of the awning had been removed by the mid 1950s.

(British Railways)

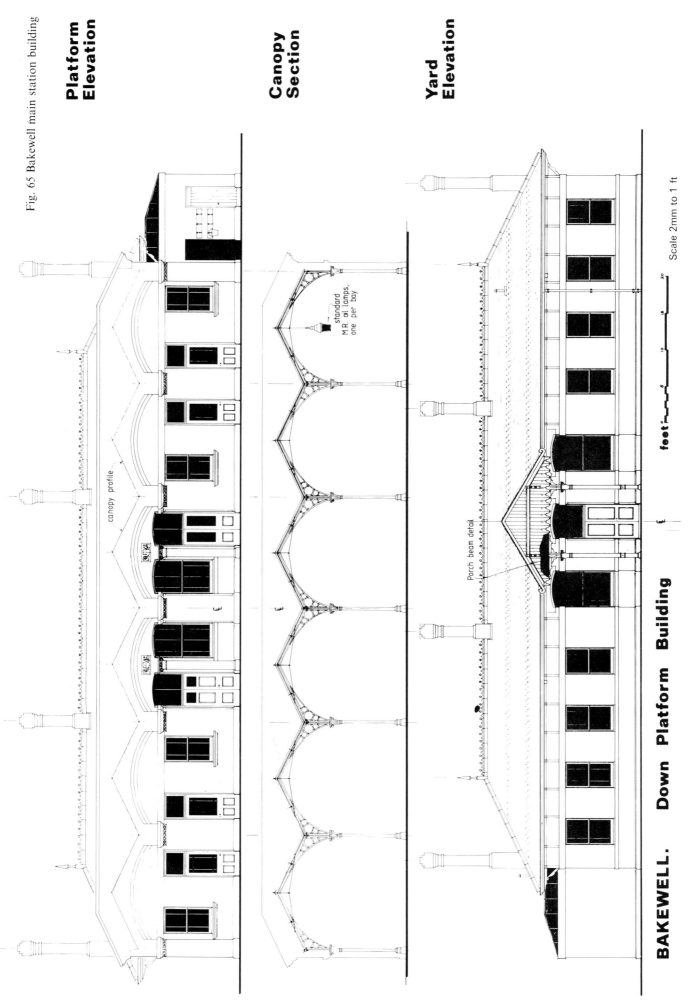

Fig. 65 Bakewell main station building

Platform Elevation

canopy profile

Canopy Section

standard M.R. oil lamps, one per bay.

Yard Elevation

Porch beam detail

BAKEWELL. Down Platform Building

feet 0 5 10 15 20

Scale 2mm to 1 ft

111

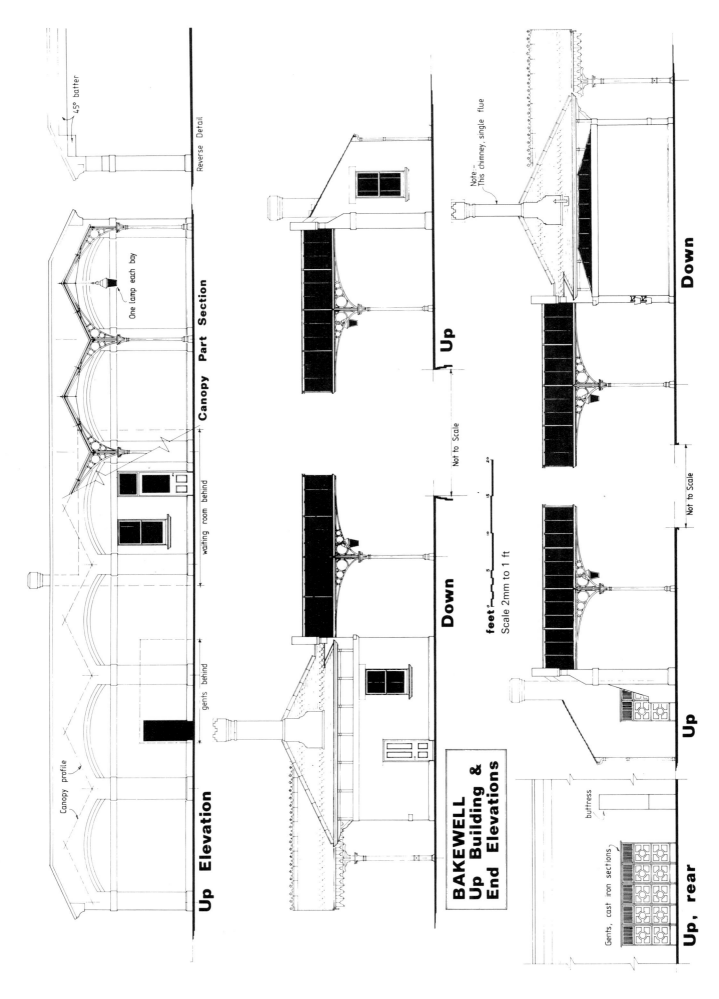

45° batter

Reverse Detail

One lamp each bay

Canopy Part Section

waiting room behind

gents behind

Canopy profile

Up Elevation

Down

Up

Not to Scale

feet 0 5 10 15 20

Scale 2mm to 1 ft

Note –
This chimney, single flue

Down

Not to Scale

Up

buttress

Gents, cast iron sections

Up, rear

BAKEWELL
Up Building &
End Elevations

112

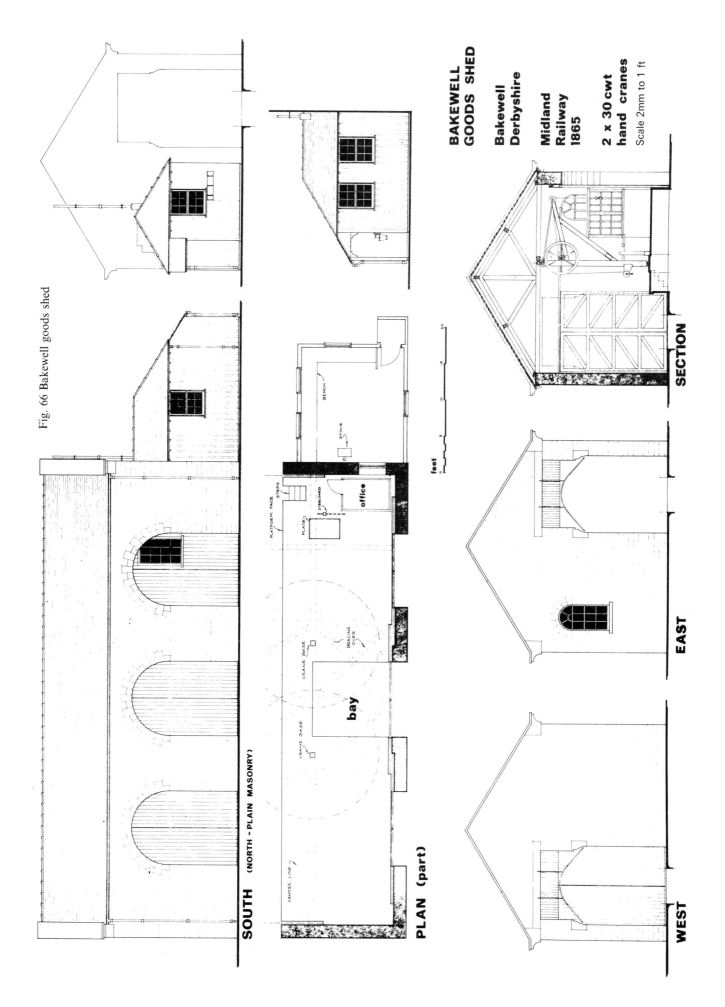

Fig. 66 Bakewell goods shed

SOUTH (NORTH - PLAIN MASONRY)

PLAN (part)

BAKEWELL
GOODS SHED

Bakewell
Derbyshire

Midland
Railway
1865

2 x 30 cwt
hand cranes

Scale 2mm to 1 ft

SECTION

EAST

WEST

feet

CENTRE LINE

PLATFORM FACE

STEPS

STANDARD

PLATE

CRANE BASE

CRANE BASE

BRACING OVER

bay

office

STOVE

BENCH

Fig. 67 Bakewell road weigh office

YARD OFFICES

**Bakewell Station
Derbyshire**

**Midland Railway
1865**

Scale 2mm to 1 ft

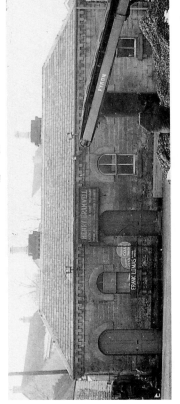

Plate 170 (above) The coal offices. This basic design was used again at Hassop, Millers Dale and Buxton.

(Author)

Fig. 68 Bakewell coal offices

Plate 168 (above) The goods shed was built in 1863 at a cost of £500, including the crane. The timber office was added in 1907/8.

(Author)

Plate 169 (above right) The road weigh office, built in 1882.

(Author)

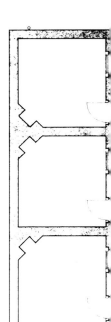

Fig. 69 Bakewell rail weigh office

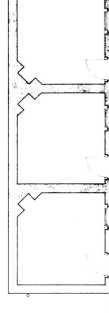

114

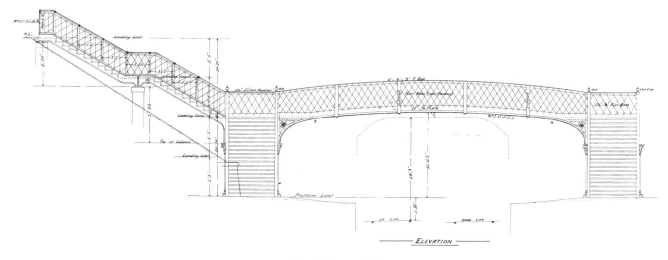

Scale 2mm to 1 ft

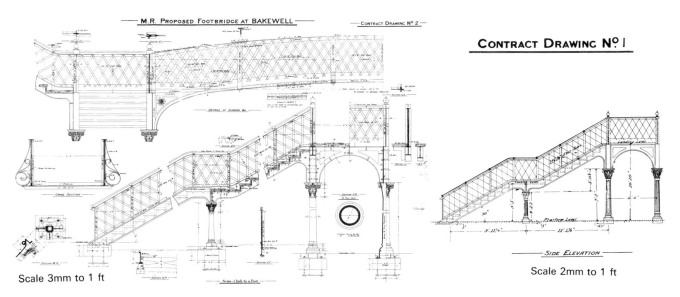

M.R. PROPOSED FOOTBRIDGE AT BAKEWELL · CONTRACT DRAWING Nº 2

CONTRACT DRAWING Nº 1

Scale 3mm to 1 ft

Scale 2mm to 1 ft

Fig. 70 Bakewell station footbridge

Plate 171 (below) The footbridge was built by the Butterley Company in 1892, some seven years after they erected the one at Cromford *(plate 55)*. With normal steps the top landing at Bakewell was much higher and therefore the arch was flatter. It was also less wide and only had four stanchions. The bridge also had an interesting extension up to the road bridge, but as few passengers came from this direction the extension was primarily an access from the station master's house. The bridge was raised in 1961, by lifting the central span about 12in, as part of a general policy in anticipation of electrification.

(Author)

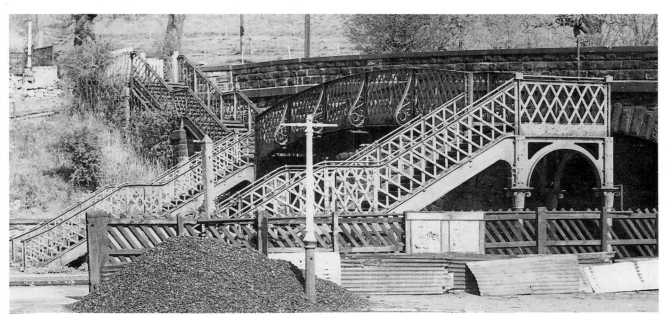

and Leicester, Worksop and Mansfield. This was in addition to those who arrived by ordinary services. Carriage stock had to be recessed at convenient locations including Buxton, Chaddesden carriage sidings, Millers Dale, Peak Forest, Great Rocks up and down lie-bys, Chinley, Monsal Dale, Hassop, Peak Forest Junction and Bakewell. In 1959, for example, some 13 freight trains were cancelled but additional guard's duties occurred at Rowsley (4), Leicester (4), Sheffield (1), Buxton (2), Mansfield (3), Nottingham (4), Chaddesden (3) and Ashton Road (2). Some idea of loadings can be be gleaned from the 10.20am ordinary ex-Nottingham/Derby (300 alighting), 10.28am special ex-Derby (330) and 10.40am special ex-Nottingham (573). High ranking railway officials, inspectors and additional staff arrived – in effect the Derby Control moved to Bakewell for the day. Even as late as 1966 a handful of specials arrived at Bakewell for the Show. Now the motorist is invited to park his car at Hassop and proceed not by railway to the show, but on a bus.

The station was one of the locations where the LMS provided holiday facilities in the shape of 'Caravan Coaches'. These were introduced in 1934, at a time when the camping holiday was growing in popularity and the venture was aimed

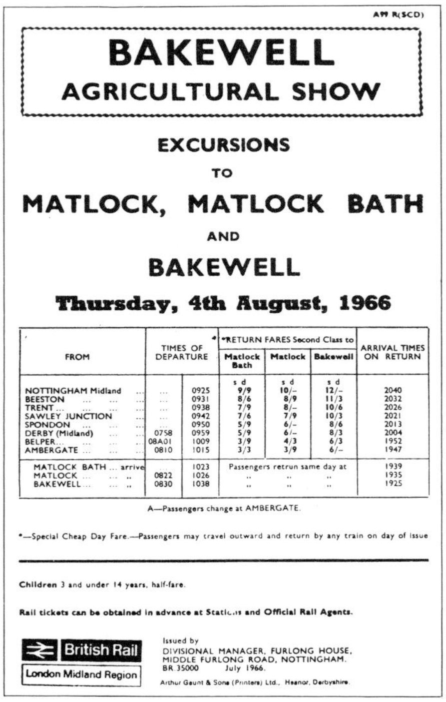
A99 R(SCD)

BAKEWELL
AGRICULTURAL SHOW

EXCURSIONS
TO
MATLOCK, MATLOCK BATH
AND
BAKEWELL

Thursday, 4th August, 1966

FROM	TIMES OF DEPARTURE		*RETURN FARES Second Class to Matlock Bath	Matlock	Bakewell	ARRIVAL TIMES ON RETURN
			s d	s d	s d	
NOTTINGHAM Midland ...	...	0925	9/9	10/–	12/–	2040
BEESTON	...	0931	8/6	8/9	11/3	2032
TRENT	...	0938	7/9	8/–	10/6	2026
SAWLEY JUNCTION ...	...	0942	7/6	7/9	10/3	2021
SPONDON	...	0950	5/9	6/–	8/6	2013
DERBY (Midland)	0758	0959	5/9	6/–	8/3	2004
BELPER...	08A01	1009	3/9	4/3	6/3	1952
AMBERGATE	0810	1015	3/3	3/9	6/–	1947
MATLOCK BATH ... arrive	...	1023	Passengers retrun same day at			1939
MATLOCK	0822	1026	..	..	..	1935
BAKEWELL	0830	1038	..	..	..	1925

A—Passengers change at AMBERGATE.

*—Special Cheap Day Fare.—Passengers may travel outward and return by any train on day of issue

Children 3 and under 14 years, half-fare.

Rail tickets can be obtained in advance at Stations and Official Rail Agents.

British Rail
London Midland Region

Issued by
DIVISIONAL MANAGER, FURLONG HOUSE,
MIDDLE FURLONG ROAD, NOTTINGHAM.
BR 35000 July 1966.

Arthur Gaunt & Sons (Printers) Ltd., Heanor, Derbyshire.

Plate 172 (Author's Collection)

at increasing traffic to and from the locations of the coaches. It was a condition of booking that users must travel to the site by rail, thus ensuring that should they then wish to tour the district, they would be most likely to use the train. In 1939 the vehicles were re-named 'Camping Coaches', and although not available during the war they were re-introduced soon afterwards. The coach at Bakewell, an ex L&Y vehicle, remained in use at least up to 1965, by which time the weekly rental in August had risen from the 1934 figure of £3 10s (£3.50) to £12 10s (£12.50), still quite a bargain! By this time, however, some members of the group taking up the bookings would arrive by road!

Day to day freight traffic was, with one exception, not quite so heavy as some of the stations we have passed through, but it was just as varied. The exception was livestock traffic which grew from 226 truck loads in 1872 to over 700 loads in 1902. During the war years the annual traffic averaged 968 trucks and it was not until the 1920s that the traffic began to decline slowly. These figures may have been influenced by the Show, but bearing in mind that most activity would be related to the weekly cattle market, it is easy to accept a former Rowsley driver's statement that "we shunted cattle wagons all day on a Monday at Bakewell". Indeed the 7.15pm cattle train to Rowsley would leave any time between 9.00pm and midnight! Related to this cattle traffic was a small shavings store near the weighbridge. It was like a small barn, with four corner posts and a roof. There were a couple of planks on edge round the base, and the shavings, which were kept in sacks, were sold to the hirers of cattle wagons, at 1s (5p) per sack.

Although a little limestone was once extracted to the west, the bulk of the tonnage shown in the coal class was indeed coal and coke, for both industrial and domestic consumers. While some of this fuel would have been used at the various mills and quarries, for heating and other processes, the dominant industrial user would have been the gas works.

Bakewell Gaslight Company was set up in 1850 on a site about 3/4 mile from the town centre adjacent to the cotton mill, on the Buxton road. Prior to the opening of the railway in 1863, coal was carted by road from Rowsley. In the early years this came from a number of small collieries in the Chesterfield area, with a small amount of cannel coal from Dukinfield Colliery, near Hyde. From the late 1870s the supply became increasingly dominated by the Sheepbridge Coal and Iron Co, who were supplying some 1,000 tons per annum, or 3–5 wagon loads per week, by the mid 1890s. In the summer of 1898 the works were purchased by the Urban District Council which immediately made a contract with John Brown and Co. to supply coal for twelve months. For the next ten years or so supplies were obtained from Browns' together with Clay Cross Co., Grassmoor Colliery Co., Nunnery Colliery Co., Rothervalve Colliery Co., J. & G. Wells Ltd. and Tom Wright. Occasional small amounts were supplied by Evesons Ltd. and Frank Lomas. In 1911 contracts were made with John Brown (500 tons), J. & G. Wells (500 tons) and Tom Wright (500 tons coal, 200 tons cannel). The latter was most likely Tinsley Park screened gas coal and Swanwick cannel. There was little change in this pattern up to 1920/21 in which period Wilson, Carter and Pearson, the Birmingham coal factors, became briefly involved. Tom Wright and J. & G. Wells shared the market up to 1924, when the former was replaced by John Brown & Co., these two companies then dominating the coal supply until the works were taken over by the Sheffield Gas Company in July 1935.

Although nominally out of context it is interesting to note that from time to time the Council purchased supplies of granite, presumably for highway purposes. For example in 1919 it ordered 300 tons each from Cliff Hill Granite Co., Groby Granite Co., and Penmaenmawr Granite Co. This would have brought 40-45 wagons from each company into the station yard.

A second major industrial consumer, at least in the early years was Magpie Lead Mine at Sheldon, a little under three miles west of Bakewell. The surface buildings were some 650ft above Bakewell Bridge and this was the height through which the coal had to be lifted by horse and cart. Chain horses were required all the way, there being only a few short 'easy' stretches en route.

Water was always a problem in the mine and although being drained by a 40in Cornish engine it closed in 1846, only to be re-opened in 1868 when a 70in Cornish engine replaced the earlier one. The period of peak coal demand was the years 1868-72, immediately prior to the driving of the Magpie sough, before which all water had to be lifted approximately 700ft to the surface. It was said of the pumping engine that it required up to 300 tons of coal monthly, all being brought to Bakewell station. It was reputed that a year's supply cost £1,432, with a further £509 for carriage. Taking into account that there was also a small steam winding engine, with its own boiler, the annual demand for coal at that time must have approached 4,000 tons.

Following completion of the sough in 1881, the coal requirements fell markedly, as water then had to be lifted only some 200ft to sough level. Thenceforth demand for coal fluctuated with the fortunes of the mine, but significant amounts continued to be required intermittently until 1919. The surface ruins of Magpie Mine remain having been made safe and are an important monument to industrial archaeology.

According to Kelly's Directory of 1881 the coal trade at Bakewell was in the hands of George Buchan, who was also described as wood agent to the Duke of Rutland; Frederick

Swallow and George Waine. In 1889 the Bakewell Almanack had an interesting advertisement for R.W. Allsop, coal merchant and colliery agent, seven collieries in the Swanwick, Butterley and Alfreton areas being mentioned. This company had its head office in Sheffield and by 1897 at least the Bakewell part of the business had been taken over by Alfred Foster.

The coal trade at Bakewell was later dominated by Frank Lomas and Henry Bramwell, both of whom operated their own wagons. The former business began on 1st January 1889, when Edward Lomas who died in 1893, purchased the interests of Mr Buchan and set up his trade in the easterly of the three coal offices at Bakewell. The company passed to Frank Lomas, whose name was originally shown by a small brass plate with black letters. This plate was moved to Millers Dale about 1926/27 when an office was opened there and was replaced at Bakewell by a very large enamelled board in dark blue, with white letters, as shown in *fig. 68*. Frank Lomas owned four wagons, two of which, Nos 1 and 2, were built by the Midland Wagon Co. in 1898 and were broken up in 1948 and 1947 respectively. They were almost certainly five plank vehicles with rounded ends, 15 x 7ft 5in x 3ft, with side doors only, painted light grey with yellow letters, shaded black. During the 1920s the business became Frank Lomas and Sons, but it is believed that the wagon livery remained unchanged. The author is unaware of any photographs of these wagons but *fig. 71* has been prepared from descriptions given by the present Frank Lomas.

Henry Bramwell, who occupied the middle office, is believed to have started in business selling coal for Messrs N. Wheatcroft & Son, Cromford. When they pulled out of the trade at Bakewell in April 1901, he set up in business on his own and put up the large sign shown in *fig. 68*. This had a bright green background (very similar to LNER apple green), with gold letters, shaded black. It is understood that Henry initially owned two wagons, painted dark red, with white letters shaded black. *fig. 72* shows the livery as ascertained from an extremely oblique photograph. During the 1940s the business was taken over by Arthur H. Bramwell, Henry's son, the words 'Prop. A. H. Bramwell' being added to the sign about 1950.

Alfred Foster gave up the third office to Wheatcroft's in August 1899, and this later passed to H.C. Rackstraw of Matlock. He is believed to have ceased trading in the early 1930s and as far as is known he never operated his own wagons. About 1925 Harry Hough started up as a coal merchant in partnership with Wm Upton of Ashford and built a small wooden hut adjacent to the coal offices. He appears to have begun in a big way with his own railway wagons and a

Ford 1 ton lorry, but it is rumoured that he was not regarded as a progressive businessman and he appears to have suffered during the depression years of the early 1930s. Certainly by 1933 the R.C.H. no longer listed him as a private wagon owner. The LMS rating plan, circa 1932, shows Hough's office under the name of R.W. Tofts but this is something of a mystery, for Frank Lomas is adamant that there never was a coal merchant by this name. It is possible that the name was related to W.N. Toft Ltd, the Derby colliery agents, who may have put some finance into Hough's business, but this is not certain. It is known however, that Harry Hough went out of business about 1939.

Frank Lomas operated three horses and carts, and a horse and dray. The latter was a platform dray, without a tailboard, very similar to the standard MR vehicle of the time. It was painted dark green, with red shafts, the wheels being lined out in red and yellow. The carts had grey bodies with red shafts, wheels and top boards. One had top boards twice the height of those on the other carts and carried the firm's name in large black letters on this board. This was used extensively to carry coke from the gas works. Under the Road Transport Order, 1918 carts and drays had to be registered and have their numbers painted on. Frank Lomas's numbers were HDBY 1880/1/2/3/4, for three carts and one dray, all 15-30cwt payload.

By 1927 F. Lomas had acquired a new Overland lorry, built by Willys Overland Crossley, Heaton Chapel, Stockport, using mainly imported parts from Willys Overland, Toledo, Ohio. This was replaced in 1937 by a Bedford 30cwt lorry and a second Bedford was purchased in 1939, at which time the company ceased to use horse transport. All the lorries were painted blue.

Henry Bramwell never owned carts. Before he bought his first lorry all his cartage was done by private contractors. One of these, Bob Hage, had stables opposite the station gates and ran a horse bus service to Sheffield on Tuesdays, Thursdays and Saturdays, leaving the Anchor Inn (now demolished) at 8.00am and arriving back about 8.00pm. Henry's first lorry was a 30cwt, 6-cylinder Chevrolet, painted bright red, acquired about 1930. This was replaced by a 2 ton Bedford in 1937, also painted red. Robert Bramwell, Henry's brother, was also a coal merchant, buying his coal from Henry and using his own dray for delivery. This was green round the edge with a green tailboard bearing his name and red axles, wheels and shafts. He had no office at the station and gave up his round in 1939. His customers were taken over by Henry and although the horse was sold shortly afterwards, the dray stood for many years in the goods yard.

Dark blue enamel, white letters

Pre 1950 bright green, gold letters black shading

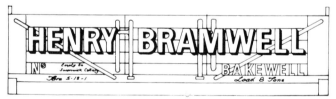

Fig. 72

H. Bramwell wagon livery

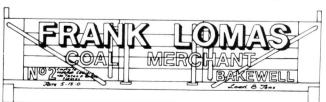

Post 1950 black, plain gold letters

Black letters, on brass plate

Plate 173 A pre-war advertisement which appeared for many years in the Bakewell Advertiser, a local trade journal.

(Author's Collection)

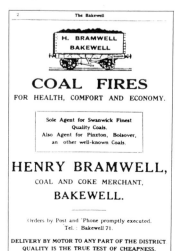

Fig. 71 The small lettering on the left reads "Empty to Watnall Colliery via Toton or Brent Sidings." The latter were included as wagons were sometimes consigned to the representative of the DP Battery Co. at Haywards Heath.

(Author)

During the 1930s several other coal businesses operated at the yard. The Bakewell & District Co-operative Society began trading in coal about 1934/35, using a secondhand 25cwt Morris Commercial lorry, painted light green. C.H. Wilkson traded up to 1939, finishing when wartime regulations required customers to register with their merchant. He operated a dark green Morris Commercial. Finally, Joseph Oldfield, a farmer from Over Haddon, ran a part time business, using a horse and dray. He would buy about 15 bags of coal at a time (that was as much as his horse could drag up the steep hill to Over Haddon) from F. Lomas & Son, for re-sale around the village. One of Joe's sons was the late Sir Maurice Oldfield, GCMG, CBE, who became head of MI6 about 1973.

With the demise of Harry Hough and Charlie Wilkson this left F. Lomas & Sons, Henry Bramwell and Bakewell Co-op to soldier on through the war years and beyond. The war brought tremendous difficulties – registration of customers, shortages of labour, spare parts for vehicles etc, etc, but there was a spirit of co-operation between the firms. They would help one another out with coal when supplies were delayed and with deliveries. The Co-op ceased trading about 1948/50, leaving Lomas and Bramwell to continue to the end of the line, by which time F. Lomas was operating three 'Thames' lorries. When freight facilities were withdrawn from Hassop on 5th October 1964, the remaining coal merchants moved down to Bakewell yard. During the final years coal was brought in by road and tipped in the yard *(plate 166)*, until all coal trading ceased at Bakewell station in the early 1970s, preparatory to the station area becoming an industrial estate.

In terms of volume merchandise traffic generally followed the pattern of other stations on the line, climbing to a peak in the early years of the century and declining somewhat after World War I, as road haulage expanded. With something in the order of 50 shops or businesses in the town in the 1920s a little over 11,000 tons of general goods passed through the yard annually, representing 12-14 wagons each weekday. These would have carried almost every conceivable item of food, furniture, building materials, animal feedstuffs, fertilizers, ironmongery etc, in every manner of packing cases, packages, tins, boxes, cartons, tubs and barrels. The latter would have included beer and it is interesting to note that the Devonshire at Sheldon, some 3½ miles from the station, received all its supplies by rail, at least up to 1939.

In addition to this general merchandise was traffic to and from the D.P. Battery works. This company was set up at Lumford Mill in premises originally built by Arkwright as a spinning mill about 1778/9. Rebuilt after a serious fire in 1868 the premises remained as a cotton spinning mill, using the railway for the carriage of both raw cotton and spun yarn, until shortly before the battery company took over in 1898. Among the more obvious traffic into the works was lead and acid, which up to the mid 1920s was delivered from the station by the railway company, who brought back finished batteries for despatch. About 1925, however, the battery company introduced their own vehicle, a battery-electric lorry, with a small rectangular cab and solid tyres. It was painted khaki-grey and had the letters 'D.P.' in black, below the windscreen. When this vehicle was introduced two of the three drays then being operated by the LMS were withdrawn. The lorry lasted until the early 1930s and shortly after it was taken off the road the LMS brought in its first motor vehicle. This was a 'cab-over engine' Karrier GH5, with a frontal nearside door. It was replaced about 1942 by a Guy Vix-Ant 4 tonner – a wartime design with a very low cab. It was said locally that the LMS had changed the lorry to make Charlie Gedney, the permanent driver, less vulnerable to low flying aircraft! The war brought extra traffic and it was not long before Bakewell had two additional railway lorries. One was an old 2 ton AEC. The other was a Dennis 30cwt, with single rear wheels, which was driven by Jessica, a local woman remembered for her good looks and smart appearance. After the war things returned to 'normal' with just Charlie and the Guy, which was finally replaced by a Ford Thames in the late 1950s. Despite protests from the driver, the old Guy was curiously lettered LMS until withdrawal.

It is worth recording that by the mid 1960s lead was received in batches of up to 10 to 15 wagons from Liverpool – extra handling staff and road motors being specially sent from St Mary's goods station at Derby to assist.

Mineral traffic, while relatively light in annual tonnage, was nevertheless most interesting. In the 18th and 19th centuries the extraction of marble from quarries near Ashford was an important local industry. The stone was processed at mills in both Ashford and Bakewell for a wide variety of internal building purposes and to produce table tops, statues, vases etc. Much of this material would have been sent out by rail, but around the turn of the century interest declined and

Plate 174 This view, taken on 4th April 1940, shows two submarine batteries from the Dujardin-Planté battery works, loaded for dispatch on a 12 ton one plank wagon. This wagon was built on 20th May 1938 as one of a batch of 1,000 to Diagram 1986, numbered 460000–460999.

(N.R.M.)

Plate 175 Around the turn of the century major renovation works were carried out on the Parish Church and this view shows a special train of GW bolster wagons from Oxford, carrying oak for the main roof timbers. It also shows the labour-intensive nature of the railways at this time.

(M.L. Knighton Collection)

competition from cheaper materials had an adverse effect. The marble works at Ashford were opened in 1748 by Henry Watson who invented the process of, and constructed the wooden machinery for, cutting and polishing marble by water power. These works at Ashford closed in 1905.

When the railway arrived in Bakewell the Wye Marble Works, near Bakewell Bridge, had been run for some years by John Lomas & Sons. John had died in 1853 and the business was being run by his sons, one of whom was Edward, the future coal merchant. During the early 1880s the business was sold to Mr Francis Norman, who then formed a partnership with Mr C.F. Groom. By 1890 Cecil Groom had come to dominate the business and was described as sculptor, builder, contractor and timber merchant. He installed the most up-to-date saws, lathes, planing machines etc, all water powered, and considerable quantities of prepared woodwork, stone and marble were dispatched to all parts of the country by rail and canal. In addition to working local material Groom imported large quantities of Belgian, Irish and Italian marble, which would have arrived at the station in large blocks, loaded in low sided wagons. He also carried immense stocks of the best English and Foreign timbers, much of which would again have arrived by rail, both as tree trunks and sawn timber.

Around the turn of the century marble working faded away, but the remainder of the business continued to prosper, being acquired later by Robert Smith, and operated primarily as Rutland Sawmills, although some general building work was continued.

A further interesting mineral was chert, a hard silicious flint-like material found locally in the higher beds of the limestone outcrops. In pottery manufacture calcined flint was ground, for combination with clay as a whitening agent. Up to the early 1770s granite stones were used for this grinding, but these gave rise to impurities in the finished product and in April 1772 Josiah Wedgwood recommended that Derbyshire chert be used in place of granite. His trials were successful and large quantities of chert were moved to the Potteries, initially by pack horse throughout, later by canal from Cromford, then by rail from Rowsley where it was sold at 15s (75p) per ton delivered in 1851, and finally by rail from Bakewell. Holme Bank Quarry, situated just across the river from Lumford Mill, was the original source of the material, with Pretoria Quarry being opened to the west of the town on the Monyash road, in the early 1900s. Both sites were worked by underground

mining and remained in operation until the 1960s, by which time road transport had taken over. Prior to this the stone was brought to the station yard where the blocks were laid out in rows along the sidings for inspection by prospective buyers. It was then loaded into wagons using a portable hand crane.

In addition to the foregoing freight traffic there was a steady traffic in cement and two ex-MR van bodies, raised on stilts were used by Messrs Earles as a store. About 1910 the Anglo-American Oil Co. set up a depot in the yard comprising three oil tanks, two being 30ft x 9ft and one 20ft x 9ft, a pumphouse and office 20ft x 9ft and a spirit store 10ft x 6ft, with a capacity limited by the MR, to 200 gallons. One of the large oil tanks was removed in June 1920 and during the 1930s three small paraffin tanks, surrounded by a brick wall, were added to the depot. Tank wagons were run down to the end of the coal sidings from where the various products were pumped by hand into the storage tanks.

During the 1930s the yard was serviced by the 10.52am stopping freight Rowsley to Hassop and the 2.00pm return working from Hassop. This was later changed to 7.20am departure from Rowsley, returning to call at Bakewell between 11.30am and 12.30pm. Some traffic was also picked up in the 1930s by the 6.50pm empty mineral from Buxton to Rowsley.

No account of the railway at Bakewell would be complete without some reference to the Rutland bus. This was part and parcel of the Rutland Arms Hotel concern and was based in the Rutland stable yard opposite the hotel, where the Midland and later the LMS had its parcels receiving office. It operated under hackney licence, being authorised to carry eight passengers and functioned like a taxi conveying passengers, luggage and parcels to and from the station where it met all trains. The exact date of its introduction, to replace an old horse bus, is uncertain but the bus of the early 1930s was a 4-cylinder Chevrolet driven by Bill Peters. It had a standard 20 seater type bus body, painted dark blue below the waist and white above. This vehicle was replaced in 1936 by a new one with purpose built body, again dark blue lower half, but cream upper half, mounted on a Bedford 30 cwt chassis. It had a front passenger entrance, with driver-operated door and double doors at the rear. Inside, there were wooden slatted seats part way along each side, the rest of the space being available for luggage and parcels. Above the windscreen, in 'gold' letters was painted 'TOWN AND STATION' and on the rear doors 'LMS PARCELS'. Although pleasing in appearance, it is said that the ride was comparable to that experienced in a Bedford 'QL', the army troop carrier.

Writing of it in his book *Derbyshire* (Robert Hale, 1950), Crichton Porteous says: "At the station the town bus was just about to start, so we scrambled on and clung to the edges of the wooden seats while the vehicle swerved and throbbed violently downhill. We were surprised at how quickly we got to the town, not because of our speed, but because of the shortness of the distance. It must be a profitable service".

The Rutland Hotel also ran a taxi, for hotel patrons only. This was a large pre-war Austin saloon, in a very nice green and black (all wings and above the waist), which was always immaculately turned out. If the bus was off the road for any reason the taxi would stand in. The bus stopped running sometime after the last war and the driver, the late Jack Gannon went to work in the 'tap room', officially called The Rutland Snack Bar, but better known among the locals as the 'Blood tub' – but that is another story altogether.

Railway enthusiasts and historians in general, are fortunate that a number of records have survived from Bakewell which give a fascinating insight into the equipment and operation of a medium size station at the close of the Midland era. At that time the staff appears to have comprised the Station Master, two booking clerks, five parcel porters, seven goods porters, three goods clerks, and a goods checker, together with the draymen and signalmen. Although no goods were collected or delivered on Sundays the draymen had an eight hour shift, at time and one half pay, in which they had to attend to their horses, clean the harnesses and messrooms and sweep up the

goods yard. There was also a two hour late duty on Saturdays to feed, water and bed down the horses. The work at the station was complex and the daily workload of the staff would cause a raised eyebrow or two among much of today's workforce. For example, the duties of the Senior Porter No. 1 can be summarised as follows:-

Early turn, on duty 6.40am
Open station and fetch in signal lamps (after daylight during winter months). Light fires in offices and rooms and couple up engine to coach of 7.24am, lighting up same when necessary. Black lead Booking Office grate once weekly.
Breakfast 7.40am to 8.10am.
Load horses and cattle and attach to trains, also attend to any vehicles detached, up to 12.30pm when late turn station porter comes on duty. After departure of 8.27am swill out urinals, brushing slates daily and go round and clean all WCs, dusting seats and mopping out pans when necessary.
Dinner 12.00pm to 1.00pm
The sweeping of platforms, up and down (except under awnings, which is done daily by parcels porter) must be done twice weekly, also the overbridge, assisted by late turn station porter. Attend to all fires and clean hearths after 1.30pm. Dust pictures in waiting rooms, chop firewood for next day's fires and riddle ashes. Assist to clean Booking Hall floor on Thursdays and up General Waiting Room on Fridays.
Off duty 4.10pm
Other porters had to deal with passengers, parcels, bill posting, cleaning windows and paintwork, polishing brasswork, trimming and filling lamps, taking messages etc.

Plate 176 The small engine policy of the MR remained much in evidence on the Manchester line until the 5XP 'Jubilees' were rostered onto the principal expressed in 1938. Here Johnson 483 class 4-4-0 pilots a Compound 4-4-0 through Bakewell with the 12.20pm Manchester Central-St Pancras express in June 1934. It is interesting to note that the finials have been removed from the signal box roof.
(E.R. Morten)

To carry out the running and administration of the station required no less than 545 different labels, forms, notices, envelopes, books and ledgers etc. In addition the following items were stocked at all times.

Indelible Stamping Ink, Slate Pencils, Penholders.
Drayman's Pen, Pens Nos 5,6,7,8,652,653 and 0505.
Tie on labels for stamped packages.
Agents blue envelopes, small and medium.
Buff envelopes, small, foolscap and largest size.
Tissue paper for copies.
Ink erasers, India rubbers.
Brown paper, small and large sheets.
Blotting paper, absorbing paper, oil paper.
Blue, black, red and French ink.
Pencils: Victoria copying, blacklead, HB, Civil Service blue, red and hard black.
Black checking and blue checking.
Single and double letter paper, single note paper
Sanitary paper.
Telegraph message carbon paper: waybill, memorandum, large memorandum, note paper, single letter, stores requisition, goods invoice, excess returns.
Brushes: carriage cleaning, sweeping, sweeping platforms, hand, yard, whitewash (flat and round), button, blacklead polishing, black lead round, scrubbing, damping, gum, paste.
Sealing wax, black lead.
Chalk, sponge cloths, dusters.
Cotton wool, lint, safety pins, splints.

Bandages: ambulance 1in, 2in, 3in, triangular.
Firewood, flags, floor flannel.
Glasses: lamp and platform.
Ink pots and glasses.
Grease knives, mops, needles, pins, pipe clay, paste.
Rape oil, harness oil, machine oil.
Nails: cut, rose and wire.
Pumice and emery powder.
Shunting poles (hickory and ash).
Disinfecting powder.
Metal polish, ambulance plaster and white rags.
Medium and thick string.
Large and small handled, loading, cask and roller sprags.
Hard and soft soap, soda, sal volatile and smelling salts.
Cattle pen scrapers.
Flag sticks: 3ft6in signal box, 2ft goods guards 1ft6in passenger guards.
Brush stails, Jacko, twine, ambulance thread.
Tapes for dating press, turpentine, whitening.
Lamp wicks, (Platform 7/8in and 1/2in, signal lamp 3/8in long burning and hand lamp).
Wash leathers, spikes 6in for securing scotches.
Spirits of salts.

Today just a hint of this atmosphere can be experienced at Bakewell, where the main building has been restored, minus awning, under the watchful eye of M.L. Knighton, a local councillor, former Mayor, and member of the Bakewell Historical and Civic Societies.

Plate 177 A 3-car Craven's dmu pauses with a Derby-Manchester local in July 1966. In a moment of quiet reflection one should compare this view with *plate 164* and perhaps wonder what the station master of the time would have thought of this dismal view.

(L.A. Nixon)

Chapter 13

Hassop

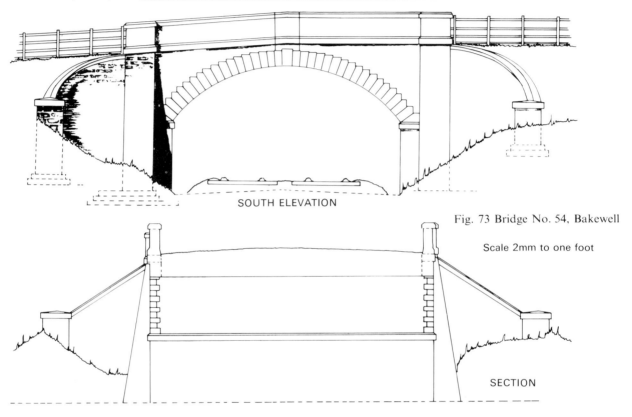

Plate 178 Bridge No. 54, Pine-apple bridge, looking north on 24th February 1985.

(Author)

SOUTH ELEVATION

Fig. 73 Bridge No. 54, Bakewell

Scale 2mm to one foot

SECTION

From Bakewell station the line ran generally northwards, curving east and then westwards on a low embankment, where it crossed two occupation bridges, Higginbotham's bridge and Pauper's bridge, before running into a shallow cutting and passing under the Baslow road at Pineapple bridge. From here the line kept more or less to natural ground level as it again curved east and then west into Hassop station, 15 miles 39 chains from Ambergate West Junction. In the vicinity of Hassop station, on both sides of the line, were to be found a pheasant, a donkey, a ram, an elephant, a sheep, together with a fox, a settee and a round table. These were all interesting

examples of the art of topiary. The bushes, all hawthorns, were first shaped in 1880 by ganger Isaiah Gilbert and at one time 15 shapes brought admiring glances from passengers who used the line.

Plate 179 (below) The art of topiary is believed to have been widely practised by gangers on the ex-CR lines of the LMS but it was rare on ex-Midland routes. This view from Pineapple bridge, however, about 1960 shows that such work was carried out in the vicinity of Hassop.

(J. R. Morton collection)

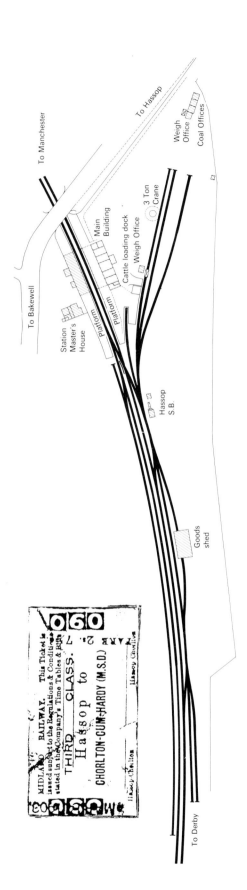

Fig. 74 Hassop track plan

(H. Townley)

Plate 180 (below) This view south from Hassop station bridge in the mid 1950s superbly captures the open nature of the landscape and the atmosphere of a station open for goods traffic only. The horizontal line just on the apex of the goods shed roof is the hedgerow marking the Baslow to Bakewell road which crosses the line at Pineapple farm seen behind the station master's house on the right. The track layout is virtually identical to Bakewell, but it is set on a westerly curve and has the down lie-by not present at the neighbouring station. The house was sold by **BR** in 1964, but was never occupied and was sold again for £31,000 in July 1986 in a somewhat sorry state, complete with self sown sycamore tree in one bedroom.

Having so far followed a course along relatively narrow valleys the railway found itself in somewhat more open countryside around Hassop. It has been argued that prior to the Pleistocene Ice Age the River Derwent south of Calver took a wide sweep to the west around the gritstone mass of Calton Pastures. This early course near Bakewell probably resulted from the ease with which the river was able to cut through the Edale Shales. When the ice stream pushed down the Wye Valley from the west it not only widened the valley where it met the shales, but it eventually blocked the course of the Derwent such that a lake formed in the vicinity of Calver. Ultimately the lake overflowed across the lowest ice free col, somewhere near the present Chatsworth House and the pent up waters quickly cut a new course to the south, rejoining the original valley near Rowsley. When the ice retreated the river was sufficiently set on its new course to adopt it permanently.

Hassop village is 1¼ miles north of the station and is little more than a few cottages, the Eyre Arms public house, a Roman Catholic church in the classical revival style and Hassop Hall. Now a hotel the latter was once the seat of the Eyre family, with distinguished Catholic traditions, who in the late 16th century virtually depopulated the area in the interests of sheep farming. When the railway was being planned the population of the village was under 100 and it is possible that a station would never have been built had it not been for the insistence of the Duke of Devonshire. It is said that if his neighbour, the Duke of Rutland, could have a station at Bakewell then he was jolly well going to have one too! Whether it was from belief in equality, status, or mere convenience, one will probably never know but both stations were built to the same general track plan, with the same basic buildings. There was a subtle difference in the main station building in that the one at Hassop had pillars between the windows on the road side, but did not have the wooden eaves brackets found at Bakewell and Rowsley. The station was built by J. Wood, who had just begun erection of the Station Master's house, in September 1862, when he won the contract for the goods shed. The coal offices were virtually identical to those at Bakewell and it is the author's opinion that they were built by the same contractor, Wm Ward, early in 1865.

In 1866 a truck weighing machine and office were erected by C. Palmer, to a design obviously copied from the coal offices, with arched windows and distinctive eaves corbelling. As traffic increased the presence of slow moving freight trains became more and more problematical and one of the earliest lie-bys to be put in on the down line was at Hassop, late in 1874. For almost 30 years down passengers had little in the way of creature comforts, for it was not until early in 1893 that the down waiting room was constructed, again very similar to that at Bakewell. In 1895 the signal box and frame were

Plate 181 LMS built 4F 0-6-0, No. 44090, carrying express freight headlamps, runs past the signal box on 29th September 1951. The box is a 15 ft period II structure built in 1895 and unusually retains the MR lamp on the front provided to allow the signalman to read engine numbers at night. A concrete WC and tubular steel steps have replaced the original structures.   (E.R. Morten)

renewed and the final construction work carried out at Hassop came in 1907, when the lie-by was extended to increase its capacity from 46 to 64 wagons. In passing it is worthy of note that the down lie-bys were put in level to give goods trains a fair chance of restarting up the bank. The increase in freight traffic in the immediate post war years again caused operating problems and in 1950 it was proposed to convert the down lie-bys at Hassop, Monsal Dale and Disley into down goods loops. Only that at Disley was implemented. The proposed loop at Hassop would have diverged from the down main line just north of bridge No.54, some 585 yards south of the signal box.

Schemes to link the Manchester line in the vicinity of Hassop with the Sheffield area frequently arose. As early as 1844/6 the North Derbyshire Union Railway proposed a line between Ashford and Dronfield. Later, in 1863, the Sheffield, Chesterfield and Staffordshire Railway failed in favour of the Midland's new line between Chesterfield and Sheffield.

An interesting proposal was the Midland Railway (Hassop and Dore) scheme 1871-2, followed by a recommendation of the Traffic Committee read to the Way and Works Committee on 16th October 1874 that 'they should proceed with the acquisition of the land for the Dore and Hassop line without delay'! Further schemes were the Hassop and Padley Railway (1885), the Grindleford, Baslow and Bakewell Railway (1903) and finally the Derwent Valley, Calver and Bakewell Railway, whose Act of Parliament was as late as 4th August 1920. Price 3s (15p) this Act was still available from the Stationery Office nearly 50 years later at a revised price of 7s 6d (37½p). That the link was not built is more surprising than if it had been constructed.

Situated only fractionally over a mile from Bakewell, Hassop could only look to the north and east for potential traffic. Prior to 1894 this sphere of influence would have extended well beyond Calver, to include Curbar, Stoney Middleton, Froggatt and Grindleford. However the opening of the Dore and Chinley line in that year, with a station at Grindleford, took much of this traffic away from Hassop, particularly for passengers to Chinley and beyond. In 1892 some 8,740 tickets were sold at Hassop, but by 1902 this total had fallen by over 50% to 4,346, a reduction from 26 passengers per week day to 13. By 1922 the number of bookings had fallen to under 2,000, or five travellers per week day. From soon after the opening of the Dore and Chinley line, Hassop became one of the only three stations between Ambergate and Chinley to make a loss on passenger traffic, but this was certainly not the case on the freight side of the business.

In 1922, when the average fare would have taken the third class passenger to Belper or New Mills and back, the station was served by five down trains. These comprised two early morning locals, together with late morning, afternoon and evening Derby-Manchester trains. Only two up trains stopped, the 7.43am and 7.15pm from Manchester to Derby. Under LMS control services declined slightly, the down trains being cut to three, with no through trains to Manchester. In the up direction the early morning train from Manchester continued

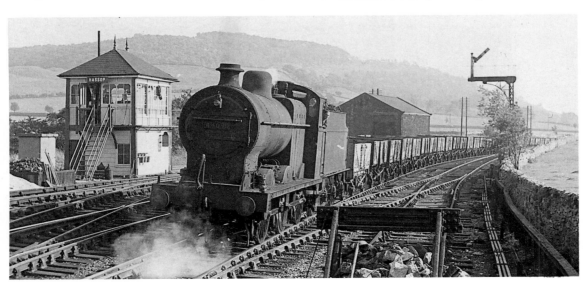

to call, as did the 12.08pm and 4.15pm Chinley-Derby services. During the early part of the war three Derby-Manchester trains each way called but the station closed to passenger traffic on 17th August 1942.

In terms of freight traffic the station fared much better as it served Great and Little Longstone, Ashford, Hassop, Pilsley, Calver and Baslow. The predominant activities around Hassop were and still are agriculture and mineral extraction. Although overshadowed by Bakewell the station saw a steady traffic in livestock, amounting to some two or three truck loads weekly, throughout the Midland period.

Coal traffic was divided primarily between domestic supplies and fuel for Baslow gas works. The trade was in the hands of Tom Wright, who set up his office in May 1888, J.W. Daybell, Roe Brothers & Co. Ltd and J. Macdonald.

Daybell's business was started by Bevan, known locally as 'Bishop' Daybell, who is believed to have sold coal for Messrs Wheatcroft. His son, John William, eventually took over and like Henry Bramwell at Bakewell, set up his own business when Wheatcroft's finished. He had a small fleet of wagons, reputedly painted grey, with white letters, shaded black. It is believed that they had a tiny JW in the top left corner and DAYBELL in very large letters below. In the bottom right corner would have been the word HASSOP in 7in or 9in letters. Two of John's sons, Bevan and Dick, continued the company, the former eventually being joined by his son Ronnie. These two were still in business when the trade was moved to Bakewell, Ronnie finally closing down about 1972, since when he became a traffic warden.

The company had a variety of lorries over the years beginning with a model T Ford and then a model A, both painted grey. About 1937 they bought a new Fordson 25cwt, painted red, but swapped this a short time later for a Morris Commercial 5 tonner, again red, which they ran until after the war. They then had a Dodge which they brought to Bakewell and finally a Bedford 2 or 3 tonner, the latter two being painted brown.

The Roe family were scrap metal merchants in Sheffield and came into the coal trade as a 'side line'. It is said that one of the four sons in the family was of delicate constitution and that his father bought the coal business for him to manage, probably in the 1920s. Although the son died early the business prospered and was moved down to Bakewell with Daybell's, where it continued until 1968/9. As far as is known the company never owned any wagons.

J. Macdonald, coal merchant extraordinaire, came to Ashford with his parents after World War I and later set up as a coal merchant in the late 1920s. He is remembered as a keen naturalist and had a bungalow built half a mile up Pennyunk Lane, on the hills west of Ashford. This was his 'H.Q.' and his 'Reception' was a box on a pole at the bottom of the lane. This location, plus his reputation as a semi-recluse who never started work before 11.00am, hardly seems a formula for a successful business, but succeed he did, until he retired in 1952 or thereabouts, aged over 70. He never owned any railway wagons and probably drew his meagre supplies from colliery agents.

Plate 182 (top) The delightful rail weigh office built by C. Palmer in 1866 copies the features of the coal offices.

(Author)

Plate 183 (below) The coal offices and road weigh office, seen here on 10th October 1971, were almost identical to those at Bakewell except that they were joined together. Consequently at Hassop the weigh office door was in the front with a slightly smaller window on that elevation.

(Author)

From time to time Frank Lomas consigned wagon loads of coal to Hassop, as he did to Monsal Dale and stations on the Buxton-Ashbourne line. These wagons would be unloaded by the customers, usually farmers taking the whole load.

The Baslow Gas Light and Coke Co. was one of the smaller gas works serving a population of around 1,500 and was probably opened around 1870, but records of coal supplies are only available on a spasmodic basis from 1914 onwards. In

Fig. 75 Hassop weigh office

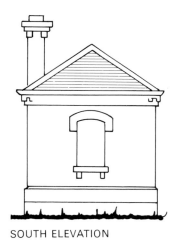

Scale 3mm to 1 ft

SOUTH ELEVATION   RAILSIDE ELEVATION   NORTH ELEVATION

125

1914/15 Tom Wright was supplying Tinsley Park best screened gas coal and Pinxton nuts. He was still active in the early 1920s, but additional supplies came in from Annesley Colliery, Barber-Walker & Co., Hoyland Silkstone Coal Co., J. & G. Wells Ltd., Sherwood Colliery and Wilson, Carter & Pearson. From the mid 1920s Tom Wright had a virtual monopoly, but around 1930 Nunnery Colliery Co. and the Hallamshire Coal Supplies Ltd began to dominate the supply. At about this time the gas company began to experience financial difficulty and was eventually sold to the Sheffield Gas Co., which took over on 1st October 1934. The annual inflow of coal to Hassop remained around 4,500 tons – 5,500 tons for much of the MR period and well into LMS days, representing 2-4 wagons daily.

Merchandise traffic was of a general nature with various shops and businesses in Ashford, Great Longstone, Baslow and Calver. Grain and animal feed of a considerable variety came in for Wm Gill & Sons of Calver Bridge, corn merchants who occupied one of the coal offices. J. Hewitt & Sons of Ashford were also corn merchants. In 1928 4,584 full grain sacks were received at Hassop, 152 for Gill (4 consignments) and 4,432 for Hewitt (70 consignments). The analysis of those for Hewitt reveals that 3,106 sacks came from Liverpool Docks, the vast majority being from Alexandra Dock. The remainder were from Manchester Docks (580), Hull (200) and the rest in small consignments from Whitwell, Bolsover, Saxby, Plumtree, Blidworth, Grimston, Radford and Farns-field. At least during Midland days raw cotton came in for Calver Mill, which was rebuilt after a fire in 1805 and continued spinning cotton until the 1920s. Much of the yarn was sent out to Leicester for use in the hosiery trade. During World War II the mill was used as a storage depot and no doubt Hassop station yard experienced one of its busiest periods at this time. Near to the loading platform at the side of the weigh office was an old coach body used for cattle cake, supplied by Bibby, Silcock etc. This was replaced in BR days by an ugly concrete structure near the goods shed. There was also a fixed 5 ton crane in the yard, which must have been of dubious reliability for Messrs Cox Wilson & Son had to sign an indemnity form for its use.

Mineral traffic included general building materials for F.Cox Wilson & Son, timber merchants & builders, Ashford;

Wm J. Eyre, builder, Great Longstone and Tom Wright, together with roadstone outwards from Cracknowl Quarry, just west of the station. In addition large quantities of spar and other minerals were brought down from the old lead workings on Longstone Edge. The Mineral Manager at Derby prepared diagrams of goods yards to show accommodation and stacking grounds for this type of traffic and the plan for Hassop is dated November 1913. Spaces allocated for stone or minerals were utilised by Spar Concessions Co. (42ft x 23ft), Hawkins (15ft x 12ft), G.G. Blackwell & Sons (15ft x 12ft) and Arthurton & Co. (30ft x 12ft). A later spar firm was Catstone Moor Spar Company of Matlock Bath who occupied 50 square yards and paid 9s 5d (47p) per month in 1924. The plan also shows the areas occupied by coal merchants as follows; W. Daybell (10ft x 72ft), with a similar amount for Tom Wright. The coal offices were occupied by Daybell, Wright and Gill and a later pencil note shows a wooden office occupied by Roe Bros by the wall side and the remark '20 yards'.

Chains and hooks were useful equipments in any small goods yard and at Hassop in September 1931 were:

No.78	5/16in	Grab hooks (14cwt)
No.80	5/16in	Wool hooks
No.81	5/16in	Cask hooks
No.84a	1/2in	Single chain (35cwt)
No.1529		Endless rope (30cwt)

Barrows on the station in 1935 consisted of a 4-wheel barrow, No.4447 (sent to Burton-on-Trent 29th September 1942), a 2-wheel barrow, No.9606 (sent to Chinley on 24th September 1941), together with a second 2-wheel barrow and a sack barrow.

During the 1930s the yard was served by the 10.52am stopping freight from Rowsley, the engine shunting the yard and returning to Rowsley with empties and outgoing traffic at 2.00pm. Later this train left Rowsley much earlier and returned just after 11.00am.

The station buildings and approach road were leased to T.I. Fearn, agricultural engineers, about 1960 and the sole member of the station staff, Leading Porter Cliff Jordan, was ejected and put into a small wooden hut nearby. Cliff, a small man who usually wore a rather long and aged railway black macintosh, was a familiar figure for many years. On Saturdays he was often conveyed into Bakewell, with a smile of anticipation, in a coal lorry which conveniently stopped by the Queen's Arms for the 'Station Master', as he was known, to alight for lunchtime refreshments.

A curious re-opening took place on 1st August 1984 when over 1,500 passengers rode from Hassop to Bakewell! Over the two Bakewell Show days a Park-and-Ride scheme operated and many service buses were diverted along the old trackbed to avoid congestion within the town of Bakewell.

Plate 185 (below) This view in May 1950, shows the down starter and the open nature of the land to the north. Further examples of topiary can be seen in the distance, on the down side of the line.

(D. Ibbotson)

Plate 184 (above) One of the companies supplying coal to both Bakewell and Baslow gas works was J. & G. Wells Ltd, owners of Holbrook and Renishaw Park Collieries, near Eckington. Wagon No. 2801 is a 1923 standard seven plank vehicle painted red with white letters, black shading. It was registered by the LNER on 28th February 1936 and was one of a batch numbered 2801–2850.

(Author's Collection)

Fig. 76 This wagon was 15ft x 7ft 6in and was painted medium grey with black ironwork, white letters and black shading. The circle was white and carried the words 'Coal Fires for Health & Comfort'

(Based on an original drawing by P. Matthews.)

Chapter 14

Great Longstone

Plate 186 (left) Bridge No.56A Printing cattle creep. (Author)

Plate 187 (above) Bridge No.58, Longstone Road bridge, was the last bridge going north which was built from gritstone. The structure was reinforced in 1929 by the insertion of four tie-bars. The ends of these were secured by cast iron bolsters from the Cromford Canal.

(Author)

Leaving Hassop the line continued to curve, passing under Station bridge, into a shallow cutting and then at natural ground level for a short distance before straightening and running onto embankment as it crossed Buxton bridge and the diminutive Printing cattle creep. It then entered a shallow cutting, curving gently northwards as it passed under Lowdale bridge. A little over 250 yards later the line left the cutting, crossed Longstone Road bridge, and curved gently westward onto a low embankment. From here the route ran almost due west, with open land to the north and the wooded grounds of Thornbridge Hall to the south. Shortly afterwards the line curved to the north, entered a shallow cutting and passed under Wagers bridge and Longstone Lane bridge, in quick succession, to arrive at Great Longstone station, 16 miles 67 chains from Ambergate West Junction. At this point the character of the line began to change and the eagle-eyed geologist on a down slow train would have noticed that Wagers bridge was constructed in limestone, not the gritstone

he had so far been observing.

The station, originally to be called Thornbridge but opened as Longstone, was built early in 1863 by Mr Charles Humphreys as part of a contract valued at £7,460 which also included the stations at Millers Dale and Buxton. It is generally accepted that the Tudor style station, with combined accommodation for the Station Master, was desgined by William Barlow. It is interesting to note that although the line was now in limestone country, the station buildings were erected in gritstone which is more suitable for building purposes. Although the up platform shelter was built at the same time it was not until 1881 that the steps were built up to the road, giving safe access to the platform. Prior to this it was "use the barrow crossing and be careful"! Following renewal of the signal box in 1902, and lengthening of the platforms early the following year, the station became one of those chosen to be fitted experimentally with long burning oil lamps. These were installed in the autumn of 1909 and appear to have comprised a base to contain the oil, a wick, and a glass cover. They were stood inside the traditional MR gas lamp top and must have proved satisfactory for they remained in use until sometime after 1950. The name of the station was changed to Great Longstone in 1913 and an unusually tall signboard on the up platform carried the name in two rows, with an additional board below lettered "FOR ASHFORD". The down platform carried the normal MR angled nameboard until almost all such identification was removed early in 1940 in case of enemy invasion.

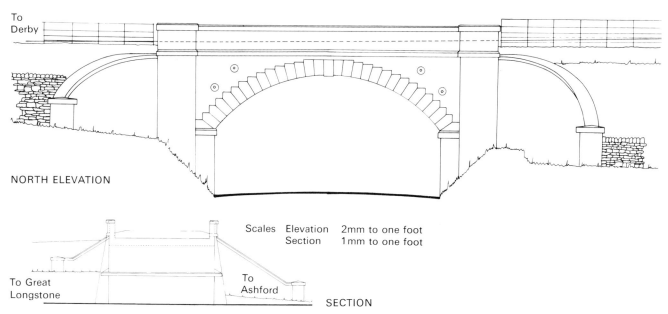

To Derby

NORTH ELEVATION

To Great Longstone

To Ashford

Scales Elevation 2mm to one foot
Section 1mm to one foot

SECTION

Fig. 77 Bridge No. 58, Great Longstone

Plate 188 Hughes/Fowler 2-6-0, No.42874, of Rowsley shed, storms under Longstone Lane bridge with a down through freight about 1952.

(E.R. Morten)

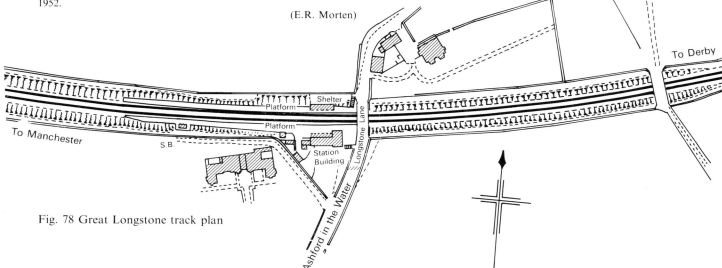

Fig. 78 Great Longstone track plan

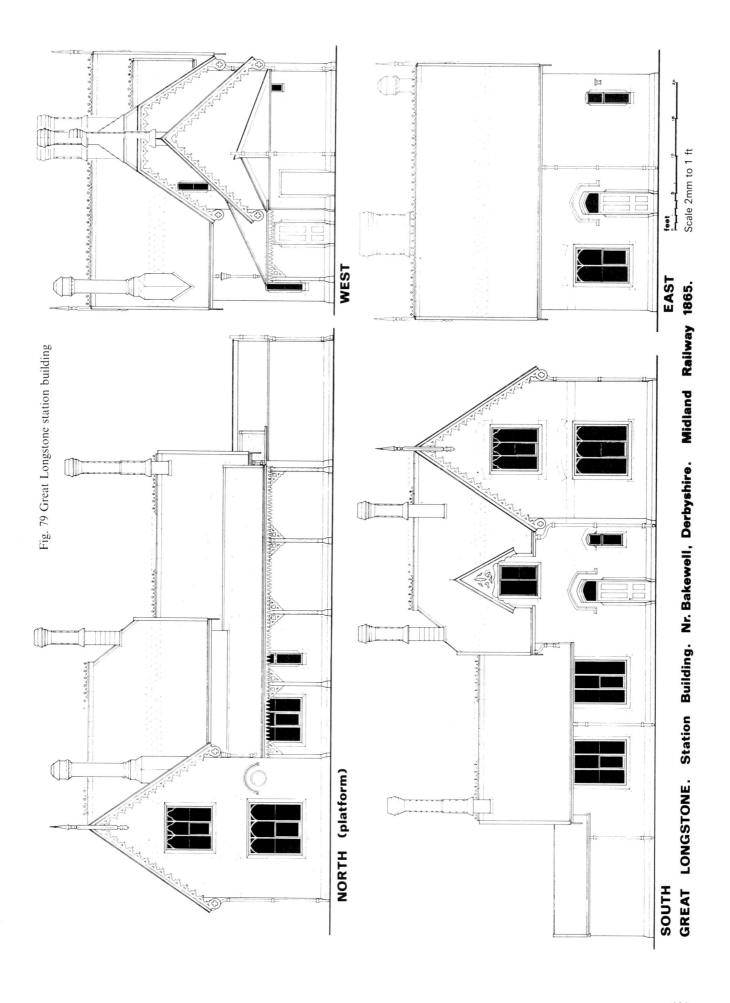

Fig. 79 Great Longstone station building

WEST

NORTH (platform)

EAST

feet

Scale 2mm to 1 ft

SOUTH

GREAT LONGSTONE. Station Building. Nr. Bakewell, Derbyshire. Midland Railway 1865.

Plate 189 (above), 190 (above right) and 191 (right) show the railside elevations of the booking hall, the north elevation and the roadside elevation respectively. Plate 192 (above right) shows the station nameboard on the up platform. A conventional angled nameboard was originally sited on the down platform just north of the station building.

The station primarily served the Longstones, Ashford and Thornbridge Hall, which together with scattered farms, gave a catchment population in the 1920s of about 1,200–1,400. There was a house on the site of Thornbridge Hall in 1790, from which time various owners carried out substantial alterations, culminating with an almost continuous period of change between 1897 and 1918 under the then owner, Mr George Jobson Marples, the son of a Sheffield businessman. He is thought to have settled at the Hall because of the proximity of his birthplace, the ease of access to London and the presence of the large estates of Chatsworth and Haddon, which he hoped to emulate. He became a director of the Midland Railway and in 1903–4 he built 'Woodlands', the imposing structure just behind the down platform. This building, in the style of the Hall itself, was built as a series of waiting rooms on the ground floor, with a huge recreation room for domestic staff and estate workers on the first floor. With his money and influence Marples became one of the very few people to have a private access to a railway station, this consisting of a gate and flight of steps to the down platform. Much of his wealth stemmed from a large shareholding in Krupps of Essen, the German munitions company, but after World War I he had lost a great deal of money and was obliged to turn Woodlands into flats, renting these out to help run the estate.

After his death the house was purchased by Charles Boot, the head of the Sheffield building company, but in 1946 ownership passed to Sheffield City Council who developed the property as a teacher training college, only to close it later owing to poor public transport in the area. Today it is a multi-purpose education centre for Sheffield and South Yorkshire.

Passenger traffic at Great Longstone grew steadily from a little over 6,000 in 1872 to over 14,000 in 1922, but these figures kept the station firmly within the 'minor' league, with an average of 43 passengers per weekday at the close of the Midland period. Interestingly, however, the number of season ticket holders had gone up from seven in 1912 to 89 in 1922. It is probable that these people worked in Bakewell or Buxton.

At this time the station was served by six trains in each direction. Of the down trains two were locals to Buxton, the remainder being Derby-Manchester services spread fairly evenly through the day. In the up direction only two Manchester-Derby trains stopped, the 7.27am and the 10.55am. The remaining four were Chinley or Buxton to Derby locals. It is interesting that the 10.50am Nottingham-Blackpool (MFO) did not stop, but the return working did. Presumably outward passengers would be fit enough to make their way to Bakewell to catch the train, but after a week in Blackpool they would be so worn out as to need dropping off nearer home. The war saw a dramatic cutback and only four down and three up trains were timetabled. With the exception of the 5.48pm Derby to Chinley, all were through trains between the two cities. After the war matters improved slightly with a morning Manchester-Nottingham train added to the service and the pre-war early evening Buxton-Derby train re-instated. At closure the service was very similar, but the Buxton train had been withdrawn previously. The station closed to normal traffic on 10th September 1962, but up to 1967 the 7.15am from Derby and a return train, stopped to allow Sister Boardman, based at one of the Buxton hospitals, to get to and from work, but not for two college girls who made the same journey! It was argued that allowing these two to travel would be tantamount to re-opening the station to regular traffic.

For many years the station was awarded more prizes for gardens, cleanliness and tidiness than any other station in the district.

Pl;ate 193 This aerial view about 1955 shows Woodlands, built by G. Marples in 1903/4, as a waiting room and recreation rooms for staff from Thornbridge Hall. The steps giving access to the down platform can just be seen opposite the white car.

(Thornbridge Hall)

Chapter 15
Monsal Dale

Plate 194 The view from Monsal Head, through Monsal Dale and Upper Dale, towards Cressbrook, must rank amongst the finest in England. In this photograph taken on 29th September 1951 an 8F 2-8-0 heads a down mineral train over the viaduct.

(E.R. Morten)

Leaving Great Longstone the passenger would have noticed only a gradual change in the scenery to begin with, but even the most nonchalant observer would have seen a startling change within a few minutes.

From the station the line curved northwards through a shallow cutting and passed under a farm occupation bridge, White's bridge. It then straightened for a short distance, curved to the left into a second cutting and passed under Orrs bridge. This time the cutting increased in depth, becoming darker as the walls became almost vertical before the line plunged into Headstone Tunnel. The traveller emerged as if in mid-air 533 yards later, for he was then some 80ft above the

River Wye on Monsal Dale Viaduct, the elegant curved structure which almost drove Ruskin to suicide. Leaving the viaduct the line curved to the north, straightened and curving southwards entered a shallow cutting, before passing under Buckley's bridge, and over Station bridge to arrive at Monsal Dale station, high on a shelf above the river. The passenger was now in Upperdale, 18 miles 20 chains from, and a little over 350ft above, Ambergate West Junction.

It was not originally intended to build a station at this location, but it is believed that representations were made by the owners of Cressbrook Mill and on 5th August 1863 the Rowsley and Buxton Construction Committee, which was still in being, recorded that "a public siding and wharf be constructed upon a site to be selected by the Engineer and Mr Alport, near to Cressbrook mills". The siding, initially known as Cressbrook siding, was laid in on the down side of the line, probably served by a simple, trailing turnout. It is known that

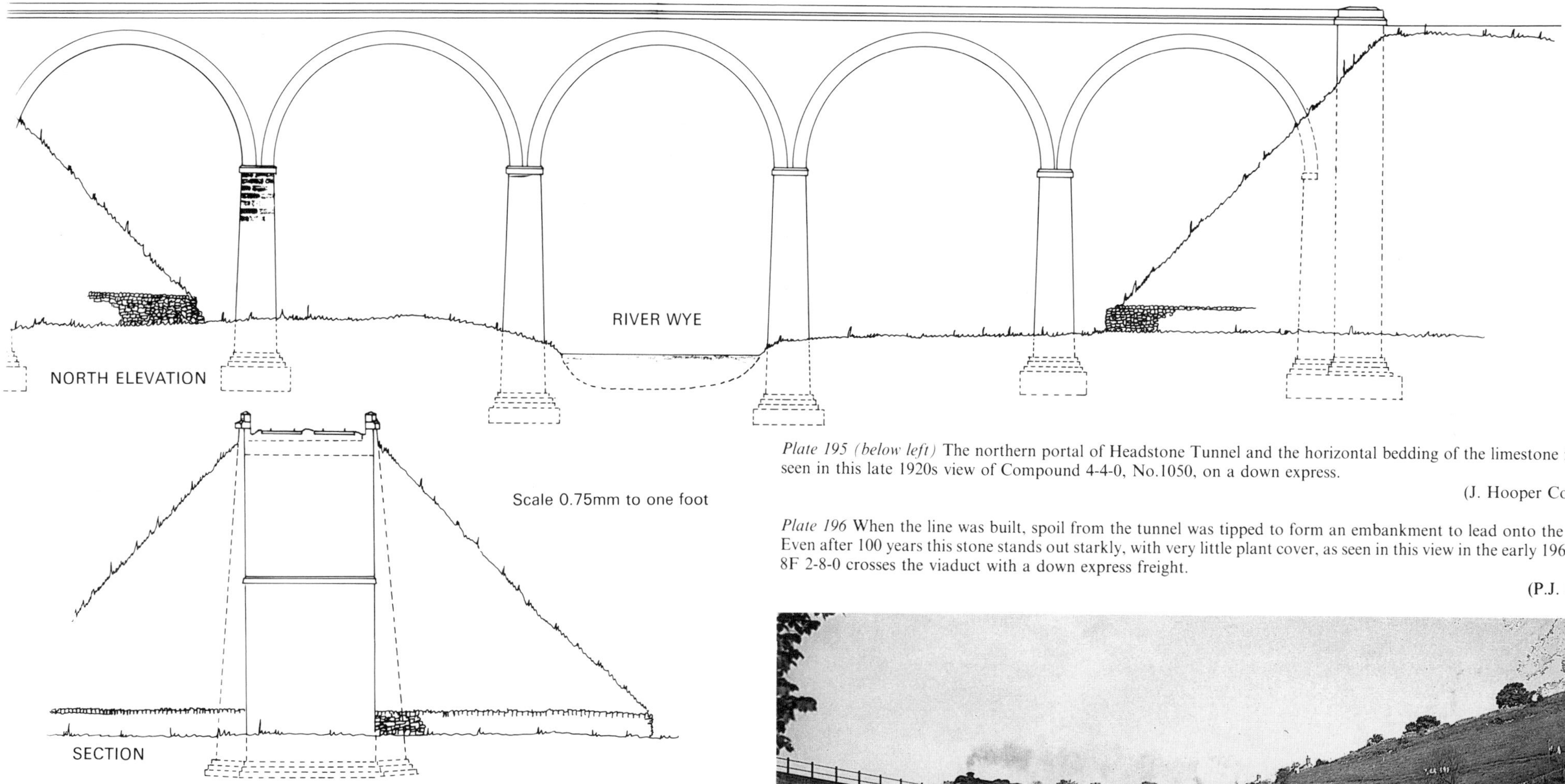

To Derby

RIVER WYE

NORTH ELEVATION

SECTION

Scale 0.75mm to one foot

Plate 195 (below left) The northern portal of Headstone Tunnel and the horizontal bedding of the limestone is clearly seen in this late 1920s view of Compound 4-4-0, No.1050, on a down express.

(J. Hooper Collection)

Plate 196 When the line was built, spoil from the tunnel was tipped to form an embankment to lead onto the viaduct. Even after 100 years this stone stands out starkly, with very little plant cover, as seen in this view in the early 1960s, as an 8F 2-8-0 crosses the viaduct with a down express freight.

(P.J. Hughes)

Fig. 80 Monsal Dale Viaduct

133

134

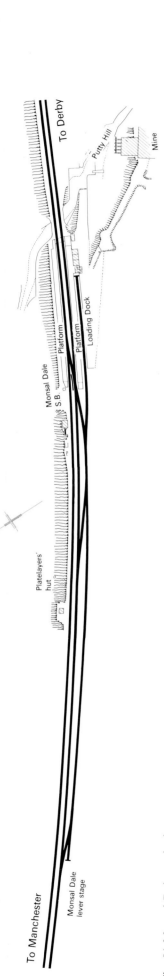

To Manchester

To Derby

Monsal Dale

Platelayers' hut

Monsal Dale lever stage

Fig. 81 Monsal Dale track plan

Plate 197 This view from the signal box on 20th April 1911 shows the line curving under Buckley's bridge, a farm occupation crossing in blue engineering brick, as it runs into the diminutive station at Monsal Dale. The down platform is built in stone and macadam, but the up side is an all timber structure supported on piles driven into the hillside. The only nameboard on the station was on the up platform, directly end on to the camera in this view, just behind the milk churn. The name was in raised letters, which at least during the 1930s, were of the serif-style used on the NSR. On the hillside to the right is the Monsal Dale spar mine, produce from which is being loaded into the three Buterley wagons for use in the company's iron works at Codnor Park. Final points of interest are the platform lamps painted chocolate, rather than the standard chocolate and cream, and the vertical paled fencing.

(N.R.M.)

Plate 198 Class 5XP No. 45650 Blake runs downhill from Cressbrook Tunnel with the 3.30pm. Liverpool-Nottingham express on 19th July 1958. The tunnel mouth is in the hillside directly above the fourth carriage. There are no signals controlling movements into or out of the sidings and everything would be done by hand signals from the box.

(E.R. Morten)

this work was carried out because payment for timber for points and crossings at Monsal Dale was authorised on 6th January 1864. The use of plural in this authorisation perhaps suggests that a second siding was put in at the same time, north of the wharf and connected to the up line by a trailing turnout and single slip. This would have been used as an up lie-by, although the others on the line were not added until some years later. At that time the route up to and under Station bridge was little more than a footpath, with a ford over the river and it must have occurred to the engineer that if he was going to the trouble and expense of building a road almost 100ft up a mountain side he may as well throw in passenger facilities at the same time. Accordingly, on 20th December 1864 he put plans before the Way and Works Committee, with a recommendation that a station be provided, subject to the work not being proceeded with until the following summer due to a dangerous slip in the cutting. This was approved, but to be absolutely safe, work the following year was restricted to construction of the access road, payment for which was agreed in December of that year. It would appear that this road did not include a bridge over the river, for Frank Lomas recalls that when his grandfather began selling coal at Monsal Dale it all came down the road by cart and if a horse stumbled, "especially in the river", the cry of "horse-down" would bring willing hands rushing out from the few cottages in the vicinity.

Although committed to the project the Traffic Committee could not have been excited about potential passenger revenue, and to keep costs to a minimum, it was resolved to move the temporary wooden station from Evesham to Monsal Dale, and the contract for this job was awarded to Charles Humphreys on 15th May 1866. The platforms were constructed between May and August, the station being opened for traffic on 1st September. Described in a newspaper as "this delightful spot", the facilities were referred to as "this singular and romantically situated (new) station". It is not certain that the buildings were completed at this time for it was not until 31st December 1866 that payment to Humphreys was authorised. The facilities at the station remained spartan and early passengers needed a strong constitution for WCs and urinals were not provided until the autumn of 1875.

Small, isolated pockets of the lower coal measures are found in parts of the Peak District and were occasionally worked for local consumption. One such site occurred near Monsal Dale, where a certain Mr Frogatt was fined £13 12s 9d (£13.64), in February 1877, for working coal under the railway without permission. He refused to pay, but promised to stop work in that part of the mine. This was not found acceptable and the and fine was enforced, together with a warning that he had

Plate 199 (above) Bridge No 67, Station bridge, immediately south of the platforms, is an unusual structure built askew and on a very steep slope. The sides of the bridge and one wing wall on the down side are built in brick, while the base of the arch is in stone. On the upside the wing walls have to carry the lateral thrust of the embankment and are in brick and concrete.

(Author)

Plate 200 (bottom) The station building was a small, secondhand structure moved from Evesham to Monsal Dale and was principally of timber construction. The chimney stacks were, of course, built in brick, as was the northern gable wall and one can only speculate that this wall was damaged beyond repair during removal.

(M.A. King)

better serve the appropriate notice in future before working under the company's land. One shudders at the possible consequences if he had carried on at shallow depth under the line.

As traffic increased the need for additional lie-bys arose, particularly for the slow moving down trains, and in 1889 the existing siding to the north of the station was connected to the down main line at the Manchester end. At the same time the siding to the wharf was connected into this lie-by, as seen in *plate 198*. The Midland Railway Distance Diagrams show the original signal box to have been sited on the down side of the line, but this was drawn thus for the draughtsman's convenience, the station being at the extreme edge of the page.

The box was in fact north of the station on the 'up' side, and when it was renewed late in 1896 the replacement was sited a little nearer the station.

It is not certain when the Monsal Dale Spar Mine Ltd began operations, immediately south of the station, but in 1914 they asked the MR to put in a private siding. This would have involved a turnout off the lie-by and considerable excavation to run the siding down the back of the station yard, where a new platform face would have been built to provide loading facilities. It seems that upon being informed that although the work was agreed, they would have to pay £320 in ten annual instalments, at 4% interest, the mine company dropped the proposal, and continued to use the public wharf. No further work was carried out at the station until early in 1924, after a land slip had occurred on the up side of the line just north of the platform, during the early hours of Sunday, 20th January, when a stretch of the breast wall some 27ft long collapsed. Rather than clear all the rubble and rebuild the original wall, which may have led to further collapse, a new length of wall was built round the slip, which was then consolidated by packing. The extra land used was subsequently purchased from the Duke of Devonshire.

The station served a very sparsely populated area, even by Peak District standards. Cressbrook and Wardlow were the only settlements of note within its catchment area and including the scattered farms, potential regular passengers probably never exceeded 400. However the area has always been popular among hikers who made up a respectable proportion of the customers, particularly in LMS days when the circular walking tour tickets were widely advertised. In this respect quite a few trains stopped on Saturdays only, but the Sunday service was withdrawn in 1916 as a wartime economy measure; few trains ever calling there on a Sunday subsequently, despite the increase in popularity of walking.

In 1922 four down and three up trains stopped on weekdays. Of these, two were through trains to Manchester. In the up direction the 7.27am Manchester-Derby slow and two early evening locals stopped. On Saturdays the 7.20pm, Derby-Manchester called. The LMS did not make any significant change to the timetable other than to include a stop by the

8.10pm Buxton-Derby on Saturdays. What is not big cannot be greatly reduced and the outbreak of war saw the loss of only two up trains. After the war the service returned to the pre-war level of four trains each way on weekdays, but with rather more activity on Saturdays. One extra down train, the 7.16pm Derby-Manchester stopped and in the up direction the 6.50pm Buxton-Derby (SO) and the 7.38pm Manchester-Derby called. The star train of the day was the 11.35am Manchester-Nottingham which on Saturdays was extended to St. Pancras.

Although rudimentary freight facilities existed traffic was always light and up to World War I consisted solely of coal and coke for Cressbrook Mill and domestic consumption. In 1872 some 414 tons of fuel was bought in and by the turn of the century this had risen to a little over 1,300 tons, an increase from approximately two wagons per week to four or five per week. With the opening of the spar mine, the construction of an engineering workshop at Cressbrook Mill, and greater use of the steam engine installed at the mill late in the 19th century, demand increased markedly and in 1922 a little over 9,000 tons of coal and coke came in, representing 27 or 28 wagons weekly. Apart from Frank Lomas mentioned earlier, the author has no record of the coal merchants involved. In the same year 185 tons of spar were sent out and 42 tons of merchandise were dealt with, but as these are the only figures known to the author no conclusions can be drawn, other than that the traffic was of little importance.

Freight was dealt with as required, by the 12.20pm Stopping Freight from Rowsley to Millers Dale, which would have taken any outgoing traffic on to Millers Dale for sorting and dispatch. With the post war growth in road traffic both passenger and freight income fell rapidly and the station was closed to all regular traffic on 10th August 1959, although some bank holiday excursions stopped subsequently.

Monsal Dale station was perhaps unique in not having a G.P.O. telephone. With the decline of freight traffic the roadway under the railway into the small station yard degenerated into a footpath. The typical Midland slatted platform fencing still remains, albeit around the perimeters of a house on a council estate in Bakewell!

Plate 201 (below) The poster notifying proposed closure of the station was an example of the hand painted posters used by British Railways when only a very small number were required.

(M.L. Knighton Collection)

Plate 202 (right) Long after closure of the station British Rail were still capitalising on the attractions of the area as this 1965 handbill shows.

(Author's Collection)

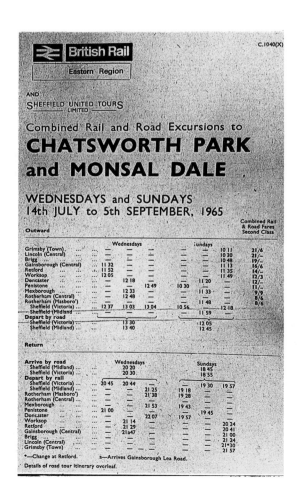

136

Chapter 16

Millers Dale

Leaving Monsale Dale station the line curved slightly to the north on a shelf high above the river, for about ¹/₂ mile and then curved gently westwards to enter Cressbrook Tunnel (471 yards) under the easterly of two neighbouring hills around which the Wye has formed two giant loops. Emerging from the northern portal the traveller found himself with one of the most spectacular views on any railway in Britain. The line was now in Water-cum-Jolly-Dale, 90ft above the river on an artificial ledge. To support the trackbed against the erosive force of the waters the embankment was held in place by a covering of individually laid stones, like a huge wall lying flat on the ground. Dramatic as the view may have been it was only for the delectation of the most alert passenger, for at 50mph the train spent just ten seconds in the open before entering Litton Tunnel. When it re-emerged 515 yards later it was in Millers Dale, high above the chimneys of Litton Mill.

Both Cressbrook and Litton Mills were built in the 1780s, but the latter earned a dubious reputation under its notoriously mean owner, Ellis Needham. Being in such an isolated area both establishments suffered from labour problems and pauper apprentices were brought in from London and other major cities. While Arkwright treated them relatively well at Cressbrook, Needham is reputed to have been a fierce and cruel taskmaster. By the 1850s Litton Mill was described as "an extensive spinning and manufacturing establishment, with a workforce of 400, using both steam and

water power". Following a fire in the 1870s the mill was rebuilt and in 1934 it was turned over to the production of artificial silk, under Litton Silk Mills Ltd. Today, under changed ownership it manufactures textured yarns.

Just beyond the mill the line passed under Litton Mill bridge, built in blue engineering brick to carry the footpath from the valley up to Priestcliffe and Taddington, and then curved southwards through a short, but deep, cutting. It then curved sharply first to the north, then south again, before curving northwards once more past Millers Dale Lime Co.'s sidings (until 1885/8 Oldham Lime siding), over the river and into Millers Dale station, 20 miles 75 chains from Ambergate West Junction.

The traveller could easily be forgiven if he now felt he was at the big station in the middle of nowhere, but a glance at the nameboards would have told him that he was at the junction for Buxton and station for Tideswell. It was originally

Plate 203 (above right) The southern portal of Cressbrook Tunnel. Without the sighting board the down home signal would be almost invisible.

(D. Ibbotson)

Plate 204 This view looking east through Water-cum-Jolly Dale, about 1911 shows the northern portal of Cressbrook Tunnel and the embankment built onto the hillside to carry the trackbed. The footpath from Litton to Cressbrook can just be seen on the left and was as popular at the turn of the century as it is today.

(M.L. Knighton Collection)

Plate 205 (right) Bridge 70, Litton Mill bridge, looking west.

(D. Ibbotson)

Plate 206 (below) LMS 4F 0-6-0 No. 4261 brings the 12.20pm stopping freight from Rowsley to Peak Forest South round Litton curves on a sunny day in June 1932. The splitting distant signal for Millers Dale can be see on the right

(E.R. Morten)

Plate 207 (bottom) 483 class 4-4-0 No.501 and Compound 4-4-0 No. 1054 sweep south through Litton curves with the 12.20pm Manchester Central-St Pancras on 6th June 1933. No.1054 was the engine involved in the celebrated non-stop run from Euston to Edinburgh on Friday, 27th April 1928, which stole the limelight from the LNER's much publicised "Flying Scotsman" introduced the following Monday. The tender was modified by fitting overhanging coal rails to carry 9 tons of coal.

(E.R. Morten)

intended to use an existing drawing for the station for on 5th August 1862 the Construction Committee ordered that "a station be constructed at Millers Dale similar to that at Hassop, and that a station master's house be constructed apart from the station". Why this instruction was not acted upon will never be known, and a smaller station similar to Great Longstone was erected. The station was built on a wide ledge carved from the hillside above the river and comprised two platform faces, on the main line, both of which were fenced along the back. The main station building was at the south end of the up platform, with a goods shed adjacent. In addition a loading dock and cattle pens were erected in the yard. In 1865 a block of four coal offices was built, just inside the yard gates, by Wm Ward using the same plans for those he had recently finished at Bakewell. There is no record of when the adjacent weigh office was built but again this is very similar to the one at Bakewell and was probably built at about this time.

Very soon after the line was opened to Manchester additional sidings were put in for the exchange of Manchester goods traffic. This in itself is most interesting and illustrates that in those early years it was considered that the main line ran to Buxton, with a branch through to Lancashire and the North West. The sidings were extended again in 1872, 1874

and 1875. The latter alterations are something of a mystery, for at a cost of £8,713 they represent major works, the single siding added the previous year having cost £310. One can only conclude that the work comprised turnouts and sidings at the north end of the station to facilitate the opening of Station Quarry. A few months later, in April 1875, it was ordered that a plan and estimate be prepared for the erection of a waiting shed on the down platform, similar to that on the up platform at Loughborough. This work was carried out by Joseph Glossop, who was paid £670 14s 9d (£670.73) in March 1877 and the building remained in use, without alterations, until the station closed. In the summer of 1875 a lie-by was put in behind the down platform and this was later extended to incorporate a run round loop to accommodate the Buxton trains. There is no record of when this work was carried out, but it was probably during the 1880s.

Traffic must have grown rapidly for on 15th April 1879 consideration was given to the purchase of land for the diversion of the footpath to Wormhill and extension of the station but the matter was deferred.

Conditions at the station continued to deteriorate and officers tried again in 1883, by submitting plans and estimates for additional accommodation to the February meeting of the

Plate 208 (top) 483 class 4-4-0, No. 413 passes Millers Dale Lime Sidings signal box with a Manchester Central-Derby slow train on 6th June 1933.

(E.R. Morten)

Plate 209 (left) Stanier 8F 2-8-0, No. 48406 of Heaton Mersey shed, passes Millers Dale Lime Works with a down freight on 30th August 1952. By this time the two lower quadrant MR signals, just visible behind the train in *Plate 208*, had been replaced by the LMS bracket signal seen here on the left.

(E.R. Morten)

Plate 210 This eastwards view of the original viaduct was probably taken in 1903 to record the scene before work began on the second viaduct. In studying the illustration one can only admire the skill of the engineers and men who designed and built such a graceful structure, much of which is hidden from today's eyes by mature trees on both banks of the river. (N.R.M.)

Way and Works Committee. These plans were looked upon more favourably and on 14th June 1883 a contract for the erection of new waiting rooms on the up platform, awnings and a subway, was awarded to J. Salt, who completed the works the following summer.

In 1890 both the station signal box and Millers Dale Lime Co.'s sidings box were renewed. At the station a tall period II box was erected, 20ft x 10ft, while a 15ft structure was put up at Lime Sidings. The final works carried out at the old station occurred in 1897 when refreshment rooms were constructed on the up platform at the request of the Hotels Committee.

By the turn of the century problems of congestion at Millers Dale were becoming intolerable. The conflict between slow moving freight trains and passenger services, almost all of which stopped at the station, was exacerbated by the movement of traffic from the rapidly expanding quarries. At the same time the Midland was approached by the promoters of the Hope & Castleton Light Railway, who had the intention of building a similar line from Millers Dale to Tideswell and required interchange facilities with the main line. The Midland would never turn down potential traffic and it was resolved that subject to the proper arrangement being entered into, the facilities would be granted.

To sort out the problems at the station called for considerable change and it was decided to add a double track loop which would result in slow and fast lines through the station in both directions. This would involve a second viaduct over the river, demolition of the main buildings and goods shed, together with cutting back the hillside to provide space for the new tracks, buildings and goods yard. Work of such magnitude required parliamentary approval and this was granted by the Midland Railway (Additional Powers) Act

1903 (Millers Dale loop). J.A. McDonald was appointed engineer and the job was split into four contracts. Those for enlarging the goods yard (£7,885 3s 4d) (£7,885.17) and building the new loop (£19,095 15s 8d) (£19,095.78) went to Messrs Whitaker Bros, Horsforth, while the Butterley Co. won the contract for building the new viaduct (£9,779 15s) (£9,779.75). The fourth one was for the erection of the new buildings and extension of the subway, but the author has no record of who carried out this work.

When the new viaduct was brought into use on 20th August 1905, the old one was closed for reconstruction by Messrs Handyside and Co. It took three years and cost £90,000 to complete the whole project, which culminated with the re-opening of the old viaduct on 1st April 1906. In conjunction with the remodelling both signal boxes had to be altered. The station box was extended by adding a further 10ft bay, which explains why a 'Period II' box exhibited a 'Period III' end, and a new 40 lever frame was installed. The Lime Co.'s sidings box was affected by the new trackwork and was replaced by a new 20ft box a little to the south.

After rebuilding, Millers Dale settled down but on 5th March 1931 the station made the headlines again when an up freight train became derailed in the station causing extensive damage to the permanent way, platform and subway. A potentially far more disastrous situation was averted the following year by the diligent observation of staff. In July 1932 the Chief Civil Engineer reported that he had put in hand emergency repairs to bridge No.75, which carried the line over the river just south of Chee Tor No.1 Tunnel. It seems that the structure was in imminent danger of collapse and it was necessary to rebuild the arch and spandrel walls at the south end, at an estimated cost of £3,500.

140

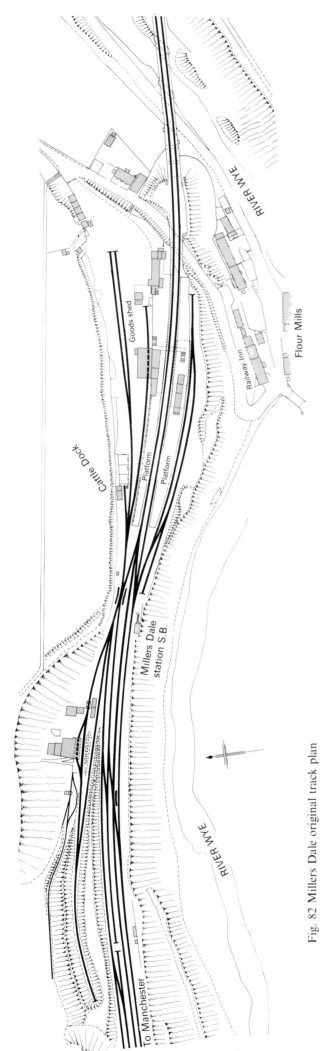

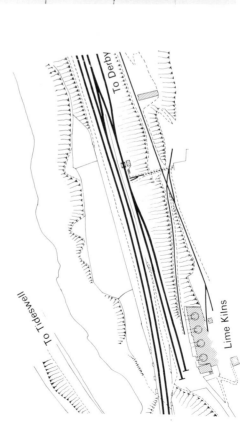

Plate 211 This view looking south around the turn of the century, shows the general layout of the station buildings. On the left is the goods shed directly behind the refreshment rooms, with the booking hall roof in the background. To the right are the down waiting rooms built to an all timber design in 1876/77.

(M.A. King Collection)

Fig. 82 Millers Dale original track plan

RIVER WYE

Flour Mills

Railway Inn

Goods shed

Platform

Platform

Cattle Dock

Millers Dale
station S.B.

To Manchester

RIVER WYE

To Tideswell

To Derby

Lime Kilns

Fig. 83 Millers Dale widened track plan

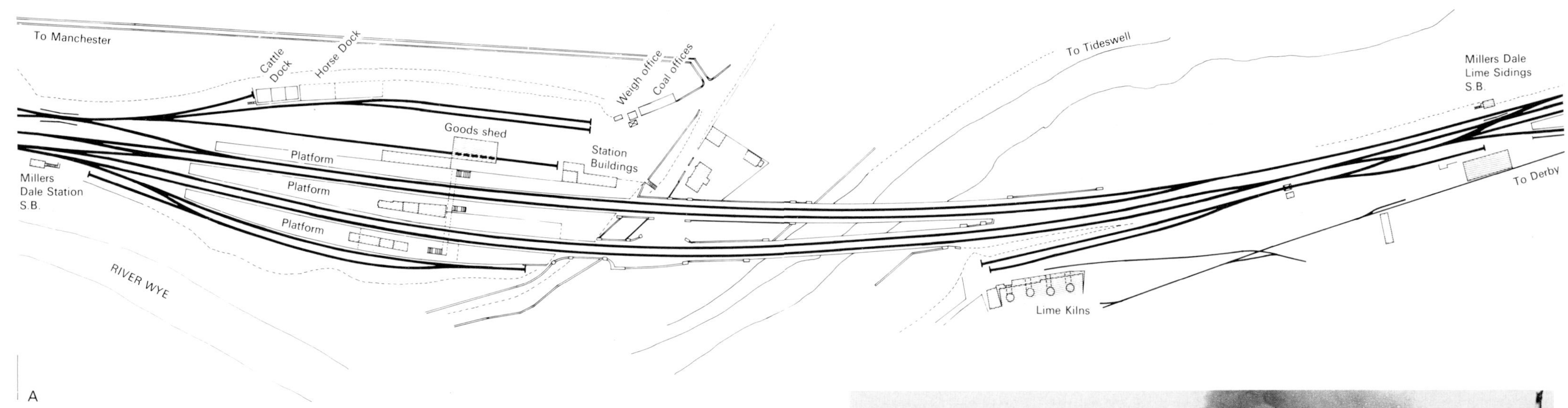

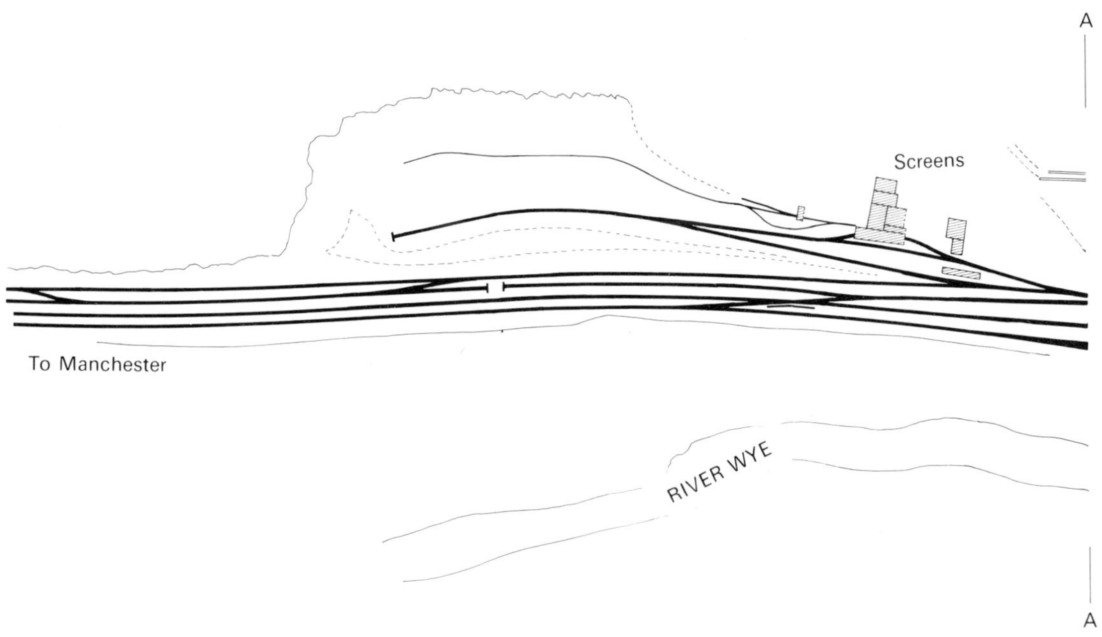

To Manchester

Millers Dale
Lime Sidings
S.B.

To Tideswell

To Derby

Lime Kilns

Weigh office

Coal offices

Station
Buildings

Goods shed

Horse Dock

Cattle
Dock

Platform

Platform

Platform

Millers
Dale Station
S.B.

RIVER WYE

A

A

Plate 212 LMS 4F 0-6-0. No. 4147 from Staveley shed. storms through the station with a down mineral train about 1946.

(W.D. Cooper)

A

A

Screens

RIVER WYE

To Manchester

Plate 213 This general view westwards on 29th September 1951, as an unidentified 5XP 'Jubilee' draws away with an up express, superbly captures the whole station and its environs.

(E.R. Morten)

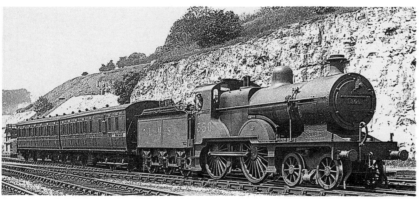

Plate 214 (above) The prime purpose of Millers Dale was that of a junction for Buxton and this view about 1930 shows Compound 4-4-0 No.1020, with a down main line local, on the left and the Buxton branch line train on the right behind Johnson 0-4-4T, No.1366. The chocolate and buff paintwork to the waiting rooms, the single colour gas lamp and the large poster board are worthy of note.

(Brookside Photographic Services)

Plate 216 (below) When the two Co-Co diesel electrics were introduced in 1947/48 one of their regular trial routes was St Pancras to Manchester and No.10001 is seen here at Millers Dale in the summer of 1948. The engines normally ran singly on these trains, but occasionally both were used.

(E.R. Morten)

Plate 215 Before the Buxton branch service became a regular motor train service about 1933/34, both tank and tender engines were used, running around at either end. This view shows 483 class 4-4-0, No. 356, arriving at Millers Dale with such a local from Buxton on 14th June 1932.

(E.R. Morten)

Plate 217 (above) In the mid 1950s the 'Britannia' Pacifics were diagrammed onto the principal Manchester trains. Here No. 70042 *Lord Roberts* stands at Millers Dale with the down "Palatine" about 1958. By this time the gas lamps had been converted to electricity and the poster boards and two-tone colour scheme had gone.

(L.M. Hobdey)

Plate 218 (below) Having crossed over from the up line, Webb 2-4-2T No.46616 draws into the bay platform to await departure with the motor train to Buxton on 12th May 1951. This engine carried the number 26616, apparently in error, from 1945 to 1948, when it became BR No.46616. It is seen here still in the 1946 block style livery.

(R.J. Buckley)

Millers Dale served a wide area, passengers being drawn from Great Hucklow, Litton, Priestcliffe, Taddington, Tideswell, Wheston and Wormhill, these settlements having a combined population of about 5,500/6,000 in the 1930s. Traffic grew from just under 16,500 in 1872 to 40,642 in 1902, declining only slightly by the end of the Midland period, at which time an average of 106 passengers purchased tickets on weekdays. With 43 departures on weekdays in 1922 this represents less than three passengers per train, but this figure belies the importance of the station as the junction for Buxton and in practice a great deal more people used the station daily. At that time the average fare represented a third class return journey to New Mills or Rowsley, but it is probable that most local passengers would be travelling from Tideswell either to Peak Forest, to work in the quarries, or to Buxton or Bakewell for shopping or work purposes.

In 1922 the main line service comprised 14 down and 15 up trains. The down trains included three St Pancras-Manchester Central expresses, the 1.25pm St Pancras-Manchester Victoria ("The East Lancashire Express"), which carried a through coach for Buxton, five Derby-Manchester trains, and the 12.00pm Nottingham-Manchester express. The Buxton branch saw 14 down trains at this period. The up London trains comprised three from Central and the "East Lancs"

from Victoria at 1.15pm. This train and the 8.55am from Central picked up through carriages from Buxton. In addition there were four Manchester-Derby services and expresses from Manchester to Nottingham and Liverpool to Derby, while 13 trains arrived from Buxton. With such an intensive timetable the LMS had little need to alter it markedly in overall terms and while the Buxton service was increased to 16 down and 15 up trains, only two extra main line trains called. There were changes, however, to the pattern of services. The "East Lancashire Express" was cut, but the St Pancras-Manchester Central trains were increased to five. With this increase the Derby-Manchester through trains were not so necessary and were cut from five to two. The three up expresses from Central to St Pancras remained but one Manchester-Derby and the Liverpool-Derby express were discontinued. In the mid 1930s five expresses in each direction passed non-stop, while one semi-fast, the 11.45pm Manchester Victoria-Derby did not call.

The wartime service was cut by virtually 50%, the brunt of which was borne by the local trains. Five down trains from London continued to call, together with four in the up direction. Three Derby-Manchester trains each way remained but the only local was the 5.48pm Derby-Chinley. The Millers Dale-Buxton service was cut to 13 each way. After the war the

timetable was expanded and the station enjoyed six London-Manchester expresses, with five in the up direction; three down and four up on the Derby-Manchester service and one each way between Nottingham and Liverpool. One train each way between Derby and Buxton was re-instated. Surprisingly the timetable continued to expand and at closure the service saw only two trains per day less than the mid LMS period. By this time the Millers Dale-Buxton service had become dieselised and to make full use of the units the frequency was increased to 19 journeys each way on weekdays.

Much of the Derbyshire limestone plateau is given over to dairy farming and up to the widespread growth of road transport, a considerable quantity of milk traffic was dispatched daily from farms within four or five miles of any station, to many destinations including the south and east side of Manchester. Very smart station working was required early in the morning to load the full churns, and again in the evenings to deal with the returning empties. With the dominance of pasture it is not surprising that Millers Dale saw a relatively high level of livestock traffic and three or four cattle wagons passed through the yard each week. It is of interest to modellers to note that the LMS usually kept a couple of cattle wagons on hand at stations normally dealing with livestock traffic, as it was not uncommon for a farmer to turn up with a few beasts and expect transport to be available immediately.

Although dominated by limestone, which will be dealt with separately in *Chapter 20*, the coal class traffic included a sizeable incoming tonnage of coal and coke. In the 1930s this consisted of some 5,000–6,000 tons per annum for the domestic market, 700–1,000 tons for Tideswell Gas Works, and other quantities for the quarries and mills. The coal trade was primarily in the hands of Tom Wright, Frank Lomas, Kirkland and Perkin, and The Tideswell and Millers Dale Coal & General Merchant Co. Ltd. The author has no evidence of the latter operating their own wagons, but if they did the livery would have been fascinating. Kirkland and Perkin were based in Buxton, but also had an office in

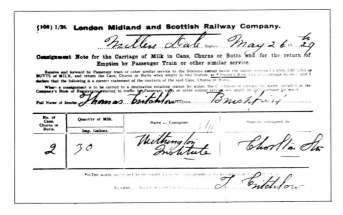

Plate 219 A milk consignment note from 26th May 1929.
(Author's Collection)

Chapel-en-le-Frith, in addition to Millers Dale and it is believed that wagons were lettered for all three stations. Very little photographic detail of these wagons has come to light but *figs 89 and 102* have been prepared from sketches in the author's collection.

The Tideswell Gas Light & Coke Co. was a small concern, at the south end of the town on the Buxton road and was probably opened in the 1870s, but records are only available from 1922. Early in that year coal was supplied by Kirkland and Perkin and Rothervale Colliery Co., but in August the company resolved to accept the tender of Nunnery Colliery Co. to supply gas coal at 27s 8d (£1.38) per ton, delivered at Millers Dale. At this time Hardman & Holden, Manchester, were buying tar from the works and their rectangular tank wagons would have been regular visitors to the station yard. For two years Nunnery Colliery had a virtual monopoly, but then Rothervale Colliery and John Brown & Co. took over,

RAMBLES

in the Peak District National Park

in conjunction with the Ramblers' Association (Notts. & Derby ...)

GOOD FRIDAY
and
EASTER SUNDAY

AMBERGATE MATLOCK
MATLOCK BATH
BAKEWELL MILLER'S
DALE & BUXTON

FROM	RETURN FARES Second Class to					
	Ambergate †	Matlock Bath	Matlock	Bakewell	Miller's Dale	Buxton
NOTTINGHAM Midland	5/6	6/6	6/6	8/6	9/–	10/–
†BEESTON	5/6	6/6	6/6	8/6	9/–	10/–
SAWLEY JUNCTION	5/3*	6/6	6/6	7/6	9/–	10/–
DERBY Midland	3/9*	5/6*	5/6*	7/–	9/–	9/6
†BELPER	1/3*	3/9*	3/9	5/9*	8/–*	8/6*
†AMBERGATE	—	3/–*	3/6*	5/6*	7/6*	8/–*

†—Bookings from Beeston, Belper and Ambergate and also to Ambergate are on April 18 only.

*—Special Day Return Fare and passengers from these stations holding such tickets are permitted to travel outward and return by any train on the day of issue.

OUTWARD JOURNEY			RETURN JOURNEY (same day)		
	April 16	April 18		April 16	April 18
NOTTINGHAM Midland	10 05	10 00	BUXTON	19 20	19 20
BEESTON		10 06	MILLER'S DALE	19 33	19 29
SAWLEY JUNCTION	10 22	10 13	BAKEWELL	19 43	19 39
DERBY Midland	10 40	10 40	MATLOCK	19 55	19 51
BELPER	—	10 52	MATLOCK BATH	19 59	19 55
AMBERGATE		10 58	AMBERGATE		20 04
MATLOCK BATH	11 04	11 10	BELPER	—	20 10
MATLOCK	11 09	11 14	DERBY Midland	20 19	20 21
BAKEWELL	11 25	11 25	SAWLEY JUNCTION	20 37	20 45
MILLER'S DALE	11 40	11 38	BEESTON	—	20 59
BUXTON	11 54	11 50	NOTTINGHAM Midland	20 54	21 10

8

Plate 220 One of the many handbills from the 1965 Easter programme.
(Author's Collection)

with occasional loads from Dalton Main Colliery and H. Nickson, Manchester.

From 1928 Nunnery Colliery again became the dominant supplier but in 1932, following an argument with the LMS over delayed carriage, arrangements were made to have deliveries by road at 21s 9d (£1.09) per ton. This arrangement only lasted three weeks and the offer of the railway to deliver to Grindleford station at 18s 5d (92p) per ton was accepted. However this still left a road journey of some eight miles, over hilly terrain and it was not long before normal rail deliveries to Millers Dale were resumed. From the mid 1930s purchase of coal was largely left to the discretion of the Gas Manager, but by about 1938 Tinsley Park Colliery appears to have become the major supplier.

With about 35 shops or small businesses in Tideswell a steady stream of general merchandise came into the station, amounting to two or three vans or open wagons daily. In addition the town had a small cotton mill, a calico weaving mill and a velvet cutting factory. These concerns together with Litton Silk Mill and Cressbrook Cotton Mill required raw materials and transport of finished goods, amounting to four or five wagons per week.

Mineral class traffic was originally restricted to sand, gravel, tiles, slates etc., for building purposes but the annual tonnage passing through the station took a marked leap upwards around the turn of the century. This resulted from the opening of quarries at Calton Hill, just south of the Bakewell-Buxton road, near Blackwell, and in Tideswell Dale, to work basalt for use as roadstone. The latter quarry closed in 1939 and probably relied heavily on rail transport, while the former increasingly used road haulage after the war until closure in 1969. Very little is known about these two quarries, but at least up to the late 1930s the majority of the output was sent away, in railway owned wagons, with 8-10 vehicles per day being involved.

The yard was serviced primarily from Buxton, although in the 1930s the 12.20pm stopping freight from Rowsley to Peak Forest was diagrammed to shunt the yard for 40 minutes. The 6.48am freight from Buxton to Millers Dale would have conveyed loaded coal and merchandise wagons, together with empty limestone wagons. This train also carried the mail for Tideswell, presumably in the guard's van, and responsibility for receiving this lay with one of the station clerks, who was also sub-postmaster for Millers Dale. The station was indeed the last one in England to have a post office on its platform. A similar train, less the mail, ran from Buxton at 1.36pm and the engine shunted the yard and quarry sidings before returning to Buxton with the 6.18pm freight. This train carried empty coal and goods wagons, loaded wagons from the mills, and loaded limestone and basalt wagons. On Saturdays the 12.48am express freight from Water Orton to Ancoats detached wagons as required, at 4.28am, but what this traffic included is uncertain.

Plate 221 Class 3F 0-6-0 No.3394 about to draw back into Station Quarry with a train of empty limestone wagons in 1935. The wagon in view, No.255 is an 8 ton vehicle converted from dumb buffers and is probably 15ft x 7ft 6in with four 7in planks at the sides and four 9in planks at the ends. The livery is mid-grey body, black ironwork, white letters, black shading. Behind the engine is the angled MR nameboard which had a second, straight board underneath reading 'Junction for Buxton Station for Tideswell.'

(G. Coltas)

Chapter 17

Blackwell Mill

Plate 222 (above) This superb view looking east on 4th July 1951 from above Chee Tor No.1 Tunnel, shows the Buxton motor train about to cross East Buxton bridge and the contrast between the densely wooded river banks in the foreground and the more open limestone plateau beyond. Above the engine is the disused East Buxton Lime Works.
(E.R. Morten)

Plate 223 (below) Compound 4-4-0, No. 931 of Derby shed, leaves Chee Tor No.1 Tunnel with the 12.20pm Manchester Central-St Pancras express on 8th May 1932. It is interesting to note that the tunnel portal is built in limestone.
(E.R. Morten)

Plate 224 (above) The western portal of the tunnel however, was built in blue engineering brick, clearly seen in this view as Fowler 2-6-4T, No.2372, leaves the tunnel and crosses Chee Tor bridge with a down local train about 1946.

(W.D. Cooper)

Leaving Millers Dale the line continued almost due west, with the river far below on the left, and immediately passed Station Quarry and East Buxton Lime Works on the right. The latter originally had independent sidings, with a crossover from the up to the down main line, controlled by East Buxton Lime Co.'s signal box. In 1933 the sidings were connected into those serving Station Quarry, the crossover and siding access was taken out and the signal box closed.

Just beyond the works the line crossed the river on East Buxton bridge, No.75, curved slightly towards the south and entered Chee Tor No.1 Tunnel. This tunnel, 401 yards in length, took the line under Chee Tor, which rises 300 ft above the river and forces the waters into a wide loop in the manner seen earlier at Cressbrook. In Chee Dale, however, the river has cut down almost vertically and this narrow, tree-lined chasm is one of the most spectacular sights in the Peak District. It is also one of the most secluded, being only accessible on foot, and then not to the casual Sunday stroller. In two places the difficult riverside path consists of a long line of stepping stones, set in the river itself, under overhanging limestone cliffs. The remainder of the path is narrow and slippery in all but the driest weather. The origin of the path is rather obscure but it may well have been 'built' by the railway as the bridge carrying it over the river at the northern end of No.1 Tunnel is MR bridge No.77A.

The passenger who blinked would have missed the view of this dale, for having emerged from the tunnel the line crossed a single arch bridge and plunged into Chee Tor No.2 Tunnel, a much shorter structure of 94 yards, under a low shoulder of rock. The route then continued south westwards on a narrow shelf before curving gently northwards and piercing a similar outcrop by Rusher Cutting Tunnel. The bore of the tunnel ran out of the strata at a very acute angle and the northern section is actually a covered way, built in coursed gritstone and supported by five massive buttresses. North of Rusher Cutting the valley begins to widen rapidly and running on embankment the line crossed the river again before diverging at Millers Dale Junction. Running almost straight ahead was the line to Buxton, while the line to Manchester veered to the right and steepened to 1 in 90.

The traveller was now at Blackwell Mill, so named from the hamlet to the south and the long closed corn mill on the River Wye. After the last few miles even the least interested passenger must have noticed that he was now in a great natural amphitheatre, carved out by the Wye and the waters which once ran down from the north, through Great Rocks Dale.

The original line to Buxton continued in a south westerly direction on an embankment built on to the hillside above the river and then through a short, deep cutting. Just beyond this the line curved slightly and passed under Needhams bridge which carried a footpath from the Mill site up to Blackwell. From this bridge, which became No.1 on the Buxton branch when the main line was constructed, the line again passed on to an embankment and was carried over the river, and a private road, by Blackwell Mill bridge. It then continued on an embankment which gradually tapered into the hillside as the line passed Blackwell Mill Halt, which was built for railway employees, and is generally accepted as having been the smallest station in the country. The line then curved gently to the north, on a shelf cut from the hillside and passed Buxton junction, where the line from Peak Forest dropped steeply down from the right. The junction was controlled by Buxton Junction signal box, which was renewed in March 1917, at which time it was moved approximately 100ft to the east.

The main line to Manchester curved sharply away from Millers Dale Junction and continued on an embankment before crossing the Wye for the last time by a five arch viaduct. It then crossed Meadow Bridge and curving to the north passed on to a shelf cut from the rock before running on to filled ground as it passed Buxton Central Lime works and approached Peak Forest Junction, where the curve from Buxton Junction came in from the left.

Plate 225 (below) This view from above Chee Tor No. 1 Tunnel in July 1951, encapsulates the character of the line as it passes through Chee Dale. In the foreground is Chee Tor No. 2 Tunnel, beyond which the line sits on a shelf cut from the hillside as it curves towards Rusher Cutting Tunnel in the distance and Blackwell Mill beyond that. On the left can just be seen the River Wye which turns through 90° and passes under Chee Tor bridge. The previous plate was taken from the roof of the platelayers' hut to the left of the tunnel mouth.

(E.R. Morten)

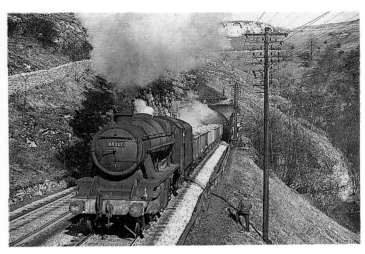

Plate 226 (left) Heaton Mersey 8F, No. 48327, storms out of Chee Tor No. 2 Tunnel with a train of iron ore for Irlam Steel Works about 1955. (W.D. Cooper)

Plate 227 (centre) Diesel multiple units were introduced on the Buxton-Millers Dale service on 14th October 1956. A 3-car Cravens unit is seen here at Millers Dale Junction with a down service on 30th April 1958. In the left background can be seen the western portal of Rusher Cutting Tunnel. (E.R. Morten)

Plate 228 (bottom) Stanier Class 5, No.44848, one of the 1944 batch built at Crewe, passes Blackwell Mill Halt with the 10.30am (Sundays only) Derby-Buxton stopping train on 22nd April 1951, as 8F No. 48279 awaits the road with a freight train from Gowhole. (E.R. Morten)

Plate 229 (opposite) This specially posed view just west of Millers Dale Junction was taken at the turn of the century to show the new MR coaching stock. It also shows some of the most spectacular limestone scenery in the country. Mentally, it is quite easy to remove the train, the embankment and the distant cutting and absorb the solitude of this inaccessible part of the Peak District. (N.R.M.)

Plate 230 (above) Climbing away from Millers Dale Junction, the main line was carried across to the northern flank of the valley on an embankment pierced by River Wye Viaduct and Meadow bridge, clearly seen here as 3F No.3233 takes a mineral train towards Peak Forest in the summer of 1932. The first nine wagons appear to comprise a 'Falk Salt' van, Butterley, three Sievewright Bacon (Manchester), unknown, W.N. Toft (Derby), unknown and S. Taylor Frith. Of the 37 wagons in the train only three can be positively identified as LMS.

(M.W. Earley)

Plate 231 (below) Class 5XP, No.5657 *Tyrwhitt* brings a down express through Peak Forest Junction about 1946.

(E.R. Morten)

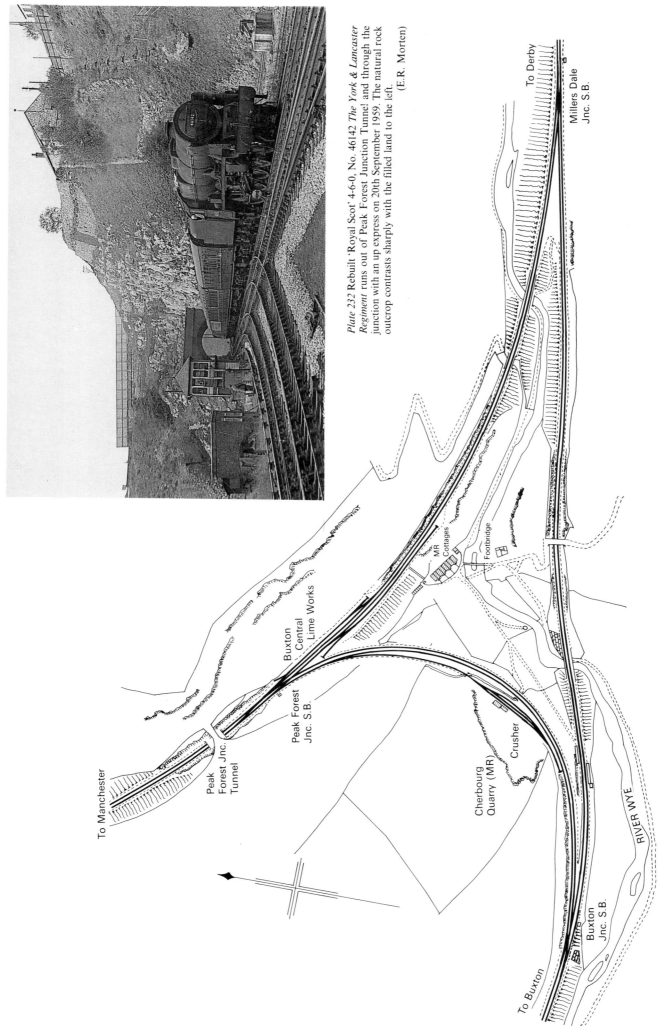

Plate 232 Rebuilt 'Royal Scot' 4-6-0, No. 46142 *The York & Lancaster Regiment* runs out of Peak Forest Junction Tunnel and through the junction with an up express on 20th September 1959. The natural rock outcrop contrasts sharply with the filled land to the left.

(E.R. Morten)

To Manchester

Peak Forest Jnc. Tunnel

Peak Forest Jnc. S.B.

Buxton Central Lime Works

MR Cottages

Footbridge

To Derby

Millers Dale Jnc. S.B.

Cherbourg Quarry (MR)

Crusher

Buxton Jnc. S.B.

To Buxton

RIVER WYE

Fig. 84 Blackwell Mill track plan
Scale: 1 in to 350 ft

153

Plate 233 This view from the Bakewell road about 1932, looking towards Peak Forest Junction and Great Rocks Dale, shows the cottages in the valley bottom, the MR Cherbourg Quarry on the extreme left and Buxton Central Lime Works. Beyond Peak Forest Junction Tunnel can just be seen the LMS dump. The train on the Buxton line, left, is headed by one of the first twelve 8Fs.

(Author's Collection)

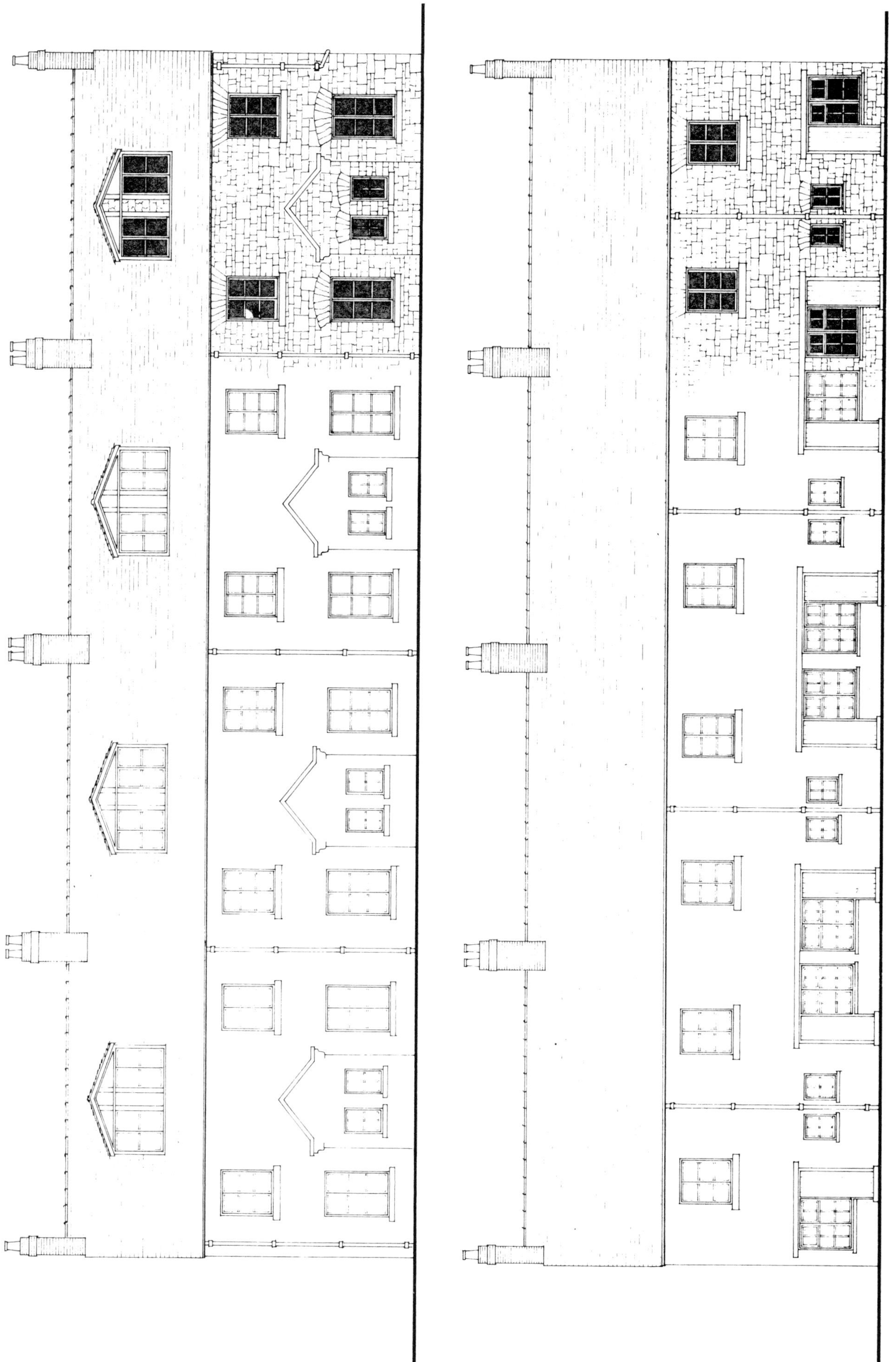

Fig. 85 Blackwell Mill cottages

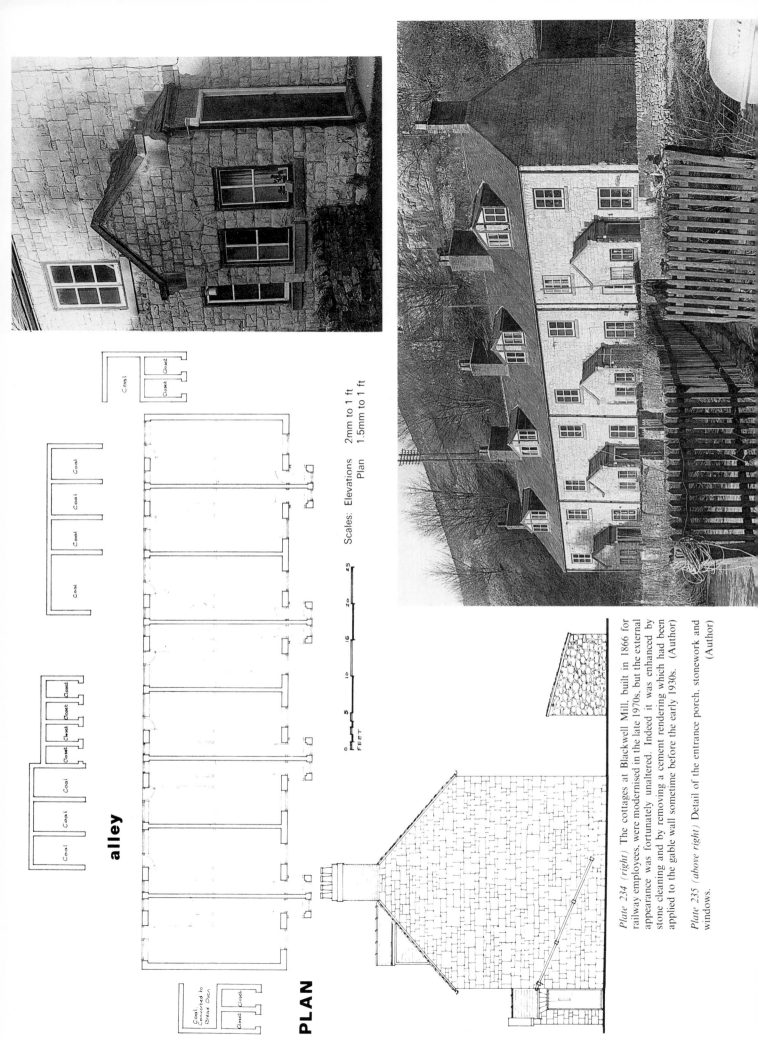

PLAN

alley

Coal

Closet   Closet

Coal   Coal   Coal

Coal

Closet   Closet   Closet   Closet

Coal   Coal   Coal

Coal   Converted to Bread Oven

Closet   Closet

Scales: Elevations   2mm to 1 ft
Plan   1.5mm to 1 ft

0   5   10   16   20   25
FEET

Plate 234 (right) The cottages at Blackwell Mill, built in 1866 for railway employees, were modernised in the late 1970s, but the external appearance was fortunately unaltered. Indeed it was enhanced by stone cleaning and by removing a cement rendering which had been applied to the gable wall sometime before the early 1930s.   (Author)

Plate 235 (above right) Detail of the entrance porch, stonework and windows.   (Author)

156

Construction of earthworks for the Manchester line were started in late February 1863 by John Ashwell, of Tideswell, who had been awarded the contract for the work up to Dove Holes Tunnel, in the sum of £48,231 15s (£48,231.75). It was not until November 1864, however, that the down line junction was put in to facilitate the delivery of permanent way materials for the completion of his contract, which also included the western curve of the triangle. In view of the isolated location it was considered necessary to provide accommodation for platelayers and the staff required to man the three signal boxes controlling the junctions. Accordingly the Construction Committee ordered that plans be prepared and tenders sought, for the erection of eight cottages. The tenders were opened on 2nd August 1865, but they were sent back for the submission of revised drawings. These were duly returned and on 4th October 1865 a contract was again awarded to J.Ashwell, in the sum of £1143, or £142 17s (£142.85) per dwelling. The cottages were built between the river and the Manchester line and were served by a private road from Topley Pike, which finally crossed the river by a ford in front of the houses. Later a footbridge was erected for pedestrians and this was known as Buxton Branch Bridge No.1A.

During the early years of railway construction the various companies were buying in ballast from many sources, some of dubious quality, but having once opened the lines, which then required constant maintenance, it seemed economic good sense to provide one's own if the railway ran through a geologically appropriate area. Thus, in September 1878, the engineer recommended that 5¾ acres of land at Blackwell Mill, adjacent to the western curve be purchased at a cost of £1,150 for the production of stone for ballast. This was agreed and following acquisition of the land, work was put in hand to open out the quarry, lay in sidings and install the necessary machinery. By August the following year work was sufficiently

advanced to invite tenders for the provision of a turbine and pipework to provide power, and in September 1879 a contract for this job was awarded to Charles Hetts, in the sum of £136.

In the late 1880s a down lie-by was put in just south of Peak Forest Junction and in 1907 this was extended to increase its capacity to 40 wagons. Now it just so happened that this siding ran directly behind the cottages and the ingenuity of railwaymen was demonstrated by the construction of a wooden chute down the embankment towards the outbuildings of the cottages. It is doubtful if this structure ever formed the subject of a report to Committee, but it is certain that the strong winds in this part of the world blew many a lump of best Derbyshire coal off the tender and down the chute to the coal houses!

Late in Midland days the availability of land, in an isolated spot just north of Peak Forest Junction Tunnel, was capitalised upon to provide a tip for used ballast, horse manure, dust, ashes etc., and a siding was put in off the up line to serve this site. By the early 1930s the nearby ballast quarry had been worked out, but the sidings were retained to store wagons which could not be immediately unloaded at the tip. While this arrangement worked in practice it was uneconomic as it was necessary to send a light engine from Buxton to shunt wagons between the sidings and the tip on a regular basis. It was therefore recommended that two additional sidings be provided at the tip, at a cost of £1,287. The scheme would immediately save £1,323 in renewing the quarry sidings, which had become neglected and would save the annual revenue costs of shunting. The schemes was approved and work was put in hand in the summer of 1935. On the original print shown at *plate 233* one can pick out the men laying the new track, which, bearing in mind that the operation was well over ¼ mile from the photographer, speaks volumes for the quality of the old plate glass cameras.

Plate 236 Class 4F 0-6-0 No.4050 struggles round the curve towards Peak Forest Junction with a Buxton-Blackpool excursion in June 1930. On the right are seen wagons waiting to be unloaded at the nearby dump.

(E.R. Morten)

Chapter 18

Ashwood Dale and Buxton

From Buxton Junction the line ran due west on a shelf cut from the hillside and crossed a loop of the river by two stone viaducts, Buxton Junction bridge and Topley Stone bridge, as it rapidly left the spaciousness of Blackwell Mill and entered Wye Dale. Leaving the second viaduct the line curved sharply to the south through a very short cutting and crossed the river and the main road by Topley Pike bridge, the first of four almost identical structures. These were originally built using fabricated segmental wrought iron girders but in 1931 it was recommended to the LMS Works Committee that the bridges, Nos 7, 9, 11 and 12, be reconstructed. This was agreed and a contract for the work was awarded to Dorman Long and Co. on 27th January 1932, in the sum of £33,270 3s 10d (£33,270 19). The main task comprised replacing the wrought iron arches with straight steel girders which were supported above the stone pillars by steel trestles. Above the girders beams encased in concrete formed the bridge deck. The final cost of the scheme, including contingencies and the relaying of the track, amounted to £440,404, £18 below the engineer's estimate.

Immediately at the western end of Topley Pike bridge a trailing turnout and single slip from the up line served Topley Pike Quarry, the crossing being controlled by Topley Pike signal box. The quarry was opened out in the early 1870s and in February 1874 it was agreed to put in siding accommodation for the owners, Messrs Newton Chambers. The sidings were extended twice in 1876 and again in 1901. In 1932 the owners granted a licence to J.Greatorex & Sons of Matlock, to erect a crushing, screening and coating plant in the quarry, and thus the latter's wagons, together with rectangular tank wagons, would have come into the sidings on a regular basis. Newton Chambers ceased production in 1955 and leased the quarry to Derbyshire Stone Ltd which put in hand an extensive modernisation programme, completed in 1964. This included the erection of lime kilns for supplying lime to the metallurgical industries, as well as a new macadam unit. Today some products leave by road, as regular travellers on the A6 know only too well, but at the time of writing a high proportion still leaves by rail, usually at 2.15am to Peak Forest, for departure at 5.00am to Widnes or Pendleton. This train is known locally as the 'Super Train' and is often loaded to carry 2,000 tons.

Plate 237 (above) The four main bridges on the Buxton line were almost identical and this view of No.7, Topley Pike bridge, taken on 30th August 1912, looking south east to Topley Pike shows the original form of the bridge. To the left can be seen the splitting distant for Buxton Junction, and the down home to protect Messrs Newton Chambers sidings.

(N.R.M.)

Plate 238 (below) 2-6-0 No. 46454 passes Topley Pike signal box with the 1.05pm Derby-Buxton local on 7th September 1955.

(E.R. Morten)

From Topley Pike the line continued along the south side of the road, curving to the north and then to the south, before passing under Kingsterndale bridge, an occupation bridge built in blue engineering brick to carry the bridle path up to the hamlet of the same name. West of the bridge the line continued in a cutting, from which it emerged on a gentle northerly curve, crossed Pig Tor bridge and, still curving, ran into Pig Tor Tunnel. This short structure of 191 yards carried the line under an outcrop of harder rock around which the river made a tight U-turn. Leaving the western portal of the tunnel the line entered Ashwood Dale and almost immediately crossed the road and river by Cowdall Bar bridge. Directly below the bridge stands a milepost, giving the distance to Bakewell as ten miles, just 1/4 mile further than the distance to Bakewell station by rail. From Cowdall Bar the line ran north west through a shallow cutting and then crossed the road and river for the last time by Ashwood Dale bridge. At this point two sidings left the line, controlled by Ashwood Dale signal box, a tall 'Period III' box erected in 1901 when the original box was renewed.

The earliest siding was that on the north side of the line and was put in late in 1876 for the Ashwood Dale Lime and Stone Co., which became part of Buxton Lime Firms Ltd in 1891. The quarry was subsequently abandoned, but on 26th April 1923 it was reported to the LMS Traffic Committee that "Mr Norman Axe had taken over Ashwood Dale Quarry sidings, which have been closed for many years". Mr Axe was at that time the owner of Hartington Quarries and in the road stone business was referred to as "that well-known Derbyshire character". Whether the venture failed, or was sold to make a profit is not known, but within a few years ownership passed to Highways Construction Ltd, who themselves sold the business to Derbyshire Stone in 1937. Today the plant is part of the Tarmac Group and specialises in the production of industrial powders, all of which now leave by road.

The second sidings were put in for the New Buxton Lime Co. in 1901 to serve its quarry on the south side of the valley and involved a substantial bridge over the river and road, which is believed to have been built in timber. The company was taken over by BLF in 1908 and in July 1924 it was reported that extensive enlargements were in hand which would require additional siding accommodation. It was further reported that the bridge was in a very poor state of repair and required renewal. Under the circumstances it was resolved to move the siding connection to the east of Ashwood Dale bridge, and lay in a new access track, which would allow the original bridge, whose abutment can be seen just east of the Devonshire public house, to be demolished. The bridge was in fact so bad that LMS engines were not permitted to cross it and wagons had to be loose shunted across. Outgoing wagons were run to the western end of the bridge, probably by horses and were picked up by an engine with a rake of wagons. The works remained in operation until 1956, relying almost totally on rail transport. Traffic to and from these quarries and Topley Pike called for several trains per day in the 1930s and while the majority of wagons were sorted at Buxton, Gowhole, Peak Forest or Millers Dale there was one block train daily direct to Cheadle sidings, leaving Ashwood Dale at 1.55pm, with a balanced return working from Cheadle at 6.30pm.

The line continued from the quarries along the northern side of the river, passing the narrowest part of the valley, where a shelf was cut from the rock to accommodate the track, before

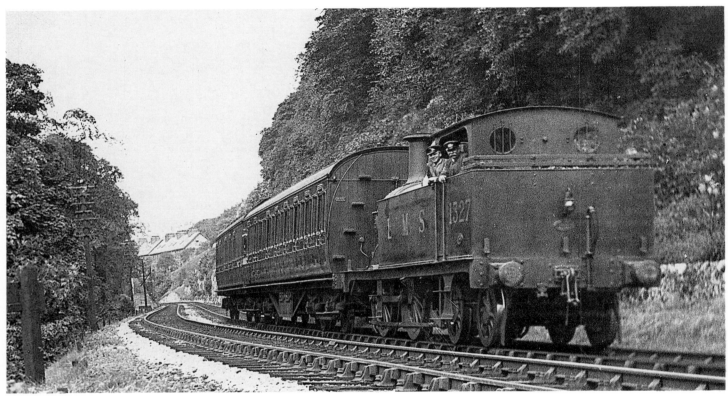

curving sharply to the north and running through Ashwood Dale Tunnel. This 100 yard bore marked a sharp change from the tree lined confines of Ashwood Dale to the urban development of Buxton. West of the tunnel the line continued to curve to the north, straightened and then began a long, tight curve to the west, as it crossed Fairfield Road bridge and passed through Buxton East Junction. At this point the line diverted with the spur to the right turning north and steepening to 1 in 84/1 in 66 as it climbed to join the LNWR at Buxton No.1 signal box. The main line continued to curve on a low embankment, passing under the LNWR Ashbourne line and over Bridge Street before finally running into Buxton station, 26 miles 29 chains from Ambergate West Junction.

Buxton originally developed as the Roman bathing town of Aquae Arnemetiae, but its fortunes then declined and the Domesday Book gave it no more than a passing mention. By the Middle Ages some semblance of recovery had occurred and a small market centre had become established on a limestone bluff, from the base of which issued the mineral spring which had attracted the Romans.

The appeal of the town as a spa re-emerged during the reign of Elizabeth I, when the Earl of Shrewsbury built a 'commodius establishment' on the site of the present Old Hall Hotel, to provide accommodation for the nobility and gentry taking the waters. It was not until 1781 however, when the 5th Duke of Devonshire commissioned John Carr, the York architect, to build the Crescent, that Buxton's modern development began. There can be little doubt that the Duke was intent on establishing a spa to rival Bath, a bold effort indeed for a town with a resident population hardly more than 600. Shortly after the Crescent was erected the magnificent Great Stables were built a little to the north and these were subsequently given to the Buxton Bath Charity, by the 6th Duke, for use as a hospital. At about the same time the Duke instructed his agent, Joseph Paxton, to lay out the Park, a residential area to the west of the stables. The growth of the town as a spa continued, its select image being contained by the poor transport facilities, but in repetition of the events at Matlock Bath, the coming of the railway in 1863 was to have far reaching consequences. In 1868 the 7th Duke ordered the building of the Palace Hotel close to the stations, followed by the laying out of the Pavilion Gardens, and the erection of the Pavilion itself in 1871, in the flamboyant iron and glass seaside pier style of the period. The final major development saw the building of the Opera House just after the turn of the century.

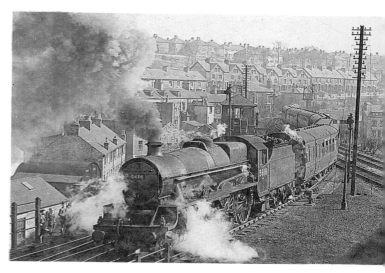

Plate 243 *(right)* Class 5XP No.5616, *Malta G.C.* in the short lived 1946 black livery brings a diverted St Pancras-Manchester express through Buxton East Junction towards the LNWR line in 1948. Such an event was rare and only occurred when both Dove Holes and one of the tunnels on the Dore and Chinley line were closed for maintenance. (E.R.Morten)

Plate 244 *(below)* Stanier Class 5, No.44847 heads the 1.05pm from Derby under the LNWR Ashbourne line and over Bridge Street as it nears journey's end early in 1953.

(E.D. Bruton)

While the population had grown steadily to just over 1,800 by 1861 it rocketed to 6,021 in the next 20 years. As a Victorian spa the town had arrived, but the aristocracy had gone. The town remained as a popular resort, with an orchestra playing nightly through the season and it reached the height of its appeal immediately before the First World War. There was a time of change however after 1918 and the habit of taking the waters declined rapidly in the 1930s. On the other hand people had begun to move out of the cities and the town was growing steadily as a commuter settlement for Stockport and Manchester.

After the Second World War and the passing the austerity years of the early 1950s, the annual holiday became commonplace for the mass of the population, but in spite of advertising by both the railways and the local authorities, it was the seaside towns, not the inland resorts, which became the centres of attraction. Today Buxton remains as a residential centre, witnessed by successful attempts to prevent closure of the direct railway route to Manchester and has now re-emerged as a tourist resort. In recent years a bold revival of the arts at the Opera House has led to the Buxton Festival gaining a good reputation.

The Midland Railway presence began in Buxton in the late summer of 1860, after the Traffic Committee had accepted the offer of a Mr Wilmot to build a small office for the company at an annual rental of £10. The development of the railway

proper began on 5th February 1861, when the engineer laid plans before the Rowsley and Buxton Construction Committee for a station at Buxton, together with the draft of an agreement with the Stockport, Disley & Whaley Bridge Company as to the positions of the two stations and the layout of the approach roads, etc. He was instructed at this meeting to arrange a meeting with the solicitors of the SD&WB to draw up a formal agreement. The following month the engineer reported that he had entered into an agreement to purchase 3 to 3½ acres of land, for the station, from Mr Andrew Brittlebank, Ashbourne, at £600 an acre. On 3rd April 1861 members were informed that agreement had been reached with the SD&WB and were shown further detailed drawings of the station, which were "severally agreed". No further action was taken on the matter until early the following year.

Historians have always commented upon the remarkable degree of similarity between the façades of the two stations at Buxton, particularly in view of the intense rivalry between the two companies. This unified design, however, was neither accidental nor a case of copying, for on 7th January 1862 the Construction Committee resolved that "Sir Joseph Paxton be authorised and requested on the part of this company to confer and agree with the Engineer and Directors of the Stockport, Disley & Whaley Bridge Company the form and style of the *front* to be constructed for the stations of the two companies at Buxton, so as to ensure a uniformity of design".

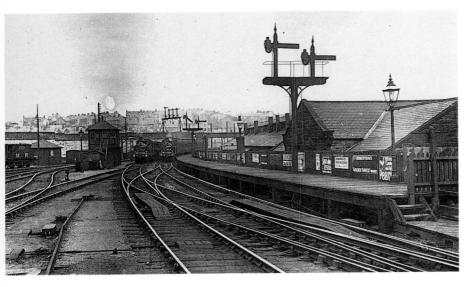

Plate 245 (left) To cater for the extensive excursion traffic at Buxton a special platform was built on the approach track to the station. In this view about 1914, a Millers Dale train has reversed out of the station to allow a local train from Chinley to run in.

(J.M. Bentley Collection)

Plate 246 (bottom) Until 1927 the twin façades of the MR and LNWR stations were linked by screen walls and wrought iron gates, but in that year the latter were removed on the grounds that they were a hazard to pedestrians.

(M.L. Knighton Collection)

It is understood that Paxton, who was a shareholder in both companies, and agent for the Duke of Devonshire who owned most of Buxton, prepared the basic designs himself, no doubt agreeing these with the Duke before he made them public. His discussions were a success and he was able to so report to his committee on 1st April 1862. The final designs for the stations were agreed in September and the contract for their construction was awarded to Charles Humphreys on 3rd November.

While Paxton may have been responsible for the basic design of the screen walls, close examination of the main Midland building reveals the characteristic detailing of Edward Walters. It would appear that it was the main buildings, platforms etc. that formed part of Humphreys' original contract, for he was awarded a further contract for "the erection of screen walls and extension to platforms at Buxton" on 20th March 1863. It is also of interest that a decision on the construction of platforms was not taken until less than two months before the station opened and on 2nd April it was ordered that such portions of the platforms as are under glass roofs, be formed of timber and the remaining parts be asphalted.

In addition to sharing the same gabled end screen walls both stations had a lightweight overall roof supported on the outer edge by cast iron columns, which on the Midland side were originally infilled with vertical wooden boarding. Both stations originally had a single track with one platform on the North Western side, but a platform either side of the Midland track. Although it may seem that the latter were preoccupied with the design and construction of passenger facilities, other aspects of running a railway were not forgotten and on 1st December 1862 it was instructed that tenders be obtained for the construction of an engine shed to hold four engines. The contract was awarded some five weeks later to J. Wood, in the

sum of £1,545. The building was of straightforward construction, over two tracks, with the appropriate offices along the rear wall, and was sited to the south of the station approach tracks, at a lower level. Hardly had the building been completed when the committee began to question their decision and on 5th August 1863 Mr Allport the General Manager and Mr Kirtley, the Locomotive Superintendent, were requested to examine and report on the most suitable site for an engine house at Buxton. It was decided at the same meeting that the tenders already received from the construction of a goods shed should be held in abeyance until it was ascertained whether or not it was advisable to convert the present engine shed into a goods shed. Such a change did not occur and the engineer was instructed to accept the best tender to hand, or seek new ones as he saw fit, for the goods shed. He was also instructed to seek tenders for the construction of a stable for three horses, that of Charles Humphreys for £120 being accepted in November 1863, but it is not known where they were sited.

Development at Buxton was rapid and in June 1864 it was ordered that plans be prepared for a station master's house, while the Traffic Committee's request for a siding and 30 ton truck weighing machine was agreed the following month. Two months later, on 6th September 1864, the General Manager recommended that a block of five coal offices be erected for Messrs Barton, Boden, Duke, Skirrow and Wheatcroft. The contract for these was awarded to J.E. Hall in May 1865, and later that year the contract for erection of the station master's house was awarded to Gyte and Thorpes, in the sum of £524. The house still stands today, just to the right of Fairfield Road bridge, as viewed from Spring Gardens coach park and is one of the few remaining MR structures in the town. Early in 1866 a two wagon cattle dock was constructed and a 5 ton stationary crane was provided. The year was most noted,

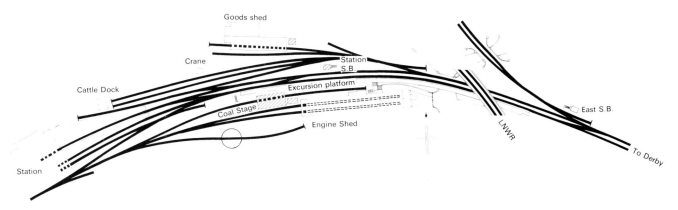

Fig. 86 Buxton MR track plan circa 1900 (part only)

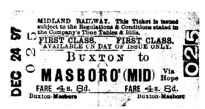

Plate 247 (above) Apart from a very interesting rake of 4 and 6-wheeled carriages, this view of the Midland station about 1880, shows the overall roof and the original timber infilling to the support columns.

(J.M. Bentley Collection)

Plate 248 (right) The construction of the timber end screens to the original roof is clearly seen in this view as a local passenger train awaits departure on 24th June 1933, behind 0-4-4T No.1247. The chocolate and buff paintwork is somewhat marred by smoke from engines which often stopped in the same position.

(H.C. Casserley)

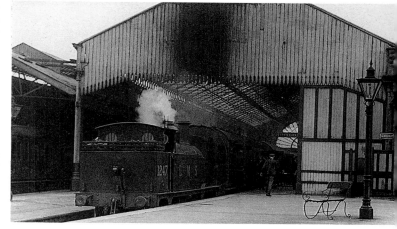

Plate 249 (below) The second overall roof was lower than the earlier one and the absence of an end screen reveals the lightweight nature of the roof trusses. The area covered was also narrower and this view on 3rd May 1934 shows that construction costs were kept down by the minimal use of glass.

(H.C. Casserley)

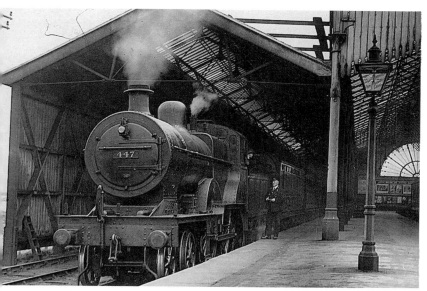

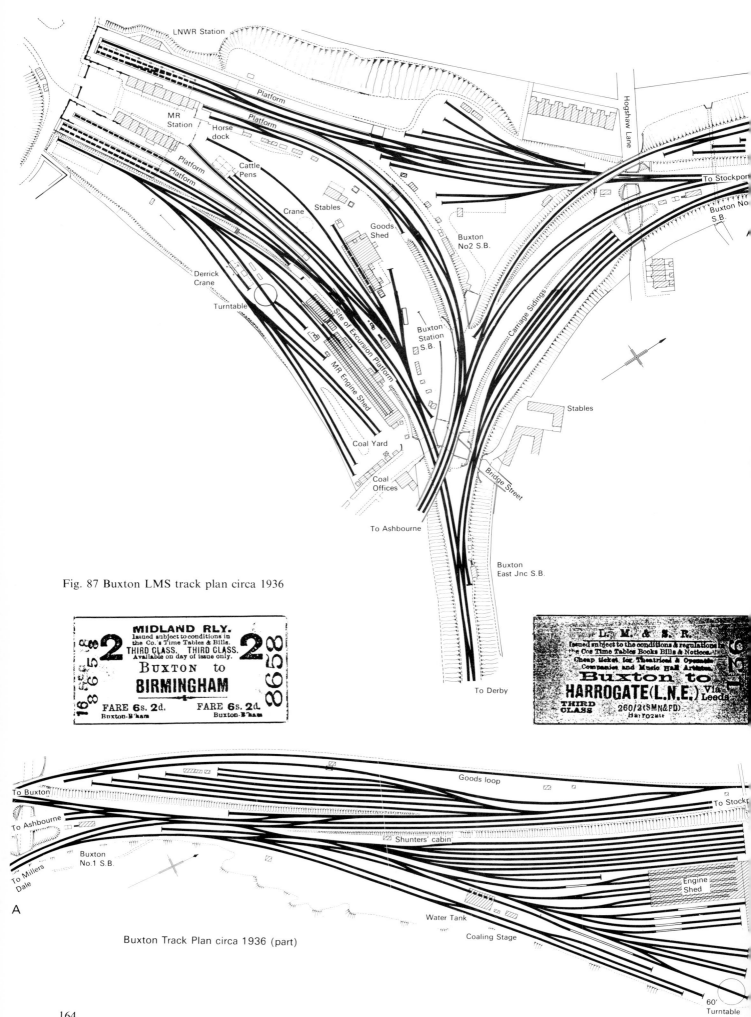

Fig. 87 Buxton LMS track plan circa 1936

LNWR Station

MR Station

Horse dock

Platform
Platform
Platform
Platform

Cattle Pens

Crane

Stables

Goods Shed

Derrick Crane

Turntable

Site of Excursion Platform

MR Engine Shed

Coal Yard

Coal Offices

To Ashbourne

Buxton No2 S.B.

Buxton Station S.B.

Carriage Sidings

Stables

Bridge Street

Buxton East Jnc S.B.

To Derby

Hogshaw Lane

To Stockport

Buxton No. S.B.

MIDLAND RLY.
Issued subject to conditions in the Co.'s Time Tables & Bills.
THIRD CLASS. THIRD CLASS.
Available on day of issue only.
BUXTON to
BIRMINGHAM
FARE 6s. 2d.   FARE 6s. 2d.
Buxton-B'ham   Buxton-B'ham
16865 2   2 8658

L. M. & S. R.
Issued subject to the conditions & regulations in the Cos Time Tables Books Bills & Notices
Cheap ticket for Theatrical & Operatic Companies and Music Hall Artistes
Buxton to
HARROGATE (L.N.E.) Via Leeds
THIRD CLASS   260/2(SMN&PD)
Harrogate

A

To Buxton

To Ashbourne

To Millers Dale

Buxton No.1 S.B.

Goods loop

Shunters' cabin

To Stockp

Engine Shed

Water Tank

Coaling Stage

60' Turntable

Buxton Track Plan circa 1936 (part)

164

however, for the first decision on substantial alterations to the station. On 31st July a plan and estimate for a new arrival platform, as requested by the Construction Committee, was put before the Way and Works Committee and passed on to the Chairman's Committee for final approval. The plan was rejected, however and a revised proposal, to include an overall roof was agreed by the September meeting of the W & W Committee. Work was put in hand the following summer and the platform and a carriage siding alongside were constructed, but the overall roof was omitted. Just why the work was not completed is unknown but the roof is not shown on the 1878 ordnance survey, while *plate 247*, thought to date from around 1880, clearly shows the original screen and roof support columns.

In April 1867 it was ordered that the excursion platform be lengthened forthwith for the proper working of traffic. This platform was a wooden construction alongside the down line, well outside the station, and had a flight of steps directly down into Bridge Street. It was almost certainly part of the original station design, for while the Midland management wanted the income from excursion and tourist traffic it was well aware, in those class-conscious times, that regular travellers would not care to mingle with 'day-trippers'. Printed Guards' Journals of 1890 curiously described this platform as Buxton Ticket Platform.

Unlike development on the Ambergate-Rowsley section of the line the 1870s were relatively quiet years at Buxton and apart from some alterations to the sidings the only work of note involved the stables and goods shed. The location of the original stables is unknown, but on 15th September 1874 it was ordered, at the request of the Traffic Committee, that a plan be prepared for moving the stables from their present position to a "more healthy" one (for the horses or the public is not certain). A few months later the Traffic Committee requested that the goods shed be enlarged. This was agreed and a contract for this work and the construction of new stables was awarded to Solomon Fox on 3rd August 1875 in the sum of £1,192 1s 2d (£1,192.07). One interesting 'might have been' cropped up in November 1876 when the Carriage and Wagon Committee recommended that plans be drawn up for providing a shed for covering about 30 carriages adjoining the station at Buxton. With the LNWR station and MR goods yard on one side and the MR engine shed, coal yard and the town centre on the other, it is rather difficult to see where this shed was to be erected. The W & W Committee gave consideration to the engineer's report in February 1877 but it was finally resolved that a carriage shed was not required at this time.

In the summer of 1881 the engine shed roof was re-slated, only three years before the shed was extended at the front to provide accommodation for four additional 0-6-0 tender engines. The following year minor extensions to the platforms were added and in February 1886 a contract was awarded to J. Slater to construct the additional platform roofing which had been approved almost 20 years earlier. The work involved the removal of the original timber infilling to the main roof supports and the erection of a new all-timber screen outside the carriage siding. Whether this screen was to protect passengers from the elements on what was a rather elevated site, or to hide the trains from the townsfolk, will probably never be known. At about the same time as this work was carried out the timber screen was built across the end of the up platform. The 1880s closed with the granting of an easement in July 1888 to the LNWR to cross the Midland's land with the viaduct for its Buxton and High Peak Junction Railway. £1,000 was paid for this privilege, a relatively small sum for the key to the whole route.

Both the coal stocking ground, to the south of the station and the goods shed were extended early in 1890, followed about twelve months later by alterations to the station buildings. This work, carried out by A. Salt, at a cost of £300 1s 1d (£300.05), comprised alterations to the booking office, together with the provision of a cloakroom and third class ladies' waiting room, which later became the enquiry office. In July 1892, the W & W Committee approved a plan for provision of a new signal box, presumed to be at Buxton East

Junction, and re-arrangement of signals at Buxton, with the proviso that the LNWR bear the full cost of construction together with all annual expenses in connection with the operation of the box. By this time relationships between the North Western and the Midland had become more amicable than they had been 30 years earlier, the former having realised that the proper interchange of traffic between the two companies would be the source of considerable revenue.

When the LNWR built its line into Buxton it was unable to find space for a traditional 'town goods yard', but it managed to squeeze in a small goods shed just east of the station. There was also a siding which ran into the yard between the two stations and then doubled back into the Midland yard. When the Ashbourne line was built both the goods shed and the siding had to be removed and the LNWR negotiated an agreement to use the MR goods facilities, which included a clause to cover equally the cost of future developments and annual maintenance. With the increase in traffic in the 1890s came an increase in the demand for cartage and on 2nd December 1892 it was ordered that a plan and estimate be prepared for erecting new and improved stabling accommodation. It was further instructed that the LNWR was to pay a proportion of the costs, the amount to be determined by the land agents of the two companies. The plan and estimate of £1,000 was approved the following month, and a tender of £788 6s 8d (£788.33), from J. Walker & Sons, was accepted on 19th January 1893.

Towards the close of the 1890s an enlightened attitude to matters of public health and staff creature comforts was shown by the instruction, in June 1897, to provide latrines at the engine shed, at an estimated cost of £85. At this time the congestion at the shed, made much worse by the access off the down main line via a short shunting neck, was becoming serious and on 16th November 1899, at the W & W Committee, the secretary read Minute No. 6217 of the Locomotive Committee, recommending the purchase of land at Buxton for a site for a proposed engine shed. He then read Minute No. 6216, which recommended purchase of land at Rowsley for the same purpose. It was resolved that the estate agent negotiate further and report to a future meeting. This he did, with some considerable success and on 9th August he was able to report that he had purchased an area of land, mainly from the Duke of Devonshire, adjacent to the LNWR engine shed. Strangely, just as at Rowsley, no further action was taken on the matter. Indeed some three years later further investment was put into the existing shed by the provision of an additional siding with an engine pit and a set of sheer legs.

In the summer of 1905 the siding which ran along the north side of the up platform and served the cattle dock, was converted to a bay platform, by putting in a crossover to the up main line, and a ground signal to control this. A little over two years later the whole operating procedure at Buxton was looked at in detail by the Traffic Committee and on 3rd January 1908 the W & W Committee agreed to several important changes. The long sidings in the goods yard, to the north of the main line, were pushed over and the up platform/bay platform was extended, primarily for excursion traffic (a more egalitarian view of passengers having now come to prevail). Various changes were also made to the crossovers and turnouts in the station throat, but the most significant changes occurred around the East Junction. Readers will recall that when the MR were authorised to build the line from Rowsley to Buxton, in 1860, the LNWR had said they would not permit through running. Thus the connecting curve at Buxton, which was built by the Midland, was double track down from the LNWR junction, but then became single track with a connection only to the up MR line. To run any through traffic on to the North Western the MR train had to draw into the station approach, set back across a trailing crossover and then draw forward at the junction until it reached the double track section. The LNWR could, of course, run straight through on to MR metals with no problem. It really was quite amazing that this situation remained as long as it did, but under these 1908 changes a normal double junction was finally provided. At the same time three carriage sidings were laid in on the down side of the curve. Coincidental with these changes to the trackwork came the renewal of the station signal box, the new box being opened on 27th November 1908.

With the general increase in the size of Midland locomotives in the early years of the century, the 40ft turntable at Buxton became more and more inadequate. Fortunately, as Chinley had become the focus of traffic, the 50ft turntable at Marple had become surplus to requirements and in July 1912 it was resolved to move the turntable to Buxton. It seems that all idea of a new shed had been abandoned, for a little over two years later, in January 1915, it was agreed to put in an additional engine pit and a breakdown van siding. Early in 1918 additions were made to the goods office accommodation and finally on 19th October 1922 a contract was awarded to G.W. Walker & Sons to construct lavatories for the goods yard staff. This was just about 25 years after similar facilities were provided at the engine shed and one wonders if it reflected the difference in status between porters, clerks and drivers.

The early years of the LMS saw no development at Buxton but in January 1927 the engineer reported that an approach had been made by the Borough Council with a request to lessen the danger to pedestrians in the station yard. An agreement was made to remove the walls and gates between the two stations, the Council to pay for and carry out the work. By this time the excursion platform had become virtually unused and it was finally removed early in 1932, at an annual estimated saving of £25 in maintenance costs. This small event reflected the general economy drive then in full gait on the LMS, and was followed on 28th June 1933 by far more significant proposals, when a scheme for the modernisation of the locomotive facilities was put before the Traffic Committee. The Midland shed, coded '20' at the time, had taken over all administrative control in 1926 but it offered no scope for expansion or improvement (although it is generally accepted as having been the better equipped of the two sheds) and attention was turned to the ex LNWR depot. This was a six road northlight shed of traditional design, opened in 1892 on a large open site to the north of the LNW station. The proposals for improvement included the filling of part of the valley at the side of the shed, on land purchased by the MR all those years before, and the addition of further storage roads, together with the provision of a new 60ft turntable and mechanical coaling and ash plants. The cost of the scheme was originally estimated at £27,150 but in May 1934 the Chief Operational Manager had to report an under estimation of almost £5,000 on the costs. Actually the question of office accommodation had been overlooked and a contract for this work was eventually

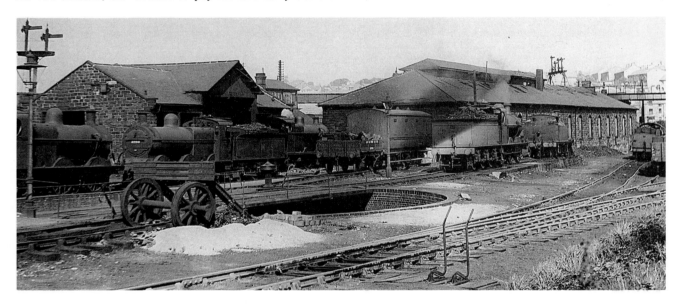

Plate 250 (above) This view in August 1934 shows the MR shed, coaling stage and turntable, all in close proximity. The extension to the shed, added in 1884, comprises that part fitted with the roof vent.

(W. Potter)

Plate 251 (below) Taken about nine months later in May 1935, this view from the station shows the cramped nature of the site and the sheer legs installed in 1903. The third track from the left is the approach road to both the shed and the coal yard and the steep slope down is quite clear. In both views the scene is dominated by 3F and 4F 0-6-0s.

(E.R. Morten)

Plate 252 This view taken on 13th April 1935, to record the new mechanical coaling stage under construction, also shows the original LNWR coaling stage, with its water tank over and the open nature of the land to the north of Buxton. In the foreground is a fascinating glimpse of the private owner wagons which were seen almost daily in the town.

(H. Townley)

awarded to Greenwoods (Mansfield) Ltd on 28th November 1934. As the modernisation scheme was drawing to a close, in the summer of 1935, approval was given to the fitting of vacuum-operated turning gear to the new turntable. On 19th August 1935 the MR depot was closed and the men and machines were transferred 'up the hill'. The next ominous rumblings of change occurred in 1956/57 when a diesel depot was constructed, almost on the site of the original LNWR engine shed, just outside the station. The two sheds ran in

Plate 253 Seen from the top of the coaling stage in June 1936 it is clear how the LNWR shed yard had been expanded and laid out to provide modern, efficient motive power facilities. Engines could quickly be coaled, move on to the ash disposal plant and then be turned before storage in the open or under cover.

(W. Potter)

tandem for some years but in March 1968 the main depot was finally closed to steam traction and the site cleared soon afterwards.

Up to the re-organisation of motive power administration late in 1935, Rowsley had been a sub-shed of Buxton and in 1933 the combined allocation of the sheds was as follows:

"Rebuilt" Johnson 4-4-0 483 class	352/56/403/12/13/ 47/48/61/62/89
Johnson 0-4-4T	1247/1420/21 (fitted for motor train working)
Johnson 0-6-0T	1759
Deeley 0-6-4T	2019/21/34
Fowler 2-6-4T	2323/24/65-71
Johnson 0-6-0 2F	2999/3001/4/48/ 3104/18/3221/70/80/ 3302/48/3445/93
"Rebuilt" Johnson/Deeley 0-6-0 3F	3268/69/71/74/75/78/ 3281/82/83/90/96/3338/ 42/87/94/3717
Fowler Midland 4F	3835/36/37/42/78/ 3900
Fowler LMS 4F	4047/48/49/50/4140/ 41/4548/49

Webb 2-4-0T	6422/25/27/28 (High Peak Section)
Webb 0-6-2T	6899/6900/04
Park N.L.R. 0-6-0T	7511/15/21/27/30 (High Peak Section)
Bowen-Cooke 0-8-2T	7896/97/98/99
Bowen-Cooke 0-8-0	9212-27
Hughes/Fowler 2-6-0	13173/74

In terms of passenger services Buxton was a terminus from whichever direction it was approached, but the town nevertheless enjoyed a comprehensive service of regular trains, a large number of excursions and a few decidedly unusual workings. In principle the LNWR station had a relatively frequent service to and from Manchester (London Road), with a very much less frequent service to and from Ashbourne and Uttoxeter. The MR station had a more diverse timetable with trains to or from Chinley and Manchester to the north, Millers Dale and Derby to the south, the Millers Dale local trains and through carriages to and from St Pancras.

In 1922 the Midland station saw nine main line departures and ten arrivals. The departures primarily comprised three early trains to Manchester, one to Derby and one to Chinley. The late morning and afternoon were quiet, with a train to Stockport and one to Manchester Victoria, while the evening saw a further service to Chinley and two trains to Derby. The arrivals consisted of early trains from Manchester, Derby and Rowsley, then a long gap punctuated only by the 2.32pm from Chinley. In the evening there were three trains from Manchester and two from Derby. The Millers Dale local service comprised 14 down and 13 up trains. To partially compensate for its branch line status the town was served by through carriages from St Pancras, no doubt originally provided to save the more genteel passengers the irksome bother of changing trains en route. It is interesting to note that on 17th November 1900 the High Peak News drew attention to the drab state of Millers Dale station and referred to it as "Patience Junction". The first down carriage was carried on the 1.25pm 'East Lancashire Express' from St Pancras and was attached to the 5.25pm from Millers Dale. This was allowed two minutes longer to Buxton, with its heavier load and arrived at 5.37pm. The carriage was cleaned and stabled overnight, before leaving the next day on the 1.58pm to Millers Dale where it was attached to the 1.15pm ex Manchester Victoria, arriving in St Pancras at 5.05pm. Two vehicles were required to operate the service and they would normally have been 1st/3rd brake composites.

This general pattern was retained by the LMS but the frequency of trains had increased by 1935 to twelve departures and twelve arrivals. The additional up trains included a very early departure to Matlock, a morning train to Chinley and an afternoon service to Manchester, but the morning train to Stockport was withdrawn. The early morning train from Manchester was withdrawn and the early train from Rowsley was re-timed to start from Matlock. Two additional services from Chinley were introduced together with afternoon trains from Manchester and Derby. The most marked change, however, related to the through London carriage workings. Early travellers to Buxton could breakfast on the way as a restaurant car was attached at Leicester to the 4.25am St Pancras-Manchester Central, which reached Millers Dale at 9.08am. There it was added to the 9.17am local to Buxton. As in Midland days a through carriage was also attached to the early afternoon train from London and a third such carriage left St Pancras on the 6.25pm to Manchester Central. This was also advertised as a through coach to Matlock and was detached at Derby, leaving five minutes later on the 9.05pm slow to Buxton.

In the up direction the first through carriage left Buxton on the 9.40am to Millers Dale, where it was attached to the 8.55am from Manchester Central, arriving in St Pancras at 1.30pm. The restaurant car was kept very busy for it was re-stocked smartly and left less than an hour after its arrival, on the 10.12am to Millers Dale. It was then coupled to the 9.46am slow from Chinley to Derby, where it was attached to the 12.00pm Derby-St Pancras, arriving in London a little

before 3.30pm. It then returned to Leicester on the 5.32pm to Nottingham. A final through working left Buxton at 2.10pm, was attached to the 1.45pm ex-Manchester Central and arrived in St Pancras at 6.13pm. Thus, unlike the Midland, the LMS provided a through service which allowed out and back travel the same day between London and Buxton, or vice versa, with almost five hours at either destination. The local service to Millers Dale was increased to 17 trains each way on weekdays, and about 1934 motor-train working (push and pull) was introduced to save running round at either end.

Following the outbreak of war most services were cut, but those to Buxton were decimated. The departures consisted of early morning trains to Chinley and Manchester, with an early evening service to Chinley. Arrivals comprised an early train from Chinley, and early evening trains from Chinley and Manchester, a grand total of six. The direct service to and from Derby and the through carriages were discontinued. By the early 1950s matters had not improved and in 1954 the station still had six weekday services. The up side saw three morning trains to Manchester and an evening departure for Derby. There were only two main line arrivals, the 1.05pm from Derby and the 5.22pm from Manchester. On the other hand the local service to Millers Dale was restored almost to its pre-war level with 17 up and 16 down journeys each weekday.

By the mid-1960s the run down of services on the main line through the Peak was well in hand and in 1967 activity at Buxton Midland had been reduced to the three early departures for Manchester, with one evening return, and an early morning train from Derby. As these main line trains were cut the town came to rely more and more on the Millers Dale shuttle service, which had been increased to 19 journeys each way, although an increasing number of passengers travelled to Millers Dale by private car. This increase was relatively short-lived however for on 6th March 1967 all stopping trains between Chinley and Matlock were withdrawn, Millers Dale station was closed and all Midland line services to Buxton ceased.

At Grouping the two Buxton stations came under the control of one station master, believed to be the Midland man, and while a detailed study of the LNWR routes to Buxton is outside the scope of the present narrative, it is felt that a brief note is necessary to complete the LMS scene. The general pattern of services had of course become established by the early 1920s, but unlike the Midland side this pattern was more straightforward and was subsequently developed in a very different manner.

The main route was to Manchester London Road and in 1919 there were eleven down trains and twelve up. Of the down trains six left Buxton between 7.10am and 9.15am with the 8.13am departure timed as an express. In the reverse direction five trains ran between 7.25am and 4.00pm, then five between 4.45pm and 6.20pm, with two in the late evening. The 5.40pm was the return express working. By 1935 the town's popularity as a commuter settlement was growing strongly and the number of trains had been increased to 19 down and 21 up. The peak period concentration remained and two trains in each direction ran as expresses. These were the 8.18am and 9.05am from Buxton and the 4.45pm and the 5.40pm from Manchester. During the war the service was cut to thirteen down and twelve up trains, but while almost every passenger train was subject to deceleration it is interesting to note that one service each way retained its pre-war express timing. This level of service continued for some time after the war, but in spite of the huge losses of traffic to the roads, the timetable had grown to surpass its pre-war level by the mid-1960s. In 1967 there were 23 down and 21 up trains on Monday to Friday. In line with modern operating practice the service was put on an hourly basis, with additional trains at the morning and evening peak periods. Today the service consists of 25 trains each way over the same period, and in weather such as that experienced in February 1986 in the Buxton area, the railway provided the only access to the towns for much of the month – despite the BBC insisting the town was "cut off"!

In complete contrast to this route was the line which curved sharply out of Buxton and ran south to Ashbourne and Uttoxeter. Conceived as a through route from Euston, via the

North Western and Midland joint line from Nuneaton to Burton and the North Staffordshire route to Ashbourne, the railway followed an undulating and sinuous route over the limestone plateau. Although a through train ran daily from London to Buxton up to 1914, the line was quite unsuitable for express running and passenger services remained compatible with the sparsely populated area the line served. At the close of the LNWR period there were four trains each way on weekdays between Ashbourne and Buxton, with a number of these originating at Uttoxeter and bringing North Staffordshire Railway locomotives and rolling stock into the heart of the Peak District. By 1935 the service had grown to five trains each way, with eight down and seven up trains on Saturdays. Of these the 10.35am and 7.50pm (SO) ran through from Buxton to Uttoxeter, while the 10.28am, 1.35pm and 9.15pm (SO) started from Uttoxeter. The wartime reductions cut the service to three trains in each direction, a level which remained into the 1950s. By then, however, all trains, except the 7.50am from Ashbourne, ran between Uttoxeter and Buxton or vice versa. In overall terms the line was lightly used and was closed to regular traffic on 1st November 1954, although it remained open for excursion traffic until 1962 and for winter emergency services up to 7th October 1963.

Before World War II the train was the only form of 'rapid transit' available to the majority of the population, and from the very inception of railways, companies were keen to promote excursion and special trains. While the financial wherewithal to indulge in day trips may have been limited to certain sections of the population before 1914, the period between the wars saw a rapid expansion in this traffic to all manner of resorts, beauty spots and places of interest, of which Buxton was a popular example. Conversely the relative isolation of the town gave rise to the demand for outward excursions to places such as North Wales and Blackpool. It was also at this time that the evening trip, both into and out of the Peak District became very popular, as did the 'land cruises' from the Potteries. Usually the trains would start from the Stoke area, one running to Buxton via Macclesfield and the Middlewood curve and the other via Uttoxeter and Ashbourne, giving passengers a choice of outward and return journeys. On odd occasions there were even more specialised trains which brought decidedly unusual visitors to the area. One could say, without fear of contradiction, that LNER J39s and GWR diesel railcars were not everyday visitors to Buxton, but *plates 256 and 257* record their presence.

In the early 1950s British Railways spent heavily on advertising to promote tourist traffic, but while the posters may have been attractive, the increasing level of private car ownership set in motion an irreversible decline in the popularity of the excursion train. Perhaps the activities of the railway preservation movement may once again bring regular special trains into Buxton, but in the meantime we must return to the 1930s and look at the lifeblood of the railways – freight traffic.

Apart from local traffic Buxton saw considerable amounts of through freight, prime amongst which was the flow of coal

Plate 254 (top) By the mid-1960s diesels were well in command and this plate shows Sulzer Type 2, No.D5287 with the 7.10am to Manchester Central on 18th June 1965. By this time the Midland station had lost its gable wall and overall roof and the virtual cessation of goods traffic allowed the yard to be used for carriage stabling.

(D. Cross)

Plate 255 (left) Fifty minutes after the previous picture, Class 5XP No.45705 *Seahorse* leaves with the 8.00am to Manchester, hauling the four coach set seen in the left background of plate 254.

(D. Cross)

Plate 256 (above) Among the special trains to Buxton were some very unusual workings. One of these was the Birmingham Railway Club's annual trip, which went out via Millers Dale and back via Ashbourne one year and in the reverse direction the next. In this view, in 1952, GWR diesel railcar No.W14W, is seen at East Junction while running empty from the LNWR side round to the MR station in readiness for the return journey.

(E.R. Morten)

Plate 257 (below) This view illustrates one of the highlights of the social calendar as LNER Class J39 0-6-0, No.1586 arrives with the team and supporters for the annual football match between Hyde and Buxton at the Spring Bank Holiday, 1937.

(E.R. Morten)

Plate 258 (right) Travel to football matches was a lucrative form of income to the railways, as this 1914 handbill suggests.

(G. Waite Collection)

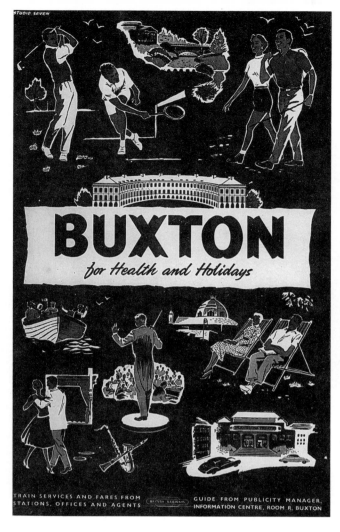

from Yorkshire, Derbyshire and Nottinghamshire to the North West. In 1932 four mineral trains from Sheffield and nine from Rowsley ran to Buxton on weekdays, with a corresponding empty flow. With the exception of an early morning service which terminated at the Midland side, these trains were worked through to the North Western exchange sidings to be sorted for the Ashbourne line, Macclesfield, Lancashire, Cheshire and North Wales. This coal traffic brought a considerable number of colliery owned wagons to the town and Mr A. Hellewell, a retired signalman can readily recall the following:

Babbington, Blackwell, Butterley, Carlton, Clay Cross, Denby, Firbeck, Gedling, Hardwick, Linby, Markham Main, Newstead, New Hucknall, J. Oakes, Oxcroft, Pentrich, Pinxton, Sheepbridge, Stanton, Staveley, Swanwick and Wingfield Manor.

While the movement of coal, coke and patent fuel was fundamental to the Midland Railway, (27,338,000 tons in 1913), the value of this traffic was at least equalled in the Buxton area by the carriage of lime and limestone products. Mention has already been made of the quarries in Ashwood Dale and the main area of production around Peak Forest will be discussed separately in *Chapter 20*. The third area of working was to the south of Buxton and warrants a brief note as the majority of the output came through the town, much of it leaving via the Midland route.

The impetus to the commercial extraction of limestone to the south of Buxton came in 1826 with the opening of the

Plate 261 (left) While the majority of private owner wagons running into the Midland side would have been destined for the coal yard, vehicles en route to more distant parts appeared from time to time. These wagons would normally have run directly up to the North Western sidings, but at busy periods they would have been sent forward from Rowsley on the first available train, to be sorted as necessary at Buxton. This view in June 1930 shows one such wagon operated by the Davies Coal & Coke Co., Llandudno. It appears to be a 10 ton vehicle, 16ft x 7ft 6in, with three 11in, one 9in and one 5in planks. The white lettering looks to have vermillion shading and the base colour was most likely mid-grey. These wagons are known to have run to Aldwarke Main Colliery.

(E.R. Morten)

171

Cromford & High Peak Railway. The immediate result of the opening of this line was the expansion of the quarries at Grin and Harpur Hill, which could send their output north via Whaley Bridge and the Peak Forest Canal, or south via Cromford to the growing industries of the Midlands. In 1861 the LNWR gained an interest in the line and following major track improvements, a new quarry was opened at Dowlow in 1874 by Richard Briggs & Sons, Clitheroe. Following the opening of the Ashbourne line in the 1890s the majority of the output went to Lancashire via New Mills and Brindle Heath. The company became part of Buxton Lime Firms Ltd (BLF) in 1891, but Briggs retained their business interests in Clitheroe and continued to operate their own railway wagons, which would have travelled regularly to Dowlow.

Around the turn of the century further quarries were opened at Brierlow, Dowlow and Hindlow. The works at Brierlow were opened in 1903 by William Spencer, on a seven year lease

The early history of the quarry at Hindlow is somewhat obscure, but it became part of BLF and is today an important part of ICI. The quarry at Grin, referred to earlier, was also absorbed by BLF, but was taken over in 1923 by Clay Cross Co., who produced crushed and screened limestone for use in its own ironworks at Clay Cross and for sale on the open market. As the company was also prominent in the mining industry they were able to make efficient use of their railway wagons by carrying coal to Buxton and bringing back limestone.

A second phase of development took place in the mid 1920s with the opening of three further quarries near Hindlow by Road Products Ltd, about 1925, Hillhead Quarries Ltd in 1927 and Ryan, Somerville & Co. in 1928. Little is known about the latter other than that they were principally limeburners. The other two began by producing roadstone, with some lime production at Hillhead. In 1935 this quarry merged with the

Plate 262 This wagon is one from a batch of ten, built by C. Roberts in 1911, numbered 181-190 and registered by the LYR. It has oil 126 axleboxes, brakes one side only and side doors. It is 15ft x 7ft 6in and has one 9in and four 7in planks on the sides. The wagon has no end sills and the end planks comprise one 11in, four 7in and one 10in. It is painted red, with black ironwork, white letters and black shading.
(Author's Collection)

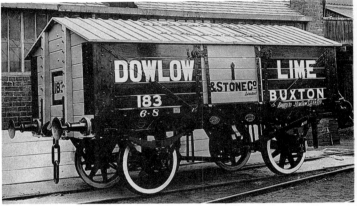

Plate 264 This wagon is one of a batch built by E. Eastwood in 1910 and registered by the LNWR. It is 15ft 9in x 7ft 9in, with four 7in and one 9in planks on the sides. It is painted red and buff, with a light grey roof and has white and black lettering respectively. In 1912 a batch of five-plank open wagons were built to a similar livery and dimensions, but unfortunately only one running number is known, 118. However, early in 1923 a further batch was built, numbered 196-215 and it is believed that these were identical.
(Author's Collection)

from the Duke of Devonshire. On expiry this lease was not renewed and BLF took over operations on a further short lease. This too was given up and in 1923 the works came under the control of Beswick's Lime Works Ltd. The managing director was Percy J. Beswick, whose father, T. Beswick had long been involved in the local limestone trade and its associated wagon building industry. As the works expanded and the number of kilns increased, a fleet of wagons was built up and by 1939 the company owned over 200 vehicles, which were used to distribute lime products and bring in coal form the kilns. The works continued as a family business until 1960 when ownership passed to Staveley Lime Products Ltd, who in turn sold out to Peakstone Lime.

The Dowlow Lime and Stone Co. began operations close to Briggs' quarry in 1898 and while the company operated a large fleet of conventional wagons it also had a number of distinctive hipped roof wagons, shown in *plate 264*. The works remained in the original ownership until the early 1960s, when it was taken over by Steetley (Mfg) Co., Minerals Division.

Hughes brothers who were then producing tarred macadam at their Waterswallows basalt quarry between Buxton and Great Rocks. Road Products Ltd, who owned a fleet of wagons about which the author knows nothing whatsoever, was also brought into this merger. The new company, Hillhead Hughes Ltd closed down lime burning at Hillhead and concentrated on macadam production at Waterswallows and the sale of dry limestone from Hillhead, principally for use in iron-making, sugar refining, glass manufacture and as railway ballast. In 1962 the company took over Settle Limes Ltd and in 1965 it became part of the Tarmac group.

In 1933 the population of Buxton was some 15,600 and this gave rise to a heavy local goods traffic which in terms of annual tonnage placed the town third in order of importance in our study area, after Matlock and Ambergate. Although large areas were occupied by quarries the predominant land use around Buxton was agriculture and the station saw an important livestock traffic. This reached a peak in the 1880s and '90s, when some 6–8 cattle trucks per week used the yard. By the early LMS period however, this traffic had fallen to one or two wagons per week, but even then the spectacle of cattle being driven through the town centre to the station still appeals to the imagination.

The coal class traffic was dominated by the output of limestone from Ashwood Dale, but considerable quantities of fuel were bought in for both industrial and domestic consumption. In the forefront of the former were supplies to

Plate 263 (left) The majority of Beswick's fleet consisted of 1923 standard 12 ton wagons, with four 9in planks. Known running numbers were 116-216 and the livery was cream with black letters.
(Peakstone Lime)

Plate 265 (left) This view shows the undulating landscape south of Buxton and the method of opening out a new quarry before the introduction of mechanised mining. The work was labour intensive and stone was loaded by wheelbarrow into the wagons, with the sidings gradually being extended as work progressed.

(C.N. Croft's Collection)

Plate 266 (below) This view not only records four workmen for posterity but shows the wagon in detail. It is a standard 1923 12 ton vehicle with four 9in planks and is painted black with plain white letters. Known running numbers are 100-110.

(C.N. Croft's Collection)

the gas company. The first gas works were opened in 1851 by the Buxton Gas, Coke and Coal Co., on a site to the west of Bridge Street. The company was acquired by the local board in 1870, but it was soon found that the works were inadequate to supply the growing demand. Construction of a new works was put in hand in 1873 on a site just to the south of Ashwood Dale Tunnel, taking advantage of the railway by putting in a siding served by a trailing turnout from the down line.

This was known as Buxton Gas siding and was controlled latterly by the ground frame seen in *plate 241*. Instructions issued in March 1899 stated that the home and distant signals worked from the Gas siding must always be kept exhibiting the 'All right' signal except when required to be placed at 'Danger' for the protection of trains stopping at the siding. The Station Master at Buxton was held responsible for appointing a competent man to be in attendance at the siding as necessary and the key of the Buxton Gas siding signal box, the key of the gate at the entrance to the gas works and the key of the points in the down main line and the siding alongside it must, when not in use, be kept in the Buxton station signal box.

Prior to 1900 records of coal supplies are rather vague but mention is made of Grassmoor Colliery and J. & G. Wells Ltd. These two concerns kept well to the fore up to about 1916, by which time several other suppliers had become involved, including Barrow Hematite Steel Co., J. Brown and Co., Kirkland and Perkin, H. Nickson and Tom Wright. For the next ten years the records become sparse again, but by 1927 the ordering of coal supplies had been made subject to the formal tendering procedure. As found elsewhere a small number of dealers came to dominate the scene and these were led by Evesons Ltd, E. Foster & Co., and J. McElvie, being joined in the early 1930s by Cawood-Wharton Ltd and the Rotherham & District Collieries Association. In the late 1920s

Plate 267 (above) **Among regular arrivals at the gas works were John Brown wagons.** This 10 ton vehicle, seen on 10th March 1941, having come to grief, was 16ft x 7ft 6in and was painted red, with white letters, shaded black.

(Author's Collection)

Fig. 88 Buxton Corporation Gas Works wagon livery
Grey, white letters, black shading.

(Courtesy D.G. Halliday)

173

the Council became aware of the advantages to be gained from operating its own railway wagons and ten standard 7-plank wagons were purchased from T. Beswick & Co. These were fitted with side, end and bottom doors and were numbered 101–110. Almost at once this move paid dividends for the dealers began to offer a discount of 11d or 1s (5p) per ton on the price of coal (then averaging 22s 6d (£1.62½) per ton delivered), if these wagons were used. It was common practice among owners to have their wagons repainted every 3–5 years and it is interesting to note that in March 1936 the wagons were repainted by F.T. Wright, Nottingham at £2 13s 6d (£2.67½) each.

The coal yard, which had siding space for 62 wagons, was adjacent to the MR engine shed, with a road access into Bridge Street. By the early 1930s the original block of five coal offices had been supplemented by three wooden sheds, and together these provided accommodation for five companies. These were Buxton Co-operative Society, Kirkland & Perkin, J.R. Lomas, H. Rains and M. Thorpe. In addition to Kirkland & Perkin, it is known that H. Rains operated his own wagons, but no records of these have yet come to light. It is not known if the other dealers had any wagons. With a catchment population in and around the town of some 16,500, the annual coal tonnage, including shops and commercial concerns, would have been in the order of 17–18,000 tons, in the 1930s, or about 38–40 wagon loads per week.

In 1922 there were some 180 shops or businesses in Buxton and in that year 16,863 tons of general merchandise passed through the joint goods yard. This traffic would have called for approximately 110 covered vans or open wagons per week, slightly over half of which used the MR line through Ashwood Dale. The goods carried covered every manner of foodstuffs, clothing, household goods, furniture etc. The variety is perhaps summed up by the example of one trader in particular, Messrs Holme & Ash, who were ironmongers, agricultural machinery merchants, dairy appliance, corn, cake, cattle feed, gun and cartridge suppliers. The demand for oil-based products was growing rapidly in the 1920s and tank wagons operated by Anglo-American Oil Co., British Petroleum Co. and Shell-Mex Ltd became regular visitors to the yard. There would also have been rectangular tar tanks bringing in tar and bitumen for Messrs Hughes Bros' macadam business. From the turn of the century there was a considerable amount of mineral traffic at Buxton, with some 40 wagon loads passing through the yard every week, but apart from the usual building materials and basalt from Waterswallows Quarry, the exact nature of this traffic has not been ascertained.

Today the Midland side at Buxton is occupied by the Peak Railway Society, which is slowly growing in status, but we must retrace our steps to Blackwell Mill and continue our journey to Chinley.

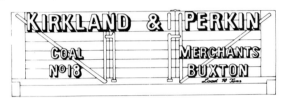

Fig. 89 Kirkland & Perkin wagon livery

Red, white letters, black shading.

(Author)

Plate 268 British Rail have removed almost every trace of the Midland Railway from Buxton but the Peak Railway Society are endeavouring to rectify this, in spirit at least. The author was fortunate enough to be on the spot when the haulage contractor delivered the Stanier 8F, No.48624, from Barry on 1st August 1981, for restoration and hopefully, service on the re-opened line to Matlock.

(Author)

Chapter 19

Great Rocks Dale and Peak Forest

From Peak Forest Junction the line continued north westwards through the tunnel of the same name and entered Great Rocks Dale. The 29 yard tunnel pierced a spur of limestone, around which the stream which cut the dale once flowed. The top of the tunnel was later used as an access to cross the line and the adjoining valley was blocked by a tip from Buxton Central lime works. Once into the dale, which was little more than 200 yards wide, with almost perpendicular edges, the line curved east, then west and finally back to the east through a long curve, taking it on to an alignment almost due north, past Tunstead Quarry. At this point a quirk of geology led the former river to make an acute 'S' bend, leaving two ridges to break up the symmetry of the valley. The southerly of the two was the lowest and this was crossed by a short, steep-sided cutting. The second, very close by, was somewhat higher and was pierced by Great Rocks Tunnel, 161 yards long. North of the tunnel the line, which was now in Peak Dale, curved gently to the west, passed under Great Rocks bridge and then to the east again as it passed Great Rocks Junction signal box. Directly beyond the box the line went under Buxton Road, straightened and after passing under Upper End bridge, curved very slightly to the east, straightened and ran into Peak Forest station, 25 miles 40 chains from Ambergate West Junction.

Although our imaginary LMS passenger would not have believed it, his early Midland counterpart would have found little but solitude in this dry, virtually treeless valley, and one is perchance to ask why a station at this location?

Just under twelve months after construction of the New Mills extension began, the Construction Committee resolved to tour the line to decide upon the location of stations, but unfortunately the minute book does not record any of the deliberations, only the outcome. The tour of inspection took place on 19th October 1863 and with a large area to cover it is fairly safe to assume that the committee came by rail to Buxton on the previous day, in order to make an early start. They would have been accompanied by the engineer, who by now would have become most familiar with the locality, and he no doubt pointed out the two roads which ran from Buxton towards the new line. The southerly of the two ran generally eastwards towards Great Rocks, Wormhill and Millers Dale.

Plate 269 (above) 'Peak' class, No.D56 *The Bedfordshire and Hertfordshire Regiment (T.A.)* passes the site of the LMS dump at the south end of Great Rocks Dale with a Manchester Central-Nottingham express on 11th May 1967. (D. Cross)

Plate 270 (below) This view looking north in May 1957, together with plate 271, shows how the Tunstead Works of ICI have come to dominate Great Rocks Dale. It also shows how crushed limestone was carried in open wagons or hoppers, but lime (bagged?) went in open wagons sheeted down. Also, modern bulk lime hoppers are beginning to appear. (British Railways)

Plate 271 (above) This view, on 23rd February 1985, shows the two spurs of land around which the river, which formed the dale, once followed an 'S' shaped course. The nearer spur was crossed by the cutting to the right when the railway was built and then again when Tunstead was developed to leave the isolated pillar of stone seen here. The second spur was somewhat higher and was pierced by Great Rocks Tunnel, 161 yards in length.

(Author)

The other ran north eastwards through Peak Dale to Peak Forest, Bradwell and Castleton. As the committee intended to travel northwards to New Mills it is highly likely that they took the northerly of the two roads out of Buxton. When they arrived in Peak Dale the engineer would have reminded them that they were on the main road to the Hope Valley. He would no doubt also have pointed out the quarrying activity which had begun in the area following the opening of the Peak Forest Tramway. They would have been quick to see the potential limestone traffic for their own railway and the decision to build a station at this point was made. Conjecture perhaps, but market research and analysis of transportation desire lines were hardly tools of the trade in the 1860s. The committee went on that day to select sites for stations at Chapel-en-le Frith, Chinley, Bugsworth and New Mills.

The station at Peak Forest, which should perhaps have been called Peak Dale, was almost identical to that at Great Longstone, but had slightly less ornate chimneys and barge boards. It was built by John Ashwell as an extension to his main contract and it is believed that the up platform shelter was built at the same time. It is interesting that even though there was a road bridge at the end of the platforms no provision was ever made for passengers to cross the line, other than by a standard barrow crossing.

In February 1871 the Traffic Committee requested that a 2 ton crane be removed from Bristol and sent to Peak Forest, presumably for use in the anticipated loading of stone. It was resolved, however, that a travelling crane be provided as certain alterations to the sidings were pending in connection with the limestone traffic. Where the crane came from or how long it stayed is not known, for the sidings in the area were extended or altered a further fifteen times up to the turn of the century. What is certain is that this crane was not the one photographed at Peak Forest about 1900 and shown in *plate 275*, for this is a 1 ton crane, and one which surely could never have run on a Midland main line. It is the opinion of David L.F. Gilbert, an authority in these matters, that this crane was an ex-contractor's vehicle, an opinion which the author tends to share. In fact, it may well have been one of the cranes used in the construction of the New Mills extension.

Plate 272 (below) 'Britannia' class 4-6-2, No.70021 *Morning Star* passes Great Rocks Junction with the 2.25pm St Pancras-Manchester Central express on 18th August 1959.

(E.R. Morten)

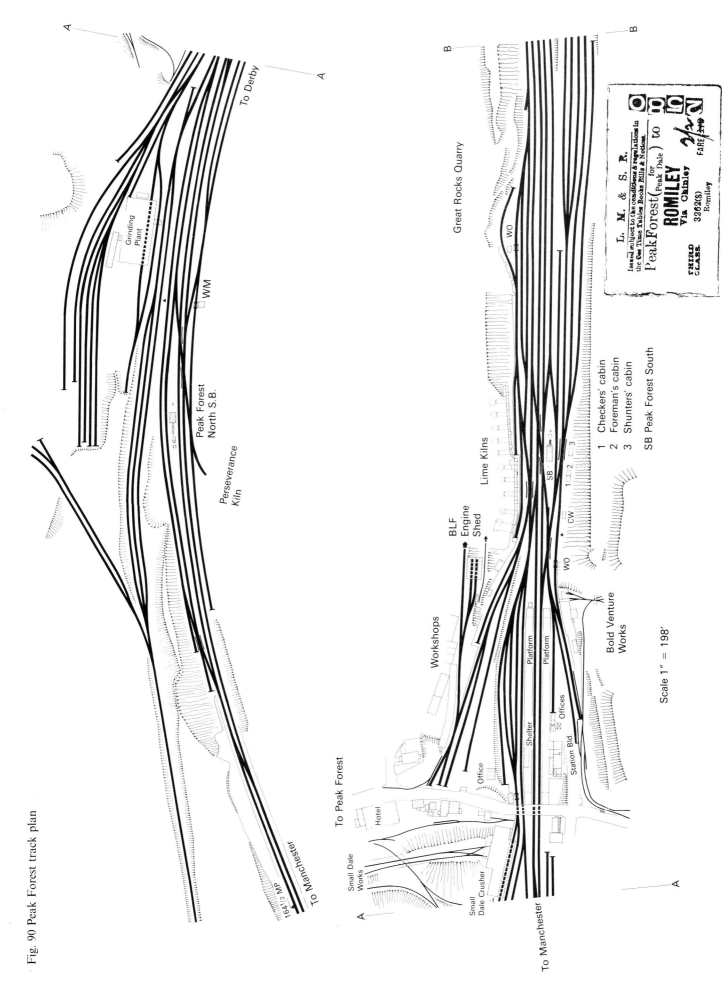

Fig. 90 Peak Forest track plan

To Derby

To Manchester

164½ MP

Grinding Plant

WM

Peak Forest North S.B.

Perseverance Kiln

A

A

A

B

B

Great Rocks Quarry

WO

Lime Kilns

SB

CW

WO

1 2 3

1 Checkers' cabin
2 Foreman's cabin
3 Shunters' cabin

SB Peak Forest South

BLF Engine Shed

Workshops

Shelter

Platform

Platform

Office

Station Bld

Offices

Hotel

Bold Venture Works

Small Dale Works

Small Dale Crusher

To Peak Forest

To Manchester

A

A

Scale 1" = 198'

177

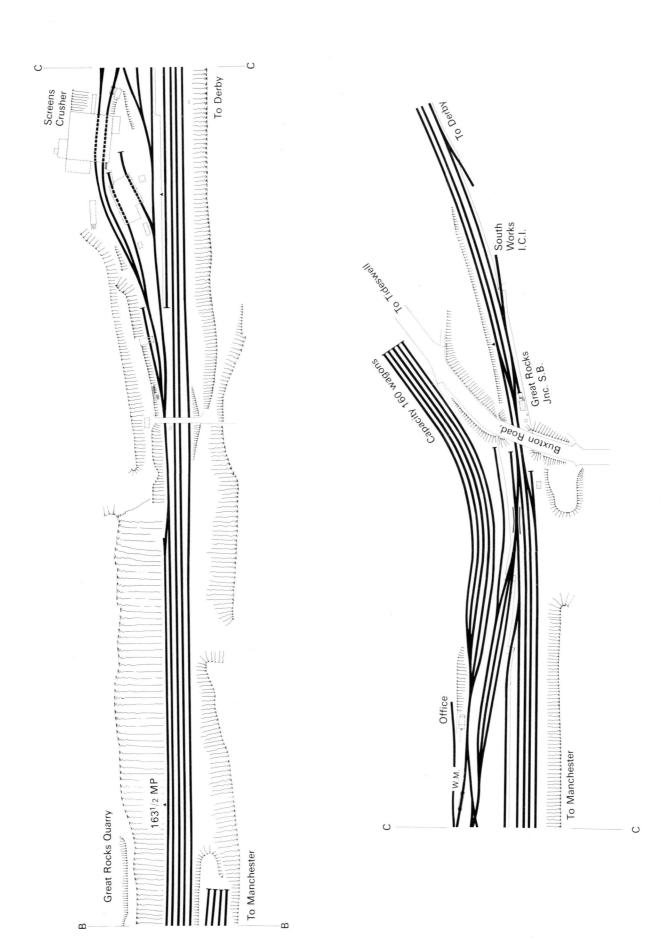

C

Screens
Crusher

To Derby

C

Great Rocks Quarry

163 1/2 MP

To Manchester

B

B

To Derby

South
Works
I.C.I.

To Tideswell

Great Rocks
Jnc. S.B.

Buxton Road

Capacity 160 wagons

Office

W.M.

To Manchester

C

C

Plate 273 (above) The industrialised nature of the valley around Peak Forest station is admirably captured by these two illustrations. This picture shows the view south as BR Sulzer Type 2, No.D5275, brings a train of hoppers past Peak Forest South signal box en route for Northwich in March 1966. Behind the train can be seen the derelict remains of the Great Rocks Lime Works.

(L. Nixon)

Plate 274 (below) This view shows Peak Forest station and the line curving round into Dove Holes Dale, as a Class 9F 2-10-0 heads a down freight towards the summit in August 1965.

(L. Nixon)

Plate 275 About 1871 a 1 ton travelling crane was sent to Peak Forest and is seen here, probably out of use, around the turn of the century. It has the general appearance of an early contractor's vehicle with its short wheelbase and cast or wrought iron wheels on square axles. The crane is fitted with an automatic counter balance weight. When a load is lifted half the weight is taken by the chain to the drum and half by the chain to the counter balance weight. In lifting the load the weight moves up the track until a position of equilibrium is achieved. When lowering the load the weight does not immediately run down the track and to prevent stress on the balance frame two large blocks of wood are placed beneath the beams just clearing the platform. These act as supports until the balance weight has been let down to the crane post. The livery in 1900 was probably red oxide with white lettering.

(N.R.M.)

To deal with local freight traffic in the station yard a weighing machine and office were constructed in 1872, and a small coal office was provided shortly afterwards. With the rapidly expanding limestone traffic a 20 ton weighbridge and office was put in on one of the sidings just south of the road bridge, in 1876. This was erected by Messrs Beresford & Sons and the office was given a flat, concrete roof. Excess stone could be removed from wagons and thrown onto the roof, where it would be available to top up any underweight vehicles. In 1878 the station yard was extended under an arrangement with Mr Joel Carrington, whereby he removed 3,570 cu. yards of soil, being paid 6d (2½p) per yard and 5,364 cu. yards of limestone for which he paid 1½d (½p) per yard. The Midland got its yard enlarged for £44, quite a bargain.

With the continued growth of through traffic and a rapid increase in shunting movements from the quarries regular changes to the trackwork took place, and in February 1888 the Traffic Committee requested the provision of an additional block post between Peak Forest Junction and Peak Forest South. Shortly afterwards further additions to trackwork were authorised and on 9th April 1891 new up and down lie-by sidings, a new down goods line, new crossover and the signal box at Great Rocks Junction were brought into use. Ten years later both Peak Forest South and North signal boxes were renewed. At the latter previous alterations to the sidings had left only limited room and a relatively unusual box on a tall narrow base was provided.

The line over the Peak was mercifully free of major accidents to passenger trains, but operating loose-coupled goods trains over steep gradients, and the presence of many sidings led to innumerable lesser incidents. The author has not been able to study the Midland records on this point, but the LMS minutes refer to three 'mishaps' in the locality. On 3rd April 1926 a number of wagons became detached in Great Rocks up sidings and running away they demolished a set of iron stop blocks, and a platelayers' hut, damaging several signalling connections in the process. A little under four years later, on 4th December 1930 an up freight train became divided in Great Rocks Dale, with 21 wagons being derailed causing extensive damage to the permanent way. In August 1938 a very similar accident happened near Great Rocks Junction when an express freight from Liverpool to Rowsley, coming fast down the bank, became divided. When such an event occurred it was often some time before the driver noticed he had lost part of his train, and by then his engine, which was still under steam but with a lighter load, would have drawn ahead of the portion freewheeling behind. Once he had noticed the problem the driver was supposed to estimate the speed of the following wagons and gently slow down his train until they caught up with him, with no more than a gentle bump. He could then

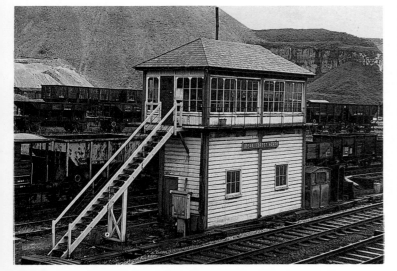

Plate 276 (left) Peak Forest North signal box, erected in 1901, was a period III design on an unusual tall, narrow base. It retained its original nameboard until closure.

(M.A. King)

stop and couple up the wagons or deal with the matter as necessary. This sounds fine in theory but in practice he was much more likely to slam the regulator shut in blind panic and apply his brakes hard, particularly in darkness. According to one ex-Midland driver at Rowsley this was standard practice among ex-LNWR men "who knew no better". A little unfair perhaps, but when the same man said "Nor-Western men only came in two sorts – drunk or with a hangover", one can conclude he was perhaps a little biased.

As a passenger station Peak Forest, (which became 'Peak Forest for Peak Dale', in 1894), was making a loss before the turn of the century, not because of the number of passengers, which grew steadily from a dozen or so per weekday to around 80 per day in the early 1920s, but because of the average fare paid. This was by far the lowest of any station between Ambergate and Chinley and one can only conclude that journeys primarily comprised shopping trips to Buxton or Chapel-en-le Frith, a few workmen's journeys to Millers Dale or Chapel and secondary school children travelling to Buxton. Nevertheless the station had a relatively frequent service of stopping trains, which in 1922 comprised nine down and eight up trains. The down timetable included four Derby-Manchester services and three Buxton-Chinley locals, while that in the up direction included four Manchester-Derby trains and two evening Manchester-Buxton services. The LMS expanded the timetable a little to provide eleven trains each way on weekdays, but the through Manchester trains were cut

Plate 277 (below) In August 1938 an up express freight train became derailed just south of Great Rocks Junction and this view shows clearing up operations at an advanced stage.

(E.R. Morten)

to two down and one up. During the war the service was cut to seven down and six up trains, three in each direction running between Derby and Manchester. Under British Railways the number of trains fell only marginally, with six down and four up services still calling at the time of closure, including the three Manchester trains in each direction.

From time to time in the 1920s and '30s express trains were stopped at Peak Forest due to the actions of a certain Station Master, who simply believed in giving his customers the best possible service. On one particular occasion he stopped a London bound train to pick up a senior director of ICI Ltd. Upon being summoned to Derby to explain his actions he merely reminded his superiors how much ICI paid the LMS each month in freight charges. No action was taken against him. If stopping passenger trains at the station did not call for much ingenuity, one unusual incident did. Directly behind the station buildings lay Bold Venture Quarry, where a 2ft 1in gauge railway provided internal transport. The owners only possessed one engine, named *Peep O'Day*, (Hunslet 297 of 1882, 0-4-0ST) which could not handle all the traffic and was supplemented by a number of horses. One day a horse slipped and rolled down the embankment in to a standard gauge wagon below. Apart from the indignity the poor animal suffered no injury, but how was it to be rescued? Following a quick conference the Station Master sent a message to one of the drivers shunting the main line sidings and in due course the wagon was brought round to the station. The door was dropped and the horse was walked out on to the platform and led back to work, none the worse for its adventure.

Freight traffic at Peak Forest was totally dominated by limestone, which is discussed in the next section, but some local traffic did of course come into the yard. In general terms

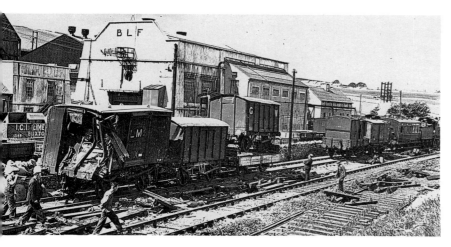

Plate 278 (below) LMS 4F 0-6-0, No. 4520, heads a down through freight past the Smalldale crusher on 10th May 1938. The first eleven wagons are 20 ton hoppers operated by the Lancashire Steel Corporation. Built for the Partington Iron & Steel Co., by Charles Roberts in 1917, these wagons are from a batch of 250 numbered 887-1136. They were 16ft 10¼in x 7ft 11¼in x 5ft 6in, with oil 112 axleboxes and were re-painted black with plain white letters, after the change of ownership in 1930. The engine has acquired a tall Stanier chimney.

(E.R. Morten)

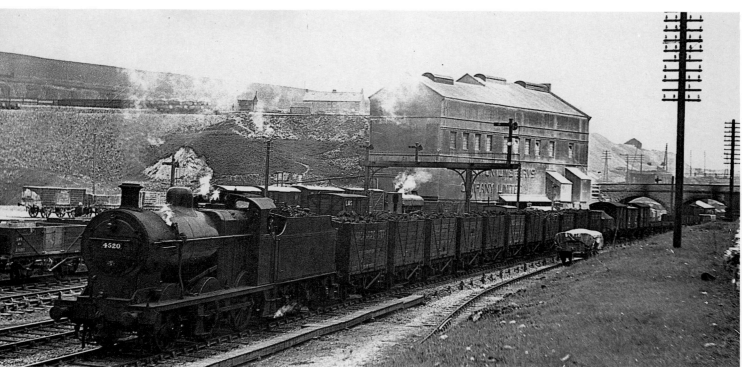

the station served an area of small villages and scattered farms, with a total population in the early 1930s of around 2,250 which would have called for 2,000–2,500 tons of domestic coal per annum. This trade was in the hands of Sidney Farrow, Great Rocks Co-operative Society and J.H. Wood. As far as the author is aware the latter never operated any wagons and while the Co-op did have two wagons for a short period, no details have survived. Sidney Farrow, on the other hand, owned four 8 ton wagons and one 10 tonner, with a further 10 ton wagon on hire. The 8 ton vehicles were 15ft x 7ft 6in, with five planks and rounded ends. They were painted red, with white letters, shaded black and *fig. 91* has been prepared from description given by the late Mr Farrow and one of his retired employees, Mr H. Heaven. The wagons normally loaded at Clay Cross, Hardwick, Williamthorpe, Nunnery or the Butterley group collieries and wagons owned by these collieries would appear in the yard from time to time. Mr Farrow generally supplied customers in Bibbington, Dove Holes, Peak Dale, Peak Forest, Smalldale, Tunstead, Wormhill and Upper End, and to a lesser extent in parts of Buxton and Chapel-en-le-Frith. To deliver this coal he used two Ford model T lorries, which were painted maroon with 'Sidney Farrow, Coal Merchant & Haulage Contractor' on the doors in gilt paint. He also owned a Thornycroft lorry and a Chevrolet, which were used more or less on general local haulage. One regular use was the carriage of limestone for local builders, but the Thornycroft was engaged for a long period in carrying bricks, which came in by rail, to Tunstead where ICI was building houses for its employees. Corn, and spent hops for use as fertilizer, were delivered to local farmers, after arriving from Bibby's of Liverpool and brewers at Burton-on-Trent respectively. In addition to lorries Mr Farrow also owned a Laffley coach, which was painted white

and was principally used on Saturdays to carry passengers from Upper End and surrounding areas to Buxton, starting at 1.45pm and finishing at 10.00pm.

There were no facilities other than the 1 ton crane, which had been removed by the early 1920s, for dealing with general merchandise, but the MR statistics indicate that some three to five wagons per week came in with this traffic in 1922. While the corn and hops referred to earlier were in this class there would also be general supplies for the few shops in Peak Forest and Upper End. By the 1930s virtually all this traffic was dealt with at Buxton, where one particularly intelligent horse was stabled. It is recalled that one carter making a regular run in the area was partial to a little liquid refreshment upon completion of his round and many was the time he fell asleep on the way back, leaving the horse to plod steadily home to Buxton, something you cannot do with a motor lorry!

The Midland Railway records show considerable volumes of mineral class traffic at Peak Forest, but it has proved difficult to ascertain the nature of this traffic. Reg Fawkes, who lived in the station house from 1926 to 1935, can recall basalt being brought into the yard by lorry for loading to rail, and a certain amount of building materials would have come in from time to time, but this traffic could not have possibly accounted for the figures shown in *Appendix III*. It may well have been that some of the quarries produced roadstone, which was classified as mineral traffic, and it is known that Wm Shepherd and Sons, Rochdale, who operated their own wagons, had an asphalt works at Great Rocks Long siding, but no detail has been uncovered about this company or its wagons.

Local freight traffic at the yard was normally dealt with by the 12.20pm stopping freight from Rowsley and the 5.10am from Gowhole to Buxton.

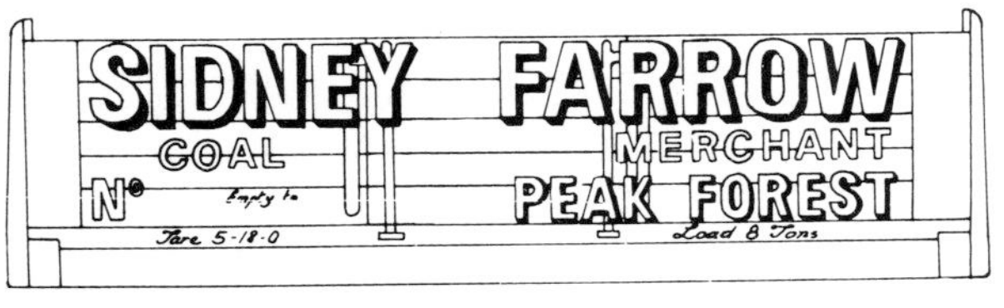

Fig. 91 S. Farrow wagon livery

Plate 279 (below) The up "Midland Pullman" at Peak Forest on 18th June 1965.

(D. Cross)

Chapter 20

The Limestone Quarrying Industry

The fact that the northern counties of England constitute the industrial heart of the nation can be attributed to a large extent to the juxtaposition of four major minerals; coal, iron ore, salt and limestone. The latter is found in many parts of the country and in a variety of geological formations, but it is the carboniferous formation which is most extensively mined. The remarkable purity of the Peak District beds, often containing 99% calcium carbonate, has made Derbyshire the most important producing county.

The use of limestone as a building material and the practice of lime burning were well established in the Buxton area by the days of the Roman Occupation. At that time it was almost certainly a part-time occupation, with farmers processing sufficient stone for their own use plus a few cart loads for sale to builders, tanners etc. Wood was once the main fuel but the attention of the lime burners and lead smelters caused such rapid deforestation by the Middle Ages that steps were taken to protect woodland. This led to the search for alternative fuels and early in the 17th century the use of coal was becoming commonplace. However, mining methods were primitive and it was only where the seams came to the surface, at the junction of the limestone and millstone grit, that supplies could be easily obtained. It was near these sites that lime burning became concentrated and the presence of coal near Whaley Bridge attracted the lime burners to Dove Holes. It is probably fair to assume that at about this time lime burning became a full time trade in its own right, setting in motion the commercial exploitation of Buxton lime.

By the middle of the 17th century the turnpike system had become well developed, but even the transport of lime by cart, which had superseded carriage by pack horse, could not satisfy the emerging industrial demands of the country. It is fortunate that men of vision were able to address their minds to the problems of mass transport and in the 1750s the Duke of Bridgewater came up with the idea of constructing artificial waterways to link centres of trade and carry raw materials and finished goods. In 1759 the hand of fate led the Duke to meet James Brindley, who was born of poor parents, near Tunstead. Although he never learnt to read or write, Brindley had a natural grasp of the principles of engineering and could both prepare and understand drawings. He was able to turn the Duke's plans into practice and their ideas caught the imagination of entrepreneurs all over the country. Another Derbyshire engineer who entered the field was Benjamin Outram who developed the concept of providing feeder routes to the canals in the shape of tramways. With the financial backing of Samuel Oldknow, the mill owner and benefactor of Marple, Outram was employed to construct the Peak Forest Canal and Tramway, under an Act of Parliament of 1794. A quarry was opened at Dove Holes the same year to provide stone for the construction of the canal which, together with the tramway, was brought into use three years later. The tramway soon led to the opening of several small quarries, and kilns were built at Chapel-en-le-Frith, Bugsworth, Whaley Bridge and Marple, to supply lime to the emerging industries of Lancashire and Cheshire. With the construction of these kilns lime burning in Dove Holes Dale virtually ceased, until Samuel Bibbington opened Perseverance Works in the late 1840s and Joel Carrington, an Oldham lime merchant, built two kilns at his new Holderness Quarry, just north of the canal company's original quarry, about 1860.

Although the opening of the Peak Forest Canal had a marked effect on the development of quarrying, this paled into insignificance with the opening of the railway in 1866. By the late 1870s several of the existing quarries had expanded and at least nine new works had been set up, seven on the Manchester line and two in Ashwood Dale. The first quarry to be directly influenced by the railway was that originally opened by the tramway company, which had been taken over by the Manchester, Sheffield & Lincolnshire Railway in 1846. By the

mid 1860s the workings had proceeded on to the route of the MR, but as relationships between the two companies were cordial, the Midland raised no objection to the Sheffield company removing the stone, which had to go anyway. Once the line was opened however, it was a different story and after considerable discussion in September 1867, the New Mills Extension Construction Committee agreed to the MS&LR putting in sidings to serve its Newline and Peak quarries. The agreement also included running powers over the line from New Mills to Peak Forest. This agreement was followed in 1869 by the provision of a siding just south of the viaduct at Millers Dale for the Millers Dale and Oldham Lime Co., together with sidings for Mr Bagshawe and Mr Ashton at both Millers Dale and Peak Forest. In 1873 sidings were laid in at Peak Forest for the Wigan Coal and Iron Co., but no details have survived regarding the last three ventures. A little after this the Buxton Central Lime and Stone Co. began operations at Blackwell Mill and the East Buxton Lime Co. opened up, just north of Millers Dale station. These were followed rapidly by Messrs Newton Chambers, Topley Pike Quarry in 1874 and T. Beswick's, Smalldale Lime Works the following year. The opening of Ashwood Dale Lime and Stone Co. and the Great Rocks Lime and Stone Co in 1876, together with Joseph Wainwright's Peak Dale Lime Works in 1877, completed the initial phase of development associated with the Midland Railway.

Meanwhile, away to the west events were taking place which were to greatly influence limestone production in the Buxton area. The vast salt deposits of the Cheshire plain between Nantwich and Northwich had already given rise to a major chemical industry, producing among others soda ash, an alkaline compound used in many manufacturing processes. Up to the early 1870s this was made by the Leblanc method, but the poisonous gases given off, including hydrogen chloride, were causing so much environmental damage that the method was outlawed. Fortunately an alternative method of manufacture was discovered by the Belgian chemist, Ernest Solvay, using limestone, salt and ammonia. In 1872 his work came to the attention of the distinguished German chemist, Ludwig Mond, who negotiated a licence from Solvay to use his process. Almost at once Mond set out with his close friend, and future partner John Tomlinson Brunner, to find a site for a factory. This search eventually led them to Winnington where a site fronting the navigable River Weaver, and with access to the CLC Railway was purchased. Construction of a plant began in October 1873 and progress was so rapid that the first soda was produced on 10th April 1874. As the works were under construction supplies of raw materials to be used in production were built up and a contract to supply 600 tons of limestone per month was signed with the Tideswell and Millers Dale Coal and General Merchant Co. Ltd on 25th October 1873, at 4s 5d (22p) per ton of 21 cwt, carriage of 3s (15p) paid, in buyer's wagons. To provide this transport twelve wagons, presumably 8 ton dumb-buffered vehicles, were purchased from Whittle Rusworth & Co. Chorley. These were painted dark red and lettered 'Brunner and Mond' in white. This was later changed to 'Brunner, Mond & Co.' following incorporation of the partnership as a limited company in 1881. So far as one is aware the first load of limestone was delivered on Monday 3rd November 1873, with the first complaint about poor quality being made the next day.

The second event which was to prove of lasting importance occurred in 1879 when Samuel Taylor purchased Joel Carrington's Holderness Quarry. Taylor had started in business as a coal and limestone merchant at Runcorn, building up a fleet of barges for use on the Cheshire/Lancashire canal system. From carrying he progressed to merchanting and then ownership of tanneries, chemical works etc, in the Runcorn and Widnes area, before adding quarrying to his list of ventures.

Although the expanding chemical industry and the invention of the 'basic' process of steel making in 1879, led to a growing demand for limestone, the industry became fraught with problems. No single producer was big enough to supply the demand and with buyers eager to secure low prices from the many producers in competition, profits slumped, making expansion and development virtually impossible. It is not surprising, therefore, that when H.A. Hubberty, of the Buxton Lime Co., began to speak of amalgamation he found sympathetic ears. Thus the majority of producers came together to form the Buxton Lime Firms Co. Ltd and in 1891 a merger of the following companies took place.

Ashwood Dale Lime & Stone Co., Ashwood Dale.

T. Beswick & Sons, Smalldale.

Richard Briggs & Sons, Dowlow.

East Buxton Lime Co., Millers Dale.

The Buxton Central Lime & Stone Co., Blackwell Mill.

The Buxton Lime Co., Grin and Whaley Bridge.

The Old Buxton Lime Co. Ltd, Harpur Hill.

W.P. Dixon, Bugsworth.

The Great Rocks Lime & Stone Co. Ltd, Peak Dale.

E. Heathcott & Sons, Dove Holes.

Millers Dale & Oldham Lime Co., Millers Dale.

J. & M. Tymm, Marple.

Joseph Wainwright, Peak Dale.

The only major operators to remain outside this combine were:

Samuel Bibbington, Dove Holes.

Gaskill, Deacon & Co. Ltd, Bold Venture Works, Peak Dale.

Great Central Railway Co., Dove Holes Dale.

Newton Chambers & Co., Topley Pike.

Samuel Taylor, Dove Holes Dale.

The formation of the Buxton Lime Firms Co. Ltd brought about a gradual, but necessary increase in prices, as buyers could not play off one producer against another and the various operators were able to improve and modernise their plant. The merger also brought together a bewildering array of wagons, which were gradually repainted and lettered BUXTON LIME FIRMS, which was shorted to BLF about 1901, although a few wagons remained lettered in full. Judging by the wagons still running in the mid 1930s however, the mood of modernisation was somewhat belated in its application to rolling stock.

Before continuing with the development of BLF it would be opportune to deal with the works which remained independent. Little detail is known about Samuel Bibbington other than that his lime and stone was sent to a wide range of markets by the Peak Forest Tramway and both MR and LNWR routes, before the firm closed in the late 1930s. Gaskell, Deacon & Co. were chemical manufacturers, at Widnes, who became part of United Alkali Ltd in the 1890s, and hence part of ICI. It seems likely that most of the output left Peak Forest in the form of lime, before the works were closed, again in the late 1930s. Newton Chambers & Co. have already been discussed in *Chapter 18*, which leads us finally to Samuel Taylor.

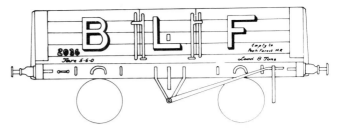

Fig. 92 Buxton Lime Firms wagon livery

This drawing shows the simplified livery as applied to an 8 ton wagon, 15ft x 7ft 6in x 2ft 9in. The fleet comprised a large number of these wagons but the author is only aware of one running number, 2036.

(Author)

Taylor's purchase of Holderness Quarry has already been noted, but in 1899 he was joined in business by Mr J. Mason Frith, who had married Samuel Taylor's eldest daughter and in 1902 the firm of S. Taylor Frith was incorporated. The company continued to expand and in 1918/19 a new quarry was opened at Bee Low, to the north east of Holderness. While much of the output was sent out by the tramway, until its closure in 1926, increasing amounts were dispatched by rail and additional sidings were provided in 1903 and 1926. The latter alterations were particularly important and began with a report to the LMS Traffic Committee on 26th April 1923. The General Manager informed the members that a considerable limestone traffic was being carried from the neighbourhood of Peak Forest station for BLF and Messrs Taylor Frith & Co., the carriage amount of this traffic for 1922 being £136,000. He further explained that since 1868 the Great Central Railway Co., and its predecessors had leased from the Duke of Devonshire a large area of land adjoining the Midland Railway, in connection with which sidings had been provided for their traffic and that of Messrs Taylor Frith. The latter had now secured the lease of the old Great Central quarry and were desirous of having new sidings, with the existing gradient of 1 in 22 on the old connection to the quarries being abolished.

In passing it is of interest to note this original steep gradient was the scene of several runaways. After one such event, Reg Fawkes, then working as a shunter, was asked by a rather arrogant railway inspector if he had any ideas about how to prevent such regular problems. "Easy" came the reply. "The problem is that before coming down the bank, all the wagon brakes are pinned down. They then get hot and expand and while they'll hold the wagons when they are first left in the sidings, once they cool, the power's not so good. The answer is to put down half the brakes to hold 'em back when they come down the bank and then pin the other half down in the sidings." "What a bright idea," said the inspector, "I'm glad I thought of it." "But it was my idea." said Reg, somewhat taken aback. "Ah, but you're only a shunter. I'm writing the report," retorted the inspector. That was the last assistance he ever received.

The proposed new siding layout would deal with 400 wagons daily, which would enable Messrs Taylor Frith to handle 1,500 to 2,000 tons of stone per day by the improved plant they were then installing. The end of the lease on the GCR quarry meant that the LNER no longer had an interest in their predecessor's sidings and these could be removed. To this effect the engineers of the two companies had agreed a price of £801 to be paid to the LNER for its share of the materials forming the sidings. The proposals were agreed, but for some reason a start on the work was delayed, the sidings finally coming into use on Sunday, 21st March 1926.

To deal with the work of the quarry the company maintained a large fleet of wagons. About 130 were in use for the carriage of lime and these were painted red with white letters, shaded black. They were built by both the Central Wagon Co. and Charles Roberts. The latter built a batch of ten late in 1911 and these are illustrated in *plate 282*. They were 15ft 6in x 7ft 6in x 3ft 6in, with three 8in and one 9in planks, brakes one side only and oil 126 axleboxes. They were numbered 79–88 and registered by the LNWR. In addition there were about 70 five plank 10 ton limestone wagons, also

Plate 280 Although the livery was shortened to BLF about 1901/2, some wagons retained the full livery, as this 8 ton wagon, photographed in 1928, shows. It was 15ft x 7ft 6in with one 9in and three 7in planks and was painted grey with white letters, shaded black.

(H. Townley)

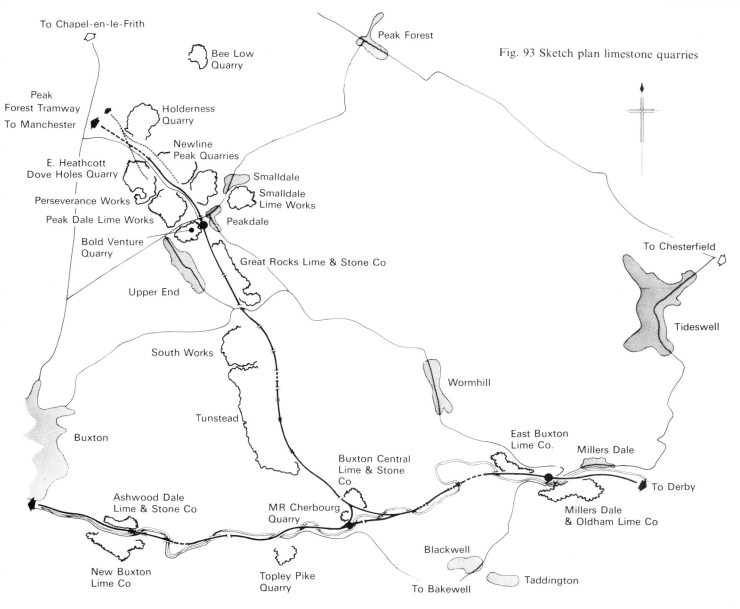

Fig. 93 Sketch plan limestone quarries

painted red. To supply coal to the kilns, and for the business as coal merchants in South Lancashire/North Cheshire the company had some 600 five plank 10 ton wagons painted black, with white letters, shaded red. As well as lime the works produced crushed stone, macadam and chippings and at busy times the coal wagons were used for this traffic. The major markets were within a 50 mile radius, particularly in the North West and Yorkshire. Coal was obtained from a variety of colliery companies including Butterley, Grassmoor, Newstead, New Hucknall, Stanton and Welbeck. The 400 wagons per day previously mentioned were broken down approximately into 20 coal, 30 lime and 150 limestone with a roughly equivalent number of empties.

In 1954 the need for heavy capital investment in new machinery and plant resulted in the business being sold to Messrs Settle-Speakman & Co. of Stoke-on-Trent, who in turn sold it to Staveley Industries Ltd, in 1966. Control has now passed to Peakstone Lime, a member of RMC Industrial Minerals Group. In line with the re-emergence of private

owner wagons the Staveley company purchased a batch of 55 38 ton hopper wagons from the Standard Railway Wagon Co. Ltd. These were numbered 14600–14654 and are shown in *fig. 94*. The base colour of these wagons was retained on acquisition by Peakstone and the present livery is shown in *plate 284*.

We must now revert to the history of BLF which, virtually from its inception, set about modernising and developing many of the quarries in the group. Soon after the turn of the century South Works was opened near Great Rocks Junction and in 1908 the New Buxton Lime Co., Ashwood Dale, was taken over. During World War I Brunner, Mond & Co., had become increasingly concerned about the supply of limestone and in 1919 it purchased a controlling interest in the Buxton Lime Firms Co. The same year saw the completion of the Smalldale crusher plant, which dominated the scene at Peak Forest station. The vast size of the building resulted largely from the fact that when it was being designed a supply of secondhand 55ft girders was available. The building housed

Plate 281 This plate shows one of the five-plank 10 ton wagons painted red with white letters, black shading. It was 15ft 6in x 7ft 6in, with four 7in and one 9in planks.
(Author's Collection)

Plate 282 This plate shows one of the 10 ton wagons built by Charles Roberts in 1911.
(Author's Collection)

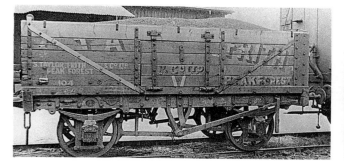

two Blake type crushers, made by Broadbent & Co., Accrington, which fed crushed stone via screens into either the Brunner Mond hopper or the gravel hoppers. The BM stone was sized as 8in ring maximum, ie it would pass an 8in hole but not a 2½in. The stone which passed through the smaller diameter screen was known as 'gravel' and was originally sold as such. However in 1921 the drying and grinding plant was erected just to the north of the crusher and the gravel was taken there for processing to dust or chicken grit. The crusher plant was fed by 2ft gauge side tipping wagons, each crusher having a capacity of 30 tons of BM stone per hour. Operation of this plant continued until 1946 when Tunstead No. 2 crusher was brought into use. After closure the machinery was

resulted in Fowler 4F 0-6-0s making their appearance on trains of up to 50 wagons. With the finance which became available on the formation of ICI it was possible to look to future limestone production. Bearing in mind that many of the existing quarries were well over 50 years old, with only limited room for expansion, it was quickly decided to open up new

Fig. 94 This diagram shows the general arrangement and original livery, which was body, frame and running gear grey enamel to BS70, lettering black, Staveley symbol Coates permanent brilliant turquoise. Axle box covers, golden yellow, bottom doors wheel (centre) orange, brake wheel (right), white.

(Based on Standard Railway Wagon Co. drawing.)

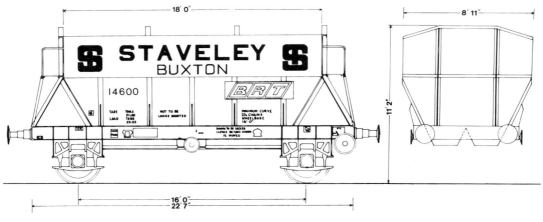

Plate 283 A wagon label from 6th August 1946.

(Author's Collection)

Plate 284 This plate shows the present livery of grey body, black lettering and dark blue symbol.

(Author)

removed and for a few years the structure housed an experimental kiln for very small stone, but it lay unused for many years before demolition late in 1986.

Soon after Brunner Mond took over, the company began to expand their wagon fleet and in 1920 they purchased a batch of 50 12 ton wagons from Charles Roberts, numbered 1001 to 1025 and 1035 to 1059. These were 16ft 5in x 7ft 10in, with five 7in, one 8in and one 9in planks, side doors only and oil 116 axleboxes. They were painted Derby red, which is understood to have been crimson lake, with white letters, shaded black. These wagons were followed by a further batch from the Central Wagon Co. These were of similar dimensions but had side and end doors, four 9in and two 7in planks and Attocks axleboxes. The fleet was again expanded in 1927 by the purchase of a batch of standard eight plank 12 ton wagons from Roberts, but the size of the order and the running numbers are not known.

Just prior to the acquisition of these vehicles Brunner Mond had merged with Nobel Industries, British Dyestuffs Corporation and United Alkali Company to form Imperial Chemical Industries, which was to become probably the largest chemical company in the world.

During the 1920s the traffic from Peak Forest to Winnington was handled primarily by unrebuilt Johnson 2F 0-6-0s, with the occasional assistance of rebuilt Kirtley 0-6-0 No. 2819. In the summer of 1928 a greatly increased demand

reserves at Tunstead, to the south of the existing BLF South Works. At that time Great Rocks Dale was little more than 200 yards wide, with scattered farms on the high land either side. These farms and the fields were linked by a number of bridges over or under the railway. The space in the valley bottom was so limited that before blasting operations could begin to open out the quarry it was necessary to provide protection for the railway. To do this appropriate signals were erected, controlled by a new signal box 12 chains south of Great Rocks Tunnel. The box was linked by telephone to the quarry where a special signal was installed. Blasting could only take place when the signal was lowered, at a time when the railway was clear of traffic. In addition, two watchmen were employed on the railway to give warning if stone fell on the line which was quite common initially. Having given the signal to begin blasting, the signalman had to take shelter in a wire cage in the base of the cabin and it was not unknown for men to refuse duty at Tunstead because of the danger. This work began in 1927 shortly after H.E. Morgan had introduced his new LMS signal box. Thus Tunstead is believed to have been the first signal box to be built to the new design, late in 1927, some four or five years before those at Broadholme and

Plate 285 (above) This view shows wagons from the batch built by Central Wagon Co., about 1920. They were painted crimson lake and known running numbers were 1162-1166.

(A.G. Ellis)

Plate 286 (right) This standard 1923 eight-plank wagon was from the batch built by Roberts in 1927. They were again crimson, with black ironwork and plain white letters.

(Author's Collection)

Ambergate, previously thought to have been the prototypes of the new standard box.

During and after construction of the sidings the various bridges in the valley were gradually eliminated. No. 84, Back Pasture bridge and No. 84A, Lower Great Rocks bridge, both cattle creeps, were filled in 1929. No. 83, Great Rocks cattle creep was closed the following year and in 1935 No. 87, Great Rocks bridge, an overbridge just north of the tunnel was pulled down. Finally No. 85, an overbridge just south of Great Rocks Tunnel and No. 88, also an overbridge, south of Great Rocks Junction, stood in splendid isolation, with no road access, until they were demolished in the late 1950s.

The sidings at Tunstead, which along with the new signal box, became fully operational on 26th October 1930, were laid out in an up to date manner to facilitate the rapid turnaround of rolling stock. Incoming empties, particularly from Winnington, crossed to the down line at Great Rocks Junction and then onto the private line, parallel to the main line, which took them past South Works and under the Tunstead hoppers. From there the loaded wagons continued down the valley into a fan of storage sidings, which had direct access on to the down main line, opposite Tunstead signal box. For the first few years much of the output was sent away as stone, but in 1935 the kilns were brought into use and subsequently large amounts of lime were produced. By the mid-1930s ICI had come to enjoy a very wide market for limestone products and in addition to the block traffic to Winnington, the following examples give an idea of the travels of the company's wagons:

Steel, Peach & Tozer, Rotherham. Iron & Steel.
Hadfields, Sheffield.
Staveley Coal & Iron Co., Staveley.
Shelton Iron & Steel Co., Stoke-on-Trent.

Plate 288 (below) Tunstead signal box, built in 1927 and brought into full use on 26th October 1930, is believed to have been the first all-timber signal box to the new LMS standard design.

(D. Ibbotson)

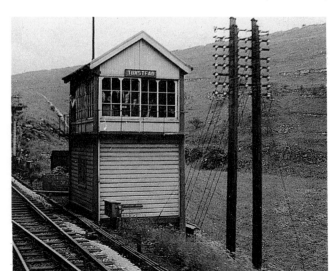

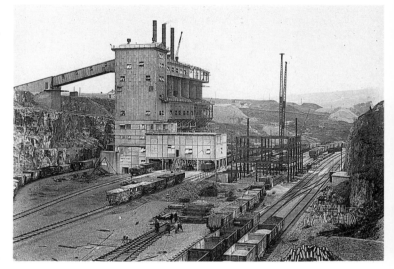

Plate 287 Development of Tunstead began early in 1927 and this view shows further development in the mid-1930s. The plate gives a good impression of the vast quantities of stone which were removed. Comparison with *plate 271* shows that the open land in the background has now been completely built over.

(H. Townley)

Albright & Wilson, Birmingham.	Chemicals.
Lifford Chemical Co., Birmingham.	
Bowaters, Scotland.	Paper making.
Pumpherston Oil Co., Mussleburgh.	Purifying purposes.
Penketh Tannery, Birkenhead.	Tanning hides.
Various works, Stoke-on-Trent.	Pottery and china.
London Brick Co.	Brick making.
Various docks, Liverpool.	Export.

This general traffic amounted to something in excess of 250 wagons per day leaving the various quarries in the group. To provide coal for the kilns approximately 30 to 35 wagon loads per day came in from many collieries including Askern, Bentley, Bolsover, Brodsworth, the Butterley group, Chatterley-Whitfield, Cortonwood, Gedling, Manton Wood, New Hucknall, Sheepbridge, Sherwood, Sneyd, the Stanton group, the Staveley group, and Unstone.

Upon its formation ICI inherited a mixed bag of wagons from BLF and three examples are shown in *plates 289–291*. At first these were repainted with both Imperial Chemical Industries and Buxton Lime Firms in full. In 1934/35 this was changed to 'ICI (Lime) Ltd, formerly Buxton Lime Firms Ltd'. Shortly afterwards as both the quarry and the kilns at Tunstead became fully operational a decision was taken to modernise the wagon fleet. To deal with the general market a batch of RCH Standard five plank mineral wagons was purchased from Gloucester Railway Carriage & Wagon Co. in 1937 and these carried the simplified livery of 'ICI (Lime) Ltd'. It is believed that these wagons were numbered 3000 to 3199, but at the time of writing the author has been unable to study the Gloucester order books, which are now at the County Record Office. Very soon afterwards the company went into voluntary liquidation in order to change its name to 'ICI Ltd (Lime Division)' and the wagon livery was changed to that shown in *fig. 95*. Approximately 120 of these vehicles remained in main line service after the war, but they were gradually withdrawn or relegated to internal user purposes, although a few remained on the main line until 1967.

In an attempt to increase the efficiency of its own traffic, arrangements were made to improve unloading at Winnington and on 28th April 1936 an order was placed with Charles Roberts to build 85 43½ ton hopper wagons, numbered 3200–3284. The general arrangement of these is shown in *fig. 96* and illustrated by *plates 294 and 295*. In order to evaluate these wagons delivery was taken over a three year period. It is a matter of history that they were a success and a second batch, numbered 3285–3319 were ordered on 3rd August 1945, with a final batch, numbered 3320–3351 being ordered on 18th June 1951. The delivery pattern and present numbers are as below:

Original No.	Date Built	Present No.
3200–3202	1936	19000–19002
3203–3229	1937	19003–19029
3230–3273	1938	19030–19073
3274–3284	1939	19074–19084
3285–3319	1947/48	19085–19119
3320–3323	1952	19120–19123
3324–3351	1953	19124–19151

The post-war wagons differed in several respects from the earlier batches. The most significant change was that the pre-war wagons had open frame bogies while the later ones had plate frame bogies. These stronger bogies allowed the carrying capacity to be increased from 43½ to 44½ tons, and they have now been fitted to the earlier vehicles. Secondly, the angle side stanchions on the pre-war wagons comprised three left hand and three right hand, whereas they were placed alternately on the later batches. The first three wagons carried the lettering ICI Ltd, but this was later simplified to ICI, which was shown by cut out letters welded to the side, the size of the letters being somewhat enlarged on the post-war vehicles. After the war the letters were picked out in white, with black edges and a narrow black band round their base. Finally the early wagons had a black frame and running gear, while the post war livery was grey body and frame, with black running gear.

In recent years there have been two accidents involving these wagons, at New Mills and Hartford and in 1983 thirteen wagons of very similar design were purchased from John Summers Steel Works to bring the fleet back up to its original

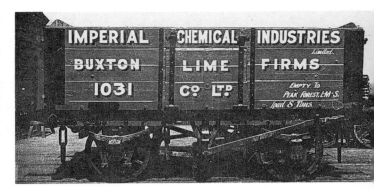

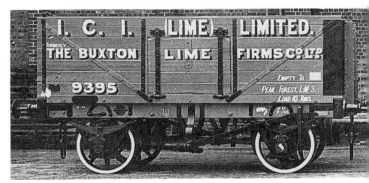

Plates 289 to 291 These three illustrations show wagons inherited by ICI. All were painted grey, with black ironwork, white letters, black shading. Wagon No.1031 (top) was 15ft x 7ft 6in, with one 11in, two 9in and one 11in planks. Wagon No.9395 (middle) was 16ft x 7ft 6in, with six 7in and one 5in planks. Wagon No.1807 (bottom) was 15ft 6in x 7ft 6in with three 9in planks. The wagons were photographed in 1934, 1935 and 1937 respectively.

(H. Townley)

Plate 292 This plate shows one of the 200 standard 12 ton wagons purchased in 1937.

(Gloucester RC&W Co.)

Plate 293 This views shows the final livery adopted in 1950, when the lettering on the right was reduced in size, and the corner plates were painted off-white.

(H. Townley)

Fig. 95 Post 1938 ICI livery. (Wagon Repairs Ltd.)

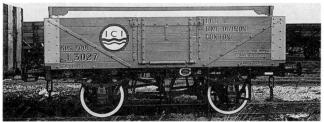

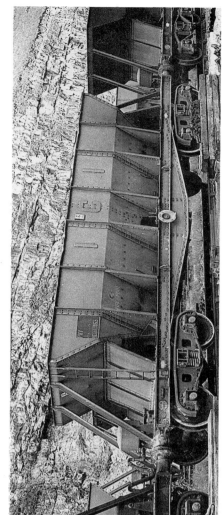

Plate 295 Wagon No.19163, one of those purchased from John Summers in 1983.

(J.B.Arnold)

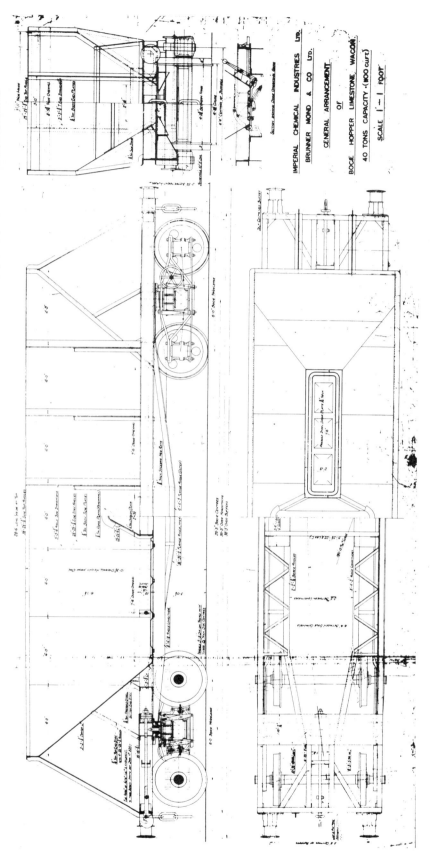

Fig. 96 G.A. ICI bogie hopper wagon
The original drawing for these wagons was produced on 18th November 1931 and revised in 1935.

(Author's Collection)

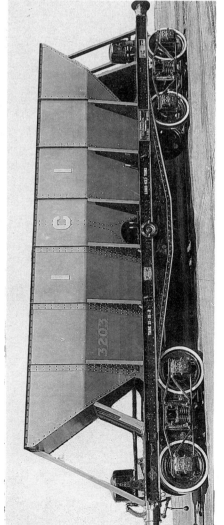

Plate 294 Wagon No.3203, the first of the 1937 batch.

(Author's Collection)

level of 152 vehicles. These wagons, built in 1952/53 and now numbered 19152–19164, differ only slightly from those built for ICI. They are a few inches lower, with eight rows of bolts on the top section of the side stanchions, as against nine rows on the original ICI wagons. They also have an end ladder, with the side rails twisted through 90° and bolted flat to the wagon ends, as distinct from the ladders fitted to some of the ICI wagons, which have their side rails bolted to the wagon ends by small right angle brackets. For the last ten years 36 of these wagons have been on hire to Road Stone Ltd. In January 1986 the prototype vehicle, No. 19000, was experimentally fitted with air brakes but in the late summer it reverted to the vacuum type.

As these wagons were delivered the trains were gradually increased until they comprised eleven vehicles, which made up the maximum load for the Class 4 engines then diagrammed for these workings. In November 1938 successful trials were conducted with the Stanier 8Fs and from the first week in December they were drafted on to the trains, which were then increased to 17 hoppers. It is believed that No. 8026 took the first full train out on 2nd December 1938. Prior to the introduction of the Class 8s, engines were turned on the Blackwell Mill triangle, but then a turntable was installed just north of the bridge at Great Rocks Junction. It is believed that this work was partially financed by ICI. For the first few years the engines regularly used on these workings were Nos 8026/44/74/87/89, of Heaton Mersey shed, three of which were stabled at the ex-CLC shed at Northwich. The Stanier engines remained the mainstay of motive power until diesels took over, but during the war the general shortage of engines led to LNER J39 class 0-6-0s being used occasionally on the empty workings. On 13th, 14th and 15th January 1957 trials were carried out with BR Standard 9F class 2-10-0 No. 92045, which took 19 wagons on the final day without difficulty. Although these tests were successful the other diagrams which would have involved these engines did not warrant such super power and it was decided not to use them on a regular basis. They did make an occasional appearance in the last few years of steam, as did the WD Austerity 2-8-0s.

Today Tunstead ranks as the largest working limestone quarry in Europe, with a main face 1¼ miles long and 120–200ft high. The annual output exceeds 5 million tons of stone, 1.7 million of which goes to Winnington. To cope with this the hopper wagons are in continuous use, with six trains running daily, except Christmas Day and New Year's Day. Motive power is usually Class 47 or Class 37 with up to 22 wagons, according to demand.

Writing in 1974, Messrs Millward and Robinson, in discussing the present industry, said that the "hungry demand of the 20th century for road metal, cement and the chemical products of the limestone industries threaten those outposts of mediaeval Wormhill with total extinction as the quarries propose to extend their territories to the eastern wall of Great Rocks Dale". That threat has now become reality and has resulted in artificial tunnels being constructed over the line at Tunstead to carry a 17m wide roadway to serve the new workings east of the railway. Completed early in 1984, by Lehane, MacKenzie & Shand Ltd, the causeway, with its precise, grass covered banks may have assured many years of continued limestone production, but it will be a long time before it forms an integral part of the scenery, as many of the older quarry workings now have.

Plate 296 This view on 27th September 1984, shows the new causeway build across the valley at Tunstead to give access for quarrying to the east of the railway. It will be a very long time before the structure blends in with the landscape.

(Author)

Chapter 21

Dove Holes

From Peak Forest station the line curved gently westwards and passed the summit of the line at 985ft above sea level, before turning eastwards and entering a deep cutting leading to Dove Holes Tunnel. A brief outline of the problems encountered in driving the tunnel, the fourth longest on the Midland Railway, has already been given in *Chapter 2*. Further evidence as to the magnitude of the task can be gauged from the fact that on 4th February 1863 a contract was awarded to Messrs Hallam and Co., to supply 3 million bricks for lining the ventilation shafts. At that time 320 men and 15 horses were engaged on tunnelling, which was continually hampered by the wet conditions. In fact, during the whole of December 1864 all work ceased due to the volume of water entering the workings. Eventually, however, the project was completed but just as the men were preparing to leave the site a serious landslip occurred at the northern end of the tunnel. On Tuesday 12th June 1866, some 10,000 tons of rock and shale came down, burying the trackbed and 17 contractor's wagons. One can only speculate on the personal thoughts of the engineer, for on 3rd July he reported to the Construction Committee that work had been put in hand to build about 70 yards of covered way and that the intervening period of some six weeks would afford an opportunity to clear further loose stone from Great Rocks Dale.

On 1st February 1867, the day the line was re-opened to traffic, following the landslip at Bugsworth, the engineer reported the costs of the tunnel to his committee. These had finally amounted to £135,986 against the lowest tender, from Messrs Rennie & Co., of £179,565 and were accepted enthusiastically by the members. This euphoria was unfortunately short lived for on the night of 18th June 1872 a London to Manchester express ran into a mass of earth and rock which had slipped a few minutes earlier at a shaft opening near the northern end of the tunnel. Seven passengers and three railwaymen were injured. The accident occurred during a tremendous thunderstorm which deluged the countryside far and wide. Passenger trains ran to and from Buxton only, until 23rd June, and then over the LNWR to Manchester, from 24th June until 19th August, normal services being resumed the

Plate 297 (above) Class 5XP No.45616, *Malta G.C.* comes over Peak Forest Summit in majestic style with the 1.50pm Manchester Central-St Pancras express on 27th March 1954.

(E.R. Morten)

Plate 298 (below) An unidentified Class 9F 2-10-0 drifts through the cutting towards Dove Holes Tunnel with an empty permanent way train about 1960.

(J.B. Bucknall)

Plate 299 (right) This view looking north was taken from almost the same spot as the previous picture and the two show the whole length of the cutting through Dove Holes Dale. The illustrations clearly show the horizontal bedding of the stone, with intermittent grass-covered ledges, and the vertical configuration left by the hand tools of the navvies. In this view 'Jubilee' No.45553 *Canada*, of Longsight Shed, heads towards the summit with the 11.35am Manchester Central-St Pancras (SO) on 16th May 1952. The photograph is particularly interesting as it was most unusual for engines from this shed to work over Midland lines.

(E.R. Morten)

Plate 300 (below) A pair of Class 20s, Nos 20134 and 20163 leave the northern end of the tunnel with a Northwich hopper train on 20th March 1985.

(Author)

Plate 301 (bottom left) The landscape north of the tunnel is completely different from that to the south. This view from above the LNWR tunnel, on 23rd June 1951, shows a Fowler 2-6-4T with the 4.25pm Buxton-New Mills local. Beyond the train is Dove Holes Tunnel signal box and Lowes bridge, with the northern portal of Dove Holes Tunnel just visible behind the signal. Above the tunnel mouth can be seen the flat area marking the covered way erected in 1866. The position of the up signal, half way up the cutting side, for sighting through LNWR Tunnel, is worthy of note.

(E.R. Morten)

following day. Between 20th June and 27th July goods trains ran over the MS&L route via Eckington, resuming the Midland route on the night of Sunday 28th July. It was reported to the shareholders by the Chairman, Mr W.P. Price, that the inconvenience to the public was very much decreased by the assistance rendered by the LNWR and that the opportunity was being taken to publicly express grateful recognition of this assistance.

The tunnel collapsed again early on Sunday 7th February 1904 and trains were diverted via the Dore and Chinley line, returning to the Dove Holes route for goods traffic at 10.00am on 17th March and for passenger traffic on Monday 21st March 1904. There was a further collapse in February 1940, due to severe storms and heavy rain after unprecedented snowfall, but the blockage was only discovered after an up freight train had ploughed into the rubble. The train was carrying, amongst others, foodstuffs and at a time of severe shortages the breakdown gangs were able to gain a little bonus as they cleared the wreckage.

Major work on relining the tunnel took place from 1954 because the brick lining had been badly affected by water seeping through fissures in the rock. The work necessitated the closure of the tunnel for eight hours nightly and required the diversion of all traffic. The job was programmed for three years.

The tunnel was notorious for dropping bits on trains, particularly on the up line as locomotive exhausts pounded the roof on the climb to the summit. An added danger in winter came from icicles which commonly formed as thick as a man's body and several feet long. In exceptionally bad weather it was customary to send a light engine through the tunnel at intervals, simply to knock off the ice. With several tons of boiler in front of the crew this was relatively safe, but with the introduction of diesel traction it must have become a harrowing experience. It is ironical that the supposedly poor state of the tunnel was given as a major reason for closing the main line through the Peak, yet it is still used regularly 363 days in the year by the limestone trains.

At the northern end of the tunnel the scenery changed as dramatically as it did when our train burst out of Headstone Tunnel at Monsal Dale. The line was now running north westwards, in a shallow cutting, towards a wide bowl in the hills, with the huge shoulder of Combs Moss towering to the south and the gritstone outcrop of Chinley Churn almost straight ahead. A few yards from the tunnel the line ran over a stream then under Lowe's bridge and passed Dove Holes Tunnel signal box, a small 'Period III' structure renewed in 1902. Opposite the box lay two short lie-by sidings, one put in about 1875, the other in 1897, but with a capacity of 13 wagons in one and 16 in the second, one wonders what real use they were, apart from storing engineers' wagons. The signal box was taken out of use on 5th March 1967.

Chapter 22

Chapel-en-le-Frith

From Dove Holes Tunnel signal box the line began to curve towards the north and passed under the LNWR Whaley Bridge and Disley line, by the appropriately named LNWR Tunnel, 104 yards long. When work started on the line from Blackwell Mill, negotiations for an easement to pass under the North Western line had not been concluded. The contract for the northern section of the Midland line, from Chapel-en-le-Frith to New Mills, which was let to Messrs Eckersley & Bayliss on 5th August 1863, began 51 chains north of the LNWR Tunnel. It was not until June the following year that the MR were able to agree an extension of this contract to fill in the remaining 81 chains to the northern portal of Dove Holes Tunnel. Leaving the LNWR Tunnel the line continued to curve towards the east, on a low embankment, crossing in quick succession Calderbank bridge, Bench Hall Carriage Drive bridge and Long Lane bridge. At this point the curve began to ease as the line entered the town, crossing Manchester Road by bridge No.100, and then Eccles Road bridge, before running into Chapel-en-le-Frith, 29 miles 16 chains from Ambergate West Junction.

Chapel-en-le-Frith was founded as a chapel in the Peak Forest about 1225, in a depression on the western slopes of the

Plate 302 (above) The Midland passed under the Stockport, Disley and Whaley Bridge line by a short tunnel, seen here looking south in June 1949. Today the conifers have gone and the tunnel has a much more spartan appearance.

(D. Ibbotson)

Plate 303 (below) The long curve across open country into Chapel-en-le-Frith is admirably captured in this view as Stanier 8F, No.48676 nears LNWR Tunnel with an up stopping freight about 1960.

(W.D. Cooper)

Plate 304 (below left) Class 20s, Nos 20163 and 20134 cross Calderbank bridge south of Chapel-en-le-Frith with a train of empty hoppers for Tunstead on 20th March 1985.

(Author)

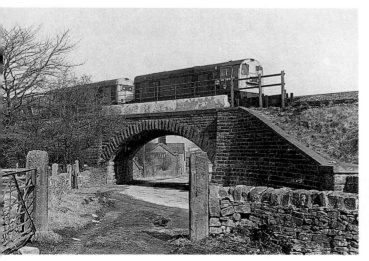

Plate 305 (below) Bridge No.100, Manchester Road bridge, was rebuilt in 1937, and is seen here on 20th March 1985 shortly after being repainted under one of British Rail's environmental improvement schemes.

(Author)

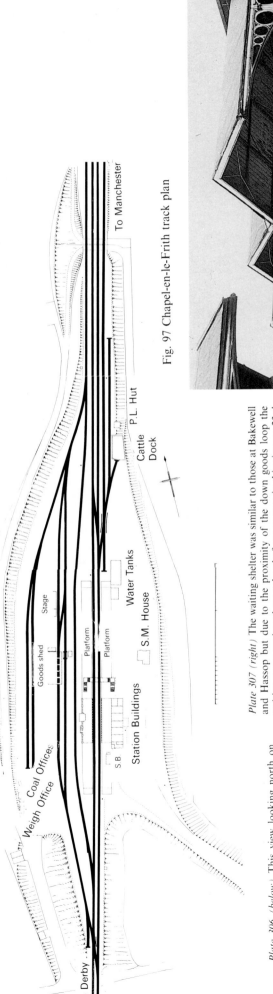

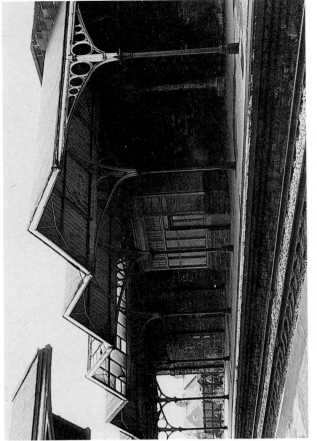

Fig. 97 Chapel-en-le-Frith track plan

Plate 306 (below) This view looking north on 15th March 1953 shows the general layout of Chapel-en-le-Frith Central, with the goods shed on the extreme left, the station house, painted white, visible beyond the twin telegraph poles, right and the chimneys of the Ferodo factory on the extreme right.

(H. Townley)

Plate 307 (right) The waiting shelter was similar to those at Bakewell and Hassop but due to the proximity of the down goods loop the waiting room projected onto the platform as seen in this view on 23rd June 1968. The glass was removed from the canopies as a wartime safety measure, but that in the centre bay was replaced in the 1950s to admit some light to the waiting room.

(M.A. King)

Plate 308 (bottom right) The back of the parapet wall, showing the rear of the waiting room and the cast iron urinal.

(M.A. King)

Pennines, believed by geologists to have been the site of a glacial lake. The settlement developed quickly and by 1250 it appears to have become a borough, that is, a place entitled to hold markets and fairs. The town was astride an important trade route across the hills, and expanded further with the construction of the Buxton-Manchester turnpike in the 1720s. With a good road system and later the Peak Forest Tramway, several entrepreneurs took advantage of the fast flowing streams in the area to set up mills at both Chapel-en-le-Frith and nearby Chapel Milton. Although well established locally as a small market and manufacturing centre by the end of the 19th century, the town is today much more widely known as the home of Ferodo Ltd, makers of friction brake linings. The founder of the company was Herbert Frood, a boot salesman, who noticed in his travels around the district that local carters and farmers often tied old boots over the wooden brake blocks of their carts to reduce wear. In 1897, in a shed at his home at Rye Flatt, two miles south west of Chapel, he invented a brake lining material using laminated hair belting impregnated with bitumen. Six years later he took over the old Sovereign Mill at Burrfields, near Chapel Milton and began making what he called 'brake-shoes'. In 1920 Ferodo became a public company and a little later built the 16 acre factory which eventually became the world's largest producer of friction brake linings.

Chapel-en-le-Frith station was built to the design used previously at Rowsley, Bakewell and Hassop, but the roof was fractionally higher, with slightly more ornate eaves brackets. In March 1866 a contract for the erection of a goods shed was awarded to J. Wood, who had previously built the sheds at Bakewell and Hassop, but while he used a broadly similar design he managed to increase his price from £500 to £670.

Perhaps his previous quotations had proved too low, for such rampant inflation was virtually unknown in the 1860s. A cattle dock was constructed when the station was built and this was extended in 1872 to accommodate four wagons. At about the same time a cart weighing machine and office was constructed near the goods yard entrance.

Mention has already been made of the quantities of water encountered in Dove Holes Tunnel and it is not surprising that this water was harnessed for use by the locomotive department. In 1866 Matthew Kirtley was instructed to provide a water supply to Chapel station, from Dove Holes. This supply was utilised again in 1874, when the smaller of the two water towers was erected by J. Berresford. There is no record of the second tower being built, but the minute books show the

submission of a plan and estimate in May 1912, for an additional water tank at Chinley. Apart from a small, relatively modern steel structure there were no such storage facilities at Chinley and it is the author's opinion that minute No.25452 of 16th May 1912 was recorded in error, the secretary writing Chinley instead of Chapel. Following alterations to both up and down sidings, and the access to the horse and carriage dock in 1875, a truck weighing machine and office was built in 1878. With the construction of the up lie-by in 1881, the down platform shelter in 1886, and the strengthening of bridge No.100 in 1891 the 19th century development at Chapel was complete.

The station was originally controlled by two block posts, Chapel-en-le-Frith South, which was on the up side of the line, 5 chains south of the station and North, which was on the down side, 6 chains north of the station. In 1905 these boxes came due for renewal and were replaced by one signal box, which was built on the up platform and named simply Chapel-en-le-Frith. A few years later the space between the main lines was widened and the platforms were raised to 3ft above rail level. Finally, in 1913, a covered footbridge was erected. By this time approximately 200 passengers per day, including season ticket holders, were using the station and a bridge was considered necessary on safety grounds. The contract for its erection was initially awarded to E.C. & J. Keay on 6th December 1912, in the sum of £348 5s (£348.25), but some irregularity must have been discovered for this was cancelled and a second contract was awarded to J. Green on 17th April 1913, in the sum of £287 7s 1d (£287.35½).

It will be recalled that in its last few weeks the Midland agreed the provision of three new Station Master's houses within our study area. The first to be erected was the one at Chapel, the contract going to R. Lehane & Co. on 25th April,

Plate 309 (left) The roof of the station was a little higher than the previous ones to the same design. Consequently the eaves brackets, which were more ornate than those at Bakewell and Rowsley, were set at a steeper angle.

(Author)

Plate 310 The weigh office, built about 1872, was a strangely proportioned building, rather tall, but with a door only a little over 5ft high.

(Author)

Fig. 98 Chapel-en-le-Frith
weigh office

Scale 4mm to 1 ft

195

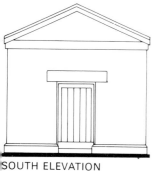

SOUTH ELEVATION

FRONT ELEVATION

NORTH ELEVATION

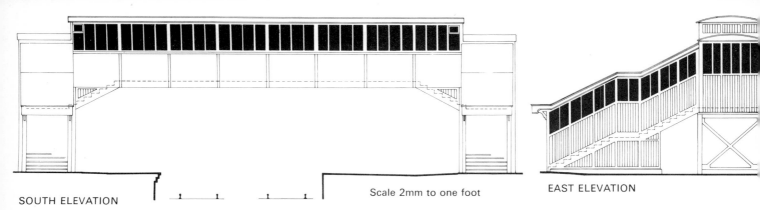

SOUTH ELEVATION

Scale 2mm to one foot

EAST ELEVATION

Fig. 99 Chapel-en-le-Frith station footbridge

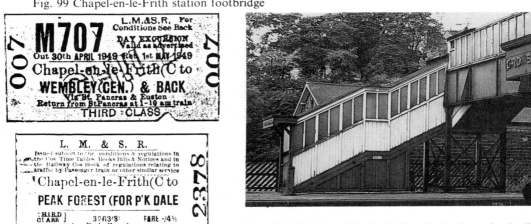

SECTION

Plate 311 This view of the footbridge clearly shows the detail of the timber staircase and the steelwork of the main girder.

(M.A. King)

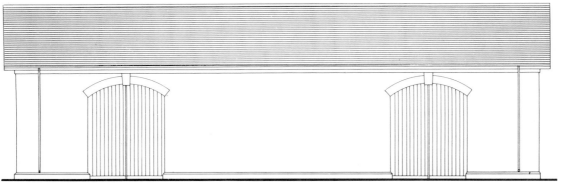

Scale 2mm to 1 ft

YARD ELEVATION

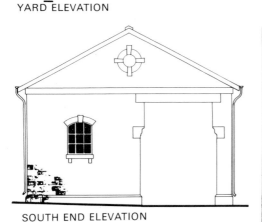

SOUTH END ELEVATION

Fig. 100 Chapel-en-le-Frith goods shed

Plate 312 Built some three years after those at Bakewell and Hassop, the goods shed at Chapel-en-le-Frith was similar, but a little lower and only had two doorways on the yard side. It did not have the timber infilling above the end door, nor did it ever receive the wooden office found at some other locations.

(M.A. King)

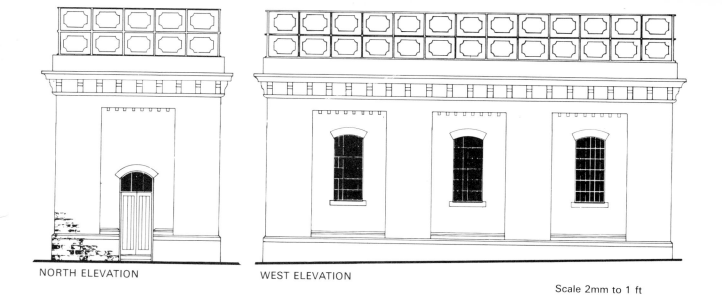

NORTH ELEVATION   WEST ELEVATION

Scale 2mm to 1 ft

Fig. 101 Chapel-en-le-Frith water tower

Plate 313 (above) An 'Austerity' 2-8-0 from Agecroft shed, brings a through freight from Brindle Heath to Rowsley out of the up loop at Chapel-en-le-Frith on 6th October 1951. The small water tower was built in 1874, and it is believed that the second one was erected about 1912.

(E.R. Morten)

1923, at a cost of £800 10s (£800.50). The design was a mirror image of that at Whatstandwell but it has not been extended in the same way and apart from new windows it remains today virtually as built. In June 1924 the suffix 'Central' was added to the MR station and 'South' was added to the former LNWR station, so that the LMS and its passengers could differentiate between the two.

It has generally been accepted that the Stanier 5XP 'Jubilees' were not permitted to run over the Derby-Manchester line until bridge strengthening had taken place. This is not strictly true for on 28th October 1936 the Chief Civil Engineer reported to the LMS Works Committee that "the superstructure of bridges No.100 and 105, carrying the railway over Manchester Road and New Chapel Road at Chapel-en-le-Frith were not strong enough to carry the engines now passing over them". He recommended that the bridges be reconstructed and that the lines be raised and subsequent alterations be

made to bridge No.101. This was of course approved and the work was carried out, but the 5XP 'Jubilees' were not diagrammed on to the principal express services until June 1938.

In terms of passenger traffic Chapel station served the town plus Chapel Milton and the scattered minor settlements to the east, with a population of a little over 6,000 in the early 1930s. In very broad figures the number of passenger bookings was comparable with Darley Dale or Rowsley, rising from just under 25,000 in 1872 to almost 55,000 in 1922. By then, however, the town had begun to develop as a commuter settlement for Manchester and the number of season ticket holders rose sharply from 74 in 1912 to 197 in 1922.

At the close of the MR period the station saw 23 stopping trains on weekdays. In the down direction 13 services stopped, including four Derby-Manchester and three early morning Buxton-Manchester. On the up line ten trains called, among which were three Manchester-Derby and three evening

Plate 314 (left) A Johnson 4-4-0 storms past the cattle dock about 1904 with an up express. The signal gantry controlled traffic from the down loops and the main line to Chinley South Junction.

(D.F. Tee Collection)

Plate 315 (centre) 483 class 4-4-0, No.332, pauses with a Chinley-Buxton local in June 1935. At that time even such a mundane service was made up of four clean corridor coaches.

(E.R. Morten)

Plate 316 (bottom) 'Britannia' class 4-6-2, No.70017 Arrow comes through the station at full cry with the 4.00pm Manchester Central-St Pancras express (SO) on 9th August 1958.

(E.R. Morten)

Manchester-Buxton services. By 1935 the LMS had expanded the timetable to comprise 14 down and 15 up trains. In the down direction there was little basic change, except that the Midland's 10.10am Derby-Manchester train was cut back to terminate at Chinley, where the 8.45am St Pancras-Manchester Central called 14 minutes later. An interesting additional local working was the 5.42pm from Chapel to New Mills, but why such a train should be deemed necessary the author cannot say. In the up direction more significant change occurred. The late morning Manchester-Derby slow was withdrawn, but a new early afternoon train left Manchester Central at 2.00pm for Buxton, replacing the 2.32pm Chinley-Buxton service. The additional trains comprised three between Chinley and Buxton, a late afternoon Manchester-Nottingham semi-fast and an early evening train from Manchester to Millers Dale. As readers are by now well aware the service was cut back sharply during the war and in 1943 seven down and six up trains called at Chapel. There were three Derby-Manchester trains each way, but the Buxton-Manchester service was cut to a single train each way, leaving Buxton at 7.25am and returning from Central at 5.23pm.

After the war the timetable remained much the same in numbers, but while the morning service from Buxton to Manchester was restored to three trains, there was still only one evening return. The up service became a little more varied and in addition to the three Manchester-Derby trains a morning Manchester-Nottingham and the late afternoon Liverpool-Nottingham called. Little general change took place in the remaining years, but by 1967 the early morning train from Derby to Manchester had been diverted to Buxton and

was replaced by the 8.26am Millers Dale-Manchester, a reminder of the 1935 LMS timetable. Of the seven down trains, five were morning services, with one late afternoon and one evening Derby-Manchester train. The up direction also saw seven stopping services, but after two early morning trains nothing stopped until the 1.10pm Chinley-Derby. The remaining trains included the late afternoon Manchester-Nottingham and Manchester-Derby services, the 5.22pm Manchester-Buxton and an evening train to Nottingham. The goods yard saw a wide and varied traffic. A cattle market was held on the first and third Thursday of each month and these markets, which stemmed from the predominantly pastoral nature of the local farms, ensured regular use of the cattle dock.

In 1922 Chapel-en-le-Frith was one of the more important stations in our study area as regards this traffic. A lot of the cattle were Irish store cattle or Irish heifers which would come over to Holyhead or Birkenhead and go to various markets along the route of the railway. Indeed such cattle arrived in Chapel well into the early 1950s and were a regular sight being driven along the main street to the market ground. There were a number of cattle dealers in the area who also bought cattle in the Scottish borders during the spring, summered them on the hills around Chapel-en-le-Frith and Chinley and finally transported them by rail to larger markets such as Northampton or Banbury. There were also locally-bred cattle moved out to the Midlands in large batches, bought by dealers with a specific market in mind. Most of this movement would be from September to November, many local farmers having insufficient winter keep or buildings for larger animals. They could, however, deal with the rearing of a calf or two through the winter for sale the following autumn.

The railway was also used, certainly up to the late 1920s, for much shorter carriage of cattle for it was common practice for farmers in the area and around New Mills, Marple etc., to send heifers into the limestone areas of the Peak (Bakewell, Millers Dale etc.,) for summer grazing. Then of course in the autumn the cattle would be returned to their home area. Occasionally top quality breeding animals would have been brought in and the odd appearance of a prize cattle van would not have been out of the question.

Apart from a little lime for agricultural purposes, the coal class traffic was dominated by coal and coke, the annual tonnage of which grew as the town developed, expanding from 3,309 tons in 1872, to a little over 8,000 tons at the turn of the century. This would have equalled about five or six wagon loads per weekday. By the close of the Midland period this figure had risen to just over 12,000 tons per annum, or seven or eight wagons per weekday. From the late 1890s to World War II the coal trade was in the hands of various dealers and was probably split about equally between domestic and industrial consumers. The earliest dealer of whom the author has records was Messrs Willcock & Co., who acquired two new wagons, Nos 19 and 20, from S.J. Claye in December 1899. These were 8 ton vehicles, 16ft x 7ft 6in x 2ft 11in with five 7in planks and full height side doors. They were painted grey, with white letters, shaded black and black ironwork. Further wagons were purchased spasmodically, from several manufacturers, up to 1908 by which time the fleet had reached eight vehicles. *Plate 317* shows one of these wagons, built by the Lincoln Wagon & Engine Co. Apart from supplying the domestic trade Messrs Willcock were the main suppliers to Ferodo Ltd and are believed to have remained in business at least up to 1939. In December 1895 they were joined in the trade by W. Potter & Sons who in that year acquired two 10 ton wagons, Nos 5 and 6. These were constructionally similar to the Willcock wagon illustrated but there are no records of the livery. At that time Messrs Kirkland & Perkin were established coal merchants in Buxton and in the early years of the century they opened an office at Chapel, with wagons bearing the firm's basic livery, but lettered Chapel-en-le-Frith instead of Buxton, as shown in *fig. 102.* The firm ceased trading, at least in Chapel, in April 1934 when their office was taken over by C.T. Cooper. There are no records to indicate that this gentleman ever operated his own wagons. At least two other dealers were engaged in the coal trade up to the late 1920s, Messrs Day and Ferguson, also

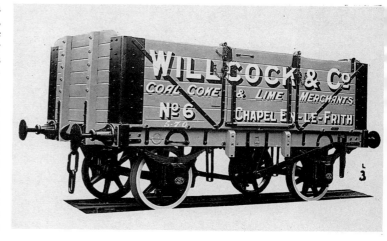

Plate 317 Messrs Willcock and Co., were established 1871 and wagon No.6 was purchased from the Lincoln Wagon & Engine Co., about 1905/6. It was an 8 ton vehicle, with side doors and a hinged top plank and was 16ft x 7ft 6in, with six 7in planks. It was painted grey, white letters, black shading.

(Cusworth Hall Museum)

Fig. 102 Kirkland and Perkin wagon livery

based in Buxton and New Mills Co-operative Society. While it is known that both these concerns operated wagons no evidence of their livery has yet come to light.

Industrial coal supplies covered a wide range of companies but they were dominated by the Chapel, Whaley & District Gas Co., who would have used some 2,000–3,000 tons per annum in the early 1930s, and Ferodo Ltd. The latter would have used a sizeable annual tonnage for powering machinery and for melting the bitumen used in the manufacturing process. Coal would also have been supplied to the High Peak Manufacturing Co., Chapel Milton and J. Lingard & Co., Bowden Hey Mill, both wadding makers; J. Kenyon & Co., rag bleachers, Chapel Milton and Town End Foundry.

In the late 1920s there were over 60 shops and small businesses in the town, almost all of which would have relied upon the railway, either to bring in supplies or take out manufactured products. In 1922 this general merchandise amounted to 4,683 tons, or about five wagon loads per weekday. The same year saw 3,318 tons of mineral traffic, and while this included building materials and bitumen coming in, there was some dispatch of roadstone from quarries near Sparrow Pit, about three miles to the east.

In the 1930s the yard was not served by a regular stopping freight and traffic was set down or taken up in the morning and evening by one of the many through freights stopping for water, or to be overtaken by faster trains. A light engine came up from Gowhole yard in the morning to shunt the yard.

On 30th June 1968 Chapel-en-le-Frith signal box closed and the down and up goods lines to Chinley South Junction were taken out of use. The block section was further lengthened on 25th August 1968 with the closure of Peak Forest North – the new block section being from Peak Forest South to Chinley South Junction.

Chapter 23
Chinley

Plate 319 (left) The Peak District is renowned for the severity of its winters but few were as spectacular as 1940, when this up freight train came to grief at Chinley South Junction, in January of that year. The view was taken from Stoddart's bridge. Today the site of the signal box is occupied by a new bridge where the Chapel and Whaley Bridge by-pass road runs under the railway.

(N.R.M.)

Plate 320 (bottom) Chapel Milton Viaduct.

(Author)

Leaving Chapel-en-le-Frith the line ran straight, towards the north east, crossed Carrington's bridge, which was widened when the down lie-by was put in, and curved gently to the west into a shallow cutting. Almost at the end of this cutting the route passed under a farm occupation bridge, Stoddart's bridge, through Chinley South Junction and then across the valley of the Black Brook, by the 15 arch Chapel Milton Viaduct, the largest structure on our journey. The viaduct was widened at its southern end in 1892/93 when the curve from the Dore and Chinley line was constructed, the subsequent junction being controlled by a 'Period III' signal box, Chinley South Junction, which remained in use until the curve was closed by British Rail. From the opening of the curve until 1902 a direct Sheffield-Buxton passenger service was operated, but with the opening of the new station these trains were diverted via Chinley.

Immediately at the north end of the viaduct the line crossed New Chapel Road by bridge No.105 and resuming its westward curve on a low embankment it passed through Chinley North Junction, where the line from Sheffield trailed in from the east. This junction was controlled by Chinley North Junction signal box which was built on the down side of the line about 1905/10, to replace an earlier box which stood in the vee of the Sheffield and Derby lines. From this junction the line continued to curve on embankment, crossed New Smithy bridge and entered a shallow cutting which was crossed by two almost identical occupation bridges, Dakins bridge and Deansgate bridge. Leaving the cutting the line resumed its course on embankment, crossed Owlerbrook bridge and entering a final shallow cutting, passed under Chinley Road and arrived at Chinley station, 31 miles 13 chains from Ambergate West Junction.

Chinley is a small settlement which grew up near a crossing of the Black Brook, close to which a number of mills were established early in the 19th century. When the railway was built the population of the village and surrounding area was well under 1,000 and it was only considered necessary to provide a small station, which was sited immediately west of

Plate 321 (above) Stanier class 5, No.44662, approaches Chinley North Junction with a Manchester Central-St Pancras express about 1955.

(H. Townley)

Plate 322 (left) The new signal box at Chinley North Junction was commissioned on 6th December 1982, and the MR cabin was demolished shortly afterwards. The modern structure may well be functional but it has none of the character of its predecessor.

(M.A. King)

Plate 323 (below) Seen here from Dakin's bridge, on 19th June 1957, Hughes/Fowler 2-6-0, No.42797, drifts through the gently undulating landscape to the east of Chinley, with a freight train from Sheffield.

(J. Hooper Collection)

Chinley Road bridge. The station buildings were virtually identical to those at Great Longstone, while the goods shed, built by J.E. Hall in 1866, was based on that at Chapel. In terms of passenger traffic in the early years the station was only marginally busier than Monsal Dale and little development took place other than the construction of an up lie-by in 1890, and the provision of two additional water cranes early in 1894.

The extra water columns were no doubt provided following the opening of the Dore and Chinley line to local passenger trains in the summer of 1894, an event which was to lead to dramatic change at Chinley. The additional traffic from Sheffield, particularly freight, placed an intolerable burden on the lines through Chinley and following authorization of the new route through Disley to Cheadle Heath, powers were sought to improve the situation. Under the MR Act 1900 (Chinley and New Mills Widening) authority was given to quadruple the tracks from Chinley North Junction to New Mills South Junction and build a new station at Chinley. The plans for this station were approved by the Traffic Committee on 20th September 1900 and a contract for its erection was subsequently awarded to Messrs Wickenson and Hardy. The new station, a little to the west of the original, was opened on 1st June 1902 and comprised five through platform faces, with a bay at the eastern end for the Buxton, Derby and Sheffield local trains. While the refreshment rooms, part of the booking hall and the waiting rooms on No.1 platform were built in gritstone, the majority of the buildings were of modular timber construction. The platforms were linked by a long, covered footbridge, which also gave pedestrian access from the road along the north side of the station, across the railway, to the main road in the centre of the village. In addition to the passenger facilities a goods shed for four wagons was provided. This was built to the then 'standard' design, of a wooden frame covered with vertical rough boarding, the joints of which were overlapped with narrow fillets. This type of construction was much cheaper than stone and was also more in keeping with the appearance of the station buildings.

When the new goods shed was completed the old one became surplus to requirements and in June 1902 approval was given for its conversion to stables, at a cost of £260. In 1911 additional stalls, with a loose box, were provided, reflecting the increase in merchandise traffic being carted by the railway at that time. By the mid-1930s motor vehicles had superseded horses and the stables were converted once again by building an internal wall to give two separate rooms, one for use as a station store, the other for use by the signal department. Additional storage facilities for the latter were provided by a wooden office built across the western end of the building, as seen in *plate 335*. In purchasing land for the widening the Midland became landlords of licensed premises, but as this activity was one of its lesser interests the Way and Works Committee readily agreed to the estate agents recommendation of 4th August 1904, that the Crown and Mitre public house be sold. One can only speculate upon the circumstances, but it is interesting to note that on 17th November 1910 the agent recommended the cancellation of the sale as no offers had been made by prospective buyers. The house still stands today, offering, one must add, a most hospitable welcome, with a fine range of Robinson's beers.

While the new station was under construction the old one, of course, remained in use, probably with a temporary up platform provided once the land had been cut back to make space for the new slow lines. Once the works were completed the old station was carefully dismantled and re-erected nearby as a private house. Before this site was cleared, engines of terminating trains were turned on the triangle at Chinley North Junction, but this was a time consuming and uneconomical practice and in December 1906 approval was given to various alterations. These included the provision of a water supply to the station from Cowburn Tunnel, the construction of additional sidings and the provision of a 60ft turntable. Shortly after this work was completed three

To Derby

Station
Building

Carriage
& Cattle Dock

Goods
Shed

Weigh
Office

To Manchester

Fig. 103 Chinley original track plan

To Derby

Station Master's House

Turntable

Cattle
Pens

Stores

Loading Dock

Chinley Station
South Jnc S.B.

Platform

Platform

Platform

Platform

Engineer's Yard

Weigh Office

5 ton
Crane

Goods Shed

P.W. Store

Chinley Station
North Jnc. S.B.

Lower Lane

To Manchester

Fig. 104 Chinley new track plan

203

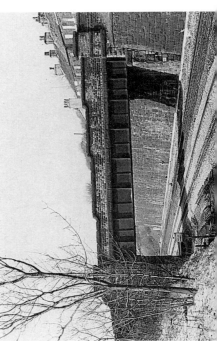

Plate 326 (above left) This view of the original station at Chinley in the late 1890s, shows the recently renewed signal box, the station buildings which were almost identical to Great Longstone, and Chinley Road bridge, with the goods shed on the right.

(M.L. Knighton Collection)

Plate 327 (below left) The new station was a far cry from the original, with its six platforms, and modular timber buildings. In this view, about 1905, Johnson 4-4-0, No.1314 (later No.302) stands in the bay with a train, probably for Sheffield.

(Author's Collection)

Plate 328 (above) The original goods shed, seen here in the early 1950s, was built in coursed random stone. It was converted to stables about 1903 and then used for storage from the mid 1930s.

(D. Ibbotson)

Plate 329 (below) Chinley Road bridge was rebuilt in 1902, using five 52ft steel girders, with stone parapets above.

(Author)

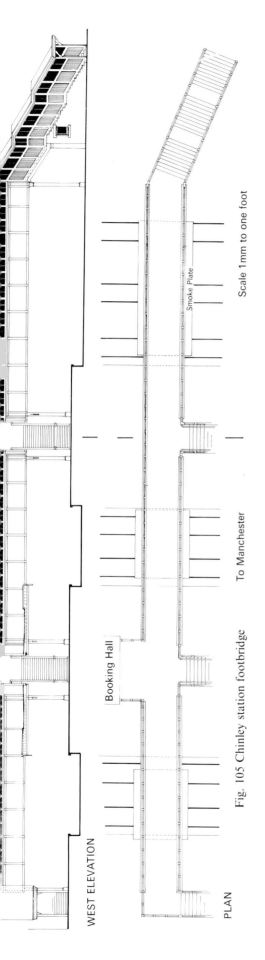

WEST ELEVATION

Booking Hall

PLAN

To Manchester

Smoke Plate

Scale 1mm to one foot

Fig. 105 Chinley station footbridge

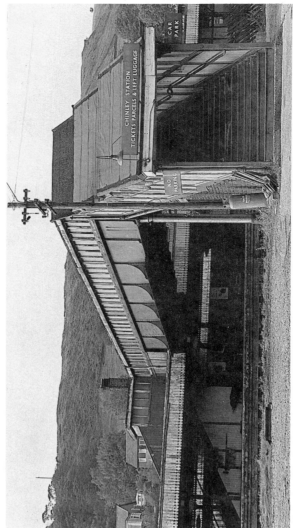

Plate 330 (left) This interior view of the footbridge clearly shows the main steel girders forming the lower half of the sides and the timber upperworks.

(M.A. King)

Plate 331 The main function of Chinley was a passenger interchange and the MR were not too concerned about creating an impressive entrance for local passengers as this view demonstrates. The footbridge did however provide a convenient right of way across the railway for residents of the dwellings to the north.

(M.A. King)

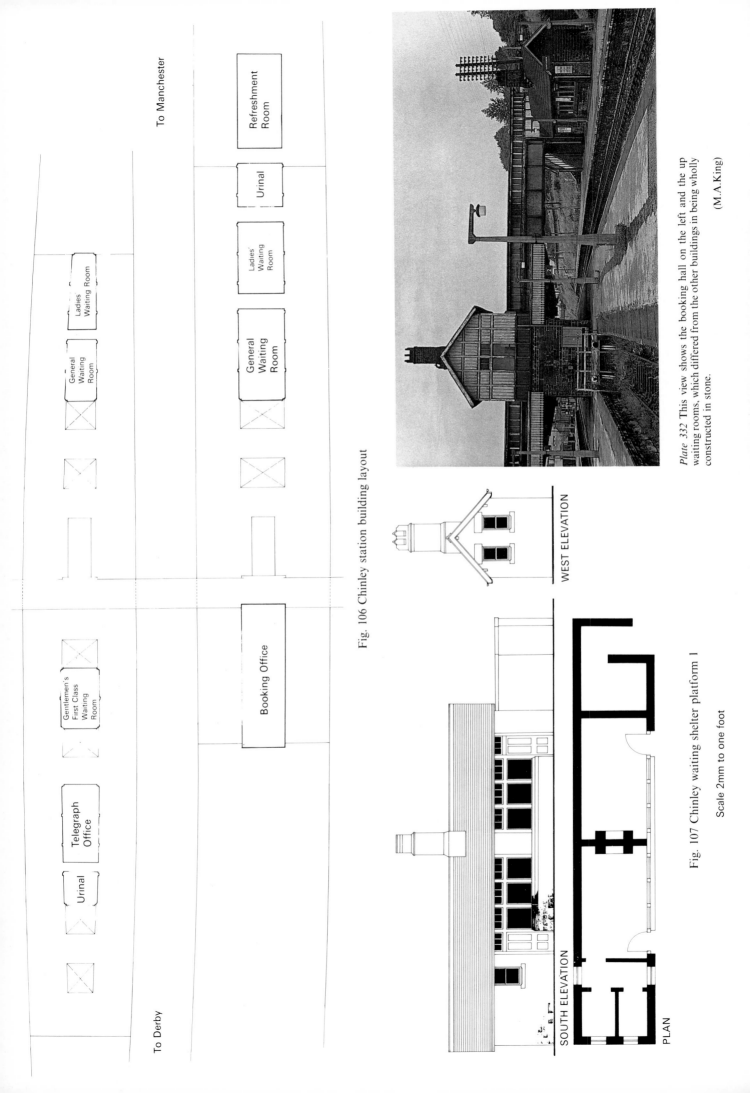

To Manchester

Ladies Waiting Room

General Waiting Room

Refreshment Room

Urinal

Ladies' Waiting Room

General Waiting Room

Gentlemen's First Class Waiting Room

Booking Office

Urinal

Telegraph Office

To Derby

Fig. 106 Chinley station building layout

WEST ELEVATION

SOUTH ELEVATION

PLAN

Fig. 107 Chinley waiting shelter platform 1

Scale 2mm to one foot

Plate 332 This view shows the booking hall on the left and the up waiting rooms, which differed from the other buildings in being wholly constructed in stone.

(M.A.King)

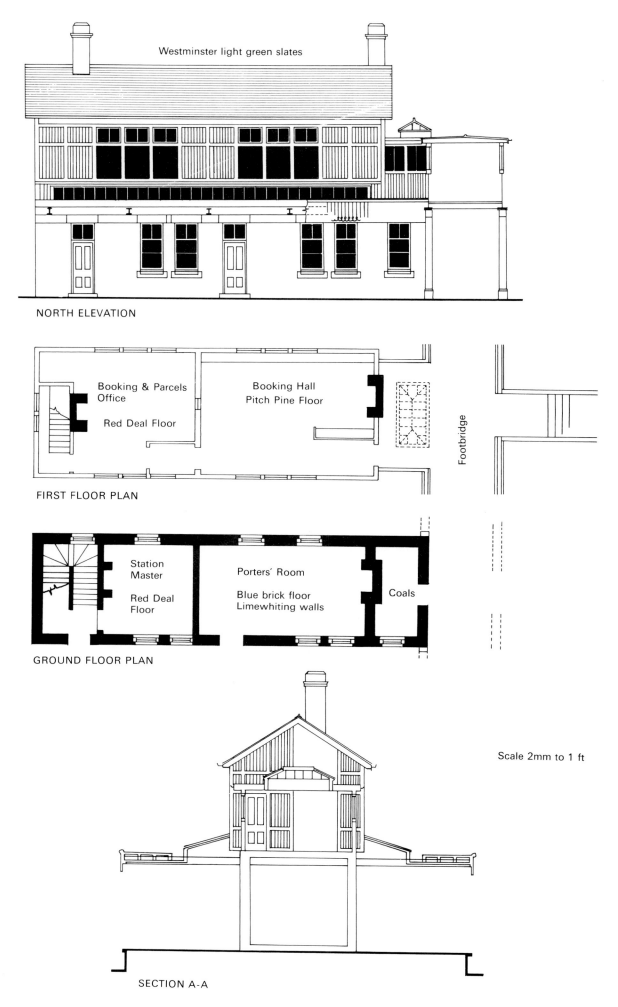

NORTH ELEVATION

Westminster light green slates

FIRST FLOOR PLAN

Booking & Parcels Office

Red Deal Floor

Booking Hall
Pitch Pine Floor

Footbridge

GROUND FLOOR PLAN

Station Master

Red Deal Floor

Porters' Room

Blue brick floor
Limewhiting walls

Coals

SECTION A-A

Scale 2mm to 1 ft

Fig. 108 Chinley station booking hall

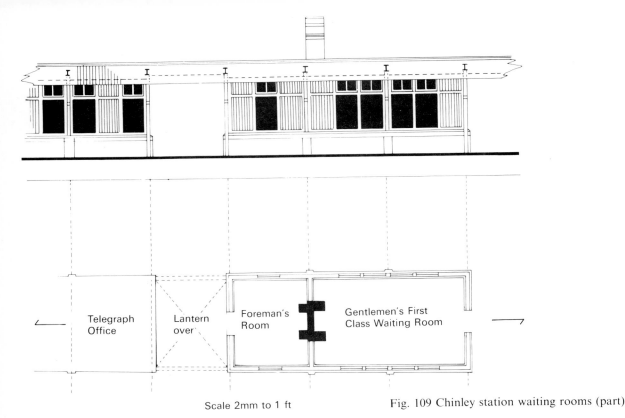

Scale 2mm to 1 ft

Fig. 109 Chinley station waiting rooms (part)

Plate 333 The majority of the buildings consisted of a stone base with a timber framed superstructure, infilled with timber panelling or glass as appropriate. This view shows the buildings at the east end of platforms 5 and 6, together with the underside of the canopy.   (M.A. King)

additional water cranes were erected and in the following summer the station was provided with long burning oil lamps. It appears that the Midland were experimenting with these at the time, but just under twelve months later, on 14th July 1910, the W. & W. Committee approved the fitting up of the station and goods shed for gas lighting. This is not to say that the oil lamps were unsuccessful but gas was much more efficient and where supplies were available they were inevitably used.

The early years of the century were troubled times for the Midland, from a safety point of view and at least five significant accidents involving passenger trains occurred between 1904 and 1913. The first, but thankfully least serious of these, occurred at Chinley, about 5.38pm on 5th January 1904, when the 5.15pm Buxton-Chinley local ran into the rear of a stationary mineral train (the 1.50pm ex-Rowsley). It was concluded that the accident was due to the negligence of the signalman at Chinley North Junction, but the inspector, Major (later Colonel Sir John) Pringle, was critical of the signalling arrangements. The railway company was not bound to take heed of an inspector's findings, but they usually did and on 19th March 1905 a plan for alterations to the signals was approved by the Way and Works Committee.

Sadly a far more serious accident happened in recent years on Sunday 9th March 1986, when the 5.30pm Sheffield-Manchester express collided head on with two light engines, almost at the same spot. In order to simplify maintenance there is a short length of single track at Chinley North Junction and the express was turned on to the wrong line at the Chinley end of this single track and met the two light engines, which had been waiting for the express to clear. The cause of the accident was an electrical fault which allowed the signalmen to turn the express on to the wrong line. Tragically the driver of the express was killed and 31 passengers were injured, two of them seriously.

Following the signalling changes of 1905 no further significant development occurred, other than the provision of an additional siding and a cart road in 1912, until early in 1931. On 25th February the Chief Engineer recommended that a sub depot be provided at Chinley, at an estimated cost of £3,615, excluding the cost of moving machinery from Derby. Construction of this depot would allow maintenance work formerly carried out under contract to be conducted by the

Plate 334 (above) Johnson 4-2-2, No.614, still in MR livery, is turned ready for its next duty on 7th August 1923, probably a portion of an express to Liverpool.

(S. Cowan)

company, resulting in economies in administration and savings on the cost of materials represented by a contractor's profit. The scheme was agreed and work put in hand to provide facilities for bricklayers, joiners, painters and plumbers.

The opening of the direct line from New Mills South Junction to Heaton Mersey in 1902, together with the completion of the new station, quickly saw Chinley replace Marple as the centre of Midland passenger activity in the North West. As this change took place the number of trains calling, and the level of bookings, increased markedly. In 1892 just under 11,000 passengers bought tickets at Chinley. Ten years later this figure had increased to over 29,000 and by 1922 it had risen sharply to a little under 67,000. By this time commuter traffic to Manchester was growing rapidly and the number of bookings continues to increase, reaching a peak of 110,106 in 1925. The following year the figure fell sharply, but then climbed again to over 81,000 by 1930, before generally falling to just under 54,500 in 1940. After the war this decline sadly continued to under 38,000 in 1962 and down to 25,468 in 1965. The purchase of season tickets also fluctuated in line with this overall pattern, increasing from three in 1892 to 192 at the end of the Midland period, reaching a peak of 980 in 1932, from whence the number slipped generally downwards to 531 in 1940, no doubt due to the depression and then the war.

Plate 335 (below) LMS built Compound 4-4-0, No.1074, runs into Chinley with the down "Peak Express" on 15th May 1938.

(H. Townley)

In our study area Chinley was fourth in terms of passenger bookings, but it was way out in front in terms of the number of trains calling, and in 1935 only five down and seven up trains ran straight through. The chief function of the station was as a junction for passenger services, partially by the detaching and attaching of carriages from or to main line expresses and partially by the origination or termination of connecting local services. The former saw the breakdown of St Pancras trains into Liverpool, Manchester Central and Manchester Victoria portions, or vice versa, while the latter comprised stopping trains to or from the Manchester stations, Liverpool, Derby, Buxton and Sheffield. The complexity of the passenger workings precludes an analysis of the growth and decline as we have noted at previous stations on our journey, but interested readers will, it is hoped, find sufficient detail in *Appendix I*.

It must here suffice to note that at the end of the Midland period 33 down and 35 up trains called, including four from London and three up to the Capital. By the mid-1930s this traffic had increased to 38 down and 40 up trains, with five from London, but only two in the up direction. Readers are by now familiar with the wartime cuts and nowhere was this more marked than at Chinley where the wartime timetable comprised 24 down and 22 up trains. After the war the growth of road traffic made restoration of the services pointless and in the mid-1950s the timetable was still more or less at its wartime level. By 1967 however, the problems of congestion in the cities and the strong growth of new commuter housing in settlements on the western side of the Peak District, had forced the railway to increase services, even though the political mandarins had different plans. Thus when local trains were withdrawn on the Peak line in 1967 Chinley was served by 26 down and 25 up trains, with the London expresses at their wartime level of five down and four up.

The majority of stations along the line saw an important milk traffic, but the only actual figures known to the author are for the period 1924 to 1937, at Chinley. In the former year 8,225 full churns were sent out, or approximately 22 per day. During the late 1920s the growth of road traffic and the emergence of centralised dairies had a dramatic effect on this traffic, and by 1930 the total had fallen to 679 churns, or about two per day. By 1937 it was down to 34, or about three per month.

Freight traffic at Chinley was dominated at the turn of the century by through traffic, much as the pattern at Ambergate, but the goods yard nevertheless saw an interesting and busy local trade. In the mid-1920s the decline in horse drawn transport was accelerating and this was naturally reflected in the number of horses carried by rail. In 1925, 144 horses were sent out, by 1928 this was down to ten and between 1929 and 1936 the average was two per year. Although cattle pens were provided at Chinley they never saw any significant use, as the area was covered by the fortnightly cattle market at Chapel-en-le-Frith. The highest annual total of traffic known to the author was 17 truckloads in 1922, while the LMS annual average was three truckloads.

Coal and coke traffic grew steadily from a little under 1,500 tons in 1872 to about 8,000 tons at the turn of the century. The market then fluctuated but in the early LMS years the annual trade was around 9,000 tons. During the 1930s the average annual tonnage had risen to a little over 14,200, or 5-7 wagons per day. The peak year for this traffic was 1940 when 17,015 tons came in. This is probably explained by the almost unprecedented severity of the weather in January and February, already graphically shown in *plate 319*.

The trade for many years was primarily in the hands of J.T. Cresswell and Messrs Booth & Fox. John Thomas Cresswell appears to have set up his business around 1900, but while his daughter, Mrs Eveline Heyworth, now in her nineties, recalls that her father operated a number of wagons, no details of the livery have survived. Mr Cresswell's business was almost equally divided between the household market and industrial consumers. The former covered much of Chinley, Bugsworth and the scattered settlements to the south. The latter included supplies to Messrs J.J. Hadfield, bleachers, at Forge Works, Messrs J. Welch & Sons, dyers, at Whitehall Works and Messrs Hollands Britannia Wire Works, Bugsworth. An interesting aspect of the business, which may well have been repeated by many other merchants, was that Mr Cresswell used to visit the cattle market at Chapel-en-le-Frith, every two weeks and sell coal, by the full truckload, to visiting farmers. The wagons would then be dispatched to the nearest station where the farmer would arrange unloading. Thus the wagons could have been seen in the yards at Chapel (Central), Chapel (South), Dove Holes, Edale, Peak Forest and Whaley Bridge.

Shortly after World War I Mr J.A. Fox started in business as coal merchant and haulage contractor and a little later he formed a partnership with Jabez Cresswell one of John's two sons. However the arrangement did not last and by the mid-1920s Mr Fox had started another company, Booth & Fox. Within ten years this partnership seems to have folded for Mr Fox was by then operating his own railway wagons, lettered J.A. Fox. These wagons were on hire, for two reasons. Firstly it obviated the need to put up the capital for the outright purchase of the vehicles. Secondly it meant that much of the administration was left to the owners, who, under the terms of the hiring agreement guaranteed that the wagons would make at least two trips per week between the collieries and Chinley. It was also implied, naturally, that the wagons would only operate on account of J.A. Fox. However, one day James was on his way by rail to Nottingham Races and he saw one of his wagons on a journey which was obviously not going to terminate at Chinley. This was a case of the owners slipping in an extra run, which would have been surreptitiously charged to the hirer's account. Quite a hullabaloo followed, but this, and Mr Cresswell's sales to farmers, are good examples of how little is actually known about the day to day operation of private owner wagons.

In addition to these two local merchants, supplies were also brought in by colliery agents, who regularly called to see clients at Chinley on their way home from the Manchester Coal Exchange. These agents, whose own wagons and those of the collieries they represented, would have appeared in the yard from time to time, included Nathaniel Attrill, Chesterfield, Burnett Bros & Co., Sheffield, The Hallamshire Coal Supplies Ltd, Sheffield and W.N. Toft, Derby. It is also known that James Oakes' wagons were regularly seen in the yard.

In the 1920s and '30s there were about 30-35 shops and businesses in Chinley and Bugsworth and a wide variety of general merchandise was handled at the station. Of particular interest were loads of steel rod and bar coming in for Britannia Wire Works. Much of this came from Middlesbrough on single or double bolster wagons, a high proportion of which would have been of LNER origin. Coils of wire, in many different sizes were sent out in low goods or merchandise wagons. Mention has already been made of Messrs J.J. Hadfield and J. Welch & Sons, both bleachers and dyers, and their activities gave rise to much interesting traffic. Cotton and other textiles for processing arrived in vans or sheeted open wagons from the North West and the Midlands, while the

Plate 336 (below) Ex-LNWR 'Renown' class, No.5155, *Irresistible* of Brunswick shed, stands at Chinley with the 12.25pm from Liverpool in July 1928. Considered by the LMS to be of minor importance the last 'Renown' was withdrawn in 1931.

(S. Cowan)

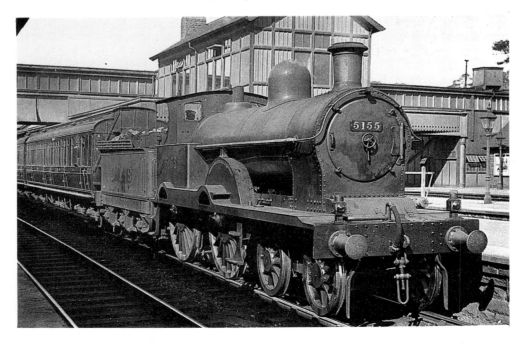

various chemicals in use arrived in boxes, barrels, drums, carboys etc. Finished goods would have been sent out primarily in covered vans. Large bales of wadding were sent out from J. Lingard Ltd, usually in sheeted open wagons.

The mineral class traffic included building materials such as sand, cement, bricks, granite setts etc., but was dominated by the output of building stone from Chinley Head Quarry, on the Hayfield road and Cracken Edge Quarry, on the eastern slopes of Chinley Churn. The latter was particularly noted for the production of paving slabs and roofing slates and remained open until about 1930. The volume of mineral traffic rose markedly to a peak of around 16,000 tons per annum in the 1890s, then declined slowly only to rise again to a second peak of almost 11,000 tons in 1929. There was a dramatic fall after the closure of Cracken Edge Quarry and by 1942 the traffic had fallen to 276 tons per annum, or about one wagon per week. This would no doubt have been incoming building material, for which there is little demand in the middle of a war.

In the 1930s the yard was served primarily by the 7.10am mineral from Gowhole to Chapel-en-le-Frith and by trip workings from Gowhole yard as required.

Today, Chinley is a forlorn relic of its former self and is served by eleven down and ten up Manchester-Sheffield local trains, these being almost outnumbered by the stone trains from Buxton and Peak Forest. Although the station is occasionally enlivened by an enthusiasts' steam special, to stand on Chinley Road bridge and look westwards at the dismal remains of the semi-derelict station can only bring back a flood of memories and I can do no better than leave the final words of this book to Jim Fox, the retired coal merchant and lifelong resident of the village.

". . . turning the engines on the turntable, the Eldorado ice-cream man, chocolates, chewing gum, Kensitas (three cigarettes and three matches in a little round tube for 2d), the name plate machines, the weighing machines. Tea and a bun, or a sandwich from the trolley, the licensed refreshment rooms, the water tower and most of all the five to five express to Manchester."

Only memories.

Bibliography

Books
Industrial Archaeology of the Peak District. (David & Charles)
Industrial Archaeology of Derbyshire. F. Nixon (David & Charles)
The Peak District. R. Christian.
The Peak District. R. Millward & A. Robinson.
Black Top – A History of the British flexible roads industry. J.B.F. Earle
A Century of Road Materials. J.B.F. Earle.
The Midland Railway. F.S. Williams.
The Midland Railway. C. Hamilton Ellis (Ian Allan) 1974.
A Pictorial Record of LMS Architecture. V.R. Anderson and G. Fox (OPC) 1981.
The Matlocks and Bakewell. Reprinted by the Arkwright Society, 1984.
Kelly's Directory of Derbyshire 1924.

Pamphlets, Journals, ets.
A History of Beswick's Lime Works Ltd 1923-1973 and S. Taylor Frith & Co. Ltd 1905-1973. Staveley Lime Products Ltd.
ICI Mond Division Technical Service Note TS/E/36.
'Limestone and Lime Products' ICI.
The Buxton Lime Trade. L. Jackson, Cement, Lime and Gravel Journal, October/November 1950.
Rockfill causeway for quarry access. The Surveyor, August 1984.
The Track of the Twenty-fives. LMS Route book No.5, c1930.
Water Softening Plant & the Utilisation of Refuse Lime. The Surveyor & Municipal Engineering, March 1918.
LMS Society Teach-in notes, Volume I. LMS Society.
HMRS Journal Vol.12 No.5, January – March 1986.

Public Record Office Documents

MR Construction Committee Minutes	
Rowsley and Buxton	Rail 491/311, 312
Buxton and New Mills	Rail 491/313
Ambergate Curve	Rail 491/322
MR Way and Works Committee Minutes	1849-1922
	Rail 491/90-135
MR Traffic Committee Minutes	1849-1922
	Rail 491/137-167
MR General Purposes	Rail 491/227-237
MR Traffic and Expenses Statistics	Rail 491/672-677
MR Distance Diagrams	Rail 491/779
LMS Traffic Committee	Rail 418/75-87
LMS Works Committee	Rail 418/93-99
Board of Trade Accident Reports	Rail 491/761

Appendix I Summary of Passenger Services

Midland Summer 1922

Down

12.00am	St Pancras-Mcr Central, calls Derby (3.45).
2.25am	St Pancras-Mcr Central, calls Derby (5.28) Carries through carriage for Mcr Victoria, dropped at Stockport.
3.55am	Derby-Mcr Victoria, calls Matlock (4.23), Stockport (5.22). Picks up carriage off 2.25am ex St Pancras.
4.25am	St Pancras-Mcr Central, calls Derby (8.07), Ambergate (8.24), Matlock Bath (8.36), Matlock (8.40), Millers Dale (9.05). Connects at Ambergate with 7.44am from Pye Bridge.
6.43am	Buxton-Chinley, calls Peak Forest (6.57), Chapel (7.05).
7.03am	Derby-Buxton, all stations. Connects at Ambergate with 6.48am Chesterfield-Derby slow.
7.05am	Buxton-Mcr Central, calls Chapel (7.23), Chinley (7.27), Bugsworth (7.36), Cheadle Heath (7.53).
7.20am	Rowsley-Buxton, all stations.
8.03am	Sheffield-Mcr Central, calls Chinley (9.17).
8.10am	Buxton-Mcr Central, calls Chapel (8.28), Chinley (8.32).
8.25am	St Pancras-Mcr Central, calls Derby (11.15), Matlock (11.42), Chinley (12.25). Carries 1st and 3rd class restaurant cars. Picks up through carriage Nottingham to Mcr Central at Derby.
8.54am	Sheffield-Chinley.
9.15am	Buxton-Mcr Central, calls Chapel (9.33), Chinley (9.45).
9.25am	Millers Dale-Mcr Central, all stations via Marple.
9.45am	Derby-Mcr Central, calls Ambergate (10.05), Matlock Bath (10.16), Matlock (10.20), Bakewell (10.35), Millers Dale (10.49), Chinley (11.09), Cheadle Heath (11.27). Connects at Ambergate with 8.10am Sheffield-Derby slow. Carries through carriage Nottingham-Mcr Victoria, dropped at Chinley.
10.10am	Sheffield-Mcr Central, calls Chinley (10.56).
10.10am	Derby-Mcr Central, all stations via Cheadle Heath. Connects at Ambergate with 9.46am Sheffield-Derby express.
10.25am	St Pancras-Mcr Central, calls Derby (1.00). Carries 1st and 3rd class restaurant cars.
10.35am	Sheffield-Chinley.
11.15am	Chinley-Mcr Victoria.
11.15am	Chinley-Liverpool Central, via Marple.
11.20am	St Pancras-Mcr Central, calls Derby (3.33), Matlock Bath (3.59), Matlock (4.04), Millers Dale (4.29), Chinley (4.50). Sets down only at Withington.
11.45am	Buxton-Stockport, via Millers Dale, calls Peak Forest (12.29), Chapel (12.37), Chinley (12.41).
12.00pm	Nottingham-Mcr Central, calls Derby (1.12), Millers Dale (1.57), Chinley (2.16).
12.25pm	St Pancras-Mcr Central, calls Derby (3.33), Matlock Bath (3.59), Matlock (4.04), Millers Dale (4.29), Chinley (4.50). Sets down only at Withington.
12.25pm	Derby-Matlock, all stations. Connects at Ambergate with 12.20pm Chesterfield-Derby slow and 12.07pm from Pye Bridge.
12.30pm	Sheffield-Chinley
1.15pm	Derby-Mcr Central, calls all stations except Nottingham Road, Cromford, Hassop, Monsal Dale. Connects at Ambergate with 12.20pm Chesterfield-Derby slow.
1.25pm	St Pancras-Mcr Victoria (East Lancashire Express), calls Derby (4.18), Matlock (4.44), Millers Dale (5.17), Chinley (5.28). Carries through carriage London-Buxton, dropped at Millers Dale and through portion for Mcr Central dropped at Chinley.
1.28pm	Buxton-Chinley, calls Peak Forest (1.41), Chapel (1.49).
1.30pm	Sheffield-Mcr Central, calls Chinley (2.12).
2.22pm	Sheffield-Mcr Central, calls Chinley (3.39).
2.25pm	St Pancras-Mcr Central, calls Derby (5.00).
2.25pm	Chinley-Mcr Victoria, calls Marple (2.38).
3.15pm	Chinley-Stockport.
3.40pm	Derby-Mcr Central, all stations to Chinley, then Cheadle Heath (6.32). Held on slow line at Darley Dale and overtaken by East Lancashire Express.
4.00pm	Sheffield-Mcr Central, calls Chinley (4.46).
4.25pm	St Pancras-Mcr Central, called Derby (7.10), Chinley (8.10). 1st and 3rd class restaurant cars. Sets down at Cheadle Heath.
5.30pm	Sheffield-Mcr Central, calls Chinley (6.37).
5.42pm	Derby-Buxton, calls Matlock Bath (6.08), Matlock (6.14), Rowsley (6.23), Bakewell (6.31), Millers Dale (6.45).
5.48pm	Derby-Bakewell, all stations.
5.48pm	Chinley-Liverpool Central, carries portion off 1.25pm ex-St Pancras.
6.25pm	Sheffield-Chinley.
6.25pm	St Pancras-Mcr Central, calls Derby (9.02), Matlock (9.37), Cheadle Heath (10.12). Sets down only at Bakewell and Millers Dale. 1st and 3rd class restaurant cars.
6.42pm	Hope-Chinley.
7.07pm	Sheffield-Mcr Central, calls Chinley (8.16).
7.20pm	Derby-Mcr Central, via Marple, calls Ambergate (7.38), then all stations except Bugsworth. Connects at Ambergate with 6.20pm Sheffield-Derby slow.
7.25pm	Buxton-Chinley, calls Peak Forest (7.38), Chapel (7.46).
8.22pm	Chinley-Liverpool Central, carries through coach off 4.25pm ex-St Pancras.
9.07pm	Derby-Buxton, calls Matlock Bath (9.33), Matlock (9.37), Bakewell (9.51), Millers Dale (10.05).
10.45pm	Buxton-Chinley (SO), calls Peak Forest (10.58), Chapel (11.06).

Up

6.03am	Mcr Central-Buxton, via Marple, all stations.
7.10am	Ambergate-Derby, workman's train, all stations.
7.20am	Mcr Central-St Pancras, picks up only Didsbury, calls Millers Dale (8.12), Derby (8.50). Restaurant car.
7.24am	Bakewell-Derby, all stations, connects at Ambergate with 7.48 Derby-Sheffield express and 8.18 Ambergate-Pye Bridge.
7.27am	Mcr Central-Derby, calls Heaton Mersey, and Cheadle Heath, then all stations, except Cromford, Whatstandwell and Nottingham Road. Connects at Ambergate with 10.05 Derby-Sheffield express.
7.35am	Chinley-Sheffield.
7.50am	Buxton-Derby, all stations except Monsal Dale and Hassop. Connects at Ambergate with 8.43 Derby-Chesterfield slow and 9.24 Ambergate-Pye Bridge.
8.10am	Liverpool Central-Chinley.
8.40am	Chinley-Sheffield.
8.55am	Mcr Central-St Pancras, picks up only Didsbury, calls Chinley (9.36), Millers Dale (10.03), Derby (10.42) 1st and 3rd class restaurant cars. Picks up through carriages ex Liverpool at Chinley, ex Buxton at Millers Dale.
9.33am	Mcr Victoria-Chinley, carries through carriages for St Pancras.
9.45am	Mcr Central-St Pancras, calls Derby (11.10). 1st and 3rd class restaurant cars.
9.48am	Chinley-Derby, all stations except Peak Forest, Monsal Dale, Hassop, Duffield and Nottingham Road. Connects at Ambergate with 10.55 Derby-Chesterfield slow.
9.55am	Mcr Central-St Pancras calls Cheadle Heath (10.10), Chinley (10.34), Millers Dale (11.00), Matlock (11.22), Derby (11.47). Picks up through carriages ex-Mcr Victoria at Chinley.
10.02am	Chinley-Sheffield.
10.55am	Mcr Central-Derby, via Marple, all stations except Bugsworth, Monsal Dale, Hassop, Cromford, Whatstandwell and Nottingham Road.
11.38am	Mcr Central-Sheffield, calls Chinley (12.18).
12.20pm	Mcr Central-St Pancras, calls Derby (1.47) 1st and 3rd class restaurant cars. Carries through carriages to Yarmouth and Lowestoft, dropped at Derby.
12.32pm	Mcr Central-Buxton (SO), calls Chinley (1.14), Chapel (1.25), Peak Forest (1.37).
12.45pm	Chinley-Sheffield.
12.55pm	Liverpool Central-Chinley.
1.15pm	Mcr Victoria-St Pancras (East Lancashire Express), calls Millers Dale (2.16), Derby (3.02). 1st and 3rd class restaurant cars. Picks up through carriage from Buxton at Millers Dale.
1.42pm	Matlock-Derby, all stations except Nottingham Road. Connects at Ambergate with 2.05 Derby-Chesterfield slow.
1.50pm	Mcr Central-St Pancras, calls Chinley (2.22), Derby (3.20). 1st and 3rd class restaurant cars.
2.00pm	Mcr Central-Sheffield, calls Chinley (2.35).
2.32pm	Chinley-Buxton, calls Chapel (2.40), Peak Forest (2.51).
2.40pm	Mcr Central-Chinley, all stations except Bugsworth.
2.45pm	Chinley-Sheffield.
3.30pm	Mcr Central-Derby, calls Chinley (4.05), Millers Dale (4.29), Bakewell (4.43), Rowsley (4.50), Darley Dale (4.55), Matlock (5.00), Matlock Bath (5.05).
4.03pm	Mcr Victoria-Chinley. Carries through coach to Nottingham.
4.07pm	Mcr Central-Chinley.
4.14pm	Chinley-Derby, all stations except Nottingham Road. Connects at Ambergate with 6.20 Ambergate-Nottingham slow and 6.25 Ambergate-Chesterfield slow.
4.25pm	Stockport-Chinley.
4.25pm	Mcr Central-Nottingham, calls Chinley (5.13), Millers Dale (5.37), Matlock (6.02), Ambergate (6.14), then via Butterley and Codnor Park. Picks up through carriage ex Mcr Victoria at Chinley.
4.35pm	Mcr Central-St Pancras, calls Derby (6.03) 1st and 3rd class restaurant cars.
4.55pm	Mcr Central-Sheffield, calls Chinley (5.30).
5.00pm	Liverpool Central-Derby, calls Cheadle Heath (5.55).
5.05pm	Mcr Central-Buxton (SX), calls Cheadle Heath (5.20), Chinley (5.43), Chapel (5.56).
5.22pm	Buxton-Derby, all stations except Hassop. Connects at Ambergate with 6.55 Derby-Sheffield.
5.38pm	Chinley-Hathersage (SX).
5.50pm	Mcr Central-St Pancras, calls Derby (7.17).
5.55pm	Mcr Central-Buxton.
6.17pm	Chinley-Sheffield.
6.45pm	Mcr Central-Chinley.
7.25pm	Mcr Central-Derby, calls Chinley (8.00), Chapel (8.12), Peak Forest (8.23), Millers Dale (8.31), Matlock (8.55), Matlock Bath (9.00).
8.07pm	Chinley-Sheffield.
8.15pm	Buxton-Derby, all stations to Ambergate. Calls Monsal Dale (SO) Connects at Ambergate with 9.42 Derby-Sheffield slow.
8.58pm	Mcr Central-Buxton via Marple, calls Chinley (9.48), Chapel (9.54), Peak Forest (10.02).
9.55pm	Chinley-Sheffield.
10.50pm	Buxton-Rowsley (SO), calls Millers Dale (11.00), Great Longstone (11.07), Bakewell (11.14).

LMS Summer 1935

Down

12.05am	St Pancras-Mcr Central, calls Derby (3.55), Matlock (4.28), carries through carriage to Mcr Victoria dropped at Stockport.
2.25am	St Pancras-Mcr Central, calls Derby (5.28).
4.25am	St Pancras-Mcr Central, calls Derby (8.06), Ambergate (8.27), Matlock Bath (8.38), Matlock (8.42), Millers Dale (9.08). Carries restaurant car Leicester to Buxton (SX) dropped at Millers Dale.
6.09am	Sheffield-Chinley.
6.30am	Buxton-Chinley, calls Peak Forest (6.44), Chapel (6.51).
6.43am	Leicester-Blackpool North (SO), via Chesterfield, calls Chinley (9.31).
7.05am	Buxton-Mcr Central calls Peak Forest (7.17), Chapel (7.26), Chinley (7.30), Buxworth (7.35), Cheadle Heath (7.52).
7.10am	Matlock-Buxton, calls Darley Dale (7.16), Rowsley (7.23), Bakewell (7.33), Great Longstone (7.41), Millers Dale (7.51).
7.10am	Derby-Buxton all stations except Nottingham Road. Connects at Ambergate with 6.21am Sheffield-Derby slow.
7.47am	Sheffield-Mcr Central.
7.50am	Mansfield-Blackpool North (SO), calls at Ambergate (8.35), Darley Dale (8.52), Rowsley (9.00), Bakewell (9.12), Millers Dale (9.30), Chapel (9.55).
8.00am	Yarmouth-Manchester Victoria (SO), calls Nottingham (12.55).
8.05am	Nottingham-Blackpool North (SO), via Chesterfield, calls Chinley (10.30).
8.10am	Buxton-Manchester Central, calls Chapel (8.28), Chinley (8.32).
8.25am	St Pancras-Mcr Central, calls Derby (11.09), Matlock (11.46), Millers Dale (12.09), Chinley (12.28), Restaurant cars. Picks up through carriages for Nottingham-Mcr at Derby (except Fridays and Saturdays).
8.25am	Sheffield-Blackpool North (SO), calls Chinley (9.22).
8.41am	Rotherham (Westgate) – Blackpool North (SO) calls Chinley (10.17).
8.45am	Nottingham-Blackpool North (SO) calls Derby (9.23), Ambergate (9.39), Matlock Bath (9.50), Matlock (9.55), Bakewell (10.09), Millers Dale (10.23), Chinley (10.43). Connects at Ambergate with 8.10am Sheffield-Derby and 8.07am Mansfield-Ambergate.
8.49am	Hope-Mcr Central, calls Chinley (9.13).
8.56am	Sheffield-Mcr Central, calls Chinley (9.42).
9.15am	Yarmouth-Mcr Central (SO), calls Chinley (4.53), Cheadle Heath (4.35).
9.16am	Buxton-Mcr Central, calls Chapel (9.33), Chinley (9.37), Cheadle Heath (10.00).
9.23am	Millers Dale-Mcr Central via Marple. All stations.
9.25am	St Pancras-Mcr Central, calls Derby (1.00), Matlock (1.24), Chinley (2.03). Carries through carriage London to Mcr Victoria (SO).

9.40am Derby-Mcr Central (SO), calls Belper (9.51), Ambergate (9.57), Cromford (10.05), Matlock Bath (10.10), Matlock (10.14), Bakewell (10.28), Millers Dale (10.41), Chapel (11.02), Chinley (11.06), Cheadle Heath (11.23). Carries through carriages Nottingham to Mcr Central and Victoria, also to Southport-Chapel Street. Connects at Ambergate with 8.10am Sheffield-Derby and 9.09am Mansfield-Ambergate. (Virtually similar train runs weekdays without Southport carriages.)

10.00am Nottingham-Blackpool North (SO), calls Derby (10.53), Duffield (11.03), Belper (11.10), Matlock Bath (11.30), Matlock (11.35), Chinley (12.37).

10.10am Sheffield-Mcr Central, calls Chinley (10.50). Carries through carriages Sheffield-Liverpool (SX) and Sheffield-Southport (Fridays and Saturdays only).

10.20am Derby-Chinley, all stations except Nottingham Road. Connects at Ambergate with 9.00am Rotherham-Derby.

10.20am Buxton-Chinley, calls Peak Forest (10.34), Chapel (10.40)

10.25am St Pancras-Manchester (SX), calls Derby (1.04), Matlock (1.33), Millers Dale (1.54), Chinley (2.13). Restaurant cars London-Manchester, through carriage to Manchester Victoria. Saturdays only runs 8 minutes later to Derby.

10.38am Leicester-Blackpool North (SO), calls Derby (11.27), Belper (11.34), Ambergate (11.45), Bakewell (12.09), Chinley (12.44). Connects at Ambergate with 10.40am Chesterfield-Derby slow.

10.43am Sheffield-Chinley

10.50am Nottingham-Blackpool North (Mondays and Fridays only), calls Derby (11.27), Belper (11.39), Ambergate (11.45), Bakewell (12.09), Chinley (12.40).

10.55am Rotherham (Westgate)-Blackpool North, calls Chinley (12.36)

11.16am Chinley-Mcr (SO), calls Marple (11.27) takes through carriage 9.40am ex Derby (runs 5 mins earlier weekdays).

11.22am Chinley-Liverpool Central, calls New Mills (11.30), Marple (11.36), Stockport (11.45).

12.25pm St Pancras-Mcr Central, calls Derby (3.00), sets down only Cheadle Heath (4.09). Restaurant cars London to Manchester, through carriages to Liverpool Central (via Mcr). On Saturdays runs 9 minutes later to Derby.

12.25pm Derby-Darley Dale, all stations except Nottingham Road (stops on SO).

12.33pm Sheffield-Chinley (SO).

12.54pm Chinley-Mcr Central.

1.11pm Sheffield-Chinley (SO).

1.15pm Derby-Mcr Central, All stations to Chinley, except Nottingham Road and Hassop. Weekdays departs Chinley 3.09 runs all stations except Strines to Mcr Central. Saturdays only runs non-stop to Mcr Central. Connects at Ambergate with 11.47am Sheffield-Derby slow.

1.28pm Buxton-Mcr Victoria, calls Peak Forest (1.41), Chapel (1.49).

1.32pm Sheffield-Mcr Central, calls Chinley (2.17).

1.45pm Sheffield-Llandudno (SO), calls Chinley (2.37).

1.45pm Mansfield-Rowsley (SO) all stations.

2.15pm St Pancras-Mcr Central (SO), calls Derby (4.58). Third class only.

2.22pm Sheffield-Mcr Central, calls Chinley (3.33).

2.25pm St Pancras-Mcr Central (SX), calls Derby (4.58), Millers Dale (5.42). Restaurant cars London to Manchester, through carriage London to Buxton. Saturdays only also calls Matlock (5.36), Chinley (6.19), Cheadle Heath (6.35).

3.05pm Derby-Matlock, calls Ambergate (3.22), Cromford (3.31), Matlock Bath (3.35), through carriage London-Matlock, off 12.25pm ex-St Pancras. Connects at Ambergate with 2.05pm Sheffield-Derby slow. Runs 9 minutes later on Saturdays.

3.09pm Chinley-Mcr Central (SX).

3.14pm Chinley-Mcr Central (SO), all stations except Strines.

3.48pm Derby-Buxton, all stations except Nottingham Road. Connects at Ambergate with 3.01pm Sheffield-Derby semi-fast.

4.10pm Sheffield-Mcr Central, calls Chinley (4.53).

4.25pm St Pancras-Mcr Central, calls Derby (7.10), Matlock (7.35), Chinley (8.14), sets down Cheadle Heath (8.32), through carriage London-Liverpool Central.

4.25pm Buxton-Mcr Central, calls Peak Forest (4.38), Chapel (4.46), Chinley (4.50), Withington and West Didsbury (5.12).

4.58pm Chinley-New Mills, Saturdays only runs to Stockport and connects with the 5.42 to Mcr Central.

5.30pm Sheffield-Mcr Central, calls Chinley (6.37), Buxworth (6.50), Cheadle Heath (7.05) then all stations to Central.

5.31pm Chinley-New Mills (SO).

5.42pm Derby-Buxton, calls Matlock Bath (6.08), Matlock (6.12), Darley Dale (6.19), Rowsley (6.25), Bakewell (6.32), Great Longstone (6.40), Millers Dale (6.49). On Saturdays leaves Derby 6 minutes later and calls additionally at Cromford (6.12).

5.42pm Chapel-New Mills (SX) calls Chinley (5,46), Buxworth (5.50).

5.48pm Derby-Bakewell (SX), all stations. Connects at Ambergate with 5.12pm Sheffield-Derby slow. On Saturdays runs 5 minutes later from Derby, does not call Nottingham Road.

5.48pm Hope-Mcr Central (SX) calls Chinley (6.12).

5.49pm Millers Dale-Chinley, calls Peak Forest (6.02), Chapel (6.09).

6.25pm St Pancras-Mcr Central, calls Derby (9.00), Millers Dale (9.45), Chinley (10.03). Restaurant cars, through carriage London-Buxton.

6.25pm Sheffield-Chinley (SX). On Saturday terminates at Hope.

7.07pm Sheffield-Mcr Central, calls Chinley (8.22) and all stations New Mills-Stockport.

7.19pm Derby-Mcr Central, all stations except Nottingham Road, Hassop and Strines. Calls Monsal Dale Saturdays only. Connects at Ambergate with 6.21pm Sheffield-Derby semi-fast.

7.30pm Buxton-Chinley, calls Peak Forest (7.43), Chapel (7.51).

8.27pm Chinley-Liverpool Central, calls Cheadle Heath (8.41), through carriage off 4.25pm ex-St Pancras.

8.35pm Sheffield-Chinley.

9.05pm Derby-Buxton, all stations except Nottingham Road, Hassop and Monsal Dale, through carriage London-Buxton off 6.25pm ex-St Pancras.

10.09pm Chinley-Mcr Central, all stations exept Buxworth and Strines.

10.57pm Derby-Rowsley (SO), all stations except Nottingham Road and Cromford. Connects at Ambergate with 8.49pm Sheffield-Derby slow.

11.05pm Buxton-Chinley (SO), calls Peak Forest (11.18), Chapel (11.25).

Up

6.05am Mcr Central-Millers Dale, via Marple, calls all stations.

6.15am Buxton-Matlock, calls Millers Dale (6.24), Great Longstone (6.32), Bakewell (6.38), Rowsley (6.45), Darley Dale (6.50).

7.20am Mcr Central-St Pancras, picks up Didsbury, calls Millers Dale (8.09), Matlock (8.27), Derby (8.50).

7.24am Mcr Central-Derby, calls all stations to Cheadle Heath, except Didsbury, then all stations Buxworth to Derby, except Whatstandwell and Nottingham Road. Stops Cromford Saturdays only.

7.32am Bakewell-Derby, all stations. Connects at Ambergate with 7.48am Derby-Sheffield semi-fast and 8.16am Ambergate to Mansfield.

7.40am Chinley-Sheffield.

7.52am Buxton-Derby, all stations except Monsal Dale, Hassop, Duffield and Nottingham Road. Connects at Ambergate with 8.46am Derby-Chesterfield slow.

8.05am Liverpool Central-Chinley, calls Cheadle Heath (9.00).

8.38am Mcr Central-Chinley, via Marple.

8.38am Chinley-Sheffield.

8.55am Mcr Central-St Pancras, via Nottingham. Picks up Didsbury, calls Chinley (9.31), Millers Dale (9.56), Matlock (10.07), Derby (10.42). Restaurant car. Picks up through carriages Liverpool to St Pancras at Chinley, and through carriage Buxton to St Pancras at Millers Dale.

9.33am Mcr Victoria-Derby (SO), calls Marple (10.04), Chinley (10.23), Millers Dale (10.48), Bakewell (11.03), Matlock (11.14), Cromfore (11.19), Ambergate (11.30). Connects at Ambergate with 11.00am Derby-Chesterfield.

9.44am Chinley-Sheffield.

9.45am Mcr Central-St Pancras, calls Cheadle Heath (9.58), Derby (11.11) Restaurant cars. Overtakes 9.46 ex Chinley at Millers Dale.

9.46am Chinley-Derby, all stations except Monsal Dale, Hassop, Duffield and Nottingham Road. Picks up restaurant car Buxton to London (SX) at Millers Dale. Held in up loop at Darley Dale on Saturday and overtaken by 9.33am ex Mcr Victoria then runs seven minutes later stations to Derby.

9.55am Chinley-Sheffield (SO).

10.55am Mcr Central-Chinley, via Marple, all stations.

11.00am Chinley-Buxton, calls Chapel (11.09), Peak Forest (11.19).

11.00am Llandudno-Sheffield (SO), calls Chinley 1.50pm.

11.44am Mcr Central-Sheffield, calls Chinley (12.14).

12.18am Chinley-Derby, all stations except Nottingham Road. Connects at Ambergate with 2.25 Derby-Chesterfield slow.

12.20pm Mcr Central-St Pancras. Picks up Cheadle Heath, calls Derby (1.48). Restaurant cars.

12.20pm Blackpool North-Desford (SO)), calls Chinley (2.42), Rowsley (3.28), Matlock (3.38), Matlock Bath (3.43), Ambergate (3.57), Derby (4.15).

12.32pm Mcr Central-Buxton (SO), calls Cheadle Heath (12.50), Chinley (1.14), Chapel (1.16), Peak Forest (1.25).

12.38pm Chinley-Sheffield.

1.00pm Llandudno-Sheffield (SO), calls Chinley (3.47).

1.04pm Mcr Central-Chinley, via Marple, all stations except Buxworth.

1.05pm Blackpool North-Mansfield (SO), calls Chinley (3.37), Chapel (3.49), Millers Dale (4.08), Bakewell (4.20), Rowsley (4.28), Darley Dale (4.35), Ambergate (4.48), then all stations to Mansfield.

1.15pm Mcr Victoria-Chinley, calls Marple (1.42). Saturdays only continues to Derby, calling Millers Dale (2.21).

1.37pm Darley Dale-Derby (SX), all stations except Nottingham Road.

1.45pm Mcr Central-St Pancras, calls Chinley (2.07), Millers Dale (2.33), Matlock (2.52), Derby (3.21). Restaurant cars. Picks up through carriage Buxton to London at Millers Dale. On Saturdays leaves 10 minutes earlier, but runs 6 minutes slower to Derby.

2.00pm Mcr Central-Buxton, calls Chinley (2.32), Chapel (2.41), Peak Forest (2.53).

2.10pm Blackpool North-Nottingham (SO), via Chesterfield, calls Chinley (4.32).

2.20pm Mcr Central-Chinley (SO), calls Cheadle Heath (2.33).

2.37pm Chinley-Sheffield.

2.45pm Mcr Central-Chinley, all stations except Strines.

2.55pm Blackpool North-Sheffield (SO), calls Chinley (5.21).

3.00pm Mcr Central-Sheffield, calls Chinley (3.32), carries through carriages Liverpool-Sheffield.

3.08pm Darley Dale-Derby (SO), all stations except Whatstandwell, Belper and Nottingham Road.

3.25pm Mcr Central-Derby, calls Chinley (4.00), Millers Dale (4.22), Bakewell (4.34), then all stations except Whatstandwell and Nottingham Road.

3.35pm Blackpool North-Leicester (SO), via Chesterfield, calls Chinley (6.07).

3.46pm Matlock-Derby (SX), calls Matlock Bath (3.50), Ambergate (4.02), Belper (4.08), Duffield (4.14).

3.50pm Blackpool North-Sheffield (SO), calls Chinley (6.20).

3.55pm Mcr Central-Hope, all stations except Buxworth.

4.05pm Mcr Victoria-Chinley, calls Marple (4.30). Carries through carriages Southport (Chapel Street) to Nottingham, and Mcr Victoria to Nottingham.

4.05pm Mcr Victoria-Nottingham (SO) calls Chinley (4.51), Chapel (4.59), Millers Dale (5.14), Bakewell (5.39), Matlock (5.53), Matlock Bath (5.58), Ambergate (6.09), then via Butterley.

4.15pm Chinley-Derby, all stations except Nottingham Road. Connects at Ambergate with 6.20pm Derby-Chesterfield slow (SX).

4.24pm Matlock-Derby (SO), calls Matlock Bath (4.27), Ambergate (4.38), Belper (4.44), Duffield (4.51).

4.25pm Mcr Central-Nottingham, calls Withington and West Didsbury (4.36), Stockport (4.43), Marple (4.57), Chinley (5.12), Chapel (5.23), Millers Dale (5.38), Bakewell (5.50), Matlock (6.01), Matlock Bath (6.05), Ambergate (6.15), then via Butterley. (Runs slow line New Mills to Chinley). Picks up through carriages from Southport and Mcr Victoria at Chinley.

4.35pm Mcr Central-St Pancras, calls Derby (5.58). Restaurant cars. Overtakes 4.05pm Mcr Victoria-Nottingham (SO) at Millers Dale.

4.55pm Blackpool North-Nottingham (Mondays and Fridays only), calls Chinley (7.00), Great Longstone (7.30), Bakewell (7.35), Matlock (7.46), Matlock Bath (7.50), Ambergate (8.04), Derby (8.19). Splits at Chinley, with portion to Sheffield departing 7.10pm.

4.55pm Blackpool North-Leicester (SO), calls Chinley (7.00) and sets down only at Bakewell, Matlock, Matlock Bath, Ambergate, Belper and Duffield, calls Derby (8.21).

4.55pm Liverpool-Derby (SO), calls Cheadle Heath (5.50), Matlock (6.45), carries through carriages Liverpool-St Pancras.

4.56pm Mcr Central-Sheffield, calls Cheadle Heath (5.09), Chinley (5.34).

5.27pm Mcr Central-Buxton (SX), calls Chinley (5.58), Chapel (6.06).

5.35pm Buxton-Derby, all stations except Hassop and Nottingham Road. Connects at Ambergate with 6.55 Derby-Chesterfield slow.

5.40pm Chinley-Buxton, calls Chapel (5.47), Peak Forest (5.58).

5.44pm Chinley-Sheffield.

5.48pm New Mills-Chinley (SO), calls Buxworth (5.58).

5.50pm Mcr Central-St Pancras, calls Matlock (6.58), Derby (7.20), (3 minutes later on Saturdays). Picks up through carriages from Liverpool at Derby on Saturdays. Restaurant cars.

5.55pm Mcr Central-Buxton, all stations from Stockport except Strines and Buxworth.

6.14pm Mcr Central-Millers Dale, calls Didsbury and all stations from Stockport except Strines and Buxworth.

6.19pm Chinley-Sheffield.

6.45pm Mcr Central-Chinley, all stations except Strines.

7.25pm Mcr Central-Derby, calls Cheadle Heath (7.39), Chinley (8.00), Chapel (8.12), Millers Dale (8.27), Bakewell (8.39), Matlock (8.52), Matlock Bath (8.56), Belper (9.15). Carries through carriages Mcr Central-Nottingham.

7.42pm Bakewell-Derby (SO), calls Rowsley (7.48), Darley Dale (7.53), Matlock (7.58), Matlock Bath (8.04).

8.05pm Rowsley-Mansfield (SO), all stations.

8.07pm Chinley-Sheffield.

8.10pm Buxton-Derby, calls all stations to Ambergate except Hassop, (Monsal Dale SO). Connects at Ambergate with 9.45 Derby-Sheffield slow.

8.20pm Mcr Central-Chinley, all stations to Cheadle Heath.

8.20pm Chinley-Buxton, calls Chapel (8.27).

8.50pm Mcr Central-Buxton, calls Didsbury (9.02) and all stations except Strines.

10.07pm Chinley-Sheffield.

10.40pm Mcr Central-Chinley (Wednesdays and Saturdays only), calls all stations except Strines.

11.10pm Buxton-Rowsley (SO), calls Millers Dale (11.19), Great Longstone (11.27), Bakewell (11.33).

11.32pm Mcr Victoria-Yarmouth (Fridays only), calls Nottingham (1.40).

11.45pm Mcr Victoria-Derby, calls Marple (12.11), carries through carriage Mcr Victoria-St Pancras.

11.50pm Chinley-Buxton (SO), calls Chapel (11.57), Peak Forest (12.09).

12.00am Mcr Central-St Pancras, calls Stockport (12.16), Marple (12.45), Derby (2.00). Picks up through carriages from Mcr Victoria at Derby.

LMS Summer 1943

Down

4.20am St Pancras-Mcr Central, calls Derby (8.40), Ambergate (8.57), Matlock (9.09), Millers Dale (9.34), Chinley (9.54). Connects at Ambergate with 8.05am from Mansfield.

5.45am Sheffield-Chinley.

6.35am Buxton-Chinley, calls Peak Forest (6.49), Chapel (6.56).

7.02am Sheffield-Mcr Central, calls Chinley (8.16).

7.10am Derby-Mcr Central via Marple. All stations except Nottingham Road.

7.25am Leicester-Blackpool North (SO), via Chesterfield calls Chinley (10.21).

7.25am Buxton-Mcr Central, calls Peak Forest (7.39), Chapel (7.46), Chinley (7.50), Cheadle Heath (8.08).

8.00am Sheffield-Chinley. Carries through carriages to Blackpool North (SO).

8.30am St Pancras-Mcr Central, calls Derby (12.05), Matlock (12.34), Millers Dale (1.02), Chinley (1.25), Cheadle Heath (1.48).

8.55am Derby-Blackpool (SO), calls Ambergate (9.10), Matlock (9.23).

10.10am Derby-Mcr Central, via Marple, all stations except Nottingham Road. Connects at Ambergate with 8.15 Sheffield-Derby slow.

12.35pm Derby-Darley Dale, all stations. Connects at Ambergate with 11.12 Sheffield-Derby slow and 11.32 from Mansfield.

12.45pm Sheffield-Mcr Central calls Chinley (1.57).

1.20pm Derby-Mcr Central, all stations except Nottingham Road. Connects at Ambergate as per 12.35 Derby-Darley Dale.

1.30pm St Pancras-Mcr Central, calls Derby (5.08), Matlock (5.34), Millers Dale (6.00), Chinley (6.21), Cheadle Heath (6.38).

2.05pm Sheffield-Mcr Central, calls Chinley (3.20).

3.30pm St Pancras-Mcr Central, calls Derby (7.00), Matlock (7.26), Millers Dale (7.52), Chinley (8.14), sets down Didsbury (8.37).

3.45pm Derby-Darley Dale, all stations except Nottingham Road.

4.35pm Sheffield-Mcr Central, calls Chinley (5.47).

5.00pm Buxton-Chinley, calls Peak Forest (5.14), Chapel (5.21).

5.30pm Sheffield-Chinley.

5.45pm St Pancras-Mcr Central, calls Derby (9.14), Matlock (9.41), Millers Dale (10.07), Chinley (10.30), Cheadle Heath (10.52), Didsbury (10.59).

5.48pm Derby-Chinley, all stations, does not call Nottingham Road on Saturdays. Connects at Ambergate with 4.37 Sheffield-Derby express.

6.50pm Sheffield-Chinley.

7.00pm Chinley-Mcr Central, all stations.

8.05pm Chinley-Mcr Central, all stations.

8.20pm Derby-Darley Dale, all stations. Connects at Ambergate with 7.07 Chesterfield-Derby slow.

9.10pm Sheffield-Chinley.

9.42pm Derby-Bakewell, all stations except Nottingham Road.

10.45pm Chinley-Mcr Central, calls New Mills (10.54), Marple (11.00), Romiley (11.06), Stockport (11.12).

Up

6.05am Mcr Central-Chinley, via Marple, all stations.

6.30am Darley Dale-Derby, all stations.

7.12am Chinley-Sheffield.

7.20am Mcr Central-St Pancras, calls Didsbury (7.31), Chinley (7.58 takes up only), Millers Dale (8.18), Matlock (8.38), Derby (9.02).

7.24am Mcr Central-Derby, via Cheadle Heath, all stations except Nottingham Road. Connects at Ambergate with 10.25 Derby-Sheffield express and 10.00 Ambergate-Mansfield.

7.25am Chinley-Buxton, calls Chapel (7.33), Peak Forest (7.43).

7.32am Bakewell-Derby, all stations, connects at Ambergate with 8.04 Derby-Sheffield express.

7.41am Chinley-Sheffield.

8.30am Mcr Central-Chinley, all stations except Chorlton-cum-Hardy, Strines and Buxworth.

8.55am Mcr Central-St Pancras, calls Didsbury (9.05, takes up only), Chinley (9.33), Millers Dale (9.56), Matlock (10.20), Derby (10.45).

9.44am Chinley-Sheffield.

10.55am Mcr Central-Derby (SO), via Marple, all stations except Nottingham Road.

12.29pm Mcr Central-Buxton (SO), calls Cheadle Heath (12.43), Chinley (1.07), Chapel (1.17), Peak Forest (1.28).

12.38pm Chinley-Sheffield.

1.04pm Mcr Central-Sheffield (SX), calls Chinley (2.12).

1.15pm Mcr Central-Sheffield (SO), calls Chinley (2.20).

1.40pm Darley Dale-Derby, calls all stations except Nottingham Road.

2.00pm Mcr Central-St Pancras, calls Chinley (2.35), Millers Dale (2.58), Matlock (3.24), Derby (3.49).

2.35pm Blackpool North-Sheffield (SO), calls Chinley (5.17).

2.42pm Mcr Central-Derby, calls all stations to Matlock, then Derby.

3.30pm Blackpool North-Nottingham, calls Matlock (6.36), Ambergate (6.53), Derby (7.10). Connects at Ambergate with 7.30 Derby-Sheffield slow.

3.55pm Mcr Central-Sheffield, calls Chinley (5.05).

5.00pm Mcr Central-Chinley, via Marple, calls all stations.

5.16pm Matlock-Derby, calls all stations except Nottingham Road. Connects at Ambergate with 5.12 Derby-Sheffield slow.

5.23pm Mcr Central-Buxton (SX), calls Cheadle Heath (5.37), Chinley (6.01), Chapel (6.11), Peak Forest (6.21).

5.40pm Chinley-Buxton (SX), calls Chapel (5.48), Peak Forest (5.58).

5.50pm Mcr Central-St Pancras, calls Chinley (6.35), Millers Dale (6.48), Matlock (7.12), Derby (7.42).

6.03pm Chinley-Buxton (SO), calls Chapel (6.11), Peak Forest (6.21).

6.41pm Chinley-Sheffield.

6.45pm Mcr Central-Derby, calls all stations except Nottingham Road (calls Monsal Dale SO).

8.10pm Chinley-Sheffield (SO).

8.45pm Mcr Central-Chinley.

10.50pm Chinley-Sheffield (SO).

British Railways Winter 1954

Down

4.18am St Pancras-Mcr Central, calls Derby (8.10), Ambergate (8.25), Matlock (8.36), Millers Dales (9.02).

6.05am Sheffield-Chinley.

6.45am Derby-Buxton Parcels (MX) calls Belper (6.57), Matlock Bath (7.17), Matlock (7.22), Darley Dale (7.37), Rowsley (7.45), Bakewell (7.55), Millers Dale (8.15).

7.02am Sheffield-Mcr Central, calls Chinley (8.55).

7.05am Buxton-Mcr Central, calls Peak Forest (7.19), Chapel (7.25), Chinley (7.32), Buxworth (7.37), Cheadle Heath (7.51).

7.10am Derby-Mcr Central, via Marple, calls all stations except Nottingham Road.

8.00am Buxton-Mcr Central calls Peak Forest (8.14), Chapel (8.20), Chinley (8.25), Cheadle Heath (8.42).

8.05am Sheffield-Mcr Central, calls Chinley (8.55).

8.15am St Pancras-Mcr Central, calls Derby (11.25), Matlock (11.49), Millers Dale (12.15), Chinley (12.34).

9.06am Nottingham-Liverpool, calls Derby (9.44), Belper (9.55), Matlock (10.11), Bakewell (10.25), Millers Dale (10.39), Chinley (10.58), Mcr Central (11.26).

9.15am Buxton-Mcr Central, calls Chapel (9.32), Chinley (9.37), Cheadle Heath (9.54).

10.15am St Pancras-Mcr Central, calls Derby (12.55), Matlock (1.18), Millers Dale (1.42), Chinley (2.00).

10.24am Derby-Mcr Central, via Marple, calls all stations except Nottingham Road.

10.55am Sheffield-Chinley.

12.08pm Spondon-Darley Dale (SO), calls all stations.

12.35pm Sheffield-Chinley (SO).

12.50pm Sheffield-Chinley.

1.05pm Derby-Buxton (SX) all stations except Nottingham Road.

1.05pm Derby-Mcr Central (SO) via Marple, calls all stations.

1.25pm Buxton-Chinley (SO), calls Peak Forest (1.39), Chapel (1.44).

2.15pm St Pancras-Mcr Central, calls Derby (4.57), Millers Dale (5.42), Chinley (6.03), Cheadle Heath (6.19).

2.20pm Chinley-Stockport (SX) all stations.

2.22pm Sheffield-Chinley (SO).

4.15pm St Pancras-Mcr Central, calls Derby (7.06), Matlock (7.30), Millers Dale (7.56), Chinley (8.16), Didsbury (8.35 sets down only).

4.30pm Sheffield-Chinley.

5.05pm Derby-Bakewell, calls all stations except Nottingham Road, Duffield and Ambergate (empty stock worked to Hassop for stabling).

5.10pm Rotherham-Mcr Central (SX), calls Chinley (6.42).

5.32pm Sheffield-Mcr Central (SO), calls Chinley (6.42).

5.50pm Derby-Darley Dale, calls all stations, but not Nottingham Road on Saturdays.

6.00pm Sheffield-Chinley (SX).

6.40pm St Pancras-Mcr Central, calls Derby (9.27), Matlock (9.51), Millers Dale (10.16), Chinley (10.34), Didsbury (10.53 sets down only).

6.55pm Sheffield-Mcr Central, calls Chinley (8.04).

7.16pm Derby-Mcr Central, via Marple, calls all stations except Nottingham Road and Strines. Calls Monsal Dale Saturdays only.

7.40pm Parcels St Pancras-Mcr Central via Chesterfield, calls Chinley to change crew 3.34am.

9.24pm Sheffield-Mcr Central, calls Chinley (10.26).

Up

12.05am Mcr Central-St Pancras, via Chesterfield (MX), calls Cheadle Heath (12.19), Derby (2.00). Mondays only runs via Matlock, calls Derby (1.46).

12.05am Mcr Central-Derby, via Chesterfield (MO), calls Stockport (12.22).

6.05am Mcr Central-Millers Dale calls all stations.

6.20am Darley Dale-Nottingham, calls all stations. Connects at Ambergate with 6.30 Derby-Sheffield slow.

7.09am Chinley-Rotherham (SX), terminates at Sheffield on Saturdays.

7.20am Mcr Central-St Pancras, calls Didsbury (7.32, takes up only), Millers Dale (8.13), Matlock (8.30), Derby (8.54).

7.24am Mcr Central-Derby, calls all stations except Nottingham Road.

7.35am Bakewell-Derby, calls all stations. Connects at Ambergate with 6.40 Birmingham-Bradford.

7.38am Chinley-Sheffield.

8.25am Mcr Central-Sheffield, calls Chinley (9.27).

9.00am Mcr Central-St Pancras, calls Didsbury (9.12 takes up only), Chinley (9.36), Millers Dale (9.57), Matlock (10.18), Derby (10.43).

10.50am Mcr Central-Sheffield, calls Chinley (12.01).

11.35am Mcr Central-Nottingham (SX), calls Chinley (12.08), then all stations to Derby except Nottingham Road.

11.35am Mcr Central-St Pancras (SO), calls Chinley (12.08), then all stations to Matlock (1.10), then Derby (1.38).

12.23pm Mcr Central-Buxton (SO), calls Cheadle Heath (12.37), Chinley (1.02), Chapel (1.12), Peak Forest (1.23).

1.04pm Mcr Central-Sheffield calls Chinley (2.13).

1.25pm Darley Dale-Derby (SO), calls all stations except Nottingham Road.

1.50pm Mcr Central-St Pancras, calls Chinley (2.23), Millers Dale (2.44), Matlock (3.02), Derby (3.26).

2.50pm Mcr Central-Derby, via Marple, calls all stations. Stands in loop at Darley Dale (4.58-5.21).

3.30pm Liverpool-Nottingham, calls Mcr Central (4.32), Stockport (4.48), Marple (5.03), Chinley (5.23), Chapel (5.32), Miller Dale (5.48), Bakewell (5.59), Matlock (6.10), Belper (6.25), Derby (6.37).

3.42pm Stockport-Sheffield, calls Chinley (4.21).

4.00pm Mcr Central-St Pancras, calls Millers Dale (4.50), Matlock (5.08), Derby (5.35). Overtakes 2.50, ex-Mcr Central at Darley Dale.

4.03pm Mcr Central-Sheffield, calls Chinley (5.07).

5.22pm Mcr Central-Buxton (SX), calls Cheadle Heath (5.36), Chinley (5.58), Chapel (6.07), Peak Forest (6.17).

5.30pm	Fleetwood-Derby Fish train (SO) calls Marple (9.00 to change engines).
5.40pm	Chinley-Sheffield.
5.46pm	Buxton-Derby, all stations except Nottingham Road.
5.55pm	Mcr Central-St Pancras, calls Chinley (6.28), Millers Dale (6.50), Matlock (7.08), Derby (7.35).
6.33pm	Chinley-Sheffield.
6.45pm	Mcr Central-Sheffield, calls Chinley (7.59).
6.50pm	Buxton-Derby (SO), calls all stations except Nottingham Road. Connects at Ambergate with 7.50 Derby-Sheffield slow.
7.38pm	Mcr Central-Derby via Cheadle Heath, calls all stations, but Monsal Dale on Saturdays only.
8.37pm	Bolton-Leicester Parcels (SX), calls Marple (11.45 to change engines) then via Chesterfield.
9.30pm	Mcr Central-Sheffield, calls Chinley (10.35).

British Railways Summer 1967
Down

4.25am	St Pancras-Mcr Central calls Derby (7.58), Ambergate (8.10), Matlock (8.22), Millers Dale (8.41), Chinley (8.59).
6.06am	Sheffield-Chinley.
7.02am	Derby-Buxton, all stations except Nottingham Road.
7.03am	Sheffield-Mcr Central, calls Chinley (8.13).
7.10am	Buxton-Mcr Central, calls Peak Forest (7.21), Chapel (7.28), Chinley (7.32), Cheadle Heath (7.45), Chorlton-cum-Hardy (7.52).
7.50am	Sheffield-Mcr Central, calls Chinley (8.48).
8.00am	St Pancras-Mcr Central, calls Derby (10.35), Matlock (10.58), Millers Dale (11.17), Chinley (11.35).
8.00am	Buxton-Mcr Central, calls Peak Forest (8.11), Chapel (8.18), Chinley (8.22), Cheadle Heath (8.36).
8.12am	Leicester-Blackpool North (SO), calls Derby (8.55), Belper (9.05), Matlock (9.22), Bakewell (9.35), Millers Dale (9.46), Chinley (10.04).
8.26am	Millers Dale-Mcr Central, calls Peak Forest (8.35), Chapel (8.41), Chinley (8.45), and all stations via Marple.
8.45am	Nottingham-Mcr Central, calls Derby (9.18), Belper (9.28), Matlock (9.44), Bakewell (9.55), Millers Dale (10.06), Chinley (10.25).
9.15am	Buxton-Mcr Central, calls Chapel (9.31), Chinley (9.36), Cheadle Heath (9.49).
9.15am	Sheffield-Chinley.
9.35am	Sheffield-Llandudno (SO), calls Chinley (10.28).
10.45am	Derby-Mcr central, calls all stations to Chinley except Nottingham Road.
12.16pm	Derby-Buxton (SO), calls all stations except Rowsley.
12.20pm	St Pancras-Mcr Central, calls Derby (2.50), Matlock (3.13), Millers Dale (3.32), Chinley (3.50),
12.45pm	Sheffield-Chinley (SO).
12.45pm	Nottingham-Mcr Central, calls Derby (1.08), Matlock (1.41), Millers Dale (2.00), Chinley (2.18).
1.10pm	Sheffield-Chinley (SX).
1.28pm	Derby-Mcr Central (SO), calls all stations except Nottingham Road and Rowsley.
2.23pm	Chinley-Mcr Central (SX), via Marple, calls all stations except Strines.
3.55pm	Sheffield-Mcr Piccadilly, calls Chinley (4.39) through train from Yarmouth Vauxhall.
4.10pm	Derby-Mcr Central, calls all stations except Nottingham Road and Strines.
4.20pm	St Pancras-Mcr Central, calls Derby (6.49), Matlock (7.12), Millers Dale (7.31), Chinley (7.49), Didsbury (8.04 sets down only).
4.30pm	Sheffield-Chinley.
4.45pm	Derby-Darley Dale (SO, 17th June-2nd September), all stations except Nottingham Road, Duffield and Ambergate.
4.45pm	Nottingham-Mcr Central, calls Derby (5.18), Matlock (5.43), Millers Dale (6.02), Chinley (6.21).
4.59pm	Sheffield-Mcr Victoria, through train from Yarmouth Vauxhall.
5.00pm	Derby-Darley Dale (SX, 17th June-2nd September), all stations except Nottingham Road.
5.30pm	Sheffield-Mcr Central, calls Chinley (6.40).
5.55pm	Derby-Bakewell, all stations (Nottingham Road SX).
6.10pm	Sheffield-Chinley.

6.35pm	St Pancras-Mcr Central, calls Derby (8.56), Matlock (9.19), Millers Dale (9.38), Chinley (9.57), Didsbury (10.14, sets down only).
7.02pm	Sheffield-Mcr Central, calls Chinley (8.06).
7.30pm	Derby-Mcr Central (SX, 17th June-2nd September), calls all stations except Nottingham Road, Whatstandwell, Rowsley and Strines. (Runs 10 minutes later on Saturdays 17th June-2nd September).
9.22pm	Sheffield-Mcr Central, calls Chinley (10.24).

Up

12.05am	Mcr Central-St Pancras (via Chesterfield), calls Stockport (12.22).
6.05am	Mcr Central-Millers Dale, all stations.
6.27am	Darley Dale-Derby, all stations.
6.45am	Chinley-Sheffield.
7.05am	Mcr Central-Nottingham, calls Didsbury (7.16, takes up only), Chinley (7.34), Millers Dale (7.51), Matlock (8.13), Derby (8.38).
7.40am	Bakewell-Derby, all stations.
7.40am	Chinley-Sheffield.
7.45am	Mcr Central-Derby, all stations except Strines and Nottingham Road.
8.30am	Mcr Central-St Pancras, calls Didsbury (8.40, takes up only), Chinley (8.58), Millers Dale (9.15), Matlock (9.37), Derby (10.01).
9.25am	Mcr Central-Sheffield, calls Chinley (10.18).
9.45am	Mcr Piccadilly-Yarmouth (SO), calls Chinley (10.21), Sheffield Midland (11.00).
10.00am	Mcr Central-Nottingham, calls Chinley (10.25), Millers Dale (10.43), Matlock (11.04), Derby (11.28).
11.45am	Mcr Central-Chinley, all stations.
12.30pm	Mcr Central-St Pancras, calls Chinley (12.55), Millers Dale (1.13), Matlock (1.34), Derby (1.58).
1.05pm	Chinley-Sheffield.
1.10pm	Chinley-Derby (SX), calls Chapel (1.14), Millers Dale (1.27), Bakewell (1.36), Matlock (1.47), Cromford (1.51), Ambergate (1.59), Belper (2.06), Derby (2.16).
1.20pm	Chinley-Derby (SO), calls Chapel (1.24), Millers Dale (1.37), Bakewell (1.46), Darley Dale (1.54), then all stations to Derby except Nottingham Road.
1.20pm	Mcr Central-Sheffield, calls Chinley (2.20).
1.20pm	Blackpool North-Leicester (SO, 24th June-2nd September), calls Chinley (3.49), Millers Dale (4.29), Bakewell (4.39), Matlock (4.52), Belper (5.06), Derby (5.15).
2.00pm	Mcr Central-Nottingham, calls Chinley (2.25), Millers Dale (2.43), Matlock (3.04), Derby (3.28).
2.28pm	Llandudno-Sheffield (SO, 24th June-2nd September), Calls Chinley (5.40).
3.25pm	Mcr Central-Nottingham, calls Cheadle Heath (3.38), Chinley (3.58), Chapel (4.04), Millers Dale (3.20), Bakewell (3.29), Matlock (3.41), Belper (3.56), Derby (4.06).
3.30pm	Mcr Central-Sheffield (SX), calls Chinley (4.22).
4.10pm	Mcr Central-Sheffield, calls Chinley (5.05).
4.32pm	Mcr Central-Derby, calls Stockport (4.49), then all stations except Strines, Whatstandwell and Nottingham Road.
4.45pm	Mcr Central-St Pancras, calls Chinley (5.10), Millers Dale (5.28), Matlock (5.49), Derby (6.13).
5.22pm	Mcr Central-Buxton (SX), calls Chinley (5.56), Chapel (6.03), Peak Forest (6.13).
6.10pm	Mcr Central-St Pancras, calls Chinley (6.35), Millers Dale (6.53), Matlock (7.15), Derby (7.39).
6.40pm	Chinley-Sheffield.
7.10pm	Buxton-Derby (SO), calls all stations except Whatstandwell and Nottingham Road.
7.22pm	Mcr Central-Chinley, calls all stations except Strines.
8.00pm	Mcr Central-Sheffield, calls Chinley (8.29).
8.15pm	Mcr Central-Nottingham (SX), calls Chinley (8.40), then all stations except Peak Forest, Rowsley, Cromford, Whatstandwell and Nottingham Road.
8.15pm	Mcr Central-Nottingham (SO), calls Chinley (8.40), then all stations except Rowsley, Whatstandwell and Nottingham Road.
9.35pm	Mcr Central-Sheffield, calls Chinley (10.36).
10.55pm	Mcr Victoria-Yarmouth (FO), calls Sheffield (12.29).

Appendix II Summary of Freight Services 1932

To give a complete breakdown of freight services over a number of years, in a similar manner to the passenger services, would not only take up far too much space, but would probably drive the reader to despair! The author has therefore taken one of the more popular modelling periods, the early 1930s, and has set down in outline the pattern of freight trains passing through the area. The vast majority of goods trains on the line passed through Rowsley sidings, and in common with the LMS working timetable, the lists below are split at this point. As with the passenger services listed previously, the lists below include the Dore and Chinley line services to show the goods traffic passing through Chinley station. Full details of light engine movements are not given.

In the lists the following abbreviations are used:

Q	Runs when required.	W	Wednesdays excepted.
M	Mondays excepted.	F	Fridays excepted.
MO	Mondays only.	FO	Fridays only.
T	Tuesdays excepted.	S	Saturdays excepted.
TO	Tuesdays only.	SO	Saturdays only.

1. Ambergate to Rowsley

Down

5.40pm (M)	Express Freight Somers Town to Rowsley, arr. 12.50am.
9.00pm (M)	Express Freight Peterborough to Rowsley, arr. 1.40am.
1.30am (M)	Mineral Derby St Mary's to Matlock, arr. 3.25am.
12.45am (M)	Express Freight Leicester to Rowsley, arr. 2.40am.
12.40am (M)	Express Freight Water Orton to Ancoats, arr. Rowsley 2.58am, deps. 3.45am, arr. Ancoats 6.27am. Detaches at Millers Dale on Saturdays.
1.20am (M)	Mineral Toton to Rowsley, arr. 3.30am.
1.30am (M)	Mineral Kirkby to Rowsley, arr. 3.20am.
2.03am (2.10am MO)	Mineral, Beeston to Rowsley, arr. 4.52am.
2.20am (M)	Mineral Wetmore to Rowsley, arr. 5.00am.
4.00am (QS)	Empties Chaddesden to Rowsley, arr. 5.12am.
3.50am	Mineral Staveley to Rowsley, arr. 5.32am.
4.30am	Through Freight, Derby St Mary's to Rowsley, arr. 5.44am.
4.40am (M)	Mineral Chaddesden to Rowsley, arr. 6.15am.
4.02am (M)	Mineral Nottingham New Sidings to Rowsley, arr. 6.50am.
5.45am (M)	Mineral Ambergate to Rowsley, arr. 6.22am.
4.30am (QMO)	Mineral Toton to Rowsley, arr. 7.02am.
5.15am (MO)	Mineral Toton to Rowsley, arr. 7.02am.
5.15am (M)	Mineral Heanor Jnc. to Rowsley, arr. 7.05am.
5.40am (MO)	Mineral Chaddesden to Rowsley, arr. 6.55am.
11.35pm (M)	Express Freight St Pancras to Rowsley, arr. 7.45am.
7.05am	Mineral Brands Sidings to Rowsley, arr. 8.28am.
7.15am (MO)	Mineral Derby St Mary's to Rowsley, arr. 8.45am.
7.13am	Mineral Kirkby to Gowhole, arr. Rowsley 9.26am, takes water arr. Gowhole 11.58am.
6.40am	Mineral Westhouses to High Peak Junction, arr. 9.35am, detaches at Johnson's Sidings.
9.00am	Stopping Freight Derby St Mary's to Rowsley, arr. 11.06am. Shunts Whatstandwell, High Peak Junction and Matlock.
10.48am	Mineral Ambergate to Rowsley, arr. 11.30am.
8.45am	Mineral Staveley to Rowsley, arr. 12.35pm.
11.05am	Mineral Avenue Sidings to Rowsley, arr. 12.48pm.
10.50am (S)	Mineral Westhouses to Rowsley, arr. 1.00pm.
11.50am	Mineral Kirkby to Ashton Road, arr. Rowsley 2.18pm, takes water, arr. Ashton Road 6.06pm.
1.35pm	Stopping Freight Matlock to Rowsley, arr. 1.48pm.
1.52pm	Mineral Ambergate to Rowsley, arr. 2.30pm.
1.20pm	Mineral Chaddesden to Rowsley, arr. 2.44pm, detaches cattle wagons at Matlock on Tuesdays and Fridays.
1.00pm	Mineral Staveley to Rowsley, arr. 4.03pm.
2.38pm	Mineral Kirkby to Rowsley, arr. 4.30pm.
4.00pm (QS)	Empties Chaddesden to Peak Forest, arr. Rowsley 5.31pm, takes water, arr. Peak Forest 6.55pm.
5.40pm	Freight Darley Dale to Rowsley, arr. 5.48pm.
4.05pm	Mineral Westhouses to Rowsley, arr. 6.00pm.
5.05pm	Freight Matlock Bath to Matlock, arr. 5.10pm, engine departs 9.00pm for Rowsley.
6.42pm	Mineral Ambergate to Rowsley, arr. 7.20pm. (Double-headed.)
7.20pm	Mineral Matlock to Rowsley, arr. 7.34pm.
7.00pm	Mineral Derby St Mary's to Rowsley, arr. 8.25pm.
7.50pm	Empties Chaddesden to High Peak Junction, arr. 8.55pm.
8.25pm (SO)	Through Freight Nottingham to Brunswick, arr. Rowsley 10.12pm, dep. 11.10pm, pass Chinley 12.32am.
9.45pm	Mineral Ambergate to Rowsley, arr. 10.35pm.
7.48pm (SO)	Mineral Staveley to Rowsley, arr. 10.43pm.
8.40pm (S)	Mineral Kirkby to Ashton Road, arr. Rowsley 10.44pm, takes water, dep. 11.45pm, arr. Ashton Road 2.40am. (Banked to Peak Forest.)
8.30pm	Through Freight Shobnall to Huskisson, arr. Rowsley 10.58pm, dep. 11.45pm, arr. Huskisson 4.20am.
9.45pm	Through Freight Wetmore to Huskisson, arr. Rowsley 11.15pm, dep. 12.20am, pass Chinley 1.50am.
10.00pm (S)	Express Freight Nottingham to Brunswick, arr. Rowsley 11.40pm, dep. 12.55am, arr. Brunswick 5.00am.
9.20pm (S)	Through Freight Leicester to Rowsley, arr. 12.20am.
10.30pm (SO)	Mineral Kirkby to Ashton Road, arr. Rowsley 12.18am takes water, dep. 12.40am, arr. Ashton Road 5.02am.
10.55pm (SO)	Mineral Heanor Junction to Rowsley, arr. 12.30am.
8.40pm (SO)	Through Freight Humberstone Road to Rowsley, arr. 12.38am.
10.05pm (S)	Express Freight Lawley Street to Huskisson, arr. Rowsley 12.58am, dep. 2.07am, arr. Huskisson 7.15am.
11.55pm (SO)	Mineral Chaddesden to Rowsley, arr. 1.50am.
11.10pm (MO)	Through Freight Chaddesden to Huskisson, dep. Rowsley 12.55am, arr. Huskisson 6.00am

Up

12.30am (MT)	Express Freight Rowsley to Leicester, pass Ambergate 12.55am.
1.50am (M)	Express Freight Rowsley to Nottingham, pass Ambergate 2.18am.
2.00am (M)	Express Freight Rowsley to Leicester, pass Ambergate 2.24am.
2.20am	Express Freight Rowsley to St Pancras, pass Ambergate 2.45am.
3.14am (M)	Through Freight Rowsley to Derby St Mary's, pass Ambergate 3.46am.
3.45am (M)	Mineral Rowsley to Ambergate, arr. 4.45am.
4.05am	Express Freight Rowsley to Birmingham, pass Ambergate 4.32am.
4.20am (M)	Through Freight Rowsley to Leicester, pass Ambergate 4.50am.
4.30am (M)	Through Freight Rowsley to Mansfield, pass Ambergate 5.00am.
4.49am (MO)	Through Freight Rowsley to Chaddesden, pass Ambergate 5.20am.
6.30am (M)	Through Freight Rowsley to Branston, pass Ambergate 7.16am.
6.55am	Stopping Freight Rowsley to Matlock Bath, shunts Darley Dale 7.04am-7.15am, Matlock 7.22am-10.30am, arr. Matlock Bath 10.35am.
7.40am (QMO)	Mineral Rowsley to Staveley, pass Ambergate 8.36am.
8.50am	Mineral Rowsley to Chaddesden, pass Ambergate 9.30am.
9.29am (MO)	Empties Rowsley to Toton, pass Ambergate 10.00am. (Runs as mineral train on Tuesdays.)
9.44am	Empties Rowsley to Ambergate, arr. 10.17am.
10.38am	Empties High Peak Junction to Westhouses, pass Ambergate 11.47am.
11.45am	Empties Rowsley to Toton, pass Ambergate 12.23pm.
11.55am	Empties Rowsley to Kirkby, pass Ambergate 12.32pm.
12.20pm	Stopping Freight Rowsley to Chaddesden, shunts High Peak Junction and Whatstandwell.
12.42pm	Empties Rowsley to Ambergate, arr. 1.18pm.
1.40pm	Empties Rowsley to Staveley, pass Ambergate 2.22pm.
2.17pm	Mineral Rowsley to Avenue, pass Ambergate 3.13pm. Picks up High Peak Junction.
3.04pm (S)	Empties Rowsley to Blackwell, pass Ambergate 3.36pm.
3.10pm	Empties Rowsley to Ambergate, arr. 3.48pm. On Saturdays runs engine and brake to Johnsons Sidings and picks up.
3.22pm (S)	Mineral Rowsley to Matlock Bath, arr. 3.55pm, sets down Matlock.
3.35pm	Stopping Freight Rowsley to Darley Dale, arr. 3.41pm.
3.40pm	Mineral Rowsley to Chaddesden, pass Ambergate 4.26pm.
4.40pm (S)	Stopping Freight Johnsons Sidings to Ambergate, arr. 4.46pm.
6.15pm	Empties Rowsley to Kirkby, pass Ambergate 6.55pm.
6.30pm	Mineral Rowsley to Staveley, pass Ambergate 7.30pm.
7.35pm	Empties Rowsley to Blackwell, pass Ambergate 8.23pm.
8.00pm	Empties Rowsley to Ambergate, arr. 8.37pm.
8.15pm	Mineral Rowsley to Chaddesden, pass Ambergate 8.50pm.
8.25pm	Empties Rowsley to Toton, pass Ambergate 9.16pm.
9.30pm	Empties Rowsley to Beeston Sidings, pass Ambergate 10.11pm.
10.00pm	Express Freight Rowsley to Derby, pass Ambergate 10.24pm.
10.15pm	Express Freight Rowsley to London, pass Ambergate 10.42pm.
10.35pm (S)	Mineral Matlock to Chaddesden, pass Ambergate 11.00pm.
10.40pm	Mineral Rowsley to Chaddesden, pass Ambergate 11.30pm.
8.10pm (SO)	Empties Ancoats to Kirkby, dep. Rowsley 11.35pm, pass Ambergate 12.10am.
11.48pm	Mineral Rowsley to Staveley, pass Ambergate 12.48am.

2. Rowsley to Manchester, Liverpool and Branches

Down

12.05am (M)	Mineral Rowsley to Ancoats, arr. 2.50am.
8.30pm (M)	Through Freight Staveley to Heaton Mersey, pass Chinley 1.49am.
6.30pm (QM)	Fitted Freight Somers Town to Ancoats, pass Chinley 1.40am.
12.25am (QM)	Mineral Rowsley to Buxton, Western Division, arr. 1.28am.
1.08am (M)	Express Freight Rowsley to Ancoats, arr. 3.18am.
9.00pm (MO)	Through Freight Duddeston Sidings to Ancoats, dep. Rowsley 1.15 am, arr. Ancoats 3.25am.
11.15pm (M)	Mineral Grimesthorpe to Longsight, arr. Buxton, WD 2.20am. (Western Division engine and men.)
11.40pm (M)	Mineral Staveley to Heaton Mersey, pass Chinley 2.44am.
1.55am (M)	Express Freight Rowsley to Ancoats, arr. 3.50am.
12.05am (QM)	Mineral Storrs Mill or 11.25pm Snydale to Liverpool, pass Chinley 3.17am.
12.15am (M)	Express Freight Stourton to Gowhole, pass Chinley 3.32am.
2.20am (MO)	Through Freight Rowsley to Cheadle Sidings, arr. 4.30am.
2.35am (M)	Express Freight Rowsley to Brewery Sidings, arr. 4.47am. (Double-headed to Belle Vue, worked by Central Division engine and men.)
10.00pm (M)	Fitted Freight Somers Town to Ancoats, pass Chinley 3.50am.
3.00am (M)	Mineral Rowsley to Heaton Mersey, arr. 6.05am. (Banked to Peak Forest.)
8.30pm (M)	King's Cross to Deansgate, pass Chinley 4.19am. (Fitted goods to Gowhole, thence LNER class 'A' Freight.)
2.40am (M)	Mineral Wincobank to Gowhole, pass Chinley 4.48am.
3.45am (M)	Mineral Buxton to Wincobank, pass Chinley South Junction 4.39am.
10.45pm (QFSO)	Express Freight (Cattle) Peterborough to Bolton, pass Chinley 4.57am.
3.25am	Mineral Rowsley to Buxton, WD, arr. 4.30am.
2.26am (M)	Mineral Staveley to Gowhole, pass Chinley 5.18am.
5.05am (M)	Mineral Peak Forest to Gowhole, arr. 5.38am.
4.35am (M)	Through Freight Rowsley to Huskisson, arr. 9.37am.
4.36am (MO)	Through Freight Rowsley to Brewery Sidings, arr. 7.20am.
5.30am (M)	Light engine Buxton to Peak Forest, arr. 5.54am.
3.15am (M)	Mineral Carlton to Cheadle Sidings, pass Chinley 6.57am. (Double-headed to Gowhole.)
5.07am (QMO)	Mineral Rowsley to Gowhole, arr. 7.18am. (Banked to Peak Forest, sets down Chapel.)
7.22am (M)	Mineral Peak Forest South to Hartford.
6.00am (MO)	Mineral Buxton to Wincobank.
3.35am	Mineral Morton to Heaton Mersey, pass Chinley 6.54am.
6.15am	Mineral Rowsley to Buxton, WD, arr. 7.28am. (Banked).
4.50am (M)	Mineral Westhouses to Heaton Mersey, pass Chinley 7.57am.
4.35am (QM)	Mineral Houghton to Glazebrook, pass Chinley 8.19am.
6.28am	Mineral Rowsley to Cheadle Heath, arr. 9.25am.
6.27am	Mineral Staveley to Gowhole, pass Chinley 8.42am.
4.55am	Express Freight Stockport Edgeley to Sheffield, pass Buxton 6.51am, Chinley South Junction 7.13am. (Western Division engine and men.)
8.30am (MO)	Engine and brake Chapel to Gowhole, arr. 9.00am.
7.05am	Mineral Grimesthorpe to Gowhole, pass Chinley 9.30am.
7.30am	Mineral Rowsley to Buxton, Midland Division, arr. 8.55am.
7.50am	Mineral Rowsley to Gowhole, arr. 10.15am.

8.52am	Mineral Rowsley to Buxton, WD, arr. 10.10am. (Sets down Ashwood Dale. Banked)
8.20am	Mineral Westhouses to Gowhole, pass Chinley 11.35am.
9.12am (M)	Through Freight Rowsley to Walton, arr. 2.43pm.
10.35am	Mineral Great Rocks Junction to Hartford (S) or Northwich (SO). (Limited to 40 wagons when worked by Class 4 engine.)
10.30am	Mineral Ashwood Dale to Buxton, arr. 10.55am. Picks up empties at Gas Works Sidings.
9.52am	Through Freight Rowsley to Ancoats, arr. 12.32pm.
11.15am	Mineral Peak Forest Junction to Peak Forest, arr. 11.32am.
10.30am	Mineral Rowsley to Buxton, WD, arr. 11.50am. (Banked)
10.40am	Mineral Rowsley to Heaton Mersey, arr. 2.35pm. (Banked to Peak Forest.)
9.55am (MO)	Mineral Westhouses to Heaton Mersey, pass Chinley 2.06pm.
10.52am	Stopping Freight Rowsley to Hassop, arr. 12.30pm. Shunts Bakewell.
12.00pm (M)	Mineral Rowsley to Huskisson, arr. 7.00pm.
2.15pm	Mineral Peak Forest South to Hartford, arr. 5.27pm. (Limited load with Class 4 engine.)
12.10pm (S)	Mineral Staveley to Gowhole, pass Chinley 2.52pm.
1.55pm	Mineral Ashwood Dale to Cheadle Sidings, arr. 4.38pm.
12.20pm	Stopping Freight Rowsley to Peak Forest South, arr. 3.10pm, shunts Monsal Dale, Millers Dale and Peak Forest Junction.
12.50pm	Mineral Rowsley to Buxton, WD, arr. 2.02pm. (Banked)
1.45pm (QS)	Mineral Rowsley to Gowhole, arr. 4.15pm.
1.15pm (S)	Mineral Avenue to Gowhole, pass Chinley 3.58pm.
2.10pm	Mineral Buxton to Wincobank, pass Chinley South Junction 3.36pm.
10.15am	Mineral Hasland to Gowhole, pass Chinley 4.44pm.
4.00pm	Mineral Great Rocks Junction to Cheadle Sidings, arr. 5.35pm.
2.10pm (M)	Mineral Grimesthorpe to Liverpool, pass Chinley 4.18pm. (Double-headed when required to Gowhole.)
2.45pm	Mineral Rowsley to Cheadle Heath, arr. 5.45pm. (Banked to Peak Forest.)
3.15pm (SO)	Mineral Buxton to Peak Forest, sets down Ashwood Dale.
3.30pm (QMS)	Through Freight Rowsley to Huskisson, arr. 9.22pm.
1.40pm	Mineral Westhouses to Gowhole, pass Chinley 5.10pm.
3.38pm (TO)	Mineral Grimesthorpe to Gowhole, pass Chinley 5.48pm.
4.00pm (M)	Mineral Rowsley to Trafford Park Sidings, arr. 9.44pm. (Banked to Peak Forest.)
4.15pm.	Mineral Rowsley to Buxton, WD, arr. 5.21pm. (Banked)
5.45pm	Mineral Ashwood Dale to Peak Forest South, arr. 6.15pm.
6.18pm	Mineral Millers Dale to Buxton, arr. 7.48pm shunts Ashwood Dale.
7.10pm	Mineral Peak Forest South to Rotherham Masborough, pass Chinley South Junction 7.36pm.
4.15pm	Mineral Staveley to Heaton Mersey, pass Chinley 7.53pm.
8.20pm	Mineral Peak Forest South to Hartford, arr. 11.13pm.
7.42pm	Mineral Rowsley to Heaton Mersey, arr. 10.33pm. (Double-headed and Banked)
8.20pm	Mineral Rowsley to Hyde, arr. 1.15am. (Double-headed)
8.50pm (QS)	Mineral Grimesthorpe to Brunswick, pass Chinley 10.46pm.
8.35pm (S)	Mineral Rowsley to Ashton Road, arr. 11.17pm.
8.35pm (SO)	Mineral Rowsley to Buxton, WD, arr. 9.50pm.
9.35pm (SO)	Mineral Buxton to Gowhole, arr. 12.00am.
10.32pm (S)	Mineral Peak Forest South to Hartford, arr. 2.00am.
10.25pm	Express Freight Grimesthorpe to Edge Hill, pass Chinley 12.03am. (Worked alternatively by Western Division and Midland Division engines and men.)
9.00pm	Mineral Rowsley to Brindle Heath.
9.25pm	Mineral Rowsley to Buxton, WD, arr. 10.52pm. (Banked)
9.40pm (SO)	Mineral Staveley to Heaton Mersey, pass Chinley 12.05am.
10.30pm	Mineral Avenue to Gowhole, pass Chinley 12.50am.
10.00pm	Mineral Rowsley to Buxton, WD, arr. 11.12pm. (Banked)
10.25pm (SO)	Mineral Rowsley to Cheadle Sidings, arr. 1.07am.
10.40pm	Mineral Rowsley to Buxton, WD, arr. 11.44pm. (Banked)
11.00pm (M)	Mineral Buxton to Gowhole, arr. 2.38am. Picks up Peak Forest South.
11.28pm	Express Freight Grimesthorpe to Huskisson, pass Chinley 12.53am.
11.25pm (S)	Mineral Rowsley to Buxton, WD, arr. 12.30am.

Up

8.55pm (M)	Through Freight Huskisson to Buxton, arr. Rowsley 1.58am, dep. Rowsley 2.55am.
12.52am (SO)	Express Freight Heaton Mersey to Hunslet, pass Chinley 2.22am.
9.45pm (M)	Express Freight Edge Hill to Sheffield City, pass Chinley 1.18am.
9.45pm (M)	Through Freight Huskisson to Sheffield, pass Chinley 3.20am.
9.35pm (M)	Through Freight Brunswick to Nottingham, arr. Rowsley 2.46am, dep. 3.38am.
12.02am (MS)	Express Freight Heaton Mersey to Carlton Sidings, pass Chinley 2.12am.
2.40am (M)	Empties Gowhole to Rowsley, arr. 4.52am.
12.15am (QWO)	Express Freight Ship Canal Sidings to Sheffield Queens Road, pass Chinley 2.20am.
12.55am (M)	Through Freight Trafford Park to Rowsley, arr. 3.02am.
1.20am (M)	Through Freight Heaton Mersey to Rowsley, arr. 3.32am.
11.25pm (QMT)	Empties Brunswick to Storrs Mill, pass Chinley 2.38am.
2.55am (M)	Empties Gowhole to Peak Forest, arr. 3.42am. (Engine turns at Blackwell Mill, arr. Peak Forest 4.30am. to work 5.05am. mineral to Gowhole.)
3.25am (M)	Through Freight Gowhole to Hasland, pass Chinley 3.40am.
1.40am (M)	Through Freight Heaton Mersey to Avenue, pass Chinley 3.50am.
3.10am (M)	Empties Heaton Mersey to Staveley, pass Chinley 4.02am.
4.25am	Empties Buxton MD to Rowsley, arr. 5.16am. (Double-headed)
3.45am (M)	Empties Cheadle Sidings to Peak Forest North, arr. 5.10am. (Engine turns at Blackwell Mill, arr. Peak Forest South 6.33am. to work 7.22am Mineral to Hartford.)
5.35am	Empties Buxton, WD, to Rowsley, arr. 6.30am.
2.32am (M)	Empties Ashton Road to Bamford, pass Chinley 5.10am.
2.42am (M)	Empties Hartford to Peak Forest South, arr. 5.32am.
5.10am (M)	Stopping Freight Gowhole to Buxton, arr. 6.25am.
4.35am (M)	Freight Gowhole to Peak Forest North, arr. 6.03am. Shunts Chapel.
4.55am (MO)	Empties Cheadle Sidings to Peak Forest, arr. 6.25am.
1.55am (QM)	Empties Brunswick to Storrs Mill or Snydale, pass Chinley 5.25am.
5.07am (M)	Empties Cheadle Sidings to Peak Forest South, arr. 6.30am. (When required runs to Ashwood Dale, arr. 8.10am.)

4.00am (M)	Mineral Grimesthorpe to Buxton, arr. 7.53am.
5.35am	Through Freight Ashton Road to Rowsley, arr. 7.54am.
6.48am	Mineral Buxton, MD to Millers Dale, arr. 7.05am, thence engine and brake to Rowsley, arr. 8.03am. Conveys mail bag to Millers Dale (mail for Tideswell).
6.10am (MO)	Empties Cheadle Sidings to Rowsley, arr. 9.00am.
6.20am (M)	Ballast train, Belle Vue to Peak Forest Junction.
6.50am (M)	Empties Gowhole to Staveley, pass Chinley 7.12am.
7.10am (MO)	Mineral Gowhole to Chapel, arr. 8.00am.
8.30am	Empties Buxton to Rowsley, arr. 9.32am. (Double-headed)
6.40am	Empties Heaton Mersey to Rowsley, arr. 9.42am.
6.40am (M)	Empties Cheadle Sidings to Blackwell Sidings, arr. Rowsley 9.57am, dep. 11.30am.
6.55am (MO)	Ballast train Belle Vue to Peak Forest Junction.
8.30am (QMO)	Empties Gowhole to Rowsley, arr. 9.57am.
6.35am	Empties Northwich to Great Rocks Junction, arr. 9.03am. (Engine turns at Blackwell Mill, arr. Great Rocks Jnc. 10.00am to work 10.35am mineral to Hartford or Northwich).
10.00am	Mineral Buxton, MD to Ashwood Dale, arr. 10.07am.
10.25am	Empties Buxton, MD to Rowsley, arr. 11.20am.
6.15am (MO)	Mineral Grimesthorpe to Buxton, arr. 11.22am.
7.55am (QS)	Mineral Grimesthorpe to Buxton, arr. 12.17pm.
11.05am	Empties Buxton, WD to Rowsley, arr. 11.58am.
9.55am	Empties Gowhole to Staveley, pass Chinley 10.05am.
6.20am	Empties Walton to Rowsley, arr. 1.05pm.
10.45am	Empties Gowhole to Wincobank, pass Chinley 11.00am.
11.20am	Empties Gowhole to Rowsley, arr. 12.44. (When required detaches at Bakewell.)
9.40am	Empties Northwich to Peak Forest South, arr. 12.18pm. (Engine turns at Blackwell Mill, arr. Peak Forest South 1.20pm to work 2.15pm mineral to Northwich.)
11.05am	Empties Cheadle sidings to Rowsley, arr. 2.00pm.
2.00pm	Stopping Freight Hassop to Rowsley, arr. 2.26pm. Picks up Bakewell.
12.40pm	Empties Gowhole to Blackwell Sidings, pass Chinley 12.54pm.
1.30pm (Q)	Empties Gowhole to Frickley Colliery Sidings, pass Chinley 1.44pm.
1.36pm	Mineral Buxton, WD to Millers Dale, arr. 2.03pm. sets down Topley Pike.
2.40pm	Empties Buxton, WD to Rowsley, arr. 3.30pm. (Double-headed)
2.50pm	Empties Gowhole to Kirby, pass Rowsley South Junction 4.22pm.
1.00pm (M)	Empties Cheadle Sidings to Staveley, arr. Rowsley 3.58pm. dep. 5.00pm Picks up Whatstandwell.
3.10pm (M)	Empties Gowhole to Rowsley, arr. 4.35pm.
4.42pm	Mineral Peak Forest South to Rowsley, arr. 6.47pm.
3.00pm	Mineral Grimesthorpe to Peak Forest South, arr. 5.48pm.
4.20pm	Empties Gowhole to Staveley, pass Chinley 4.34pm.
3.55pm	Empties Cheadle Sidings to Bamford, pass Chinley 4.50pm.
3.32pm (S)	Through Freight Moston Sidings to Rowsley, arr. 7.34pm.
5.35pm (S)	Empties Gowhole to Avenue, pass Chinley 5.50pm.
6.10pm	Empties Gowhole to Avenue, pass Chinley 6.24pm
4.50pm (M)	Empties Cheadle Sidings to Staveley, pass Chinley 6.35pm.
6.50pm	Empties Buxton, WD to Rowsley arr. 8.20pm. (Double-headed, picks up Ashwood Dale and Bakewell.)
2.45pm	Through freight Huskisson to Rowsley, arr. 8.28pm. (Double-headed to Millers Dale Junction, pilot turns and arrives Peak Forest 7.54pm to work 8.20pm mineral to Hartford.)
4.45pm	Mineral Grimesthorpe to Buxton, arr. 8.22pm. (Double-headed when required.)
7.00pm	Empties Gowhole to Blackwell Sidings, pass Chinley 7.13pm.
6.30pm	Empties Cheadle Sidings to Ashwood Dale, arr. 9.10pm.
6.55pm (SO)	Fitted Freight No.1, Ancoats to St Pancras, pass Chinley 8.12pm.
7.35pm	Express Freight Ancoats to Rowsley, arr. 9.26pm. (Double-headed when required.)
8.55pm (S)	Empties Buxton, WD to Rowsley, arr. 9.51pm.
7.30pm	Through Freight Trafford Park to Rowsley, arr. 10.02pm. (Sets down London fitted traffic at Gowhole.)
9.50pm (S)	Empties Gowhole to Wincobank, pass Chinley 10.05pm.
8.10pm	Through Freight Ancoats to Rowsley, arr. 10.35pm. (Runs to Kirkby Sidings on Saturdays.)
8.22pm (S)	LNER class 'A' Goods Deansgate to Colwick, pass Chinley 9.30pm. (Limited to 33 wagons.)
7.00pm (QFS)	Fitted Freight No.2 Garston Docks to Carlton Sidings, pass Chinley 9.36pm.
6.25pm	Through Freight Langton Dock to Birmingham, arr. Rowsley 11.00pm, dep. 12.20am. (On Mondays shunts Millers Dale when required.)
6.55pm (S)	Through Freight Huskisson to Rowsley, arr. 11.18pm. (Double-headed to Millers Dale Junction, pilot turns and runs light engine to Cheadle Sidings.)
9.20pm (S)	Through Freight Ancoats to Rowsley, arr. 11.45pm.
10.55pm	Empties Peak Forest South to Buxton, MD, arr. 11.32pm.
10.10pm (SO)	Empties Gowhole to Staveley, pass Chinley 10.23pm.
10.30pm (T)	Empties Gowhole to Sheffield Engine Shed Sidings, pass Chinley 10.44pm.
9.30pm (SO)	Empties Cheadle Sidings to Staveley, pass Chinley 11.30pm.
9.20pm	Through Freight Ancoats to Birmingham, arr. Rowsley 11.45pm dep. 1.39am. (Runs as Express Freight from Rowsley.)
9.25pm	Through Freight Moston Sidings to Rowsley, arr. 12.10am. (Central Division engine and men.)
9.50pm (S)	Express Freight Ancoats to Rotherham Masborough, pass Chinley 11.15pm.
9.35pm	Through Freight Trafford park to Rowsley, arr. 12.17am.
10.18pm (S)	Through Freight Cheadle Sidings to Rowsley, arr. 12.34am.
10.15pm (S)	Through Freight Heaton Mersey to Rowsley, arr. 12.56am.
8.00pm (S)	Express Freight Huskisson to Hunslet, pass Chinley 11.28pm.
10.45pm (S)	Fitted Freight No.1 Ancoats to St Pancras, pass Chinley 12.03am.
10.15pm (SO)	Through Freight Heaton Mersey to Blackwell Sidings, arr. Rowsley 1.05am.
10.50pm (QTO)	Express Freight Trafford Park to Rowsley, arr. 1.04am.
11.00pm (S)	Through Freight Cheadle Sidings to Sheffield Queens Road, pass Chinley 12.59am.
11.25pm (S)	Through Freight Ancoats to Rowsley, arr 2.10am.
9.15pm (SO)	Express Freight Edge Hill to Sheffield Engine Shed Sidings pass Chinley 1.28am.
2.25am (S)	Empties Gowhole to Kirkby, arr. Rowsley 4.15am, dep. 4.40am.

Appendix III   Sample Traffic Statistics

Date: 1872

	Season Ticket Holders	Number of Passengers Booked	Receipts £ Passengers	Parcels Horses Carriages dogs	Livestock No. of trucks in and out	Coal coke, lime & limestone in and out	Carted in and out	Not carted in and out	Mineral class in and out	Tranships	Expenses at £ station
Ambergate	not in use at this date	28297	1934	161	122	77282	457	5398	6665	-	1298
Whatstandwell	-	9793	450	47	1	114	163	871	8313	-	315
Cromford	-	24141	1538	226	-	-	-	\ -	-	-	100
Cromford Wharf	-	-	-	-	-	11320	306	-	-	-	80
Matlock Bath	-	44078	4451	370	-	5668	106	5658	1894	-	359
Matlock Bridge	-	47245	3743	842	190	22548	4270	7521	8815	81	732
Darley Dale	-	12888	624	205	-	5243	575	3154	4887	-	259
Rowsley	-	23236	2328	31	-	17568	137	683	44381	-	248
Bakewell	-	34395	3027	516	226	6830	2178	5872	1546	-	362
Hassop	-	8913	875	107	91	4411	2220	5493	2898	-	490
Great Longstone	-	6276	384	60	-	-	-	-	-	-	83
Monsall Dale	-	4342	250	28	-	414	-	-	-	-	103
Millers Dale	-	16451	1211	262	111	16609	1657	2774	1321	304	654
Buxton	-	51651	8915	1069	122	9164	2314	2795	1750	273	1162
Peak Forest	-	4874	152	31	-	17568	137	683	44381	-	248
Chapel-en-le-Frith	-	24844	1449	312	151	3309	1070	959	794	-	343
Chinley	-	5750	194	100		1404	1286	1207	175	-	299

Notes. Reference Rail 491/672

Date: 1902

	Season Ticket Holders	Number of Passengers Booked	Receipts £ Passengers	Parcels Horses Carriages dogs	Livestock No. of trucks in and out	Coal coke, lime & limestone in and out	Carted in and out	Not carted in and out	Mineral class in and out	Tranships	Expenses at £ station
Ambergate	20	77297	3840	386	91	91,548	1756	16424	10676	-	2396
Whatstandwell	25	27094	1158	435	56	8994	1176	6659	16816	-	731
Cromford	6	32747	1734	-	-	-	-	-	-	-	340
Cromford Wharf	-	-	-	-	-	13,656	84	-	-	-	67
Matlock Bath	19	55302	4306	538	-	5320	628	7494	4228	-	1082
Matlock Bridge	18	107633	8296	1736	206	77642	10967	18169	39547	50	2141
Darley Dale	21	43320	1662	713	43	16087	1975	4664	23012	-	813
Rowsley	10	42204	2599	1604	118	9007	1470	15487	25978	-	2534
Bakewell	87	54952	5103	1156	733	9808	4171	9559	2045	-	1088
Hassop	2	4346	199	250	84	5864	707	5287	11141	-	454
Great Longstone	7	13,564	835	311	-	-	-	-	-	-	339
Monsall Dale	-	6754	351	30	-	1337	-	-	-	-	214
Millers Dale	11	40642	2632	1013	209	119228	1414	4676	13234	78	2647
Buxton	35	98479	16425	2223	323	74921	5478	8202	14945	822	4608
Peak Forest	4	23635	541	363	-	456901	482	2531	82002	-	1517
Chapel-en-le-Frith	15	46209	1908	745	201	8388	1315	4209	4234	387	2034
Chinley	11	29143	1462	341	-	8001	1181	11011	11386	-	1209

Notes. Reference Rail 491/675

Date: 1922

	Season Ticket Holders	Number of Passengers Booked	Receipts £ Passengers	Parcels Horses Carriages dogs	Livestock No. of trucks in and out	Coal coke, lime & limestone in and out	Carted in and out	Not carted in and out	Mineral class in and out	Tranships	Expenses at £ station
Ambergate	371	90517	8297	1400	152	229231	1090	16771	33251	-	9635
Whatstandwell	108	25517	2252	570	1	10857	674	2046	4832	-	1922
Cromford	67	20884	2390	1662	-	-	-	-	-	-	1211
Cromford Wharf	-	-	-	-	-	-	-	-	-	-	-
Matlock Bath	96	46336	7542	194	-	11686	936	7454	9637	-	2779
Matlock bridge	204	134825	23823	2851	64	71001	9861	15255	100576	-	6388
Darley Dale	96	64835	4210	1397	42	19142	1044	3759	22154	-	2496
Rowsley	105	42770	4563	4049	85	6920	892	12923	8592	-	4277 + line staff 15518
Bakewell	47	47414	8280	2664	475	11858	6013	5596	3359	-	3509
Hassop	1	1760	347	523	147	6544	251	3171	5272	-	1294
Great Longstone	89	14284	1714	1109	-	-	-	-	-	-	1018
Monsall Dale	6	4223	434	193	-	9284	21	21	185	-	827
Millers Dale	40	38659	4954	2146	171	233136	1190	4112	19700	-	7159
Buxton MR	368	95714	35181	2090	50	188822	3966	4836	11533	1113	14824 &
Buxton LNWR		117656	24512	1251	144	14246	2929	5132	3502	-	5031 Goods
Peak Forest	26	29497	1716	905	-	505764	478	3082	29557	-	5360
Chapel-en-le-Frith	197	54731	7237	3698	100	12170	2201	2482	3318	66	4904
Chinley	192	66854	10529	743	17	9665	1670	4553	3464	-	6215

Cromford Wharf closed Sept. 30 1921

Notes. Reference Rail 491/677.

APPENDIX IV Ambergate to Chinley and Buxton Branch

List of Bridges and Tunnels

No.	Type	Name or location	Built or altered	Distance from St Pancras
1	Underbridge	Heage Road	1863 rebuilt 1891	138m 6c
1A	Footbridge	Ambergate Station	1885	138m 10c
2	Underbridge	Chesterfield Road	1863	138m 17c
3	Underbridge	Goods Yard Bridge	1875	138m 17c
4	Underbridge	Chesterfield Road	1847 widened 1876	138m 23c
5	Viaduct	River Amber	1847 widened 1863	138m 26c
6	Occupation bridge	Poyser's Bridge	1847	138m 31c
7	Overbridge	Hay's Wharf	1847	138m 43c
8	Overbridge	Mold's Wharf	1847	138m 61c
8A	Overbridge	Chase Bridge	1883 raised 1912	139m 30c
8B	Footbridge	Whatstandwell Station	1894	140m 14c
9	Tunnel	Whatstandwell	1847	140m 19c/26c
9A	Culvert	—	1847	140m 46c
10	Viaduct	River Derwent Bridge	1847 rebuilt 1892	140m 51c
11	Occupation bridge	Meerbrook Cattle Creep	1847	140m 57c
12	Culvert	Meerbrook Sough	1847	140m 74c
13	Occupation bridge	Homesford Cattle Creep	1847	141m 7c
14	Overbridge	Homesford Bridge	1847	141m 15c
15	Viaduct	High Peak Bridge	1847 rebuilt 1887	141m 33c
15A	Underbridge	High Peak Bridge	1915	141m 33c
16	Aqueduct	High Peak	1847	141m 40c
17	Tunnel	Leawood	1847	141m 42c/56c
18	Aqueduct	Leawood	1847	141m 57c
19	Viaduct	Leawood Bridge	1847 rebuilt 1888, 1911	141m 58c
20	Occupation bridge	Leawood Cattle Creep	1847 Filled in 1931	141m 66c
20A	Footbridge	Brown's Bridge	1883	141m 78c
21	Culvert	—	1847 lengthened 1883	142m 46c
22	Occupation bridge	Arkwright's Bridge	1847	142m 60c
23	Viaduct	Cromford Viaduct	1847	143m 3c/6c
23A	Footbridge	Cromford Station	1885	143m 9c
24	Tunnel	Willersley	1847	143m 13c/48c
24A	Footbridge	Matlock Bath Station	1887	143m
24B	Station Approach Bridge	over River Derwent	1847	143m 67c
25	Occupation bridge	Gas House Bridge	1847	143m 78c
26	Tunnel	High Tor No. 1	1847 extended 30ft 1894	144m 6c/20c
26A	Covered Way	High Tor No. 1A	1894	144m 21c/24c
27	Tunnel	High Tor No. 2	1847	144m 24c/41c
28	Occupation bridge	Lime Tree Bridge	1847	144m 52c
29	Viaduct	Boathouse Bridge	1847	144m 9c/62c
29A	Underbridge	Boathouse Bridge	1847 rebuilt 1891	144m 62c
30	Overbridge	Green Lane	1847 demolished c1960	144m 64c
31	Tunnel	Holt Lane	1847	144m 65c/71c
32	Overbridge	Holt Lane	1847	144m 76c
33	Footbridge	Matlock Station	1875 Covered 1889	145m 0c
33A	Occupation heading	—	Not known	145m 13c
34	Occupation bridge	Cawdor Cattle Creep	1847 Filled in 1929	145m 19c
35	Viaduct	Cawdor Bridge	1847 rebuilt 1908	145m 39c/43c
36	Occupation bridge	Carnell's Bridge	1847 rebuilt 1891	145m 59c
37	Occupation bridge	Gregory's Cattle Creep	1847 rebuilt 1891	145m 62c
38	Occupation bridge	Broomhead's Cattle Creep	1847 rebuilt 1891	146m 21c
39	Overbridge	Warney Lane	1847 steps added 1911	146m 74c
40	Culvert	Warney Brook	1847 rebuilt 1891	146m 76c
40A	Footbridge	Darley Dale Station	1911	147m 11c
40B	Footbridge	Church Lane Crossing	1911	147m 47c
41	Culvert	Hoe Brook	1847 rebuilt 1891	148m 50c
41A	Culvert	Hoe Brook	1847	148m 50c
42	Overbridge	Bakewell Road	1847	149m 34c
42A	Subway	Rowsley Station	1891	149m 36c
43	Underbridge	Rowsley Road	1862	149m 41c
44	Viaduct	Rowsley	1862	149m 47c
45	Occupation bridge	Duke's Private Road	1862	149m 50c
46	Underbridge	Church Bridge	1862	149m 54c
47	Occupation bridge	Park Lane	1862	150m 4c
48	Tunnel	Haddon	1862	150m 49c/151m 17c
49	Overbridge	Greave's Bridge	1862	151m 38c
50	Viaduct	Combs Lane	1862	151m 76c
51	Occupation bridge over	Outrake Bridge	1861	152m 45c
52	Overbridge	Station Road	1861	152m 63c
52A	Footbridge	Bakewell Station		152m 64c
53	Cattle Creep	Higginbotham's Bridge	1861	153m 7c
53A	Cattle Creep	Pauper's Bridge	1861	153m 9c
54	Overbridge	Pineapple Bridge	1861	153m 31c
55	Overbridge	Hassop Station Bridge	1861	153m 69c
56	Underbridge	Buxton Road	1861	154m 23c
56A	Cattle Creep	Printing Cattle Creep	1861	154m
57	Overbridge	Lowdale Bridge	1861	154m 37c
58	Underbridge	Longstone Road	1861	154m 50c
59	Cattle Creep	Hawley's Bridge	Filled	154m 56c
60	Occupation bridge over	Wager's Bridge	1861	155m 3c
61	Overbridge	Longstone Lane	1861	155m 11c
62	Occupation bridge over	White's Bridge	1861	155m 25c
63	Occupation bridge over	Orr's Bridge	1861	155m 51c
64	Tunnel	Headstone	1861	155m 62c/156m 6c
65	Viaduct	Monsal Dale	1862 rebuilt 1907/8	156m 11c/15c
66	Occupation bridge over	Buckley's Bridge	1862	156m 32c
67	Underbridge	Station Bridge	1861	156m 42c
68	Tunnel	Cressbrook	1861/62	157m 1c/22c
69	Tunnel	Litton	1861/62	157m 33c/56c
70	Occupation bridge over	Litton Mill Bridge	1861	157m 76c
71	Occupation bridge over	Morley's Bridge	Pulled down 1909	158m 24c
72	Viaduct	Millers Dale old	Strengthened 1906	159m 8c/14c
72A	Viaduct	Millers Dale new	1905	159m 7c/14c
73	Underbridge	Buxton Road old		159m 16c
73A	Subway	Millers Dale Station	1884 lengthened 1905	159m 20c
73B	Underbridge	Buxton Road new	1905	159m 16c
74	Occupation bridge	East Buxton Lime Co. tip bridge	1876	159m 47c
75	Viaduct	East Buxton Bridge	1861	159m 56c
76	Tunnel	Chee Tor No. 1	1860–62	159m 64c/160m 2c
76A	Over river	Chee Tor Bridge	1862	160m 3c
77	Tunnel	Chee Tor No. 2	1861–62	160m 5c/9c
77A	Footbridge	Over River Wye	1862	160m 3c
77B	Footbridge	Over River Wye	1862	160m 6c
78	Tunnel	Rusher Cutting	1862 lengthened 1897	160m 28c/33c
79	Viaduct	Millers Dale Junction Bridge	1862	160m 39c
80	Viaduct	River Wye	1865	160m 56c
80A	Footbridge	Over River Wye	1865	160m 56c
81	Occupation bridge	Meadow Bridge	1865	160m 61c
82	Tunnel	Peak Forest Junction	1865	161m 8c/9c
83	Occupation bridge	Great Rocks Cattle Creep	1865 Filled 1930	161m 49c
84	Occupation bridge	Back Pasture Bridge	1865 Filled 1930	161m 77c
84A	Occupation bridge	Lower Great Rocks Bridge	1865 Filled 1930	162m 12c
85	Occupation bridge	Lower Great Rocks Bridge	1865 Pulled down	162m 20c
86	Tunnel	Great Rocks	1865	162m 25c/32c
87	Occupation bridge over	Great Rocks Bridge	1865 Pulled down 1936	162m 46c
88	Occupation bridge over	Great Rocks Bridge	1865 Pulled down c1950	162m 64c
89	Overbridge	Buxton Road	1865	163m 6c
90	Occupation bridge over	Upper End Bridge	1865	163m 27c
91	Overbridge	Peak Forest Road	1865	163m 69c
92	Tunnel	Dove Holes	1863–1865	164m 43c/166m 19c
93	Culvert	within tunnel	1863	164m 55c
93A	Culvert	down side	1872	166m 11c
94	Culvert	double culvert	1865	166m 32c
95	Occupation bridge over	Lowe's Bridge	1865	166m 33c
96	Tunnel	LNWR Railway Tunnel	1865	166m 44c/49c
97	Underbridge	Calderbank Bridge	1865	166m 67c
98	Occupation bridge	Bench Hall Carriage Drive	1865	166m 78c
99	Underbridge	Long Lane	1865	167m 13c
100	Underbridge	Manchester Road	1865 rebuilt 1937	167m 27c
101	Underbridge	Eccles Road	1865	167m 33c
101A	Footbridge	Chapel-en-le Frith station	1913	167m 43c
102	Occupation bridge	Carrington's Bridge	1865 widened 1893	167m 57c
103	Occupation bridge over	Stoddart's Bridge	1865	167m 69c
104	Viaduct	Chapel Milton	1865	168m 6c/14c
105	Overbridge	New Chapel Road	1865 rebuilt 1937	168m 21c
106	Overbridge	New Smithy Bridge	1865 lengthened 1902	168m 46c
106A	Culvert			168m 51c

No.	Type	Name or location	Built or altered	Distance from St Pancras
107	Occupation bridge over	Dakin's Bridge	1865 lengthened 1902	168m 61c
108	Occupation bridge over	Deansgate Bridge	1865 lengthened 1902	168m 69c
109	Culvert	Ottersbrook culvert	1865 lengthened 1902 closed 1902	169m 3c
110	Culvert			169m 9c
111	Occupation bridge under	Owler Brook Bridge	1865 lengthened 1902	169m 11c
112	Overbridge	Chinley Road	1865 rebuilt 1902	169m 25c
112A	Footbridge	Chinley Station	1902	169m 39c

BUXTON BRANCH

No.	Type	Name or location	Built or altered	Distance from St Pancras
1	Overbridge	Needham's Bridge	1862	160m 72c
1A	Footbridge	Blackwell cottages over river	1862	160m 72c
2	Viaduct	Blackwell Mill Bridge	1862	160m 79c
5	Viaduct	Buxton Junction Bridge	1862	161m 20c
6	Viaduct	Topley Stone Bridge	1862	161m 32c
7	Viaduct	Topley Pike Bridge	rebuilt 1932	161m 48c
8	Occupation bridge over	Kingsterndale	1862	162m 3c
9	Viaduct	Pig Tor Bridge	1862 rebuilt 1932	162m 13c
10	Tunnel	Pig Tor	1861/62	162m 32c/41c
11	Viaduct	Cowdall Bar Bridge	1862 rebuilt 1932	162m 44c

No.	Type	Name or location	Built or altered	Distance from St Pancras
12	Viaduct	Ashwood Dale Bridge	1862 rebuilt 1932	162m 54c
12A	Viaduct	Ashwood Dale Quarry Bridge	1901	162m 70c
13	Occupation bridge	Gas Sidings Bridge	1862	163m 58c
14	Tunnel	Ashwood Dale	1862	163m 69c/74c
15	Underbridge	Fairfield Road	1862	164m 27c
15A	Culvert	Hogshaw Culvert	1862	164m 31c
15B	Viaduct over	LNWR Railway Viaduct		164m 37c
16	Underbridge	Bridge Street	1862 reconstructed 1897	164m 38c
17	Underbridge	Charles Street	1862	164m 38c
18	Underbridge	Hogshaw Lane	1862	164m 47c
18A	Culvert	Hogshaw Brook Culvert	1862	164m 50c

BLACKWELL MILL NORTH CURVE

No.	Type	Name or location	Built or altered	Distance from St Pancras
4	Cattle Creep		1865 lengthened 1878	0m 6c
3A	Bridle road over			0m 11c
3	Bridle road under		1865	0m 14c

Note: All names used in the schedule are official MR local names as entered in the bridge register book.

Rails in the Landscape. A Tunstead-Northwich hopper train negotiates the sweeping reverse curves past Great Rocks Junction, at the south end of Peak Dale. The train comprises 18 hoppers, one more than the normal load, and may well have been one of the rare occasions in the declining years of steam, when motive power consisted of a BR Standard 9F class 2-10-0.
(Greater Manchester Museum of Science and Industry)

Index

AU REVOIR
MIDLAND . . .

Outrake Bridge, Bakewell 24th February 1985.

. . . WILL PEAK RAIL RETURN?

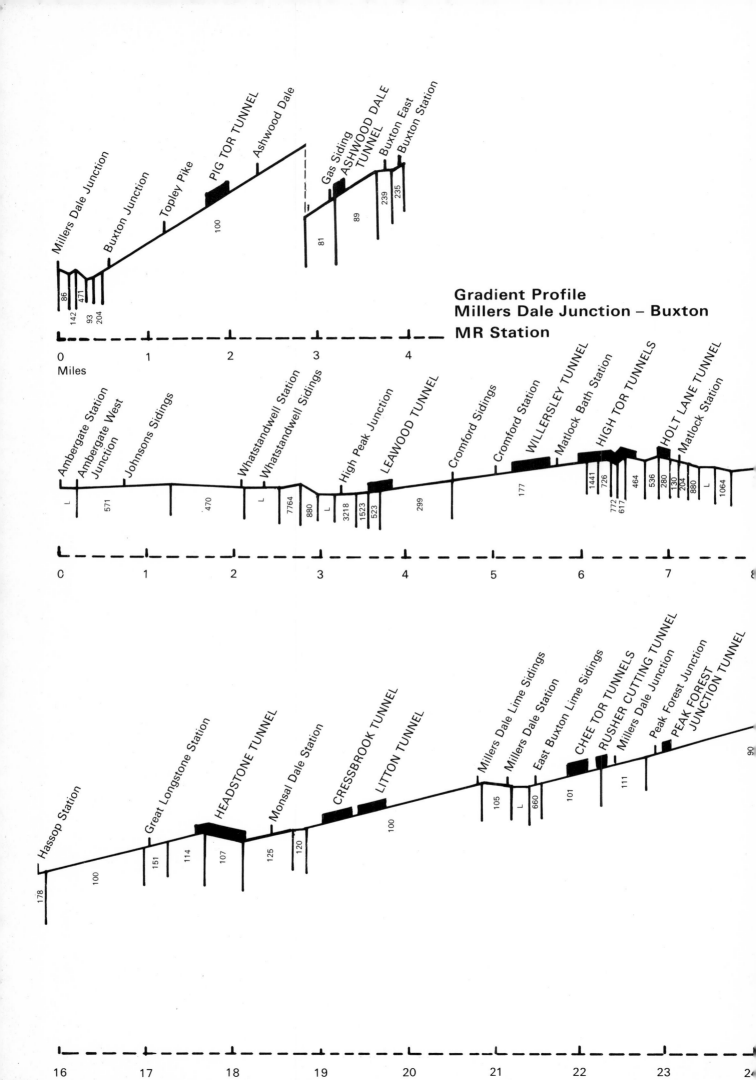

**Gradient Profile
Millers Dale Junction – Buxton**

MR Station

Miles